MW01620337

Angels

in our midst

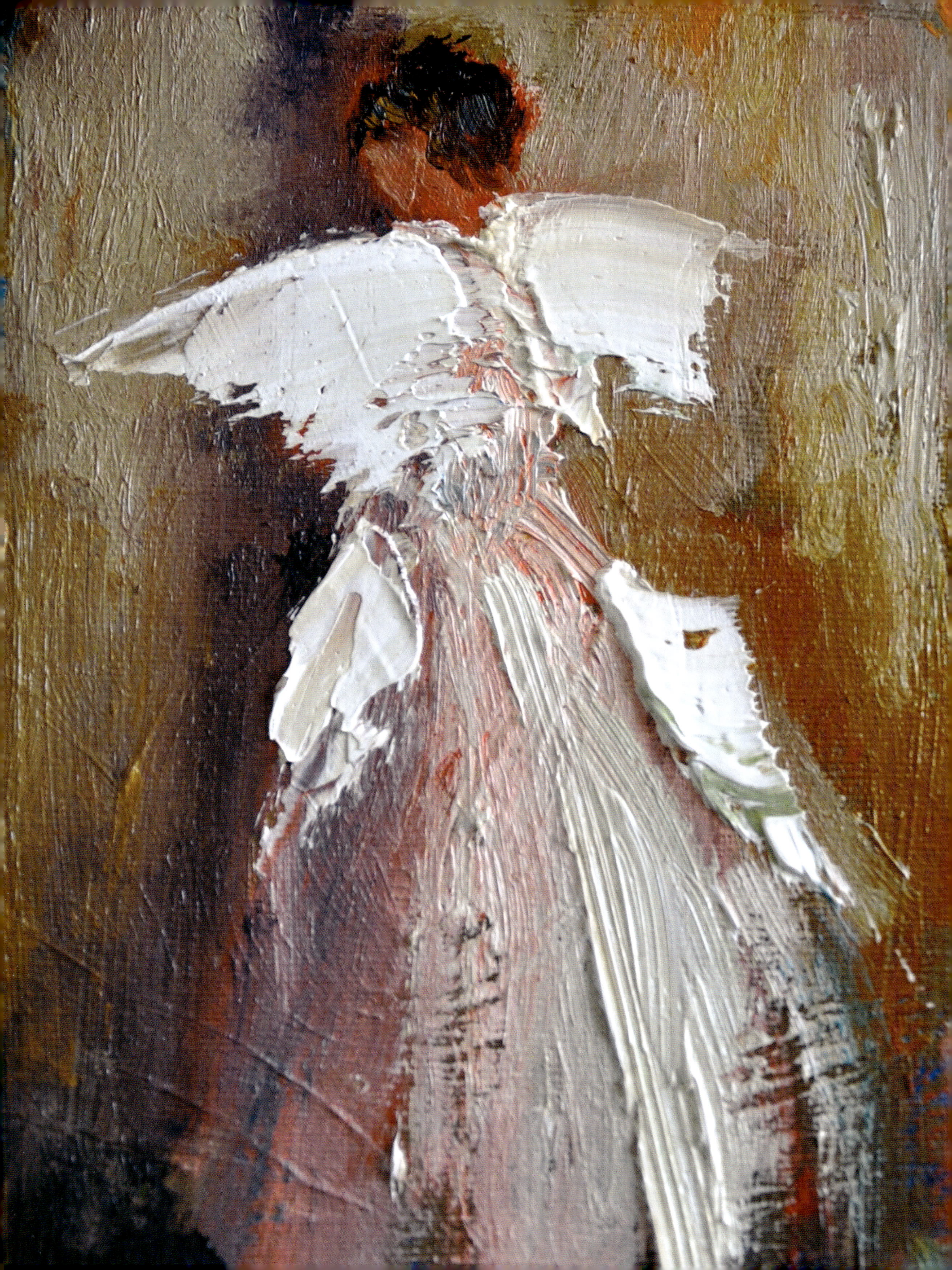

Angels in our midst

ANNE H. NEILSON

Foreword by Ron Hall

AHN Designs
Charlotte, North Carolina

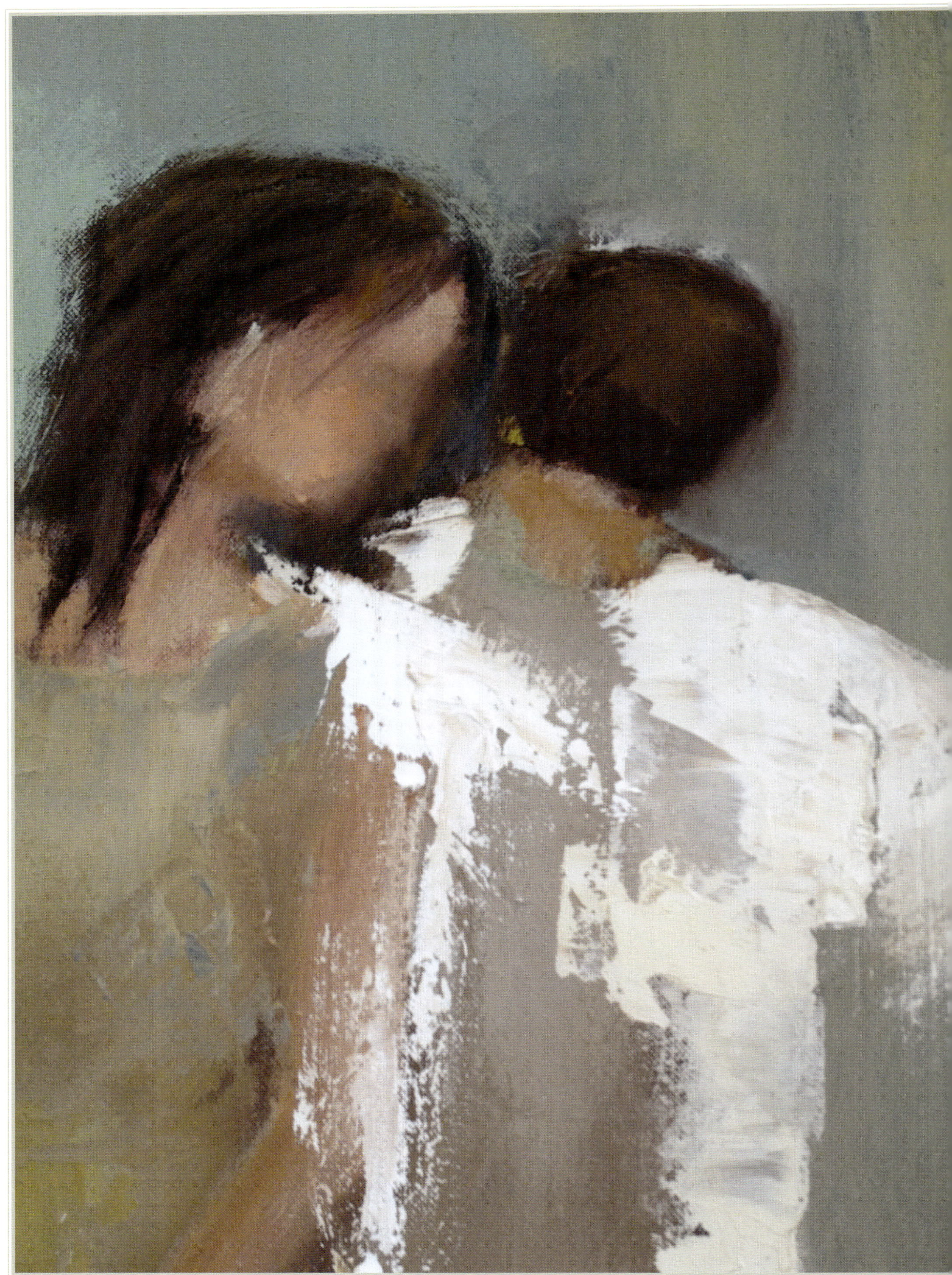

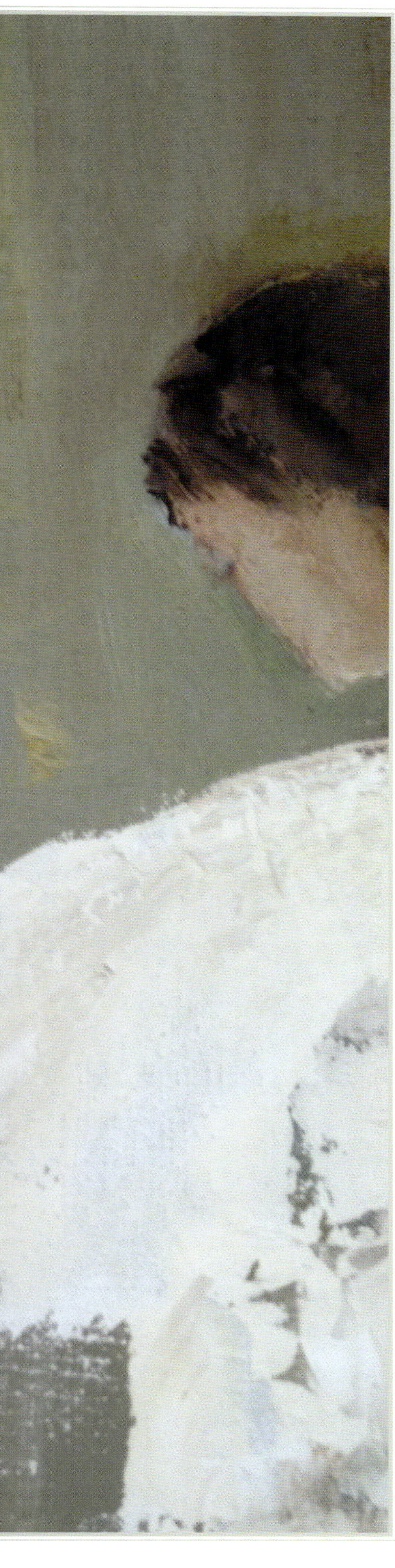

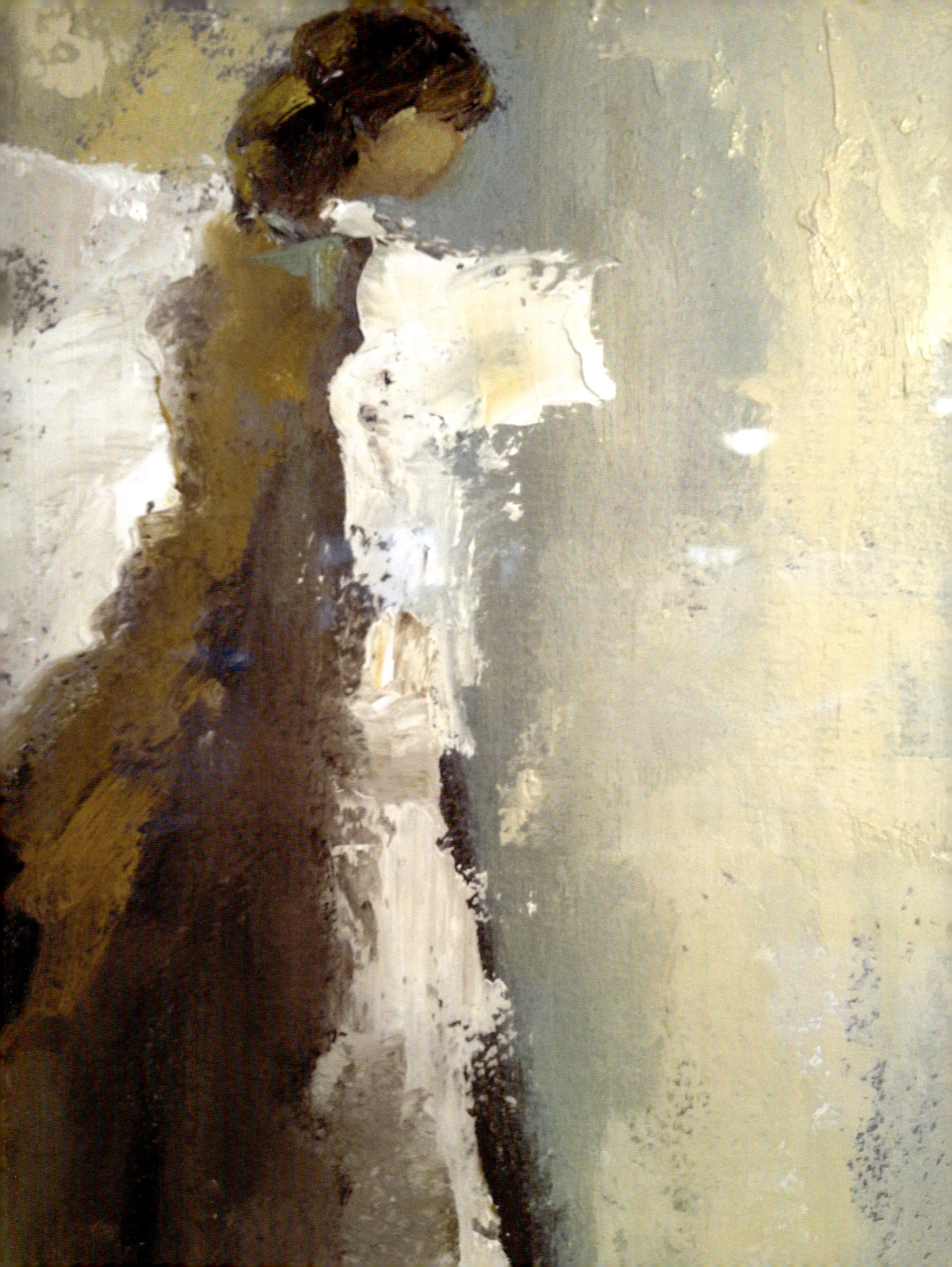

FOREWORD

by Ron Hall

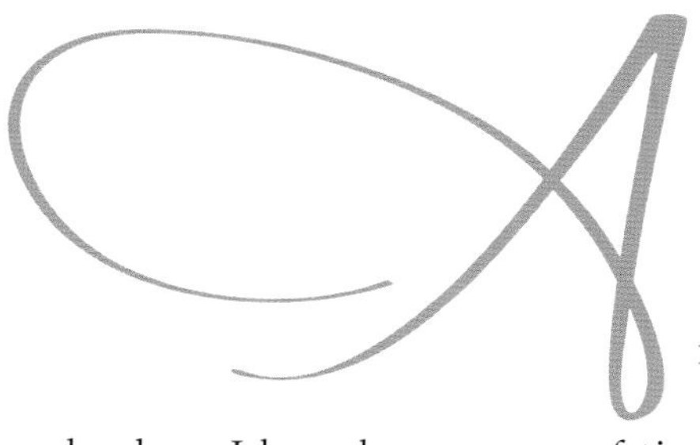

ngels have been woven into the fabric of my life. They come in many sizes and colors. I have been aware of time spent with them and I believe I've experienced their presence unaware.

Once a skeptic, my first encounter with an angel was life-changing. Fourteen years ago, a homeless man told me he believed my wife, Deborah, was an angel. As believers, we knew better, even though she was clearly one of God's messengers. We are taught to believe that's the role of real angels. Strangely, Deborah in her heart believed he was an angel too, even though it was not sound theology; he was, without question, one of God's messengers too.

Not long after that encounter, when Deborah was preparing to leave this Earth, she was surrounded by a multitude of angels, real ones, as she cried out to God for her own wings. I was there as a witness. I felt the flutter of their wings. I believed. Sometimes life-changing encounters skip our heads and move our hearts to feeling the angelic qualities of God's earthly messengers. *Angels in Our Midst* does that for me.

Using the extraordinary combination of her God-given talent and her divinely inspired vision, Anne Neilson provides a double blessing, not only for those who read this book, but also those who benefit from its success. Open the pages of this well-written book and invite angels into your midst. Some say seeing is believing. I say believing is seeing.

—RON HALL, Author of the *New York Times* Bestseller, *Same Kind Of Different As Me*

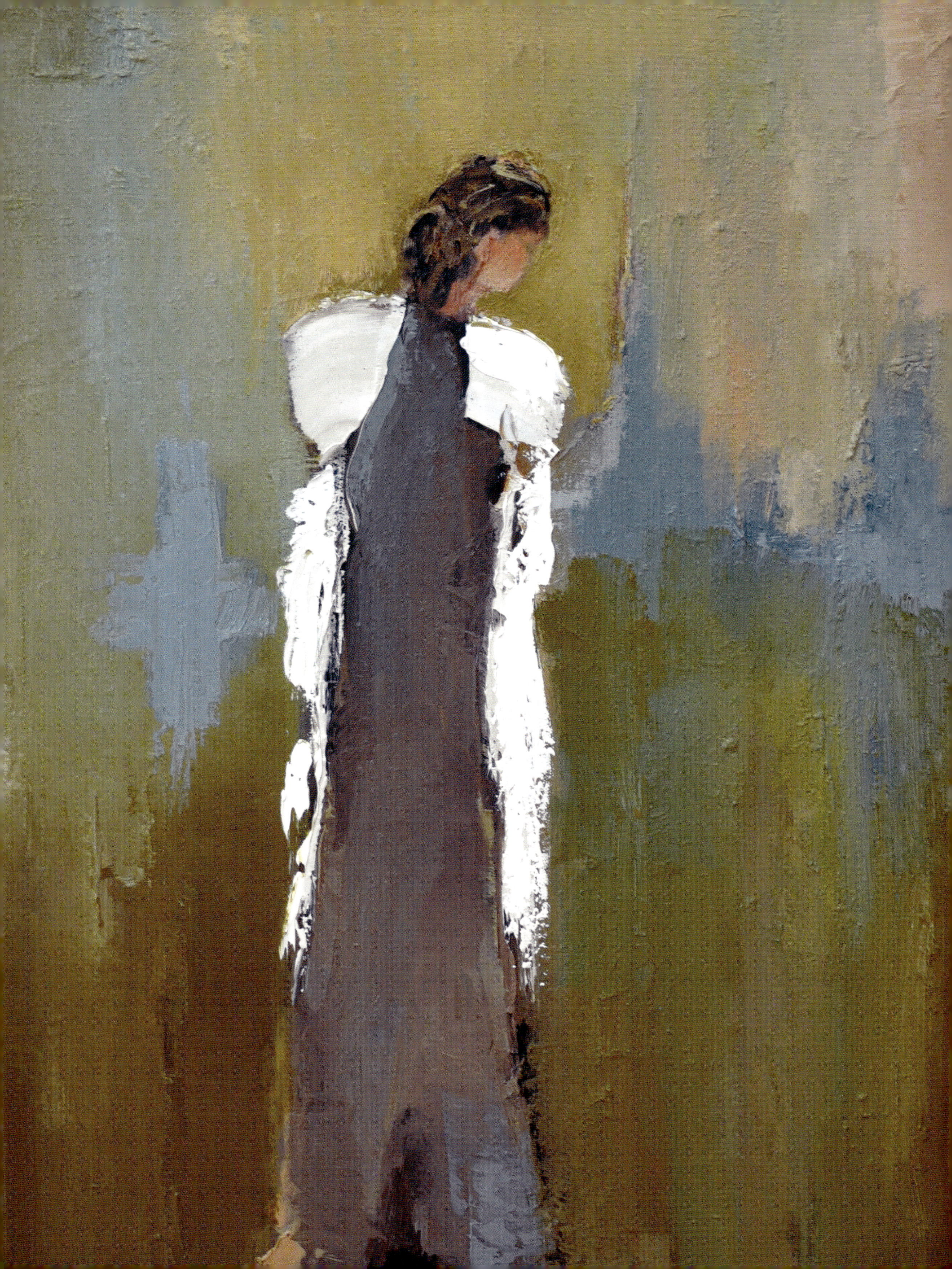

Angels

in our midst

INTRODUCTION

by Beth Bowen

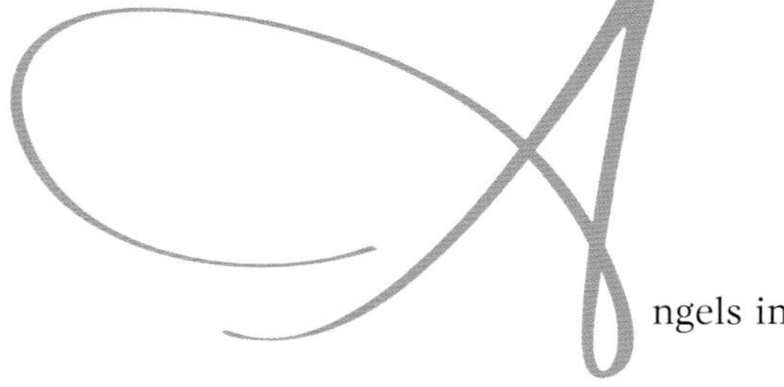

ngels in Our Midst *is truly a treasure. Within its pages you will catch a glimpse into the heart of a remarkable artist who has fully committed her life to the Lord and has obediently and passionately followed where He has led. Like many people, I have a collection of beautiful books on my coffee table and find that often I will simply flip through and admire the colorful pages, without pausing to carefully read the details or fine print. I urge you not to skim through this book, but instead savor these personal stories and experiences of encouragement, faith, compassion, love and hope.*

It has been my privilege to be the sister to this amazing artist and to witness her life's journey unfolding in living color. I can so clearly remember us as little girls, sitting at the kitchen counter while I watched her doodle for hours on end and practice her signature in more fonts that you would find today on the World Wide Web. It was obvious Anne would be an artist. But when and how were yet to be determined. In Anne's search for identity and purpose, she found the saving grace of our Lord, Jesus Christ. From that point on, the artistic gift God gave her has been revealed and shared with people around the world all for His glory.

I will never forget sitting at my computer late one night when an email came from Anne with a

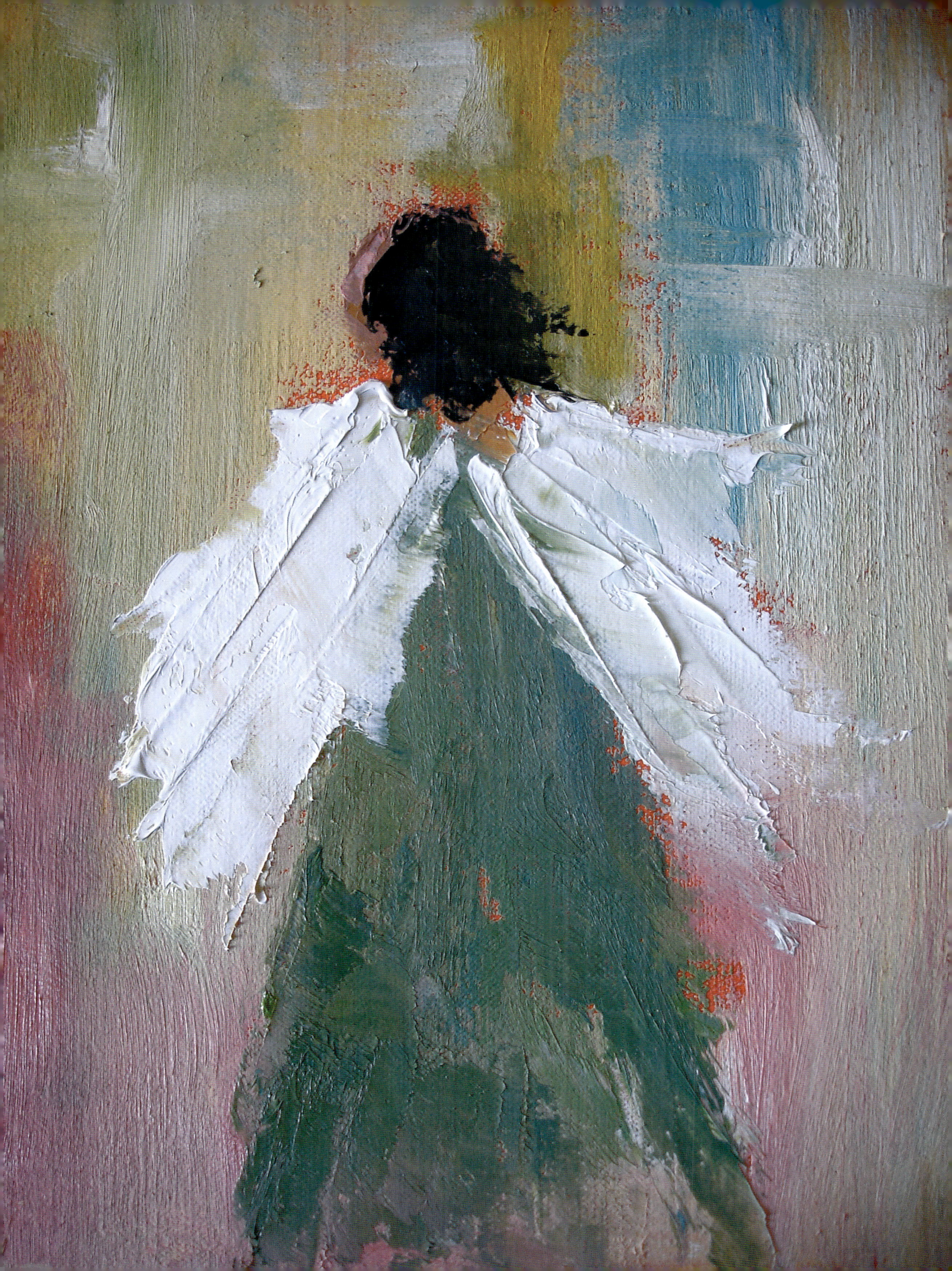

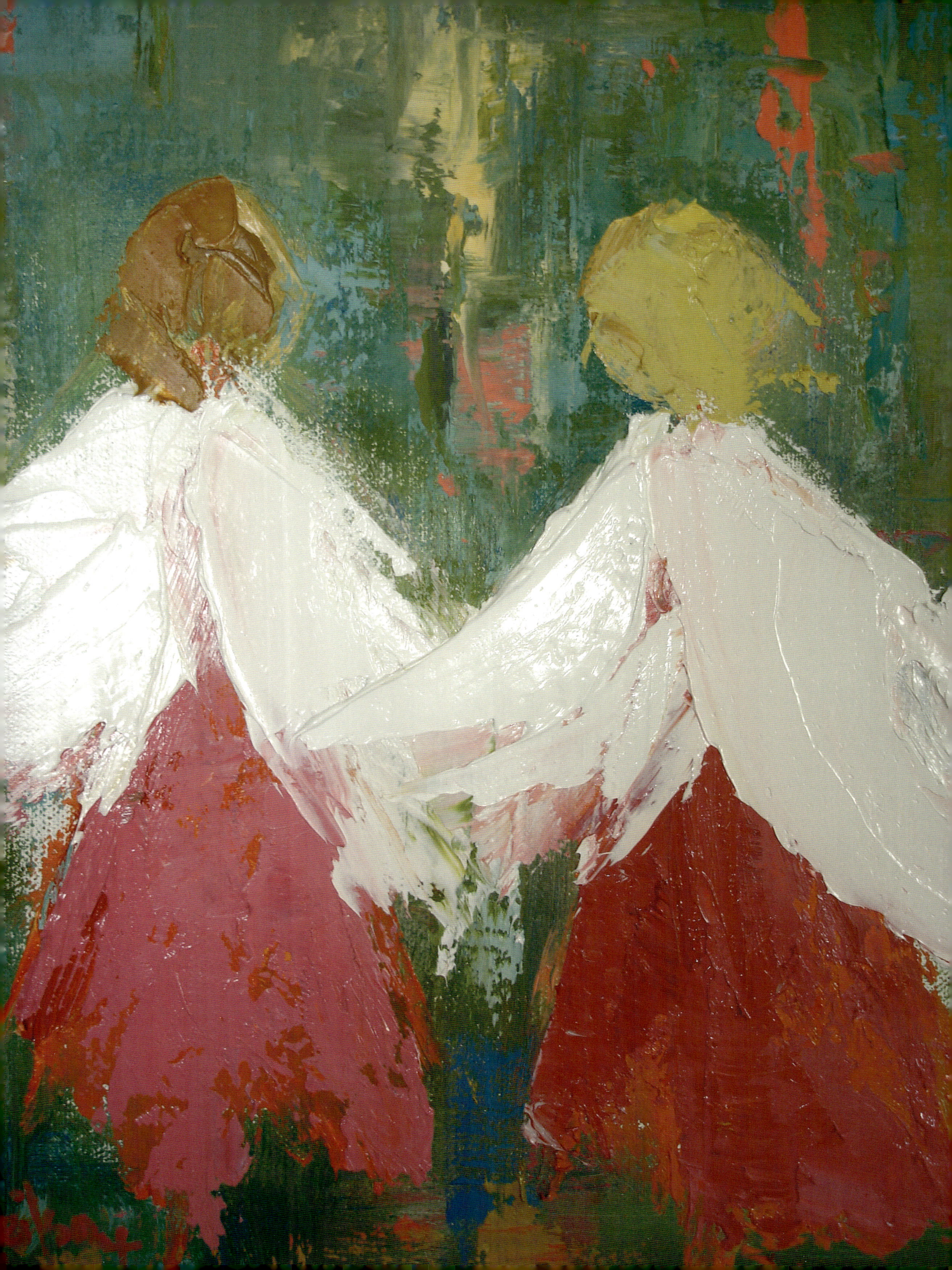

photo of her first angel painting, asking: "What do you think?" Immediately, I recognized the beauty, mystery and movement she had captured on this little canvas. That night I told her that "she had found her voice," but what I did not yet realize was that this "voice" would become her life's song, lifted high in praise of our God and used to bring joy, comfort, love and healing to His people. Anne's talent is unquestionable. Her limitless energy would exhaust the average superhero. But for those of us who know her, we know that she relies on the strength and leading of God's Holy Spirit – in Whom all things are possible. What my precious sister has done is so much more than simply paint. Through her art and encounters with just about anyone and everyone, she has boldly invited all to: "Come and see what the Lord has done, the amazing things he has done on this Earth."

Anne's art is a gift. Her passion is an inspiration. This book gives witness to God's faithfulness in our ordinary and everyday lives when we choose to submit to Him and live in obedience. I pray that the testimonies and Scripture verses found in these pages will call each of us to live as boldly and confidently in the strength, power and love of the Lord as my beloved sister.

Enjoy!

—BETH BOWEN

FOR WHERE YOUR TREASURE IS,
THERE YOUR HEART WILL BE ALSO.

MATTHEW 6:21

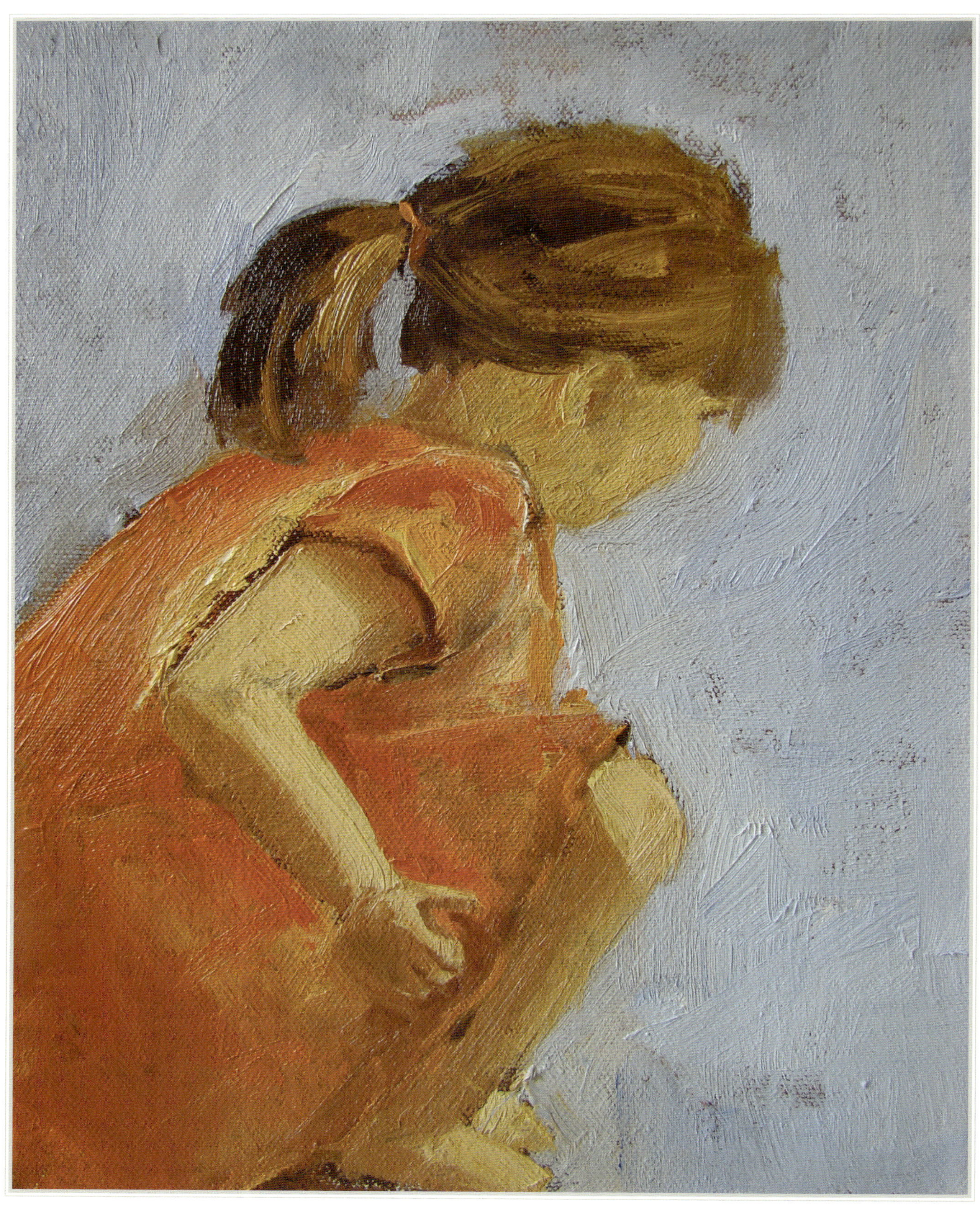

EVERY CHILD IS AN ARTIST. THE PROBLEM IS HOW TO REMAIN AN ARTIST ONCE HE GROWS UP.

—PABLO PICASSO

THE STORY BEHIND THE ARTIST

Ever since I was little, I have known that I was made to be creative. I recently found a paper that I wrote in 1972 entitled: "When I Grow Up." I outlined my desires of what I wanted to be as an adult, and chief among them was to be an artist. I was forever drawing people, animals, flowers and doodling in my notebooks in class. I took art classes, hoping that one day I would be able to have a career that utilized my creative energies. However, I did not pursue my dream right away. I graduated from high school in 1981, attended Florida State University for two years, and graduated from Jacksonville University with a Bachelor of Arts degree in Elementary Education.

The desire to be an artist bubbled up inside of me as a third grade teacher, where I was able to tap into that creative spirit in the classroom. I had the most imaginative bulletin boards in the classrooms and the most creative art projects. I tried to tie in an art project to any subject that I was teaching. For one science project on sea life, I went down to the local fish market and purchased about a half a dozen whole dead fish. The next morning, I brought the fish to school in a cooler. We coated the fish with paint and began to make 'impressions' of them on construction paper - scales and all. Less than an hour into the project we were all complaining about the smell. Even though it was the dead of winter, we finally had to open all the windows, and spend the rest of the day working in our coats and mittens. But when completed, the art project hung proudly outside our classroom walls and was one that would never be forgotten.

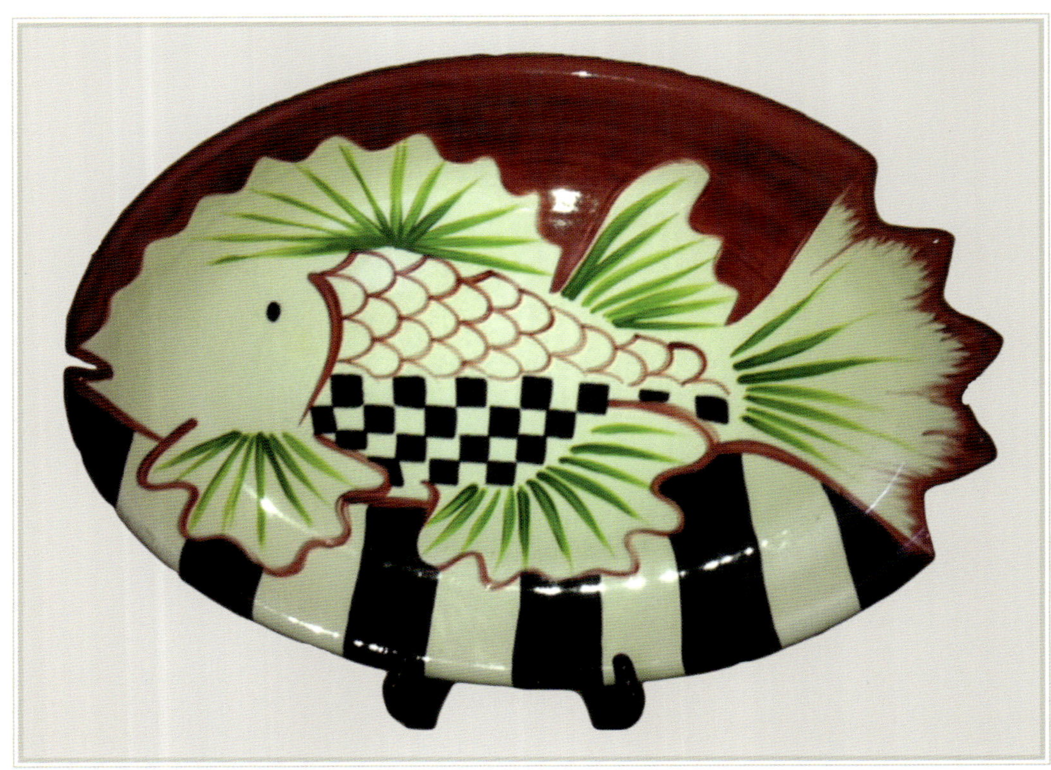

Shortly into my teaching career, I began to paint pottery. I would create designs on greenware, which is the semi-hardened clay before it has been shaped but has not yet been bisque fired, which converts it from clay to ceramic. The more I painted, the more I felt that I was reaching my goal of becoming an artist. I loved every minute of it. Eventually, I began to sell the pieces of pottery for wedding gifts and house-warming gifts to my friends, family and co-workers. I knew I was on to something.

When I moved to Charlotte in 1989, I started Herring Designs, Ltd., a hand-painted dinnerware line. I quit my job as an elementary teacher and focused on developing and designing a line of dinnerware. I spent countless hours painting plates, platters and bowls with designs of fish, flowers and fruit. I did not own a kiln early on in this new career adventure, but it was my desire to eventually have one of my own. I painted several pieces at a time at my home, then carefully loaded up the car of all the fragile painted green-ware and took it to a little craft store - BJ Crafts. The owner, BJ, had several large kilns in the back of the shop where I loaded up my pieces to be fired. Then I would return a day or two later to glaze the pieces and re-fire for the finishing touch.

BJ sold countless sizes of platters, pitchers, bowls, platters in green-ware, and I would go there to choose the newest and latest pieces for my dinnerware line. I wore myself out making the necessary trips back and forth to

BJ's. Frustrated, I asked my father if he would invest in a kiln for me. My sales were paying all my bills at the time, but I did not have enough saved up for a kiln. His reply was no at first, but during a trip to Alexandria, Virginia, he stopped at a little gift store and noticed one of my fish designs that was for sale. I received a call from him later that day asking if I still needed that kiln. Shortly after installing it in the basement of my home, Herring Designs was making a name for itself through home shows and sales representatives, and the pottery line was being sold up and down the Southeast.

In 1993, I married my precious husband, Clark, and settled in to start our family. After my second daughter was born, I decided to sell the kiln and pottery supplies and put the artist dream on hold until my children were older. Before I knew it, my family had grown to six and I was enjoying every minute of raising my three girls and little boy. Life was full and satisfying. When my girls were little they would climb on my bed with a box of crayons and markers and color for hours on the homemade coloring sheets I made. I had requests for underwater scenes, unicorns, flowers, and more. Whatever the favorite item of the day was, I created them on paper for the girls to fill in with vibrant colors.

In May 2000, Clark and I realized we had quickly out-grown the home that we had loved, and knew that it was time to either move or build. I had always wanted to build a house and got really excited at the prospect. We began the process, and prayed for wisdom and discernment. We met with our builder and architect on a weekly basis. We were not sure we were doing the right thing by stepping out in faith and building a home, but as we prayed and turned it over to God, we had peace. In April 2001, six months after we had bought the lot, I felt the Lord quietly whispering in His word from 2 Chronicles 1:10-12: *"Give me wisdom and knowledge, that I may lead this people, for who is able to govern this great people of yours?" God said to Solomon, "Since this is your heart's desire and you have not asked for wealth, possessions or honor, nor for the death of your enemies, and since you have not asked for a long life but for wisdom and knowledge to govern my people over whom I have made you king, therefore wisdom and knowledge will be given you. And I will also give you wealth, possessions and honor, such as no king who was before you ever had and none after you will have."* I knew in my heart that this was a Word from the Lord confirming our decision to build this house.

I began to journal and document scripture during my prayer time about the process of building this home. The verse that we all prayed (including the architect) was from Psalm 127:1 "*Unless the LORD builds the house, its builders labor in vain*." We began to commit every detail to the Lord. From the foundation to the framing, from the electrical to the sheetrock, from the stair-cases to the finishing touches, every detail was prayed over and surrendered to the Lord. It was not easy. During the building process, the economy took a downhill turn. My husband grew anxious and made a few references that we were building a spec house. But I knew that we were building God's house. A house that we would eventually use to serve Him by hosting events such as Bible Studies, Young Life Events, a little children's Bible Study that a neighbor and I formed called Art and Soul, and even a house that had my own studio. I knew that God had a plan for this home.

The days before we moved in, my husband and I were talking with our landscaper at the house. As we were drove out of the driveway, we looked back at the three large oak trees that stood grouped together on the side of our home. We noticed that on one of the trees there was a large cross. All of us saw it and were stunned. I knew that was our sign that when we let go, when we truly surrender the things that we hang on to, God can show up mightily and display His wonder.

We moved into our new home in December 2003, and I settled in to painting in my brand new sunny studio. I took workshops with different artists and painted with well-known local artist Andy Braitman. After experimenting with different subjects, I painted my first angel in 2004. The paintings were small at first as I experimented with color, texture and values.

During this early time in my painting career, I also began volunteering at the Harvest Center, which is a local shelter that feeds the homeless. I came to know about the Harvest Center when the founder, Barbara Brewton Cameron, came and spoke to our Sunday School class. Her story was captivating. The Harvest Center was a powerful place to serve, and leaving there one day, I struggled with where I should invest my time. Did I need to choose between my love of painting or the call to serve others? As always, I just had to hand it over to God in prayer and ask Him to direct my path. I heard a still, small voice say: "Paint and give back." I arrived home that afternoon to a call from a local boutique, 3 French Hens, that was selling my paintings. A lady had come into the

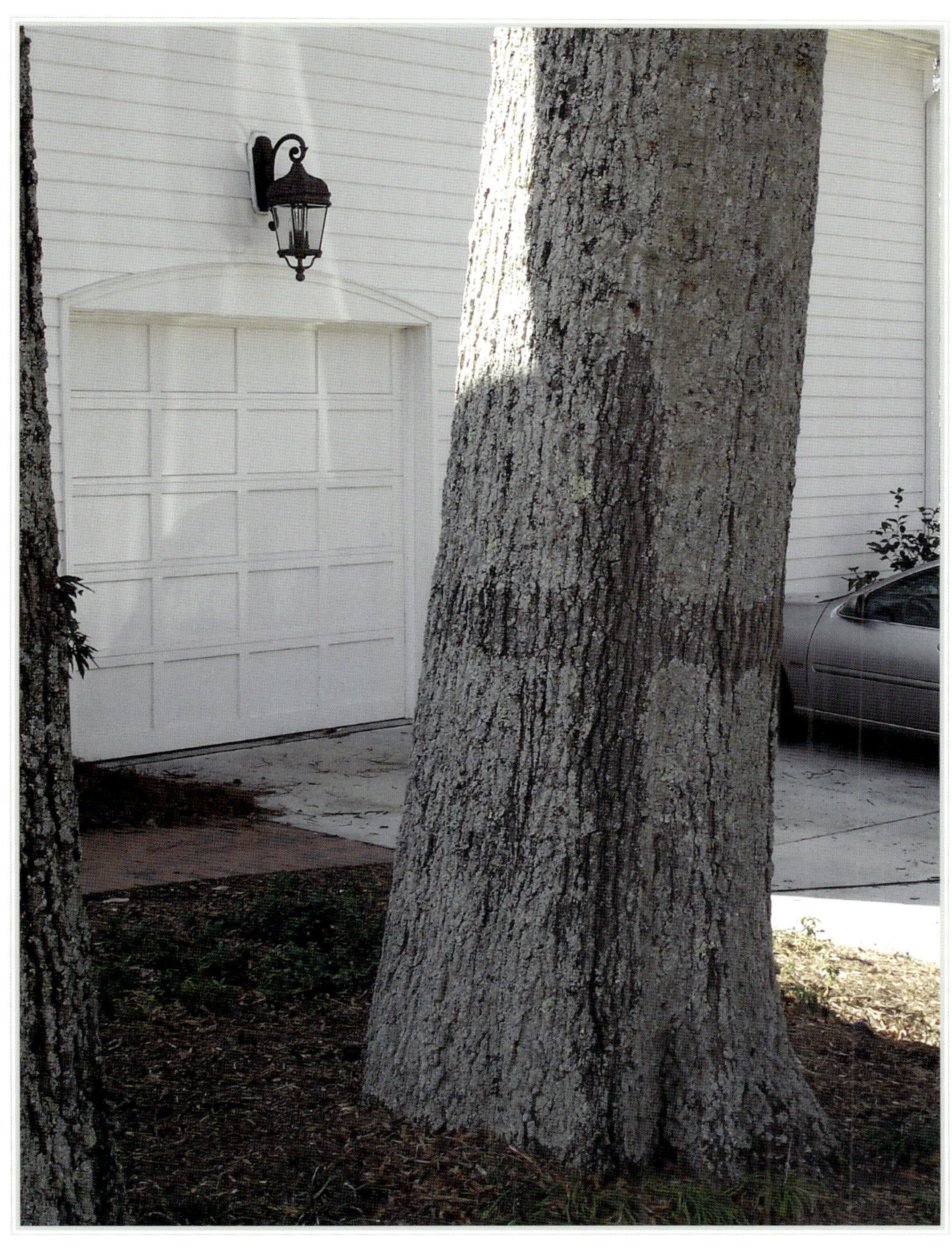

UNLESS THE LORD BUILDS THE HOME, ITS BUILDERS LABOR IN VAIN.

PSALM 127:1

store and purchased three angel paintings. This was confirmation. I now knew I could use my painting to serve others. That started the journey of "Angels in Our Midst."

I wanted to use this gift – this talent from God - to give back, and to give Him glory each step of the way. I cannot take credit for the success of the angels and the journey that it has taken me on. It has been a journey of partnering with the homeless, children with disabilities and even helping a young talented girl reach her dream to become an artist. It has brought me more joy in my life knowing that the gift that has been given to me can be given back to others.

I give God all the glory for the path He has had me on these past 49 years. I am a daughter, a sister, a teacher, a wife, a mother of four incredible children, and now an artist sharing God's glory though each painting.

Each painting starts out the same: as a blank canvas. Then a toned undercoating of paint. Next there is layering upon layering of paint, creating texture and color with each stroke. It looks like a mess until the very end, when each stroke is in place and the blank canvas becomes somewhat complete. Most of the paintings are very similar, yet each one draws the viewer in different ways.

Our lives are much like the process of creating art. Each of us is created with a purpose. As we grow and become who we are – most often we go through trials and tribulations. As we allow the hand of God to move and work in our lives, it is difficult to figure out sometimes why certain events are happening, and what purpose they serve. But one day, we will be able to look back and see the masterpiece – without this color, turn, or sidetrack, none of the other great things could have worked to come together.

EVERY GOOD AND PERFECT GIFT IS FROM ABOVE, COMING DOWN FROM THE FATHER OF THE HEAVENLY LIGHTS, WHO DOES NOT CHANGE LIKE SHIFTING SHADOWS.

James 1:17

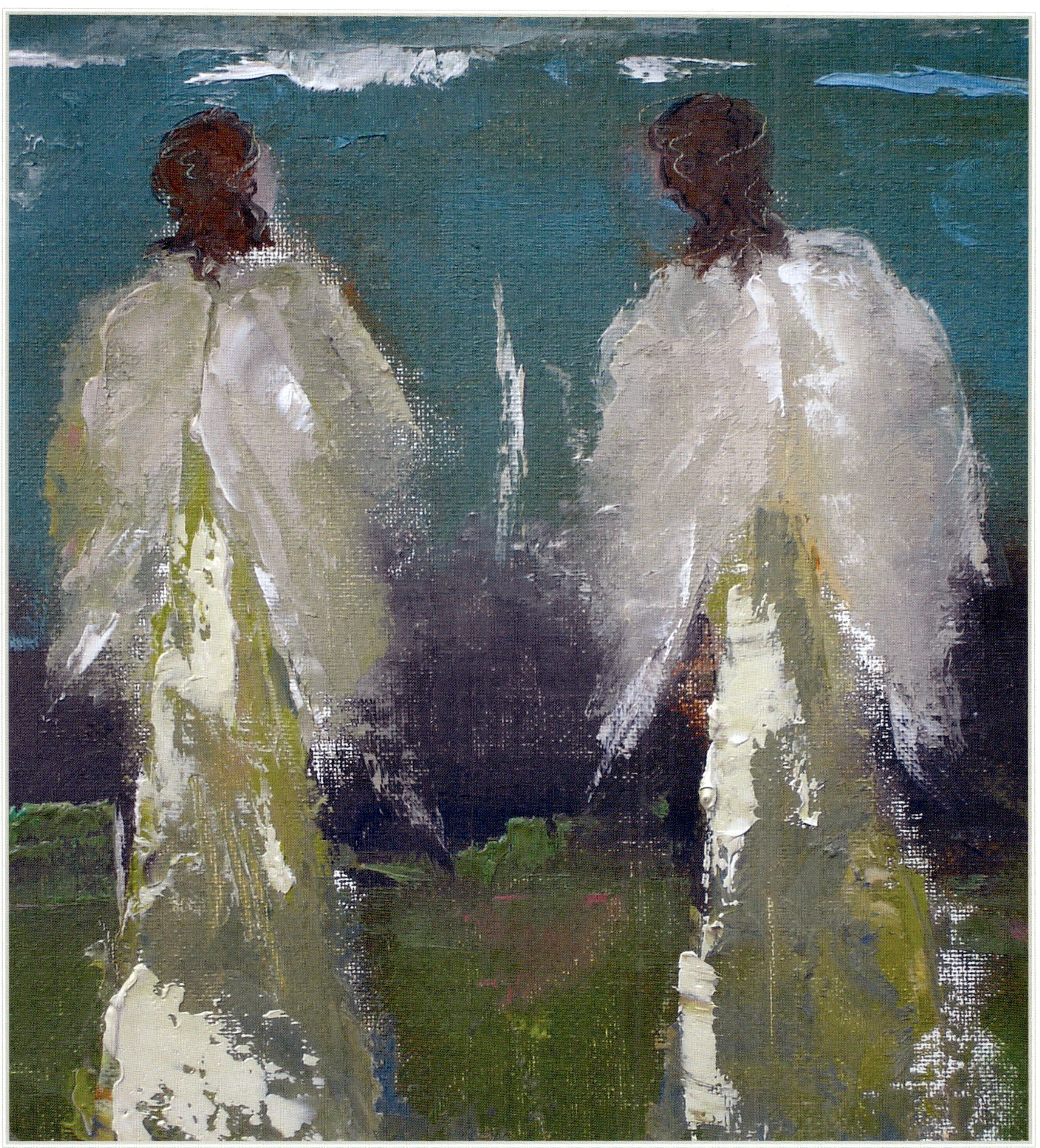

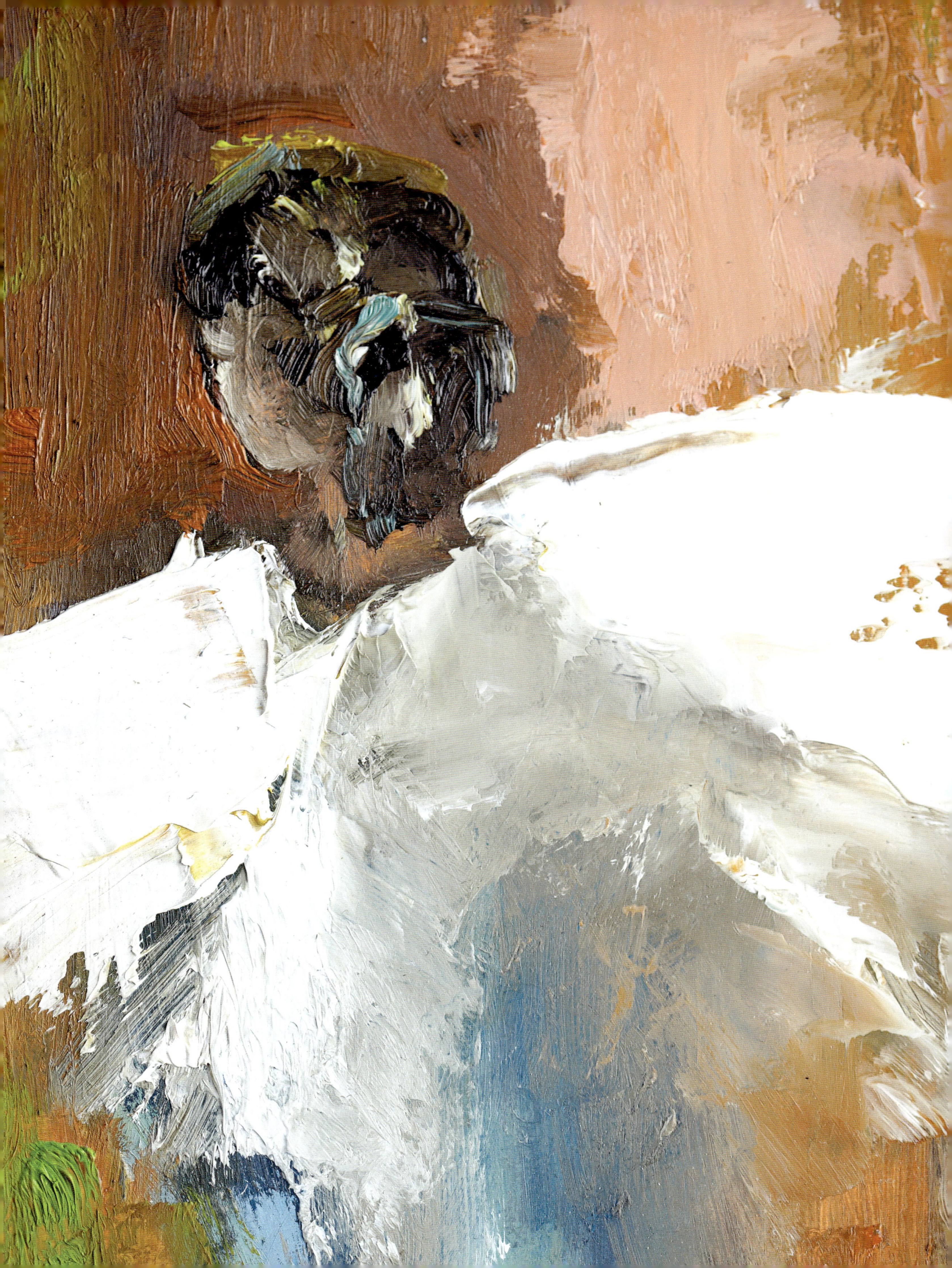

CONSIDER IT PURE JOY, MY BROTHERS AND SISTERS, WHENEVER YOU FACE TRIALS OF MANY KINDS, BECAUSE YOU KNOW THAT THE TESTING OF YOUR FAITH PRODUCES PERSEVERANCE. LET PERSEVERANCE FINISH ITS WORK SO THAT YOU MAY BE MATURE AND COMPLETE, NOT LACKING ANYTHING.

JAMES 1:2-4

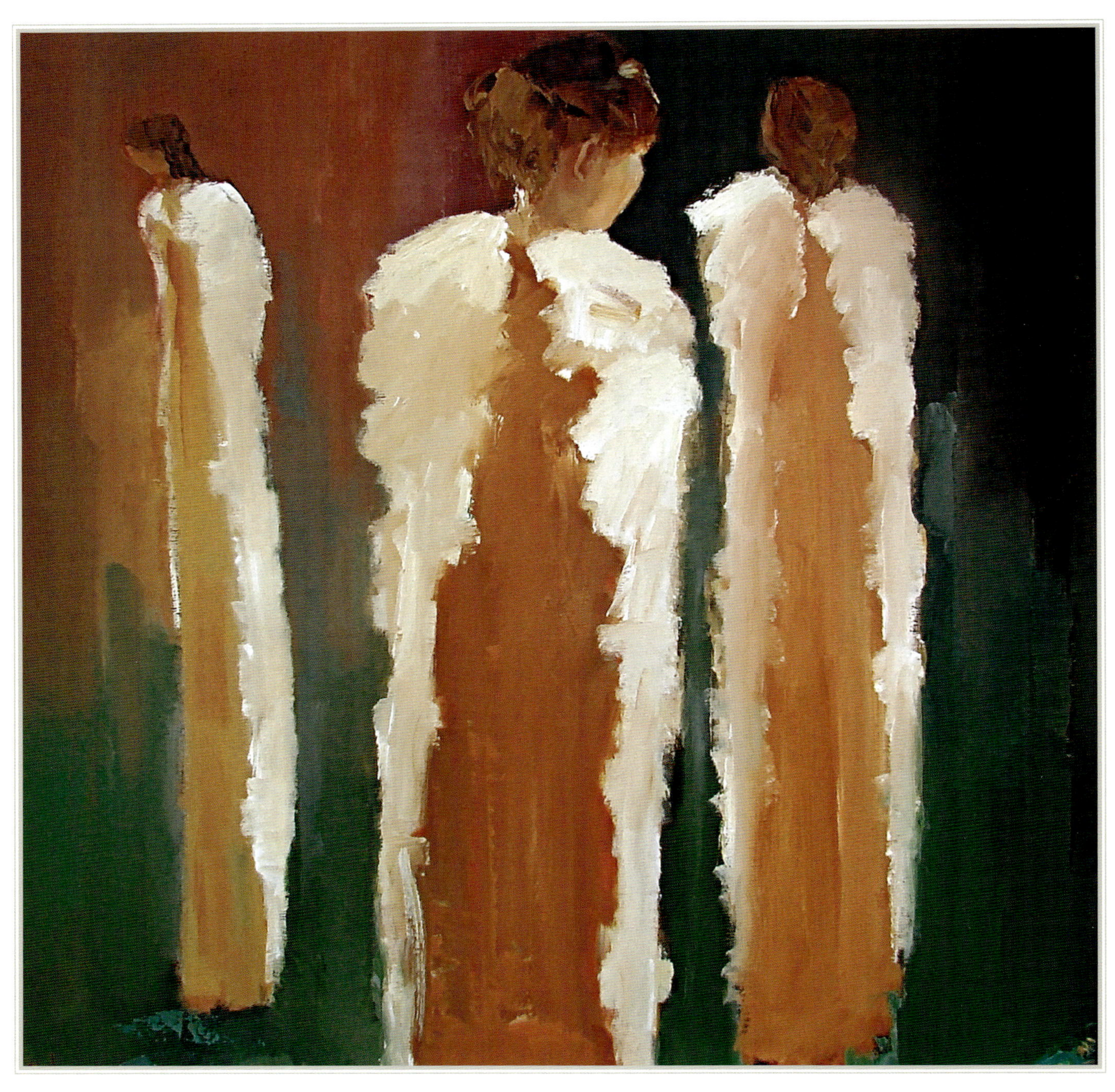

IN THE BEGINNING, GOD CREATED . . .

Genesis 1:1

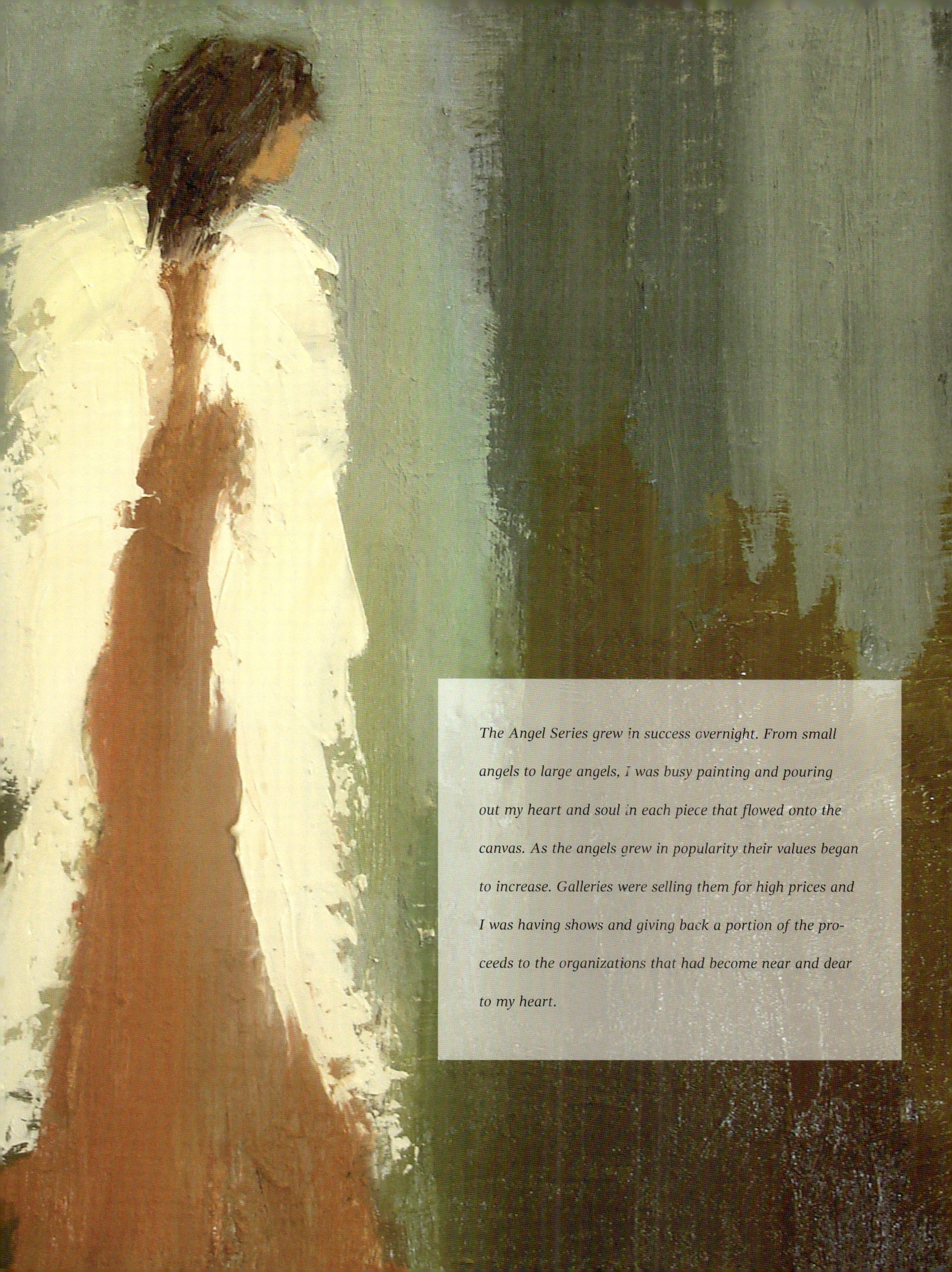

The Angel Series grew in success overnight. From small angels to large angels, I was busy painting and pouring out my heart and soul in each piece that flowed onto the canvas. As the angels grew in popularity their values began to increase. Galleries were selling them for high prices and I was having shows and giving back a portion of the proceeds to the organizations that had become near and dear to my heart.

ABOUT THE BOOK

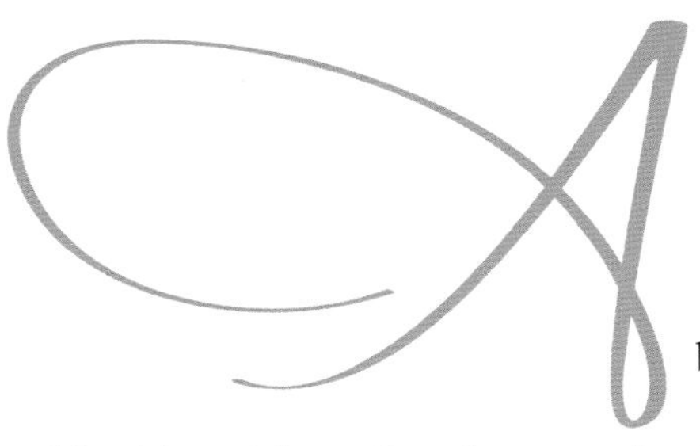

bout a year ago, after reviewing hundreds of images from the Angel Series and looking at how they have evolved over the past several years, I decided to create this book to display the journey of the art and the many stories behind the paintings. *Angels In Our Midst* is composed of over 100 images from the Angel Series, landscapes from various travels, figures and still-life studies. It is also intertwined with personal devotions and stories connected with the paintings.

I will continue to paint Angels as well as landscapes, figures and still life studies, all representing my favorite moments in life. Thus the journey continues . . . from the heart to the canvas . . . and it truly is a blessing to use the Gift that was given from above to help others in our world.

A portion of proceeds from the sale of this book will go to the charitable organizations highlighted within.

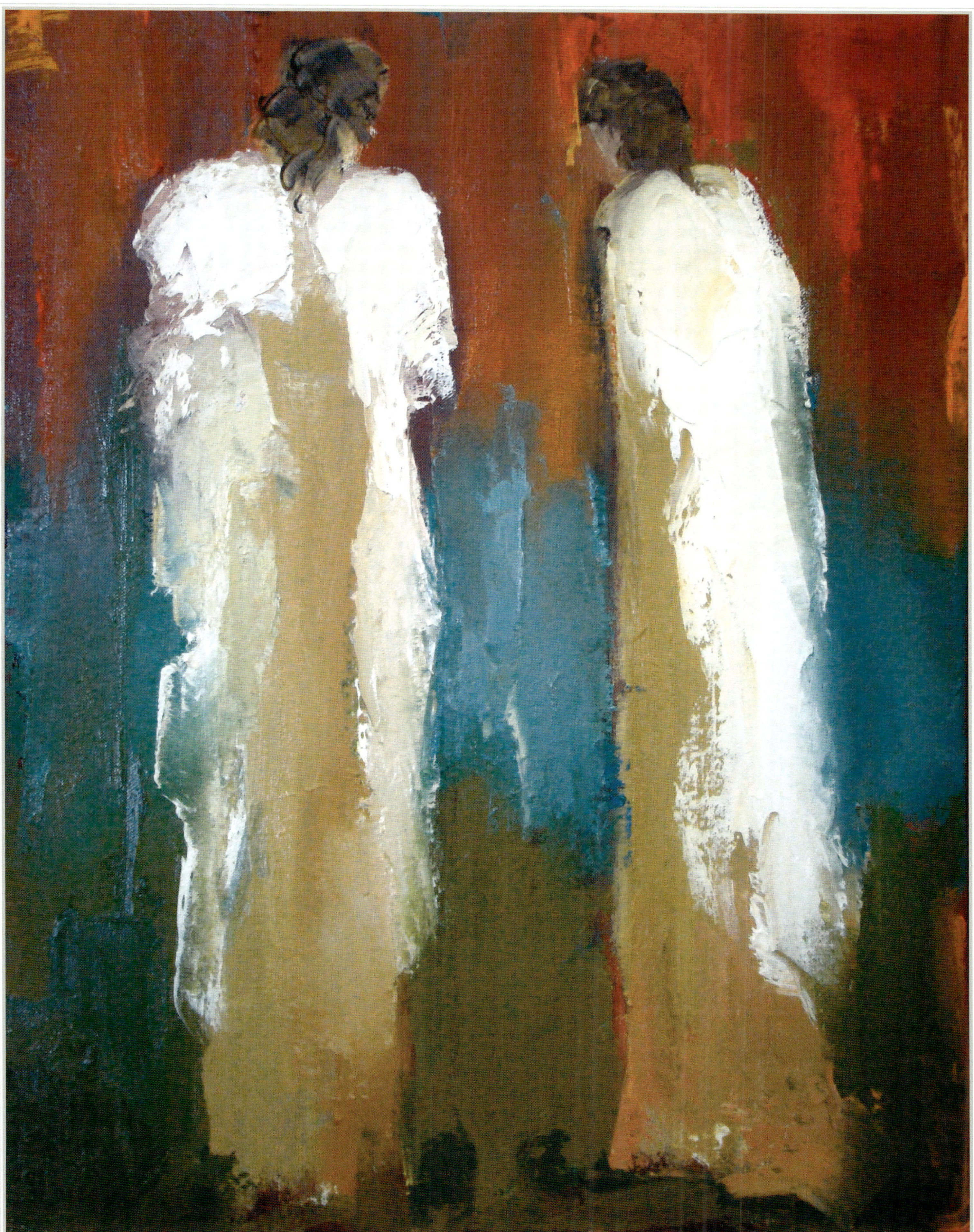

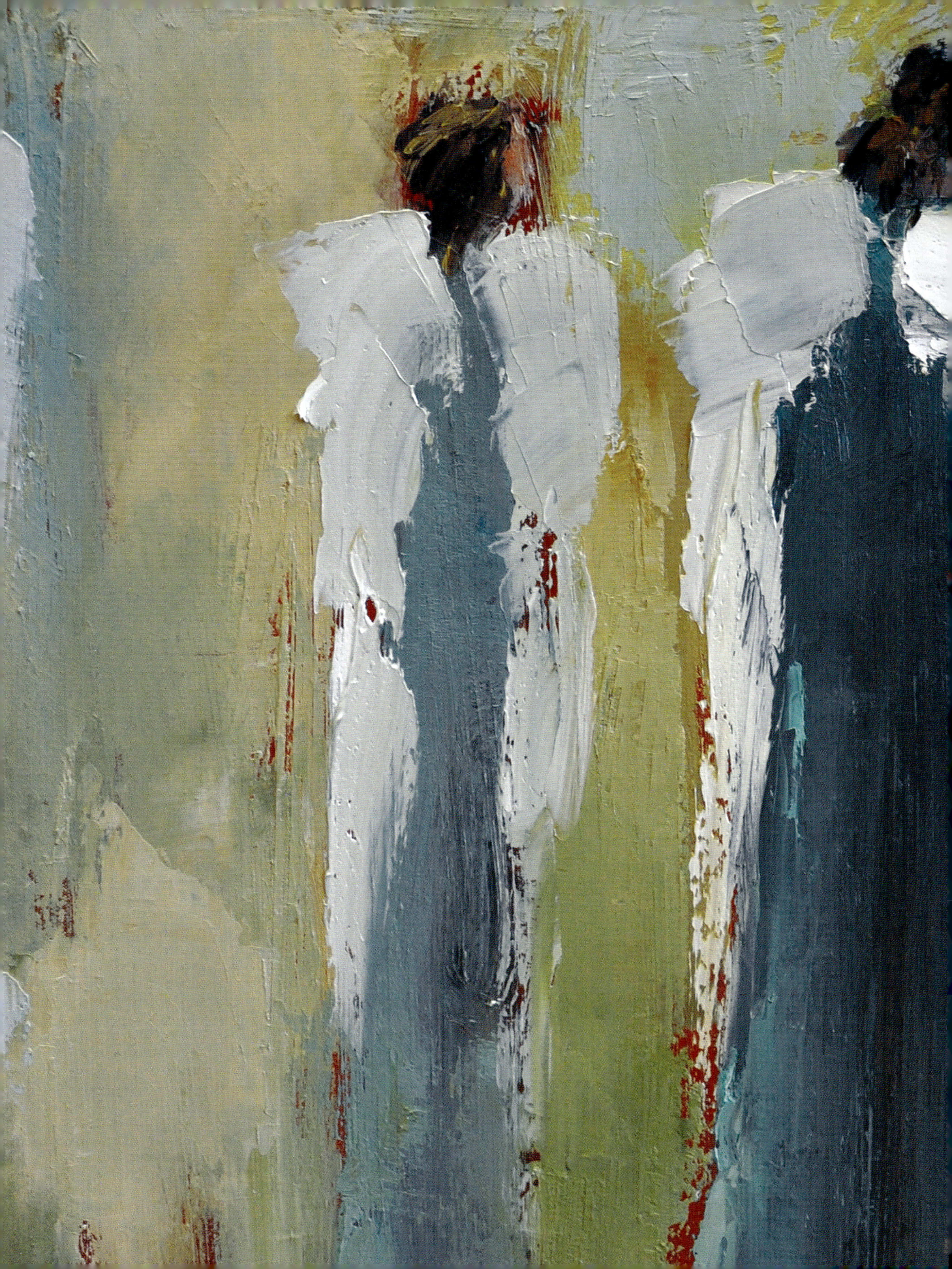

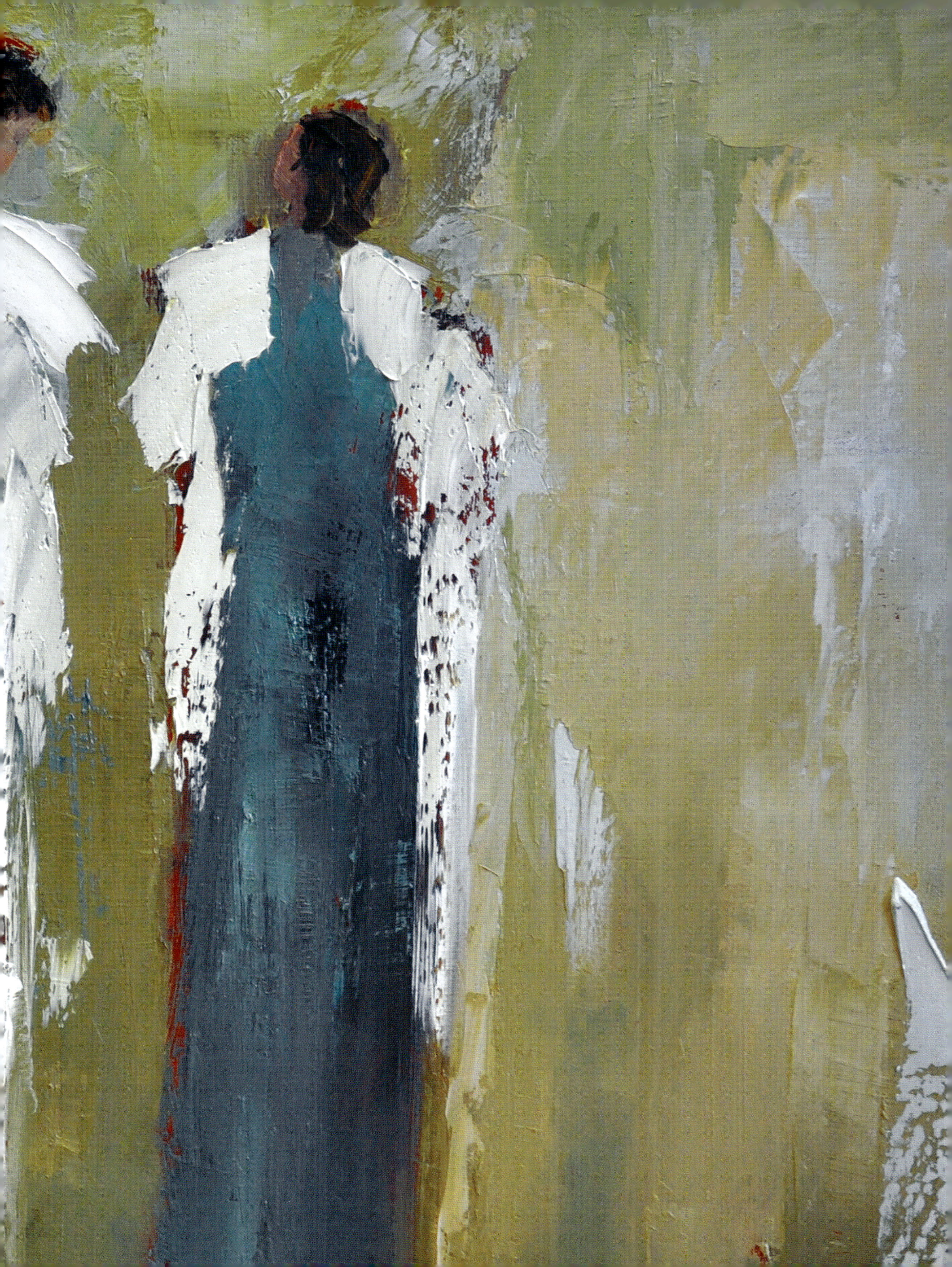

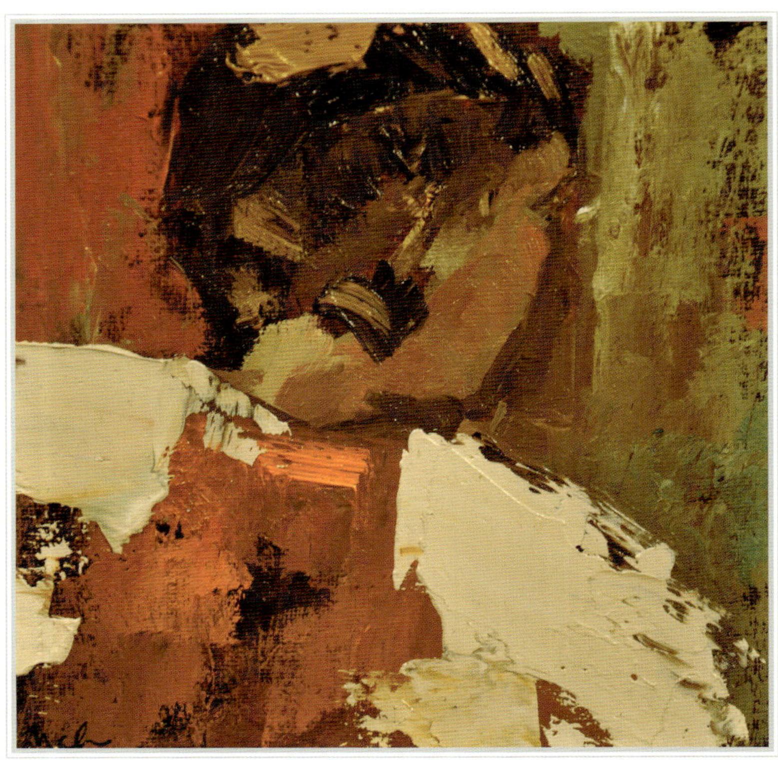

ANGELS IN OUR MIDST

Judith MacNutt, co-founder of Christian Healing Ministries, is known and respected for her extraordinary gift of discernment combined with love and compassion. She is not only gifted in praying for inner healing, but also gives many talks on the ministry of angels. Judith MacNutt's latest book is Angels Are For Real.

The foundation of Christian Healing Ministries (CHM) was founded by Francis and Judith MacNutt in 1980. CHM is a ministry bringing the healing message of the Gospel, the message of healing prayer, to the world - both by teaching and by praying for the sick, so that every person throughout the world may understand the message.

My mother, Joy Lamb, author of Sword of the Spirit the Word of God, *became very involved with Christian Healing Ministries, heading up their intercessory prayer team. I was 25 at the time and got to know both Judith and Frances, and spent time at the Ministry either in prayer, at conferences under the leadership of the MacNutts, or just helping my mother with her work. I was honored and blessed when Judith agreed to share a glimpse of her story about angels.*

ANGELS

by Judith MacNutt

Thomas Aquinas said, "We are like children who stand in need of masters [or teachers] to enlighten us and direct us, and God has provided for this by appointing his angels to be our teachers and guides." Isn't that encouraging? Psalm 91 reads: "*He will give His angels charge of you concerning your ways. They will guard you in all of your ways.*" Psalm 34:7 declares that: "*The angel of the Lord encamps around those who fear him, and he delivers them.*" Guarding, protecting, and guiding: these are just a few of the activities that the Lord has directed His angels to accomplish here on Earth.

A Gallup Poll in 1994 revealed that 72 percent of Americans believed that angels are real. Interestingly, that number was up 22 percent from a poll taken in 1988. And the latest polls now show that over 80 percent believe in angels. The growing belief in angels is amazing. Something has been happening in our lives that is making us aware of the supernatural realm. Why? What is the explanation?

My life work has been in the area of counseling and in the area of supernatural healing. The reason I wrote *Angels Are For Real* was to share with the public the wonderful stories of angel encounters that have been sent to me over the years (many having to do with healing), and to teach about angels from a Biblical foundation. What a comfort to know that God, in His compassionate mercy, created these wonderful beings to help us, to heal us, and to encourage us on our journey. It is especially comforting to know that they will come to usher us into the kingdom of God when our time comes to leave this Earth!

In the sixteenth century, St. John of the Cross said: "The more people's miseries increase, the more God multiplies [His] mercies." Today's hardships have increased to the point that many are living in despair. To counteract this, God is allowing people who are not even religious to see angels! Many ordinary people quickly come to believe in God after these majestic angels appear to them! Of all the angelic interventions I have heard about, the ones that mean the most to me are angelic appearances to those people who are in the deepest trouble, desperate people who have deep needs.

Who can see angels? First of all, let me say that to be able to see an angel does not signify holiness. Just because someone has seen an angel does not mean the person has unusual faith either. We know this because we can read about the people Jesus healed in His three-year public ministry in the Bible. None of them were Christian. They did not even know who Jesus was.

Angels will appear not because of our great faith or holiness (although the great saints did experience many visitations), but many times, because of our great need. And then I hear the occasional story where one is left to wonder why an angel appeared because no apparent reason can be found. Seeing angels is a privilege and changes us for the rest of our lives. It brings us into the awareness

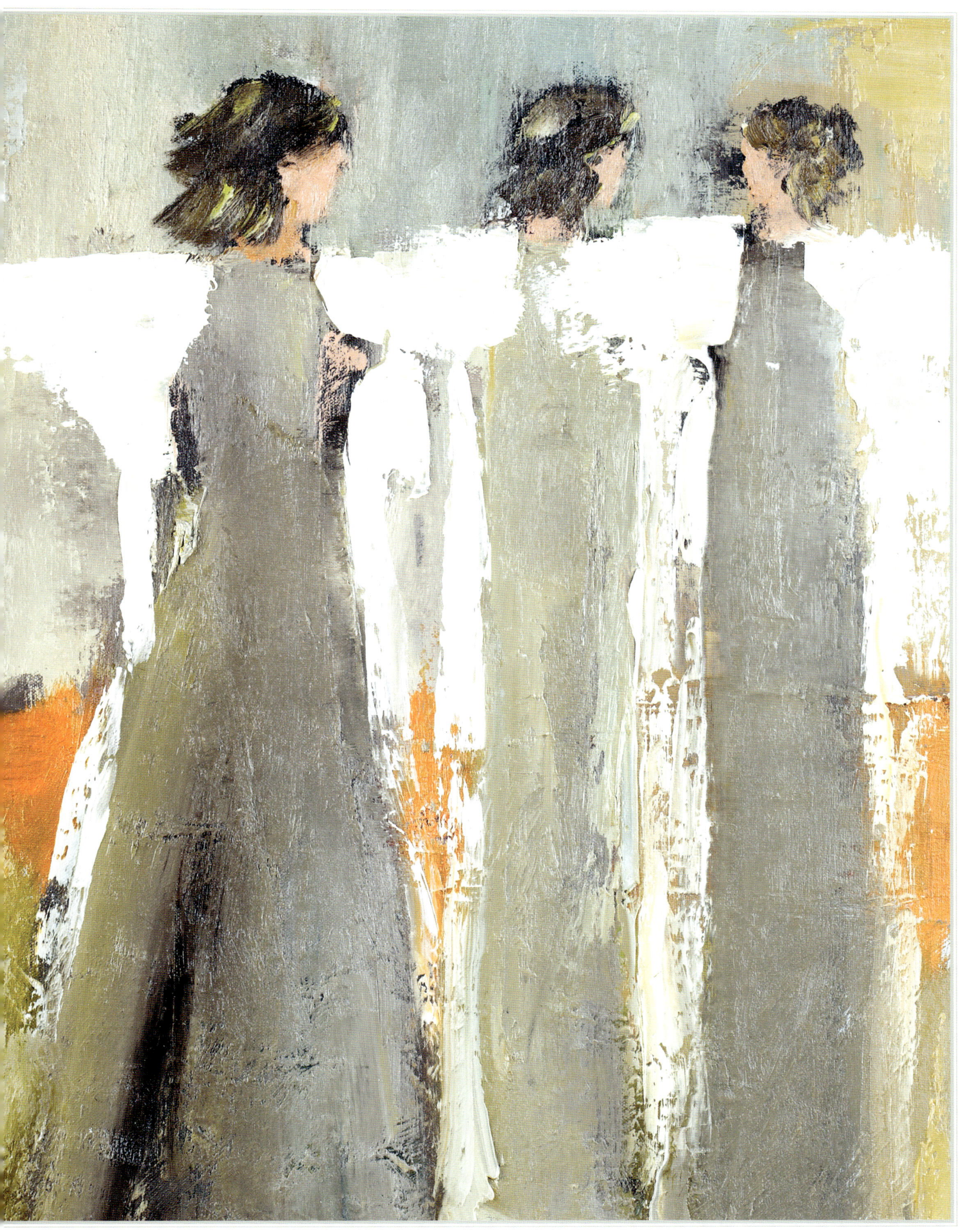

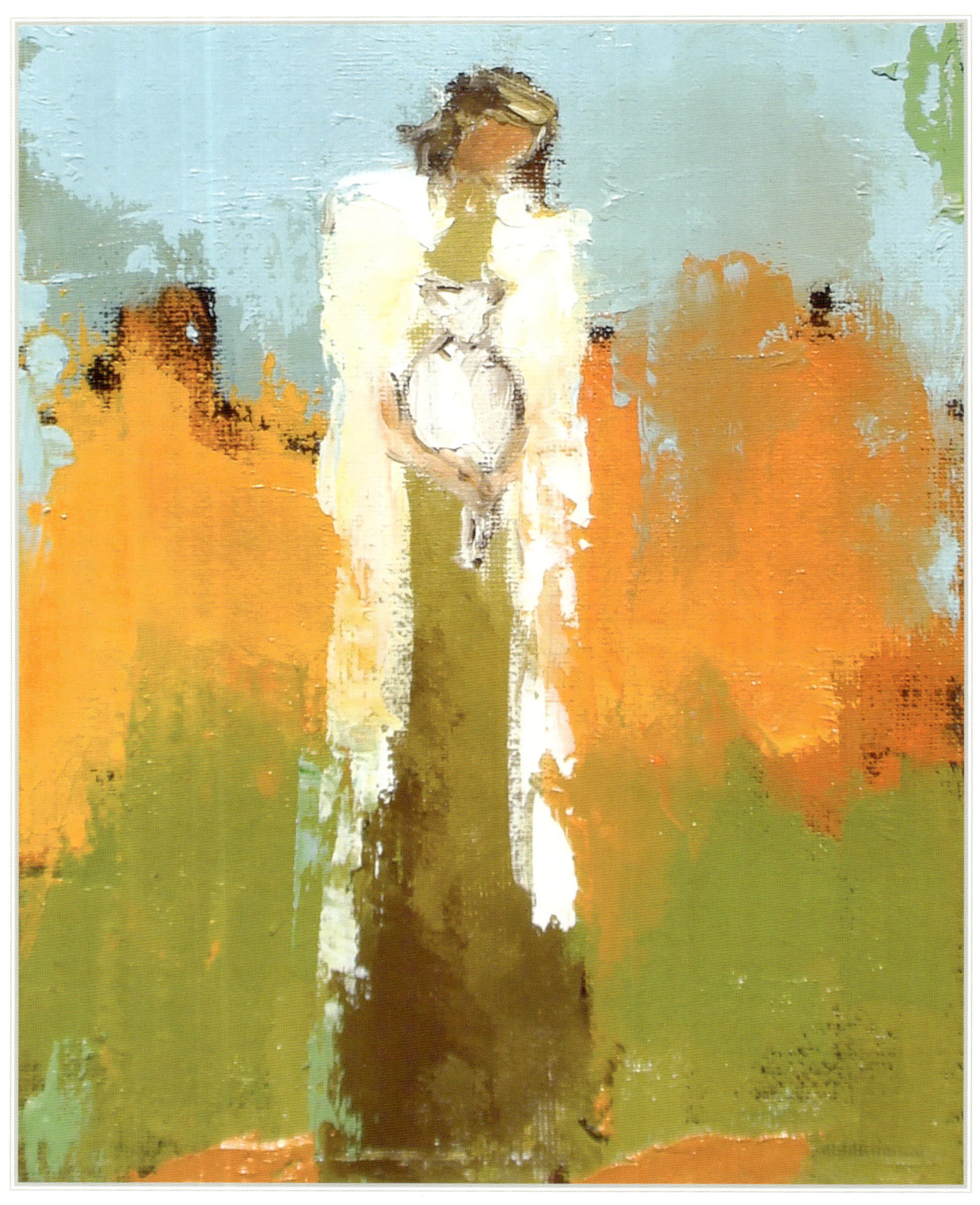

FOR GOD COMMANDS HIS ANGELS TO GUARD YOU IN ALL YOUR WAYS.

Psalm 91:11

of that other dimension – the spiritual dimension – where connection with the supernatural is never dull, never boring, and always active.

I have heard many testimonies from people over the years who have seen angels in their bedroom at night. Sometimes they appear in the form of light, sometimes as a figure in the corner of a room. I always encourage people to pray and ask God why this is happening and what it means.

At times, God allows us to catch glimpses of the spiritual world. St. Paul and St. John saw into the spiritual world and described it. They were no different than you or me. They just happened to be people who were allowed to catch these glimpses into the spiritual realm. When the angel appeared to Daniel, he was the only one who saw the vision; the men with him "*did not see it, but such terror overwhelmed them that they fled and hid themselves.*" (Daniel 10:7) The veil that separates us from the spiritual realm is lifted for some people, but not for everyone.

Angels are real, and I believe angels take a significant role in our lives. God has allowed me to see angels at times, but not all the time. Many of us never really think of angels as having a key role in our lives. They are created beings who existed before the foundations of this world were laid. Simply defined, angels are messengers. The Greek word for angels, angelos, means one who is sent, or a messenger.

Angels are mentioned in the Bible multiple times, showing that they are important and significant in the Kingdom of God. Part of the Lord's prayer: "*Thy kingdom come, thy will be done on earth as it is in heaven,*" (Matthew 6:10) describes part of the activity of angels. Angels are members of God's kingdom and their roles include guiding, guarding, sending messages, and comforting. They are with us now. They will be with us for all of eternity.

—JUDITH MACNUTT, Author of *Angels Are For Real* and President of Christian Healing Ministries

I MYSELF DO NOTHING. THE HOLY SPIRIT
ACCOMPLISHES ALL THROUGH ME.

—WILLIAM BLAKE

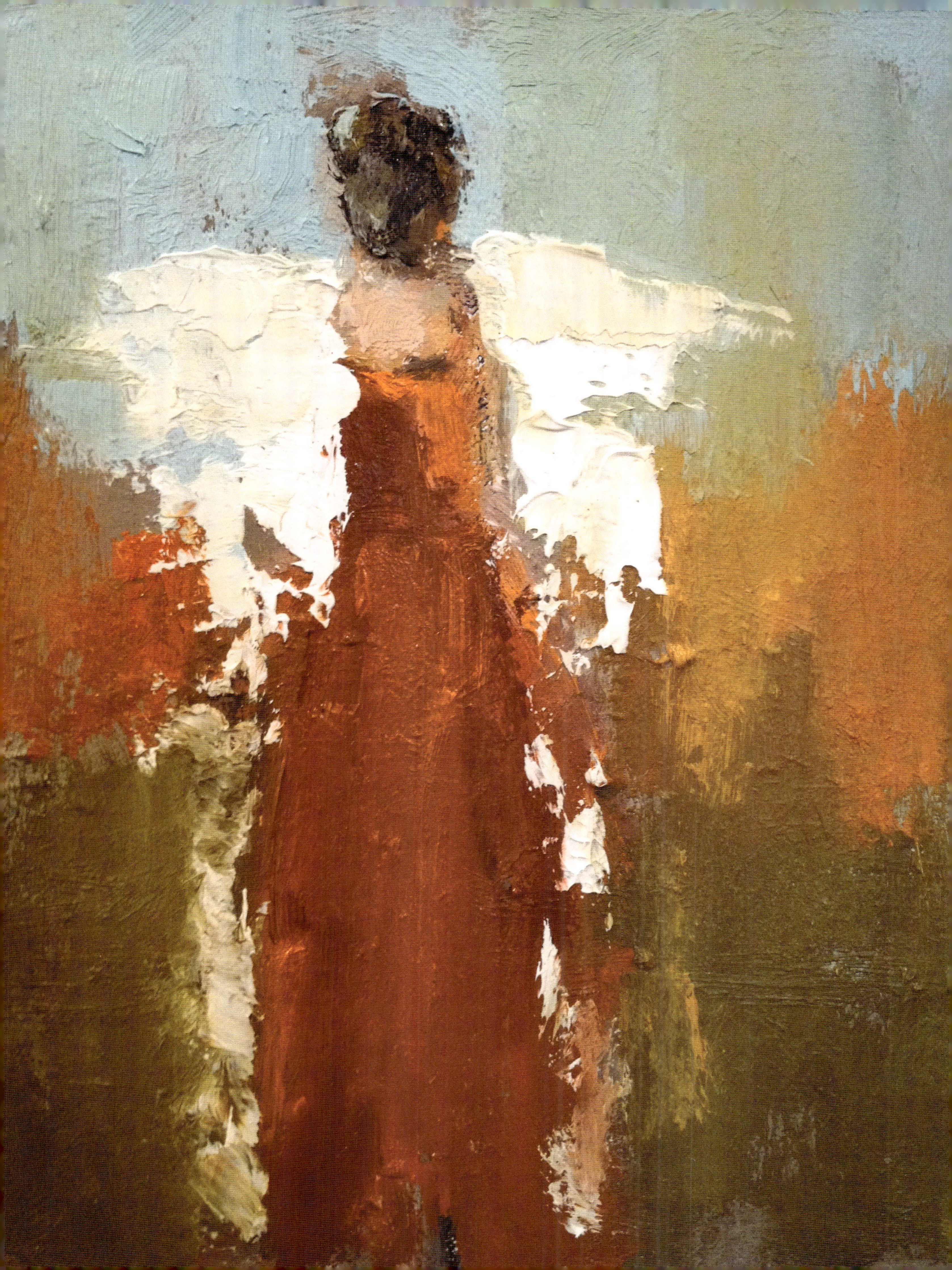

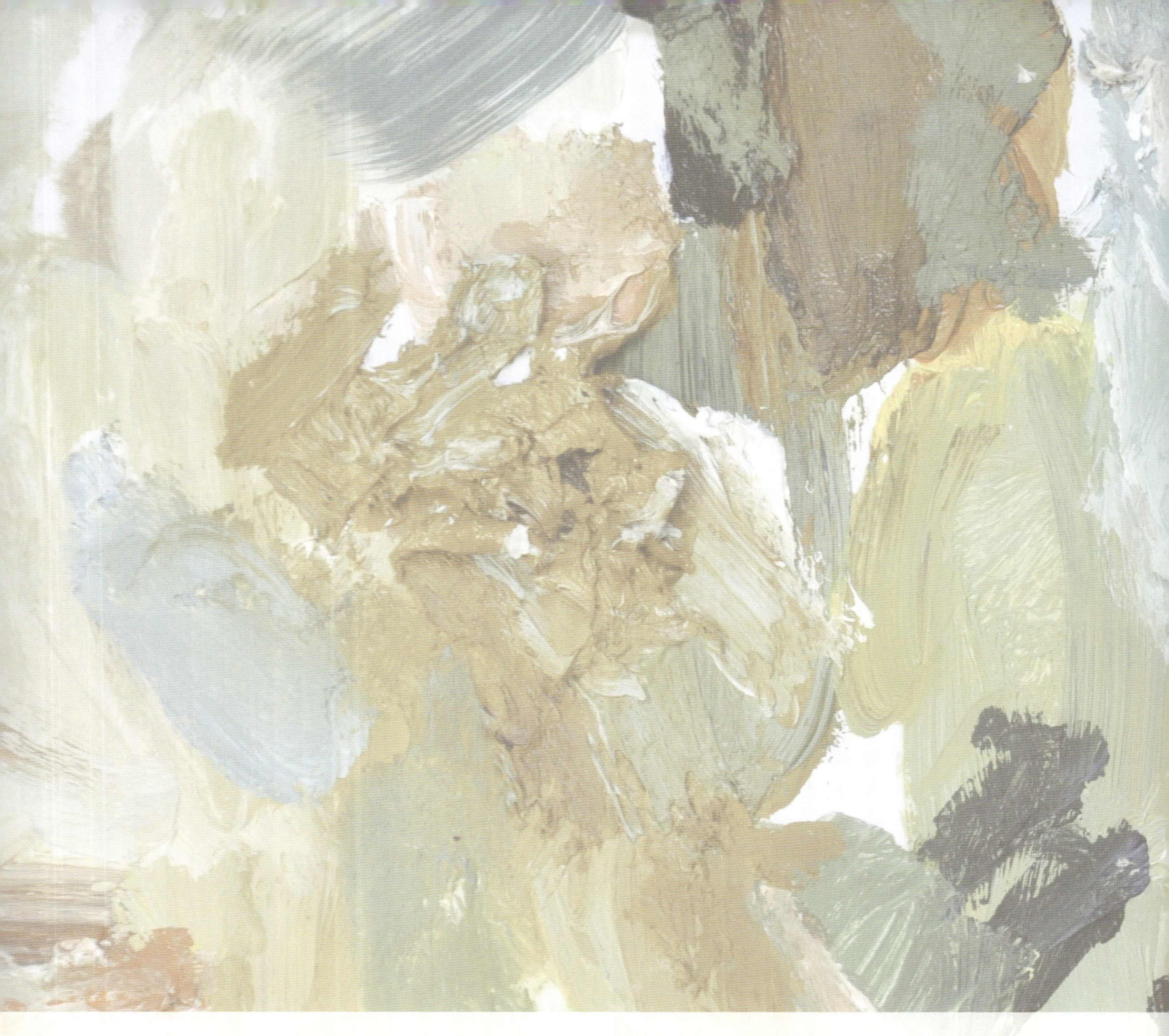

JESUS REPLIED: 'LOVE THE LORD YOUR GOD WITH ALL YOUR HEART AND WITH ALL YOUR SOUL AND WITH ALL YOUR MIND.' THIS IS THE FIRST AND GREATEST COMMANDMENT. AND THE SECOND IS LIKE IT: 'LOVE YOUR NEIGHBOR AS YOURSELF.'

MATTHEW 22:37-39

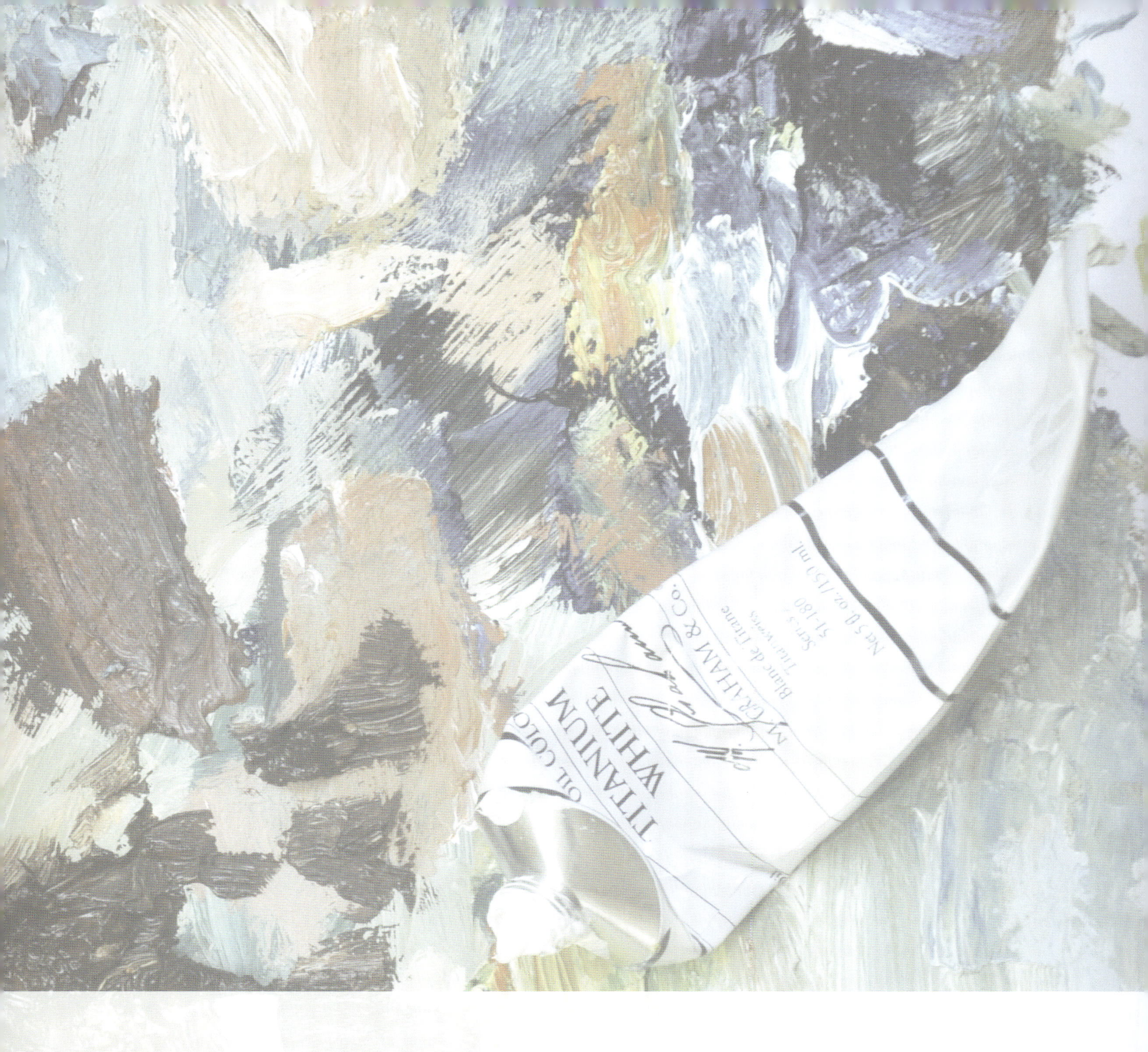

LOVE

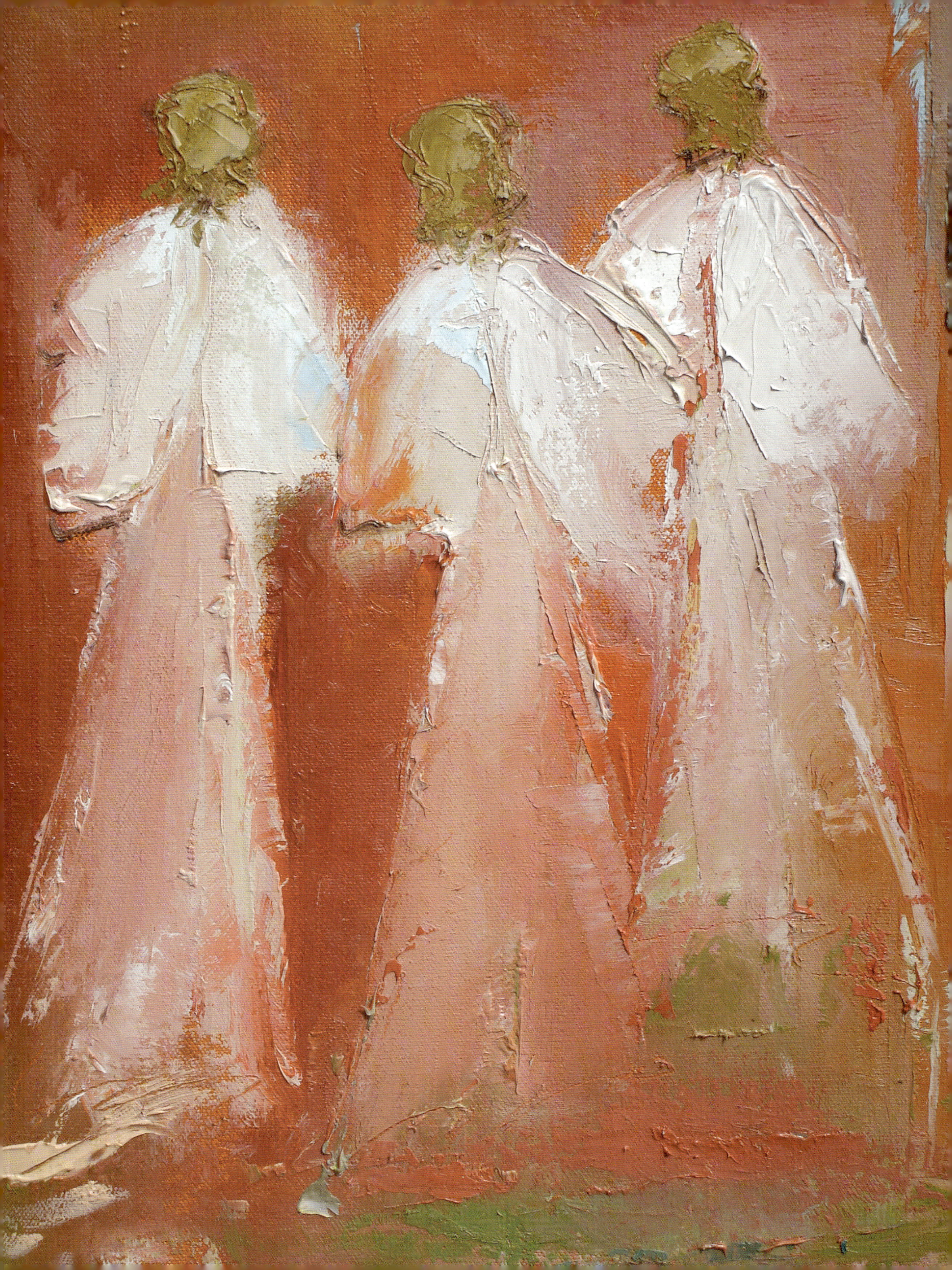

WHAT GOOD IS IT, MY BROTHERS AND SISTERS, IF SOMEONE CLAIMS TO HAVE FAITH BUT HAS NO DEEDS? CAN SUCH FAITH SAVE THEM? SUPPOSE A BROTHER OR A SISTER IS WITHOUT CLOTHES AND DAILY FOOD. IF ONE OF YOU SAYS TO THEM, "GO IN PEACE; KEEP WARM AND WELL FED," BUT DOES NOTHING ABOUT THEIR PHYSICAL NEEDS, WHAT GOOD IS IT? IN THE SAME WAY, FAITH BY ITSELF, IF IT IS NOT ACCOMPANIED BY ACTION, IS DEAD. BUT SOMEONE WILL SAY, "YOU HAVE FAITH; I HAVE DEEDS." SHOW ME YOUR FAITH WITHOUT DEEDS, AND I WILL SHOW YOU MY FAITH BY MY DEEDS.

JAMES 2:14-18

FAITH AND DEEDS

The Harvest Center of Charlotte
by Marion Shields, Board Member

Enter the Harvest Center and you enter a place where love abounds - from the hugs of Barbara, the greeter and the smiles on the faces of the volunteers, to the warmth and tangible comfort of a hot meal. People come to The Harvest Center in search of food, clothing, or housing. What they find is a place where God's love reaches out to them through the staff, volunteers, and residents and draws them in so that they can begin the process of transformation.

The Harvest Center was started by the late Barbara Brewton Cameron in the Double Oaks neighborhood of Charlotte, North Carolina where she grew up. While walking home from work in 1973, Barbara's husband was murdered, and she and her three small children left the neighborhood, vowing never to return. Nine years later, she felt God calling her back to this neighborhood, and she reluctantly returned to start a simple meal ministry on the sidewalk, serving soup and sandwiches to the homeless. She invited her sister, Rosa, to help in the effort. Pastor Cameron and Rosa were committed to revitalizing the neighborhood that was full of guns, gang activity and drug-dealers. The neighborhood was transformed and their simple ministry grew into what is now The Harvest Center of Charlotte.

The Mission of The Harvest Center is to create an environment where Jesus Christ transforms members of

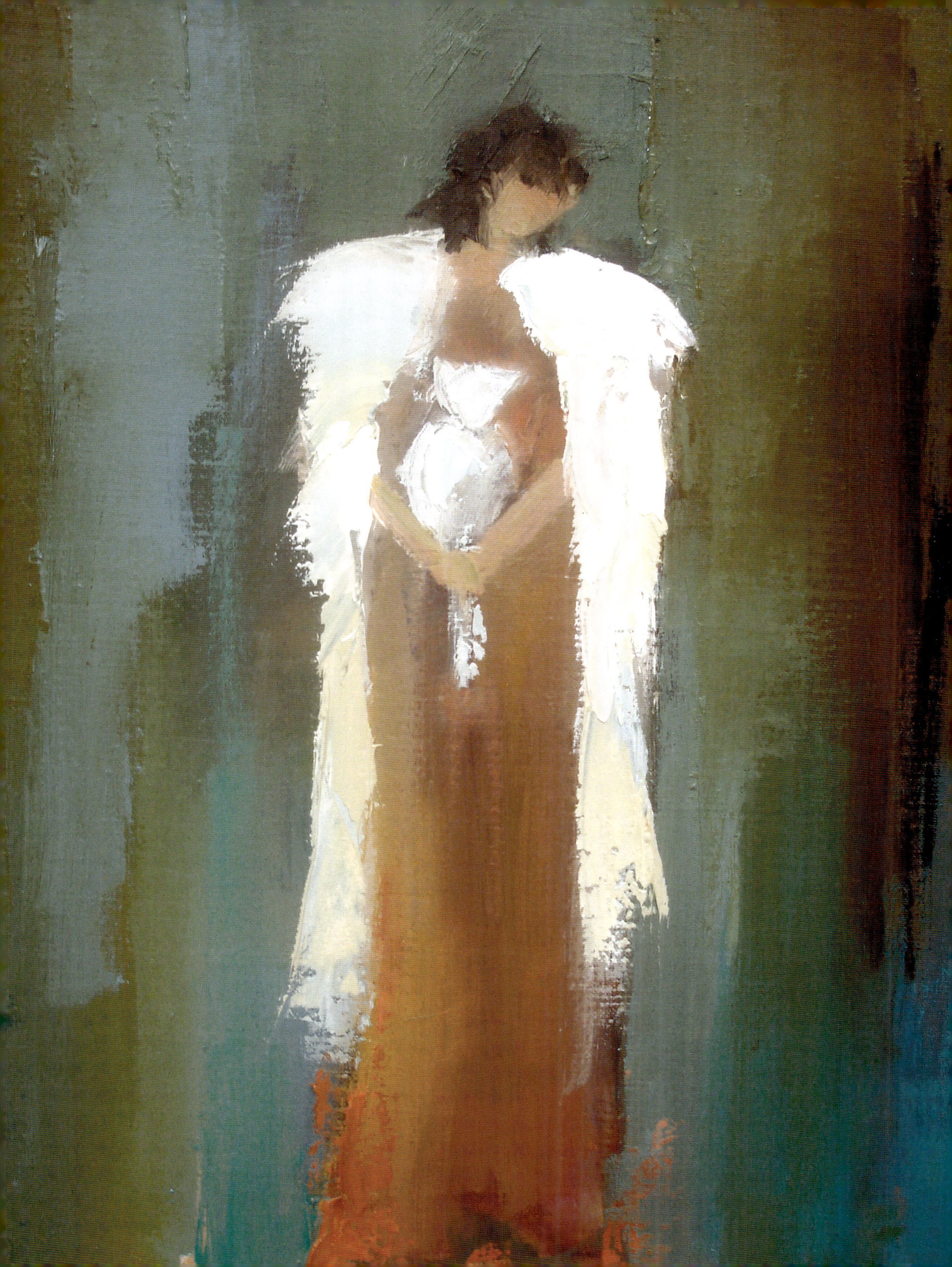

WHOEVER IS GENEROUS TO THE POOR LENDS TO THE LORD, AND HE WILL REPAY HIM FOR HIS DEED.

PROVERBS 19:17

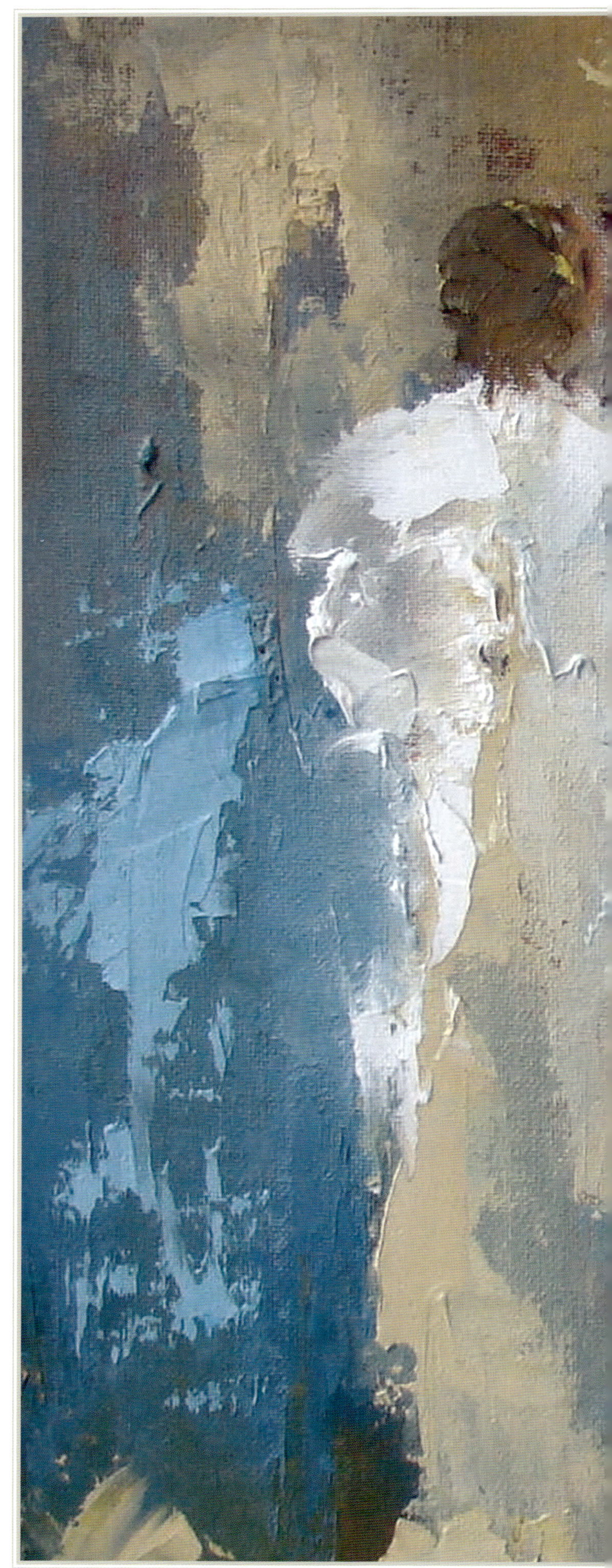

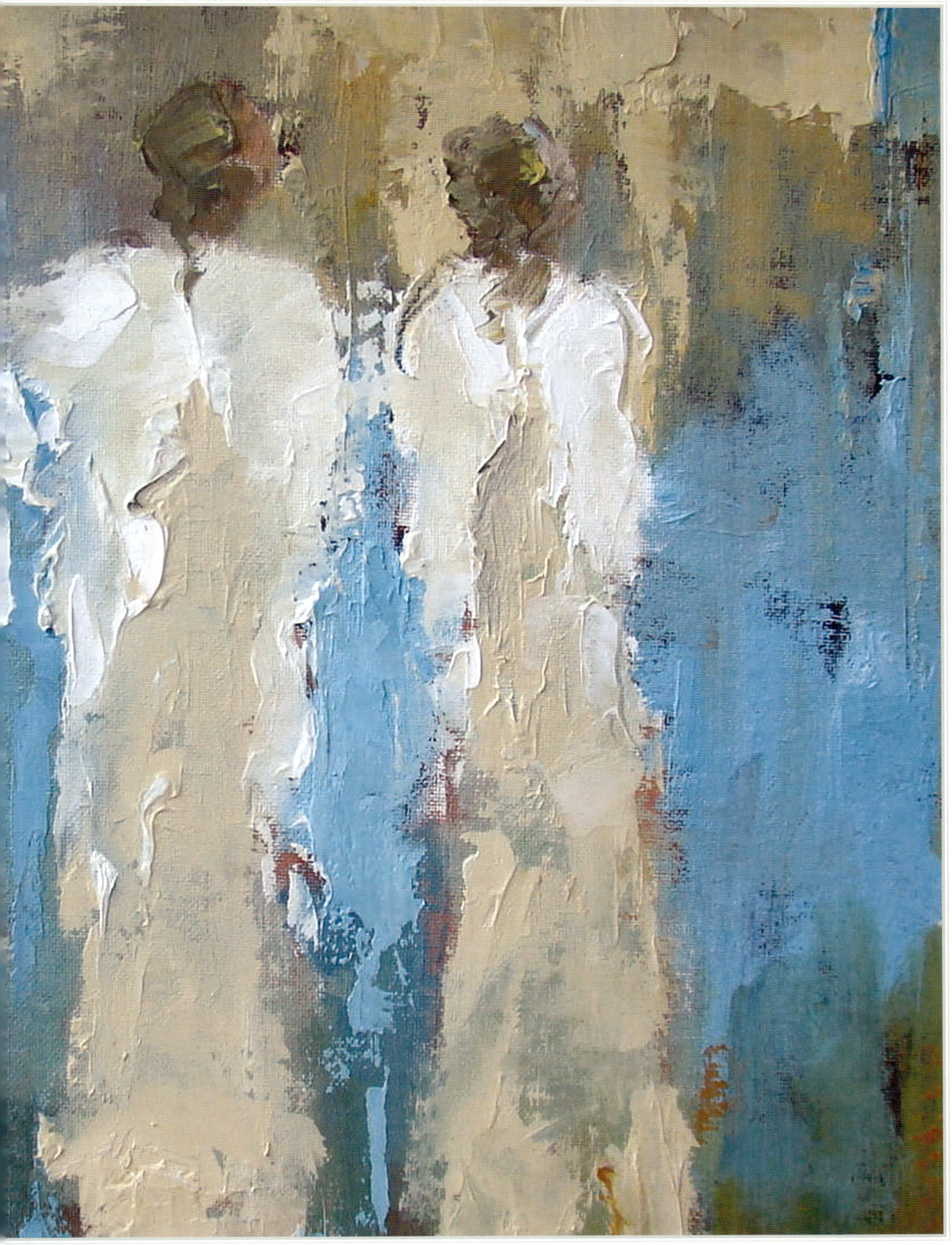

our community to their full potential by providing food, clothing, housing, education, counseling, and recovery services and referrals. We serve over 1,000 of Charlotte's homeless and low-income individuals every week, offering hot meals and giving out clothing and blankets on Tuesdays and Wednesdays. The Harvest Center also operates a Food Pantry that distributes groceries to over 30,000 individuals each year. The food and clothing ministry attracts clients to The Harvest Center, where we are then able to develop relationships of trust and care so that the transformational process can begin.

As part of The Harvest Center's Transformational Program, a variety of programs are offered which assist our clients in becoming contributing members of our community. Literacy and GED preparation classes, job skills and readiness classes (in collaboration with Jacob's Ladder), addiction recovery meetings, Bible Study classes, an entrepreneur and small business development program, and a Winter basketball program for men and young men are part of this growing arm of The Harvest Center. Our goal is to truly transform the lives of those we serve, ultimately hoping to end homelessness in our community one life at a time. In the words of one of our program participants: "I was a part of something just by getting up and going to work at The Harvest Center every morning at 6:00 am. By having to be there, I started to turn around. I looked forward to it. I felt a part of a community."

The Harvest Center's Vision is to be a community of guests, volunteers, and staff whose lives are mutually transformed by the love of Jesus Christ. This transformation is equally evident in the lives of volunteers. In the words of one volunteer: "I used to be afraid of the homeless, but after volunteering at the Harvest Center, I now see that they are individuals just like me, yet their lives have taken a wrong turn (for a variety of reasons). I really look forward to my weekly volunteer time at the Harvest Center – first, because it's such a joyful place, and second, because I can help my homeless neighbors and offer them some small comfort and friendship, while the atmosphere allows them to keep their dignity."

In the New Testament, Jesus's brother, James, writes: *Dear Friends, do you think you'll get anywhere in this life if you learn all the right words but never do anything? Does merely talking about faith indicate that a person really has it? For instance, you come upon an old friend dressed in rags and half-starved and say, "Good morning, friend! Be clothed in Christ! Be filled with the Holy Spirit!" and walk off without providing so much as a coat or a cup of soup – where does that get you? Isn't it obvious that God-talk without God-acts is outrageous nonsense!* James 2:14-17 (The Message). The Harvest Center is a place where God-talk and God-acts come together and where the love of Christ is shown to all through His faithful servants. Love abounds!

LET LOVE OF THE BRETHREN CONTINUE. DO NOT NEGLECT TO SHOW HOSPITALITY TO STRANGERS, FOR BY THIS SOME HAVE ENTERTAINED ANGELS WITHOUT KNOWING IT.

HEBREWS 13:1-2

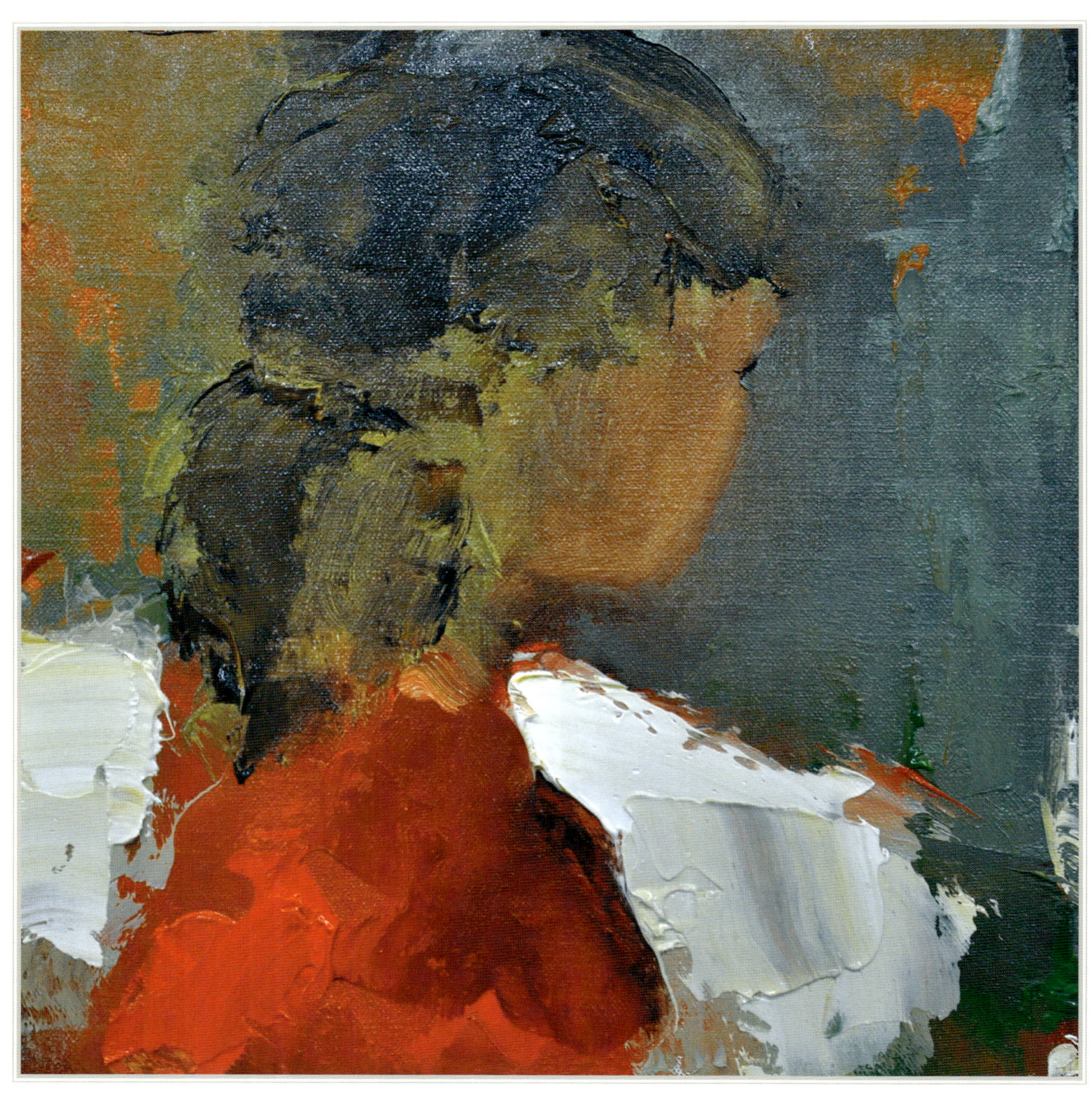

IN OUR LIFE THERE IS A SINGLE COLOR, AS ON AN ARTIST'S PALETTE, WHICH PROVIDES THE MEANING OF LIFE AND ART. IT IS THE COLOR OF LOVE.

—MARC CHAGALL

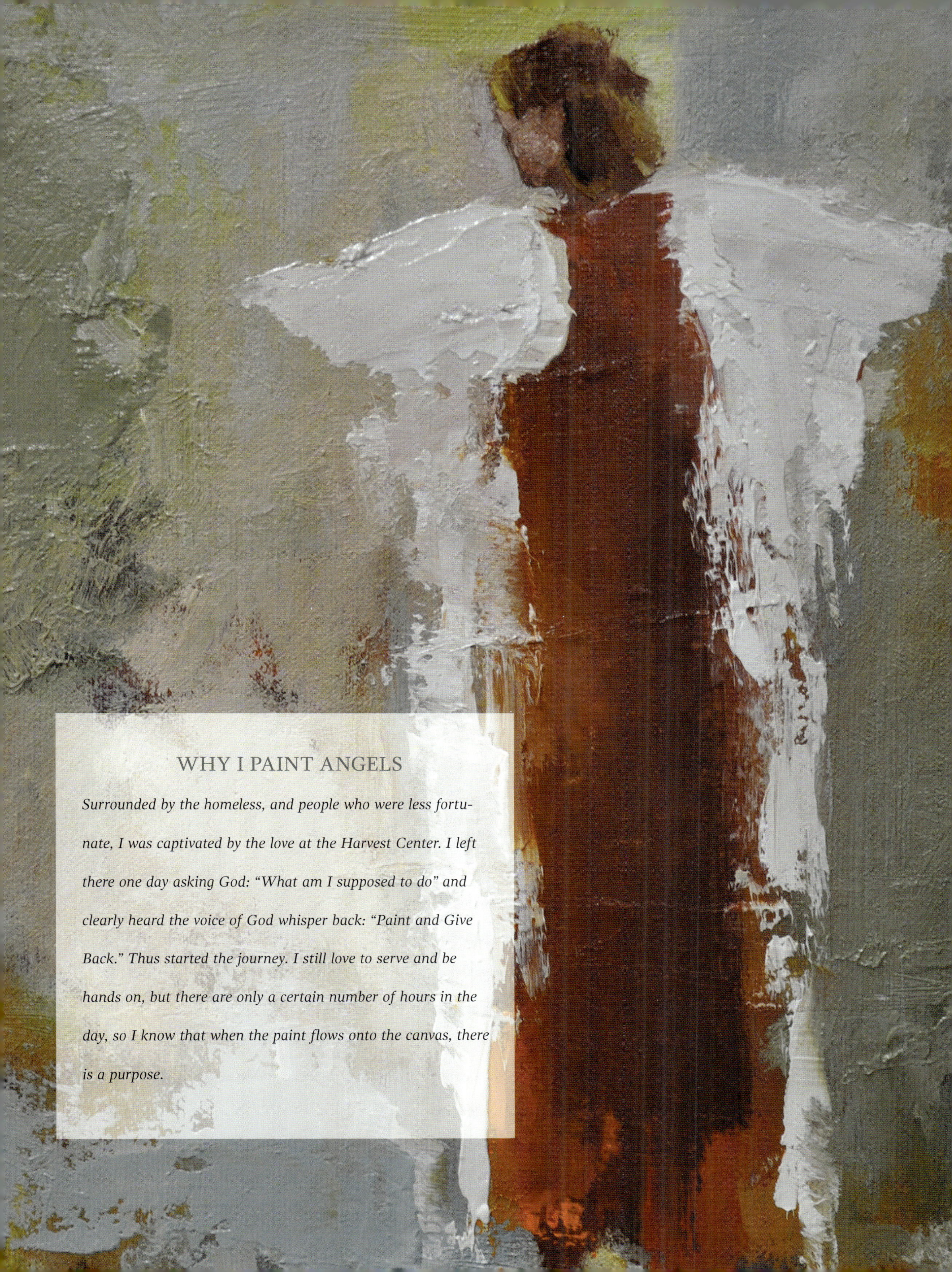

WHY I PAINT ANGELS

Surrounded by the homeless, and people who were less fortunate, I was captivated by the love at the Harvest Center. I left there one day asking God: "What am I supposed to do" and clearly heard the voice of God whisper back: "Paint and Give Back." Thus started the journey. I still love to serve and be hands on, but there are only a certain number of hours in the day, so I know that when the paint flows onto the canvas, there is a purpose.

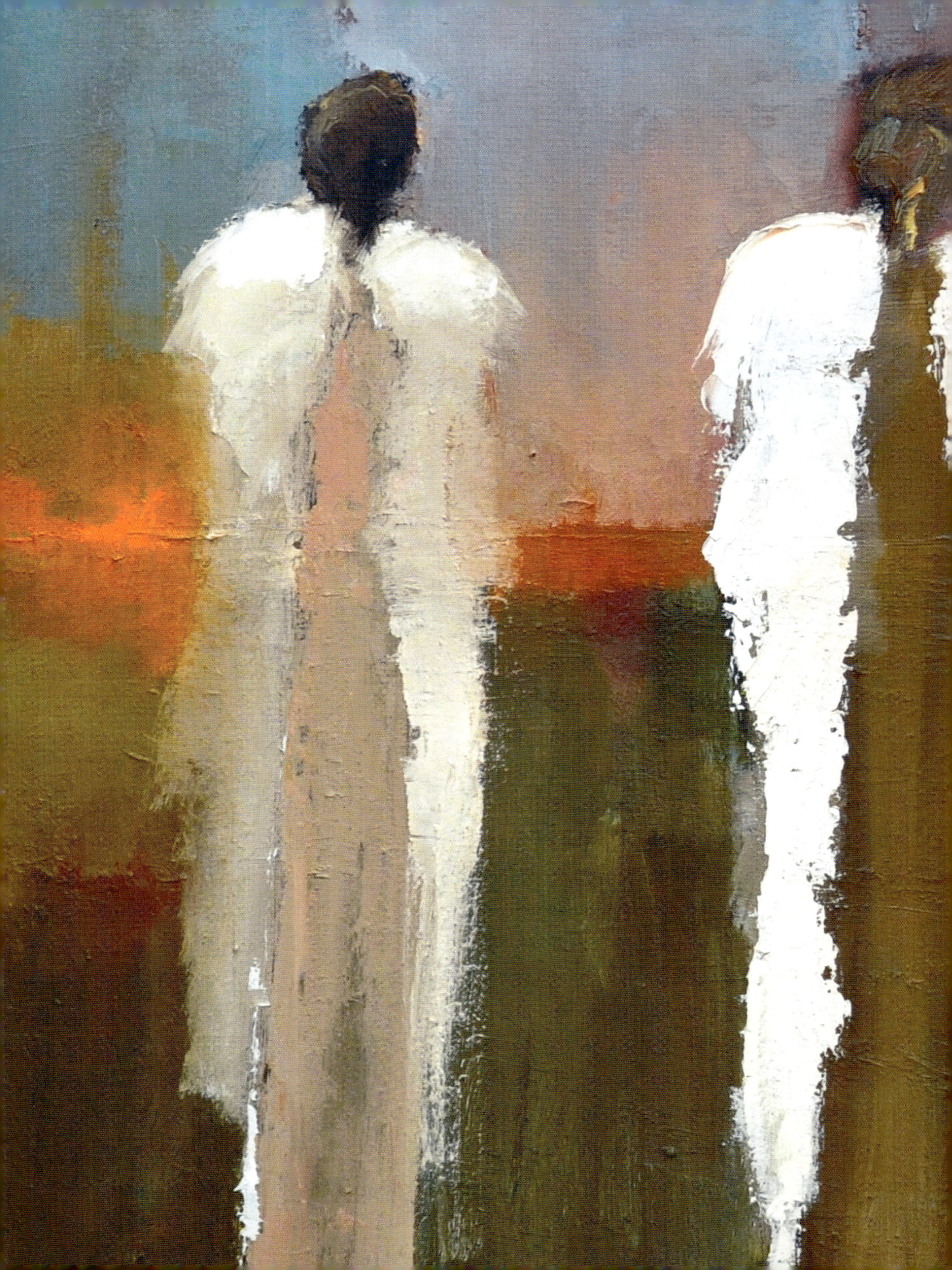

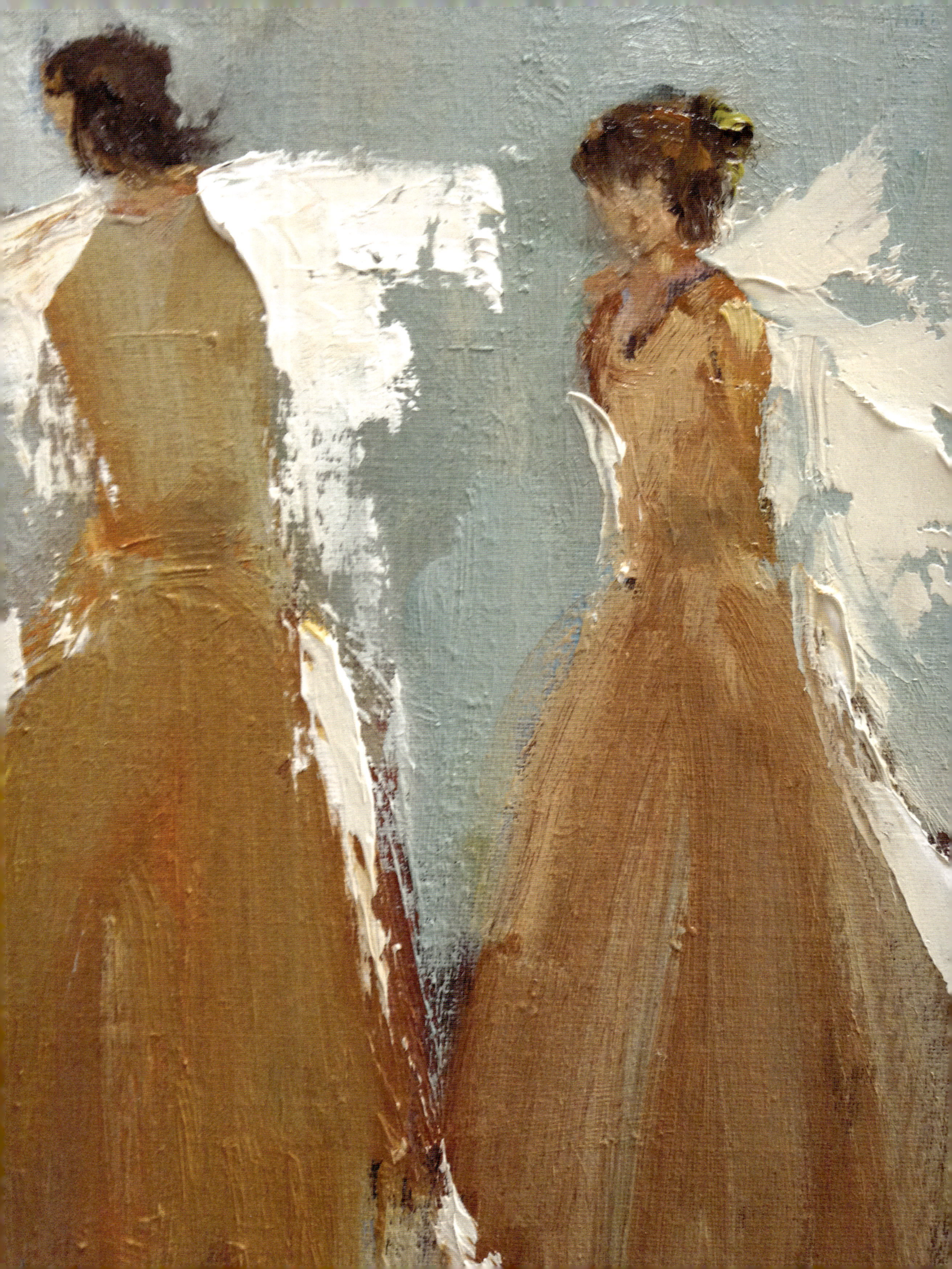

LOVE IS PATIENT, LOVE IS KIND, AND IS NOT JEALOUS;
LOVE DOES NOT BRAG AND IS NOT ARROGANT, DOES NOT ACT
UNBECOMINGLY; IT DOES NOT SEEK ITS OWN, IS NOT PROVOKED,
DOES NOT TAKE INTO ACCOUNT A WRONG SUFFERED, DOES NOT
REJOICE IN UNRIGHTEOUSNESS, BUT REJOICES WITH THE TRUTH.
LOVE BEARS ALL THINGS, BELIEVES ALL THINGS, HOPES ALL THINGS,
ENDURES ALL THINGS. LOVE NEVER FAILS. NOW ABIDE FAITH, HOPE
AND LOVE, THESE THREE; BUT THE GREATEST OF THESE IS LOVE.

I Corinthians 13:4-8, 13

GOOD AND FAITHFUL SERVANT

Same Kind of Different As Me

My husband Clark and I were coming back from a road trip and I was desperate to dig in and read this book, *Same Kind of Difference As Me*. The first few pages were captivating and I was hooked. This amazing story is about an international art dealer, Ron Hall, and a homeless man, Denver Moore. My husband wanted my attention to keep him company and help him stay awake, so I decided to read the book aloud to him. He drove for four and a half hours while I read the story about Ron, his wife Debbie, and Denver.

When I finished the book, I knew that Ron needed an angel painting. I spent the next few weeks in the studio painting and praying for these men, and an Angel was created on the canvas that I entitled: "Good and Faithful Servant." A few months later, the painting was shipped. I will never forget the afternoon when I received a phone call with the caller ID: Ron Hall. What an honor to hear first-hand more of their story, their journey and the incredible friendship that was formed between these two men.

In May of 2009, Clark and I had the privilege to be a part of a fundraiser "Carry the Torch" in Knoxville, Tennessee, where Ron and Denver would be speaking. I was asked to donate an original oil painting: "*An Angel*

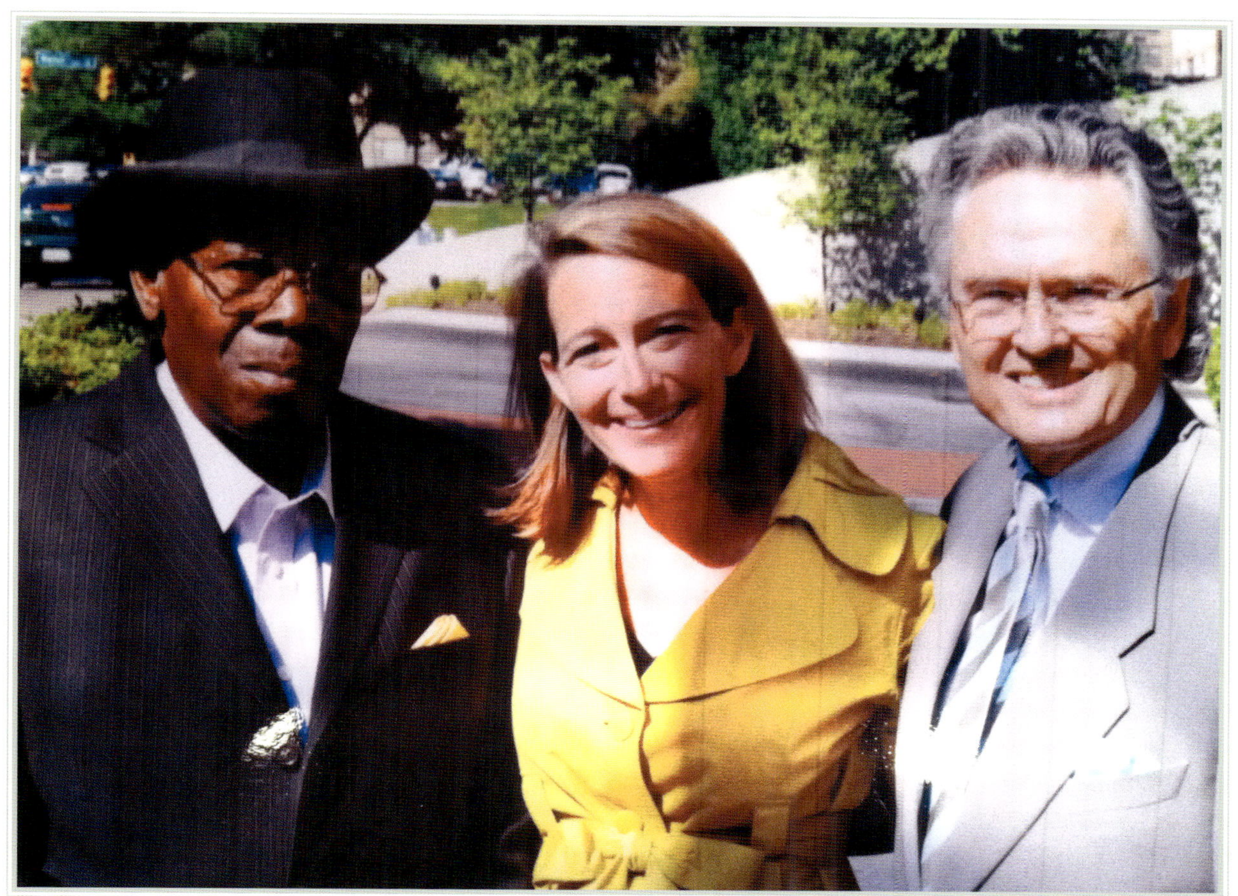

In Our Midst" that hangs in the center today. In addition, prints of the original oil were made and sold at the fundraiser to benefit the Volunteer Ministry Center. We spent two days with Ron and Denver, and were so inspired by these men's humbleness and faith. Denver was a man of few words, but when he spoke, his words were full of wisdom and grace. Giving God the glory for all things, he spoke words of truth with great conviction.

Their story is one of courage, forgiveness, undeniable faith, redemption and love. It is a story worth reading, and I encourage you to do so knowing that everywhere we go, everyone we meet, there are Angels among us.

DENVER MOORE
1937–2012

Denver Moore was born in Shreveport, Louisiana, on January 30, 1937. He was raised on a cotton plantation in Red River Parish. In the mid-to-late '50s, he left Louisiana for the first time and lived briefly in Fort Worth, Texas, before moving to Los Angeles. He left LA in the mid '60s, riding the rails before returning to Texas then Louisiana. He was living in Dallas at the time of his passing.

Though his lips were always flappin' like Bible pages, he would say he never claimed to be a preacher, just a sinner saved by grace with a message of hope for those that didn't have any.

His story, well known by millions, is told in *Same Kind of Different as Me*, a word-of-mouth best-selling book that spent three and a half years as a *New York Times* bestseller. His follow-up book *What Difference Do It Make*, tells the rest of his story.

Denver, formerly homeless, spent much of his life on the streets of Fort Worth, Texas, until Deborah Hall (Miss Debbie to him) dreamt of this poor man with wisdom that would change the city. And did he ever! A few years after her dream, Denver was honored as the Philanthropist of the Year for his ministry and fund-raising for the homeless in Fort Worth. Upon accepting that honor, he shared the story of his transformation that he first told on the Tavis Smiley Show on PBS. "God is in the recycling business," he said. "What most folks in Fort Worth thought was trash on the streets, God turned into a treasure!" Amen to that.

In 2007 Barbara Bush selected *Same Kind of Different as Me* to be featured at her Celebration of Reading fund-raisers in Dallas and Washington, D. C. Denver was honored to meet the President and attend a private

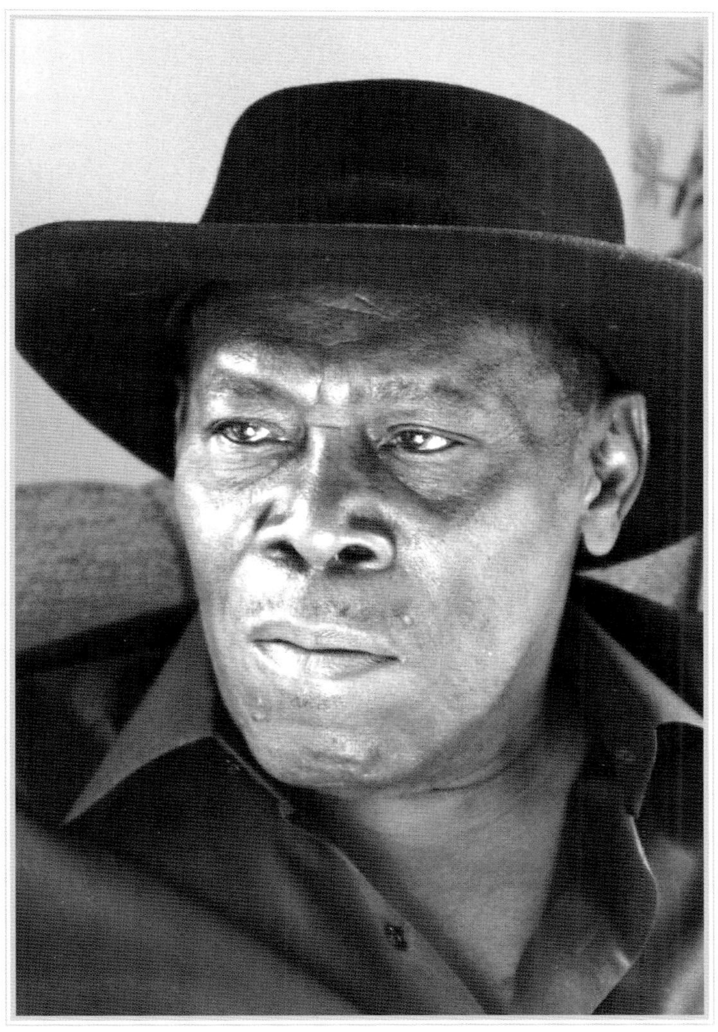

luncheon in the White House with Bush family members and four other best-selling authors. As he pulled away from the White House in a long blue limousine, he told his co-author, Ron Hall: "I done gone from livin' in the bushes to eatin' with the Bushes. God bless America," he exclaimed. "This is a great country!"

Since 2005, Denver had spoken at more than 400 fund-raising events and countless radio and TV shows. He attained rock star status with his fans, but the only introduction he ever wanted was, "Tell 'em I'm a NOBODY that is tryin' to tell EVERYBODY about SOMEBODY that can save ANYBODY." And he did. That "SOMEBODY" was Jesus, and Denver woke up in His arms on March 31, 2012. His famous quote and the final words in his book are, "We are all homeless workin' our way home." Welcome home, friend; you were a good and faithful servant.

—RON HALL

I found out everybody's different – the same kind of different as me. We're all just regular folks walkin' down the road God done set in front of us. The truth about it is, whether we is rich or poor or something in between, this earth ain't no final restin' place. So in a way, we is all homeless – just workin' our way toward home.

DENVER MOORE

Author, *Same Kind of Different as Me*

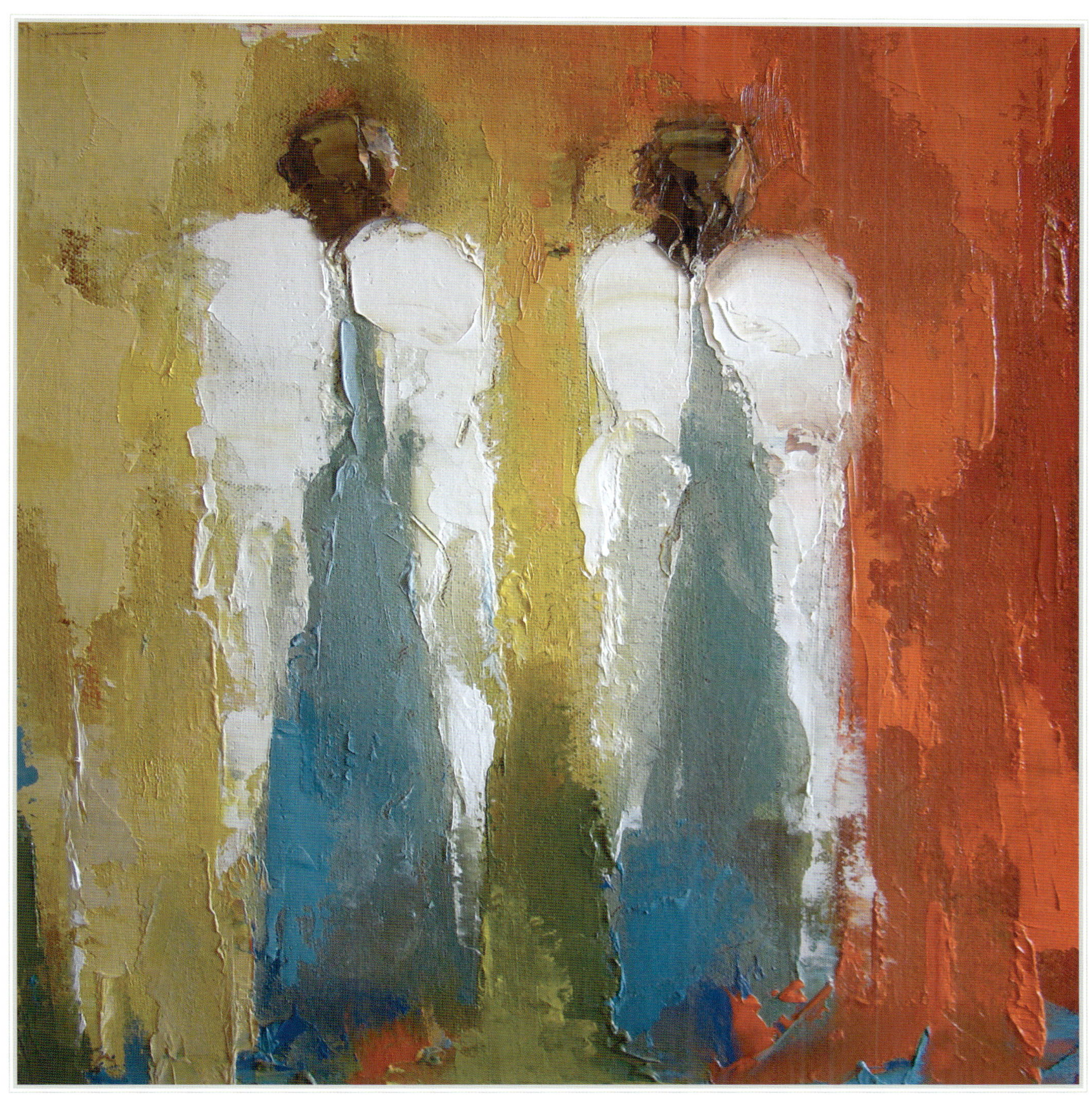

WE LOVE BECAUSE HE FIRST LOVED US.

I John 4:19

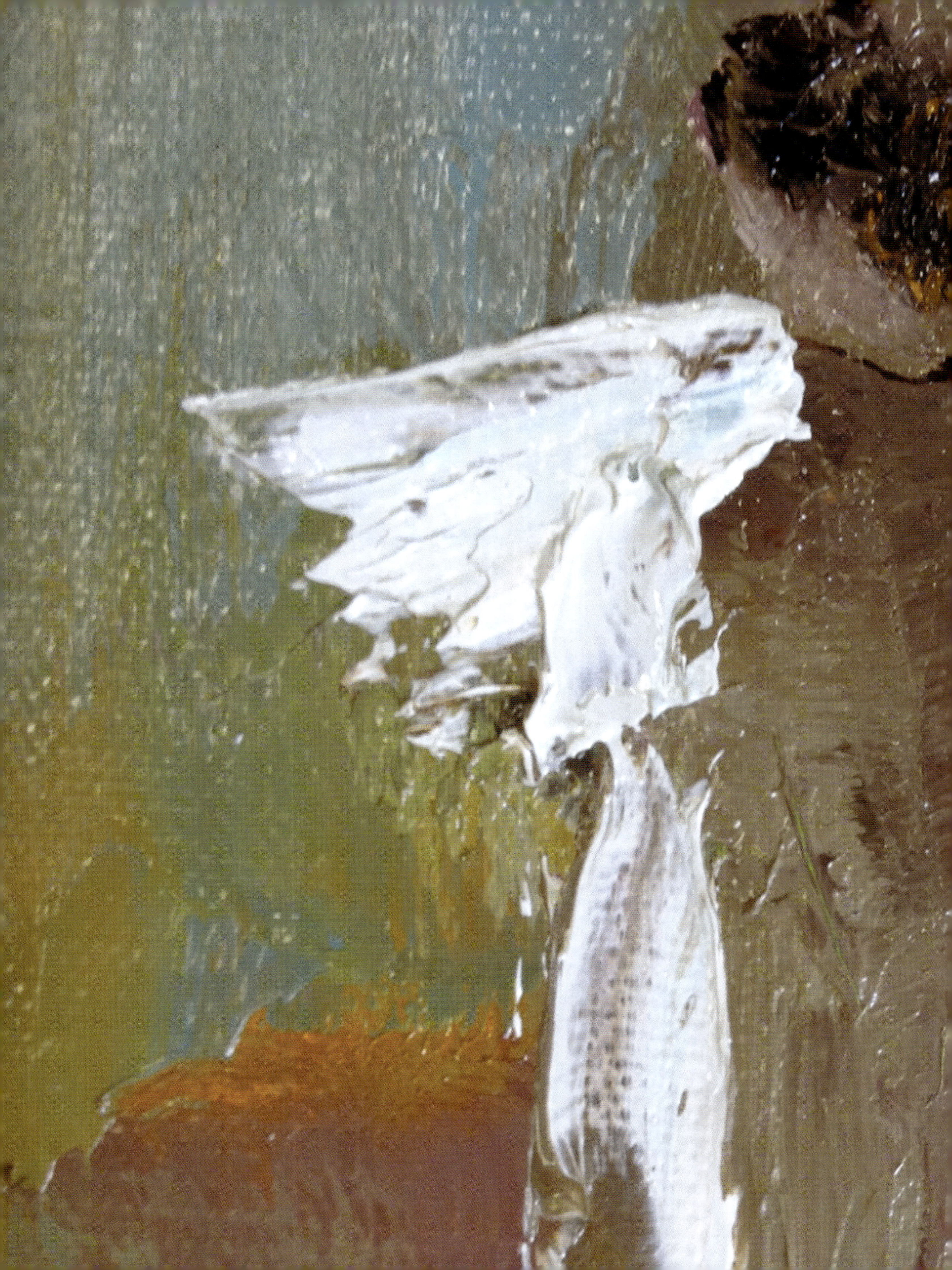

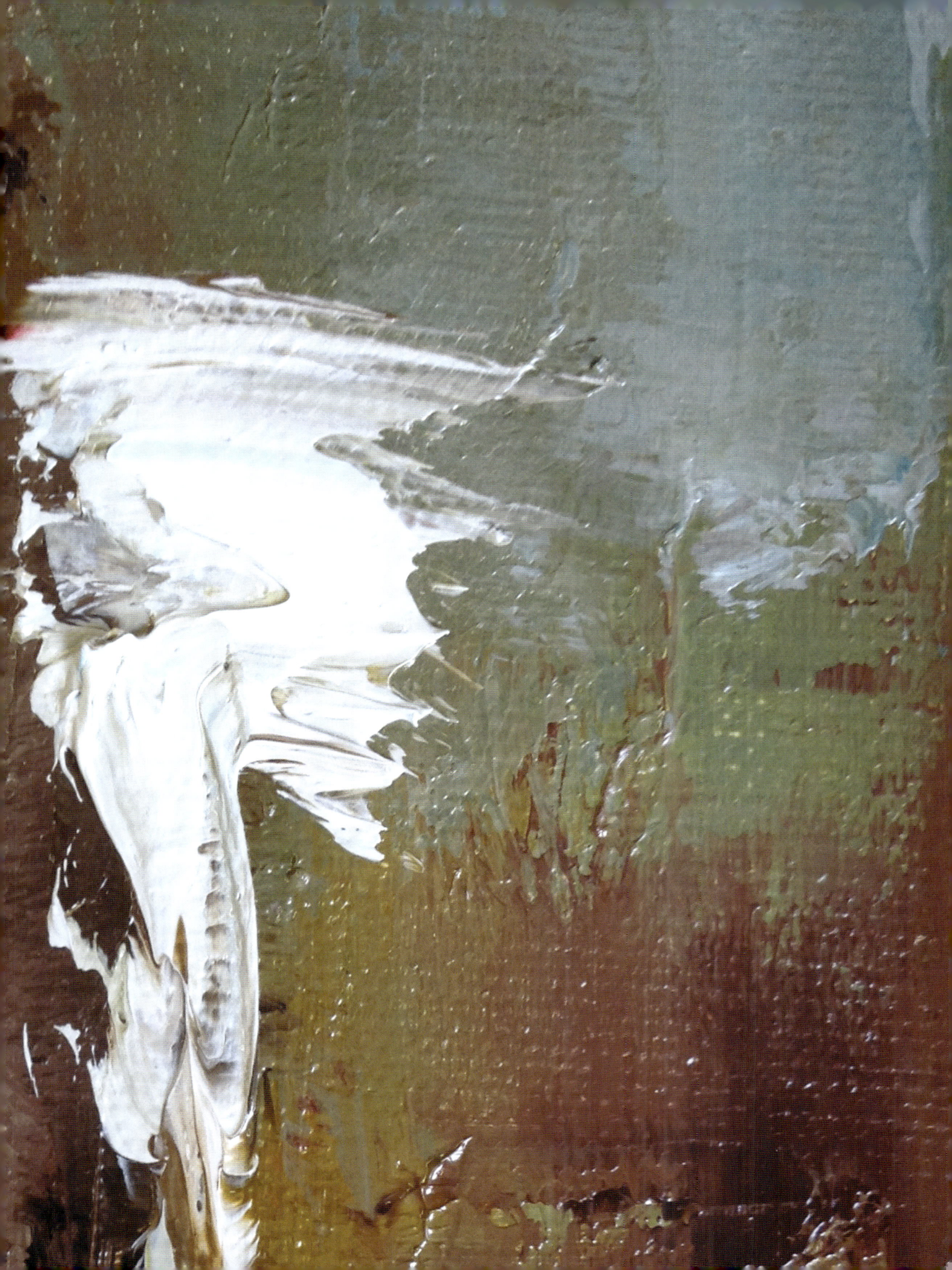

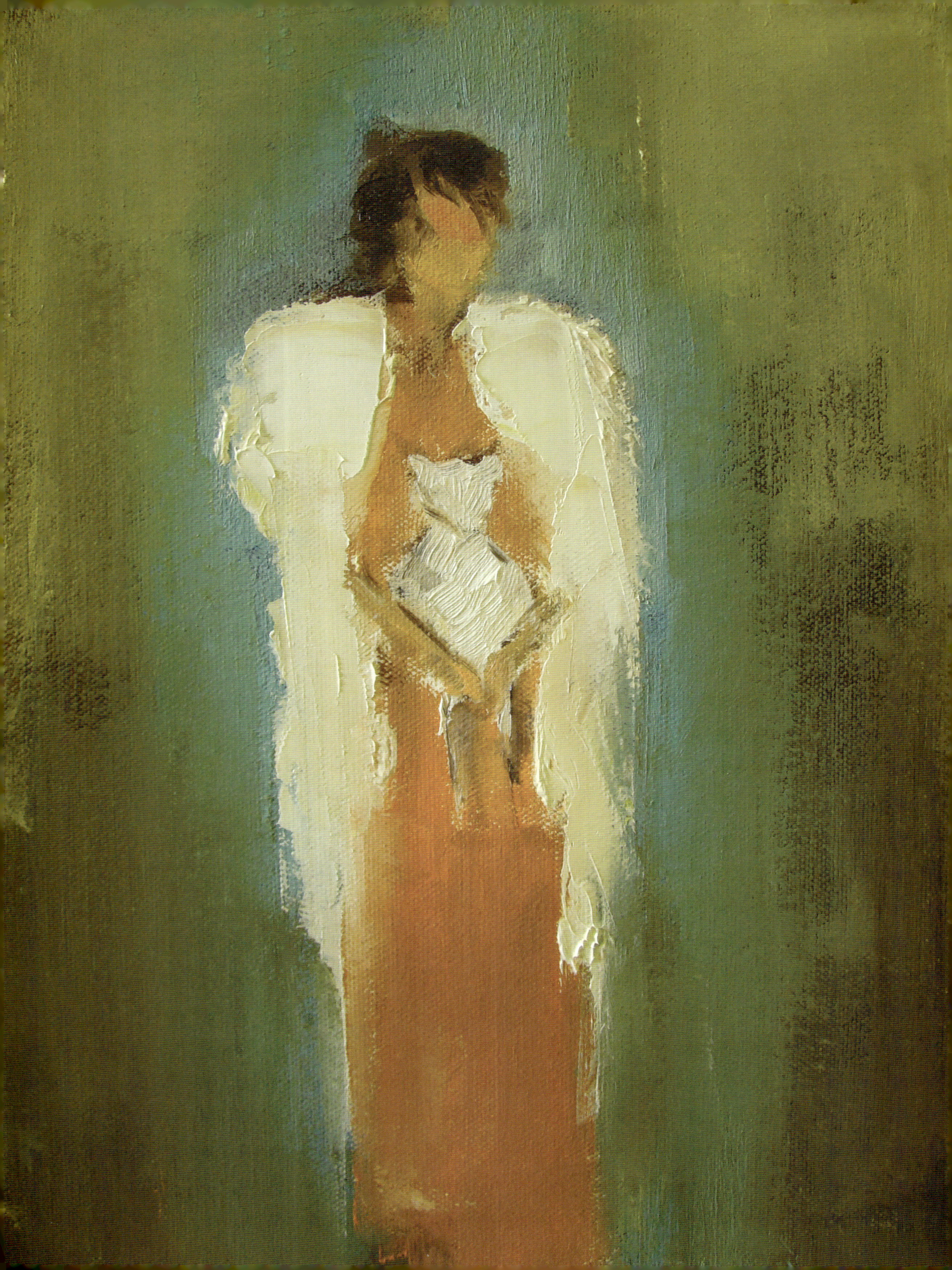

ART IS NOT WHAT YOU SEE BUT WHAT YOU MAKE OTHERS SEE.

—EDGAR DEGAS

FOR I WAS HUNGRY AND YOU GAVE ME FOOD, I WAS THIRSTY AND YOU GAVE ME DRINK, I WAS A STRANGER AND YOU WELCOMED ME, I WAS NAKED AND YOU CLOTHED ME, I WAS SICK AND YOU VISITED ME, I WAS IN PRISON AND YOU CAME TO ME.' THEN THE RIGHTEOUS WILL ANSWER HIM, SAYING, 'LORD, WHEN DID WE SEE YOU HUNGRY AND FEED YOU, OR THIRSTY AND GIVE YOU DRINK? AND WHEN DID WE SEE YOU A STRANGER AND WELCOME YOU, OR NAKED AND CLOTHE YOU? AND WHEN DID WE SEE YOU SICK OR IN PRISON AND VISIT YOU?' AND THE KING WILL ANSWER THEM, 'TRULY, I SAY TO YOU, AS YOU DID IT TO ONE OF THE LEAST OF THESE, MY BROTHERS, YOU DID IT TO ME.

MATTHEW 25:35-40

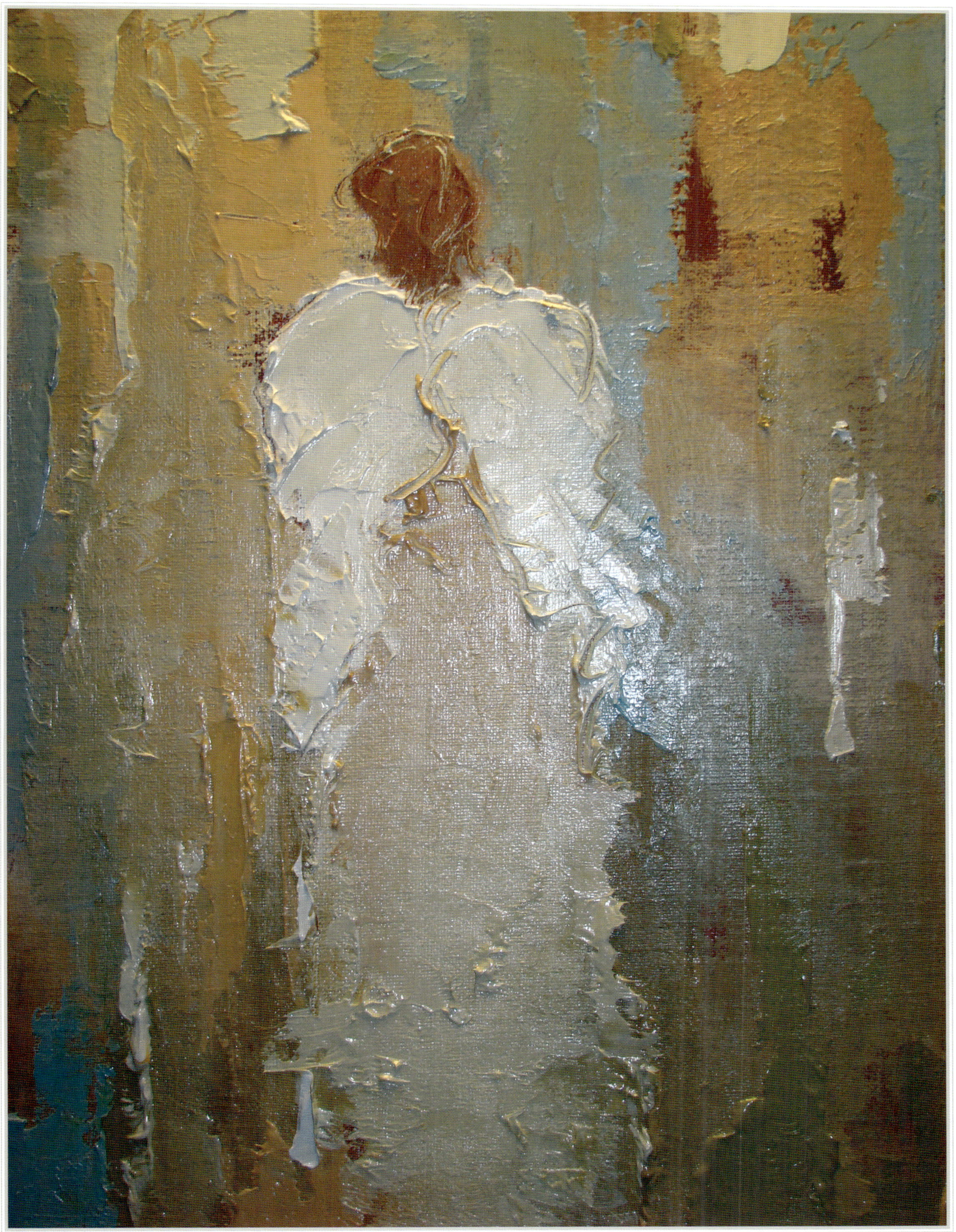

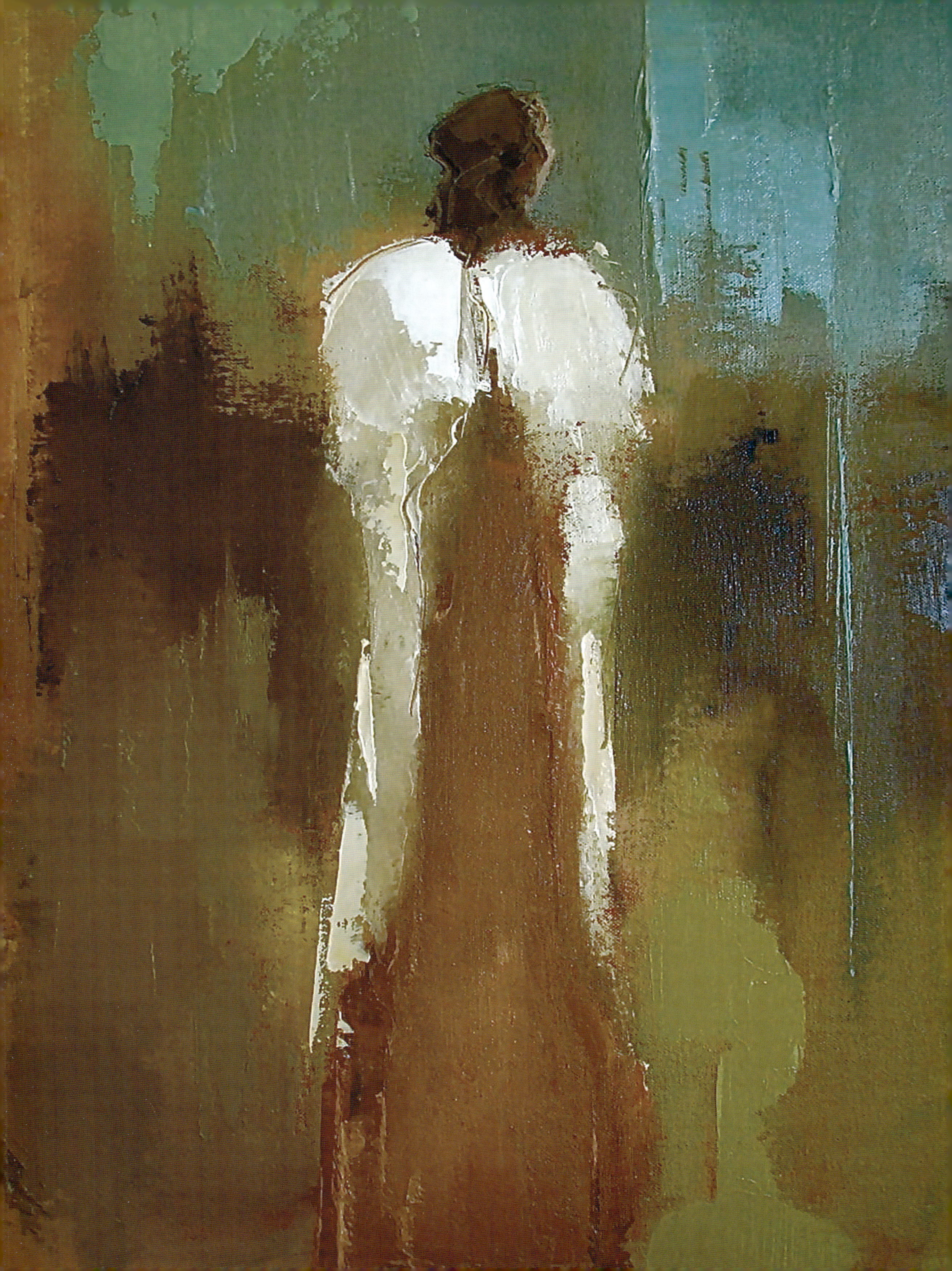

Anne Neilson's painting hangs prominently in my collection with the best artists of this generation. I am drawn to her sense of color and the skill with which she applies paint on the canvas. They are hauntingly beautiful and when I stand before them, I know I am in presence of Angels.

RON HALL

Art Dealer and *New York Times*
Bestselling Author of *Same Kind of Different As Me*

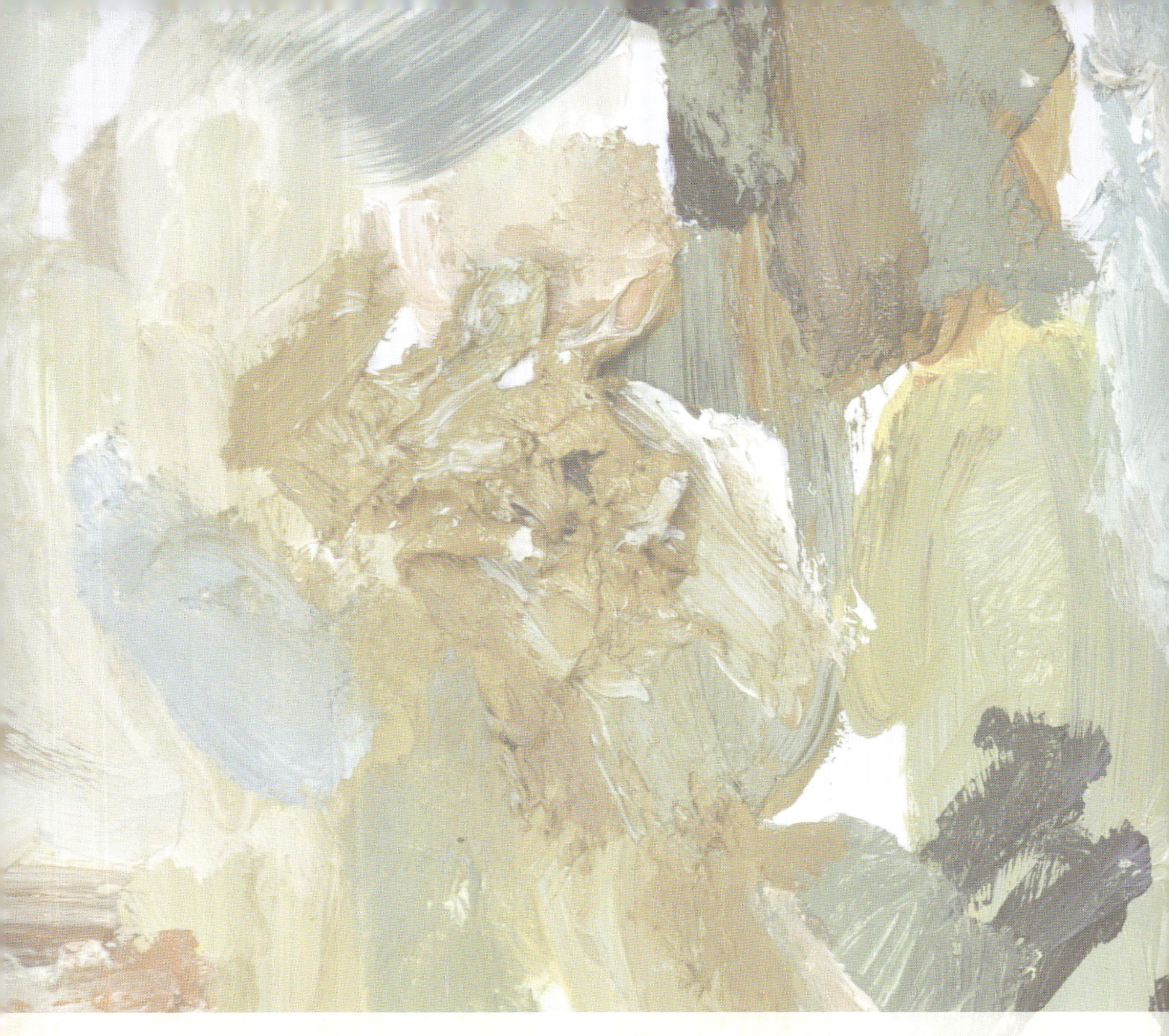

YOU WILL GO OUT IN JOY
AND BE LED FORTH IN PEACE;
THE MOUNTAINS AND HILLS
WILL BURST INTO SONG BEFORE YOU,
AND ALL THE TREES OF THE FIELD
WILL CLAP THEIR HANDS.

Isaiah 55:12

M. GRAHAM & CO.
TITANIUM
WHITE
Blanc de Titane
Titanweiss
Series 3
51-180
Net 5 fl. oz./150 mL

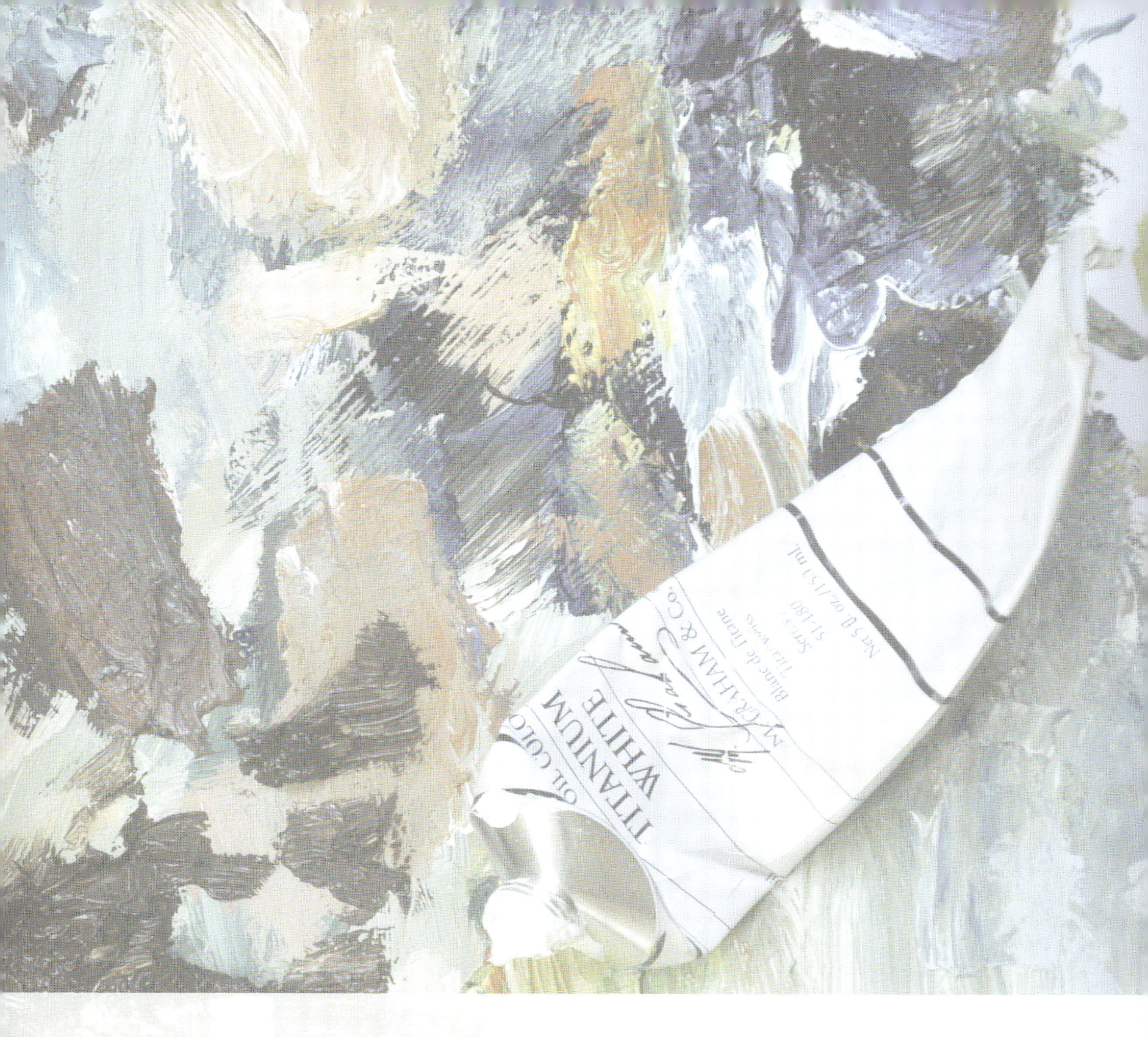

JOY

BUT LET ALL THOSE WHO TAKE REFUGE AND PUT THEIR TRUST IN YOU REJOICE; LET THEM EVER SING AND SHOUT FOR JOY, BECAUSE YOU MAKE A COVERING OVER THEM AND DEFEND THEM; LET THOSE ALSO WHO LOVE YOUR NAME BE JOYFUL IN YOU AND BE IN HIGH SPIRITS.

Psalm 5:11

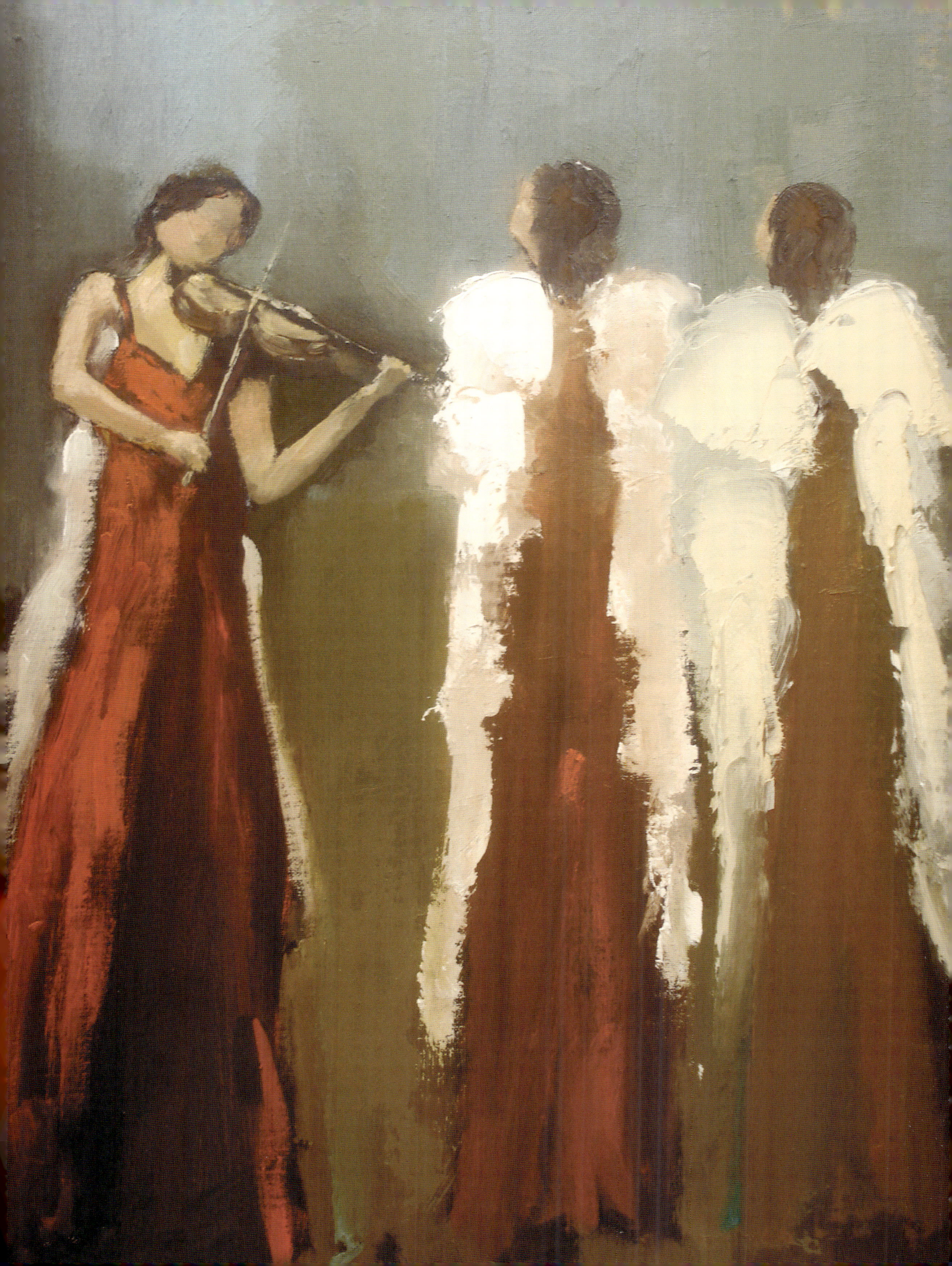

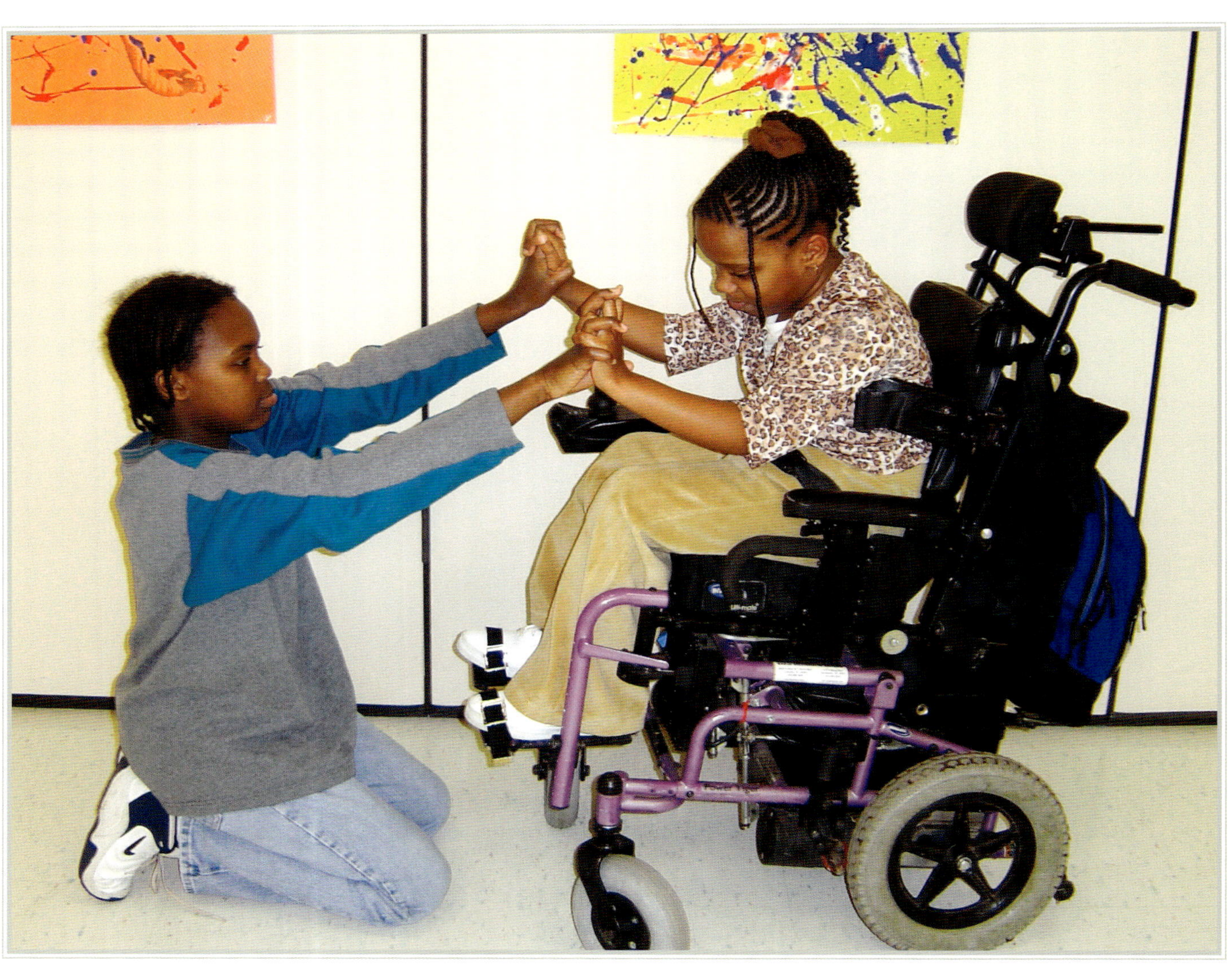

THE ALLEGRO FOUNDATION

A Champion for Children with Disabilities

In the spring of 2008 I became aware of a local, non-profit organization, The Allegro Foundation. Through free classes every week they teach more than 500 children with mental retardation, Down's syndrome, orthopedic challenges, spina bifida, cerebral palsy, learning disabilities, muscular dystrophy, visual and hearing impairments, and children with cancer. An art collector had recently given an Allegro board member one of my Angel paintings.

Upon receiving this gift, the board member immediately contacted me with the desire to introduce me to Founder, Pat Farmer and their Chief Operating Officer, Jane Fastje. The next thing I knew, I was sitting in a meeting with these two dynamic women and brainstorming about how to incorporate my angels into their fundraising efforts. It was decided that I would donate a large angel painting for an upcoming live auction.

Before starting on this painting for the fundraiser, I attended one of the Allegro classes. From the moment I entered the room, I was overwhelmed by the JOY on each child's face. As I watched the children in their wheelchairs or with the assistance of a volunteer "partner," the magical movement to music and their contagious smiles moved me to tears. It was powerful. I knew that I was in the presence of angels. Precious children created in the image of God. Knowing that each child there was indeed fearfully and wonderfully made and could do all things through Christ who strengthens them.

I went back to the canvas later that week with the images of the children in my heart, which poured out onto the canvas.

The night of the auction, my painting was the highest bidding item (that even out-bid a leased Mercedes), netting more than $15,000 for the Allegro Foundation. Once again, I knew that this talent was a gift and was to be used to give back to others.

A year later, we were back at the table brainstorming on ways to raise more awareness and funds for the Allegro Foundation. In October 2009, I hosted my first "Angels in Our Midst" solo show, giving back fifty percent of proceeds to the Allegro Foundation. The Charlotte community stepped up to help out in making this event a huge success. We had five restaurants offering their food, with donated beverages as well as beautiful arrangements of orchids from well-known Campbell's Greenhouse in Charlotte. We raised $10,000 just from selling art. This showed me that I was to surrender my talent for painting over to God, and watch where He would lead me.

> Anne Neilson's Angels reflect an inner beauty found within all mankind but often overlooked in the medically fragile bodies of children with disabilities served by Allegro Foundation. With the transformative stroke of her paint brush, Anne glorifies God's creations and encourages us all to celebrate the life we have been given.
>
> PAT FARMER
>
> Founder/President of Allegro Foundation

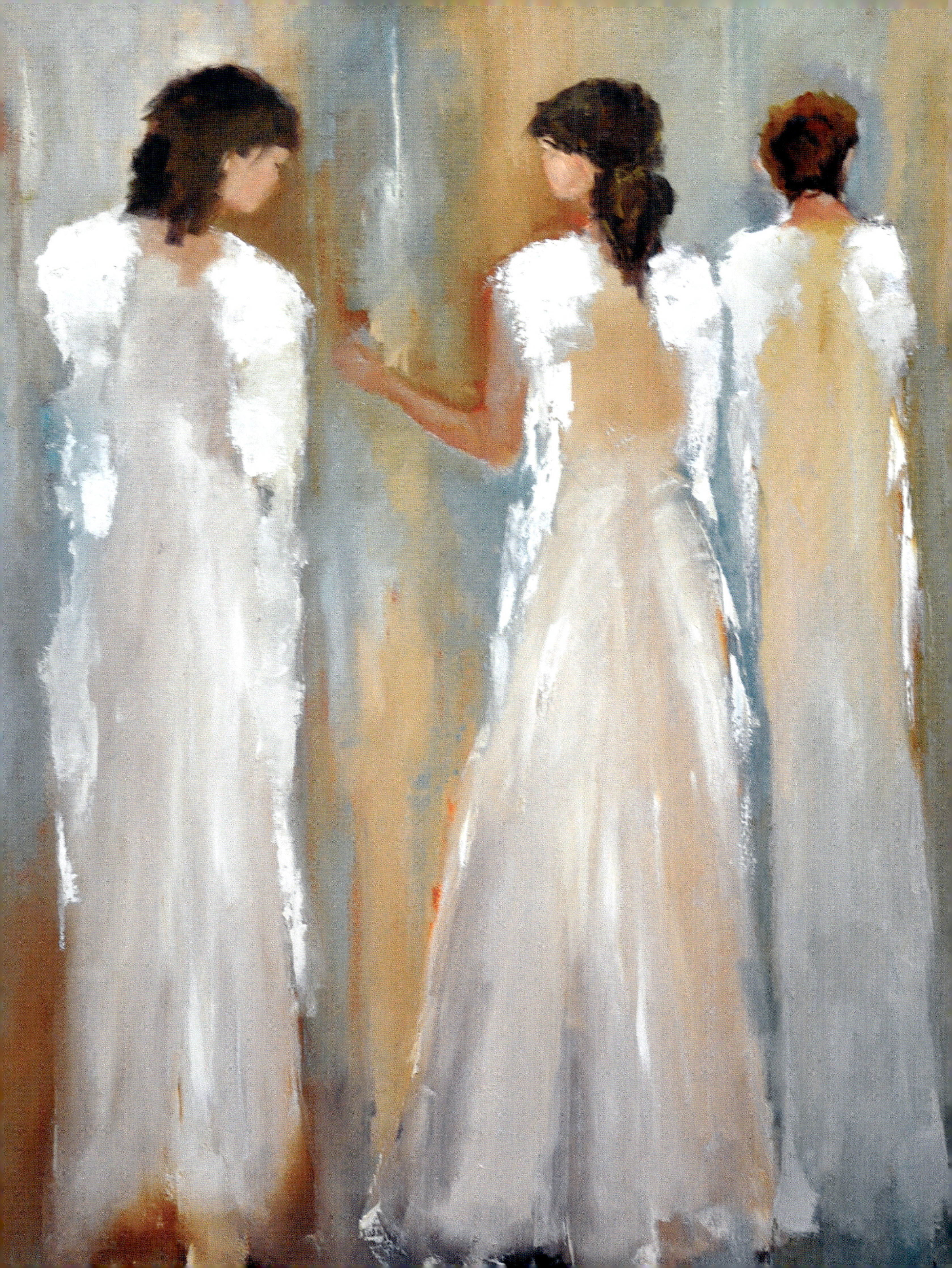

REJOICE IN THE LORD ALWAYS; AGAIN I SAY, REJOICE!

Philippians 4:4

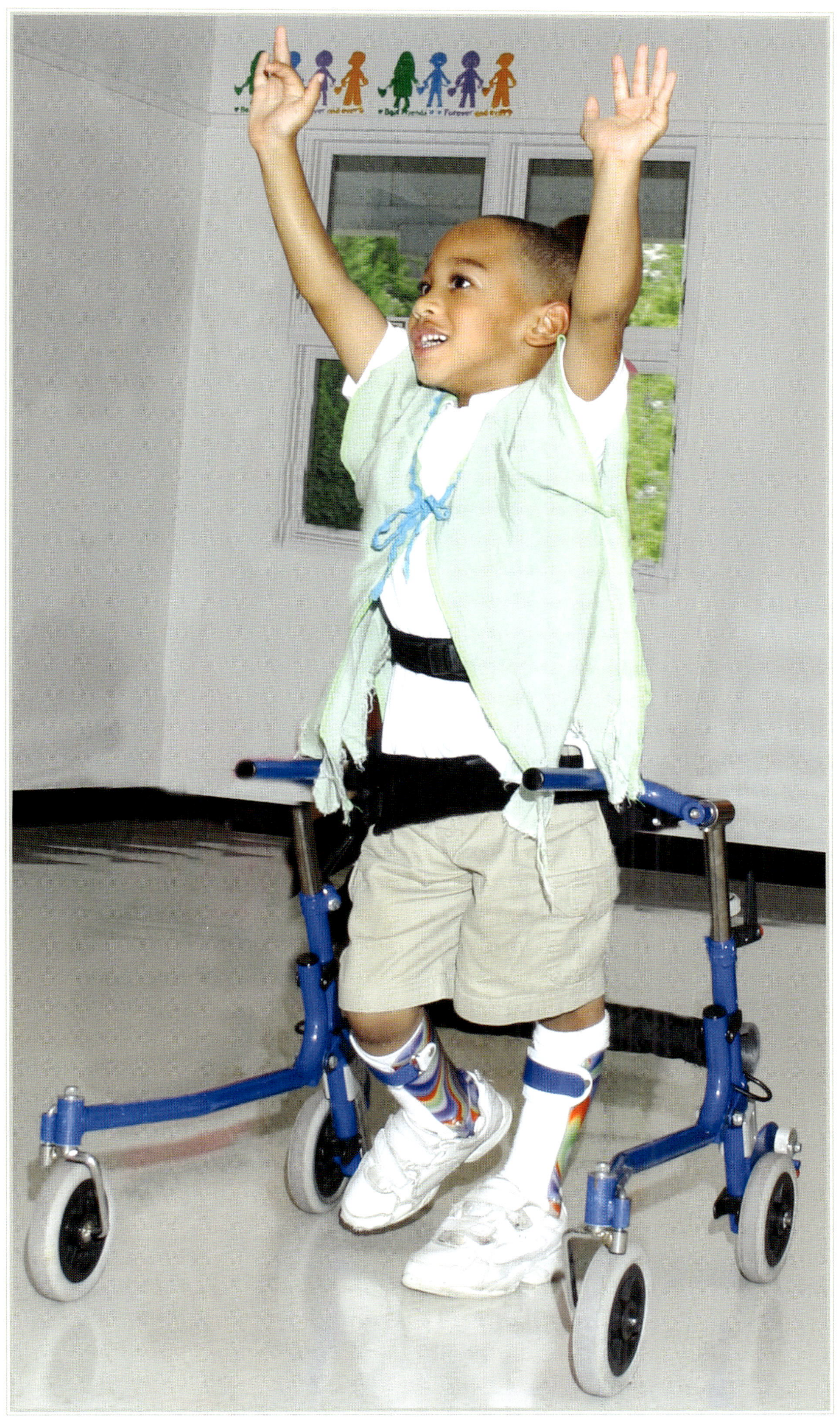

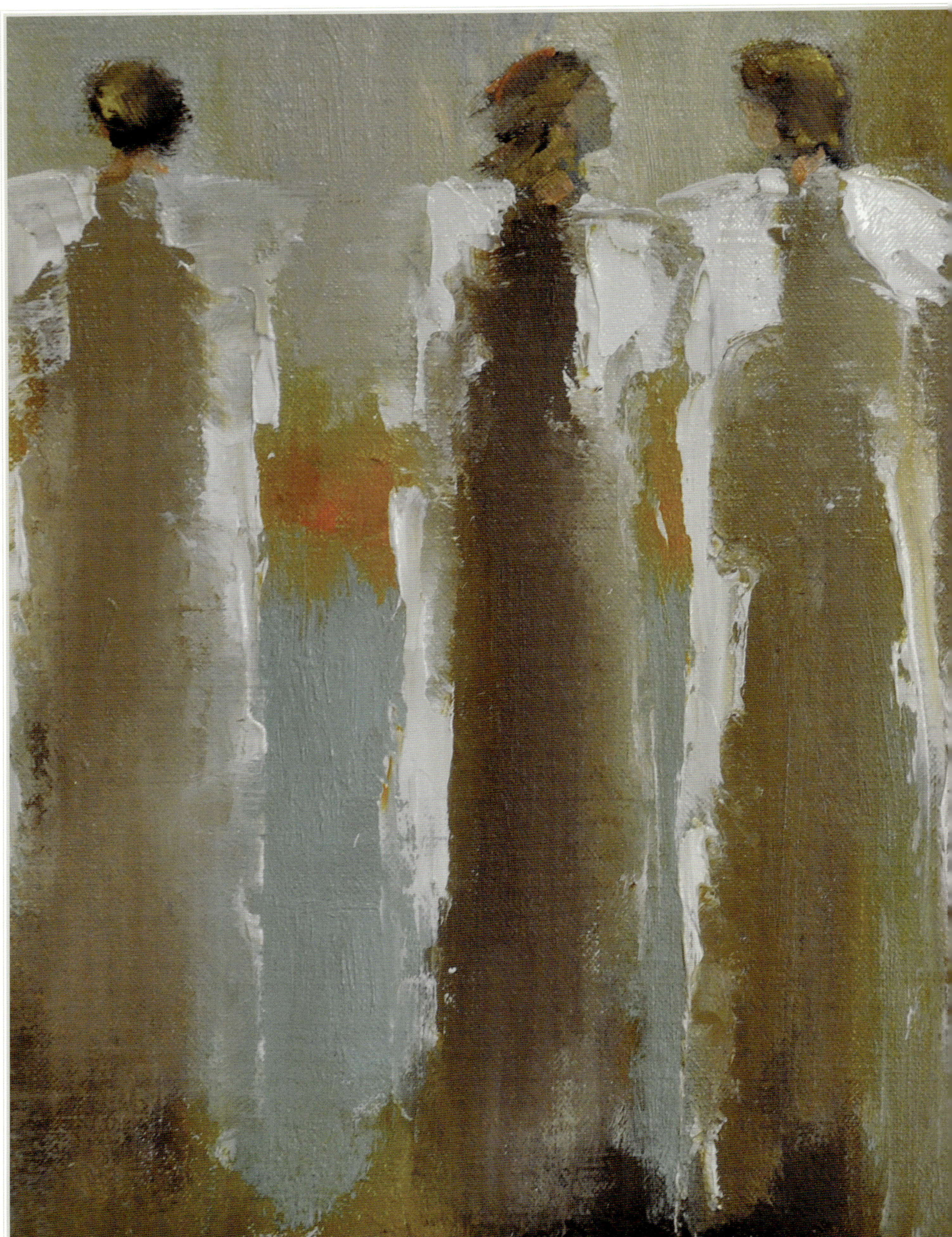

Over many years, the talented artist and philanthropist, Anne Neilson, has spent tireless hours in her studio crafting magnificent works of art for auction to help fund Allegro's free movement education classes for children with disabilities. Local Charlotteans and individuals as far away as Monaco alike display Anne's Angels in their private collections, a testament to both her artistic talents and commitment to Allegro's children with disabilities. Bless you, Anne, for giving the world your Angels and inspiring Allegro Foundation's Angels to learn in a new way.

JANE FASTJE

Chief Operating Officer, Allegro Foundation

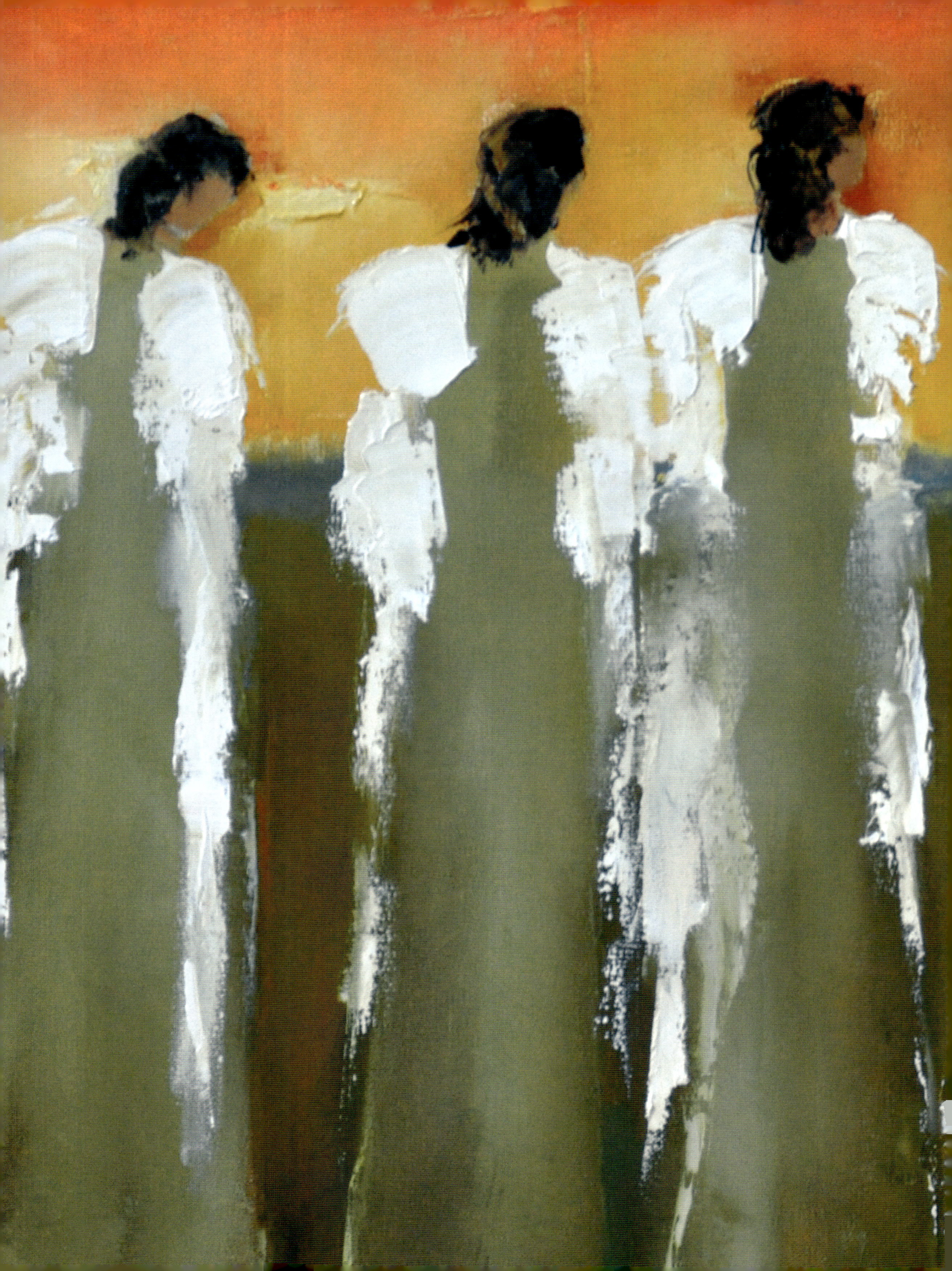

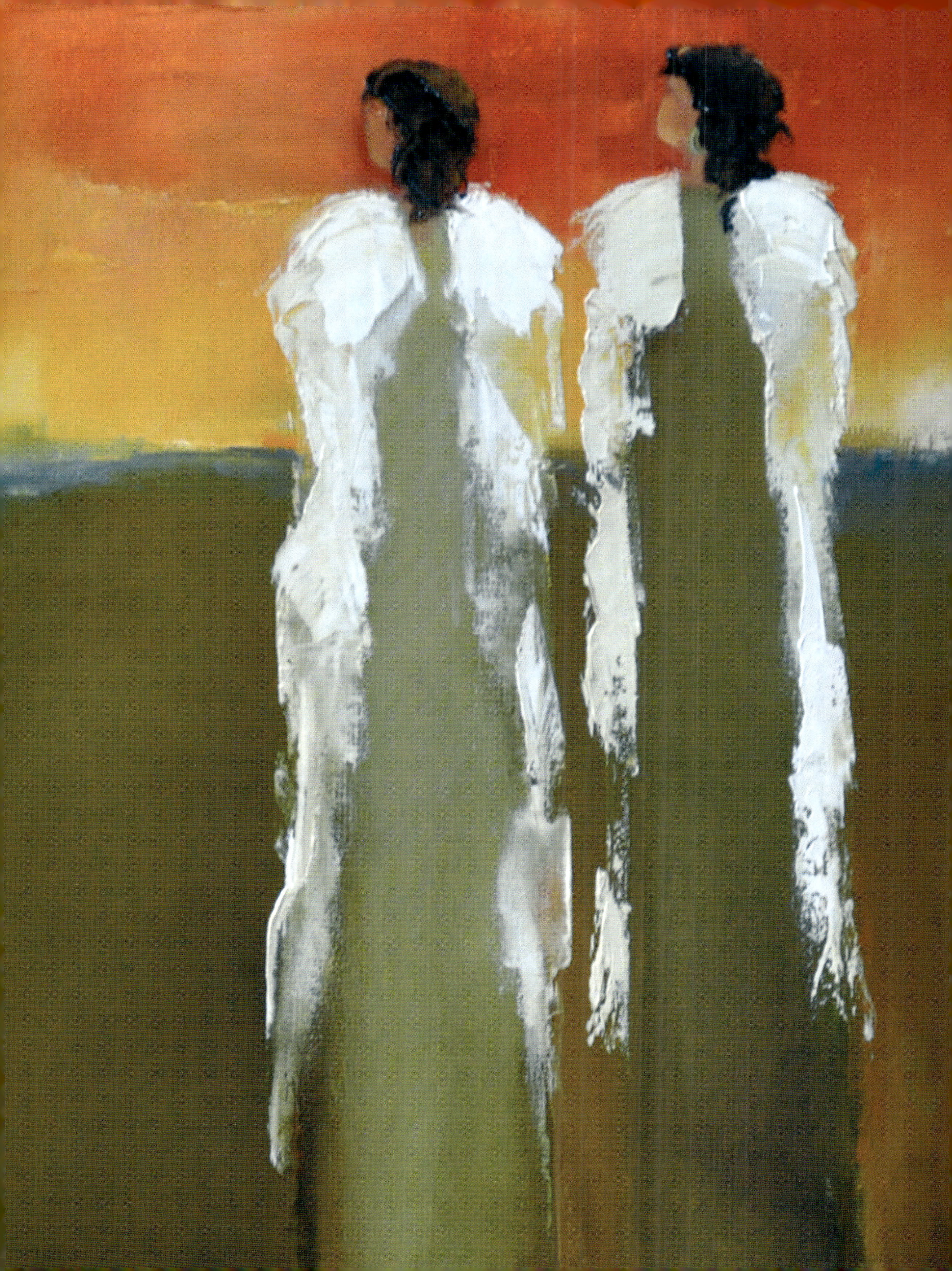

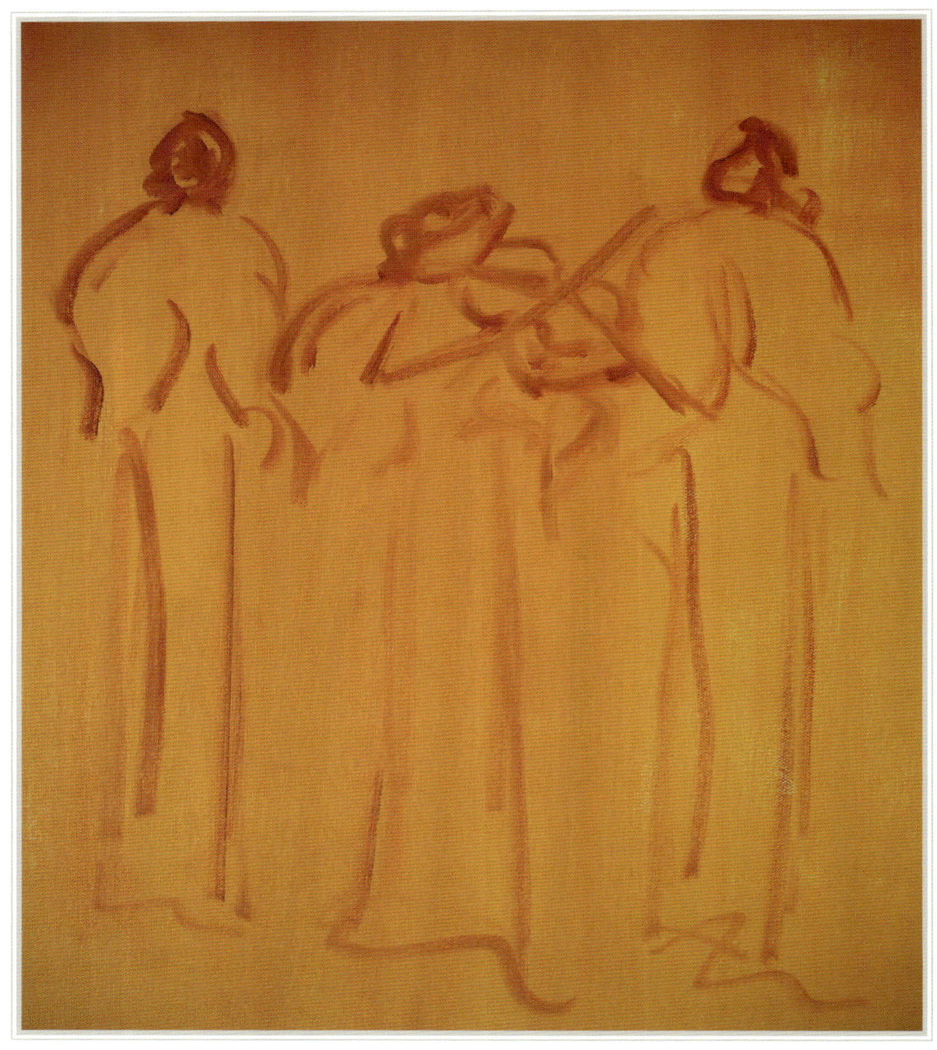

There is magic around the beneficent activities of the Allegro Foundation. It is the work of extraordinary people who know how to create an imaginary world around children who have not been granted an equal sharing of blessings. Anne Neilson's beautiful paintings are the perfect illustration of the innocent children whose grace appears in their smiles or of the Guardian Angels who protect and guide them.

GILLES A. NOGHÈS

Ambassador of the Principality of Monaco
Permanent Observer to the Organization of American States

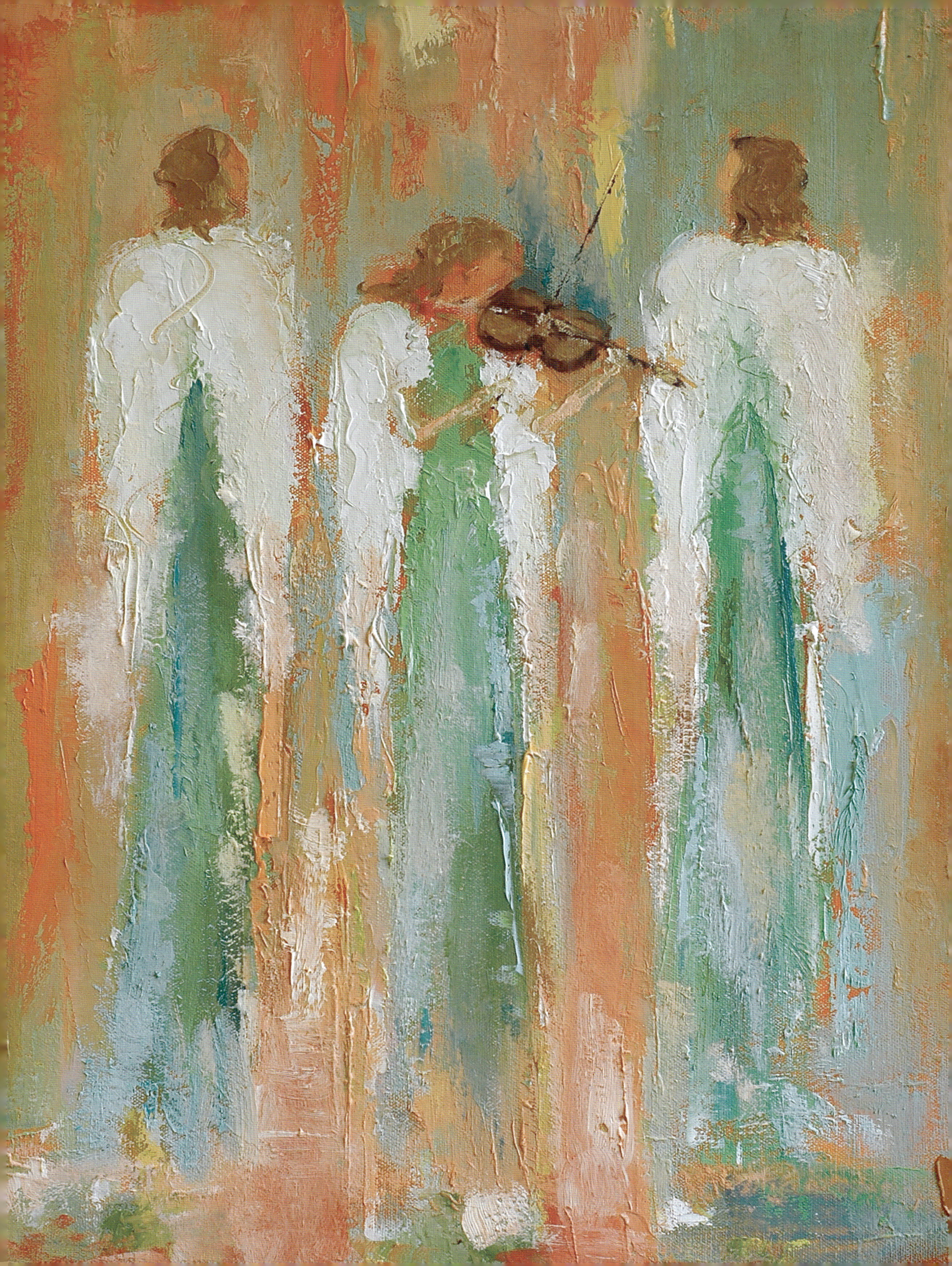

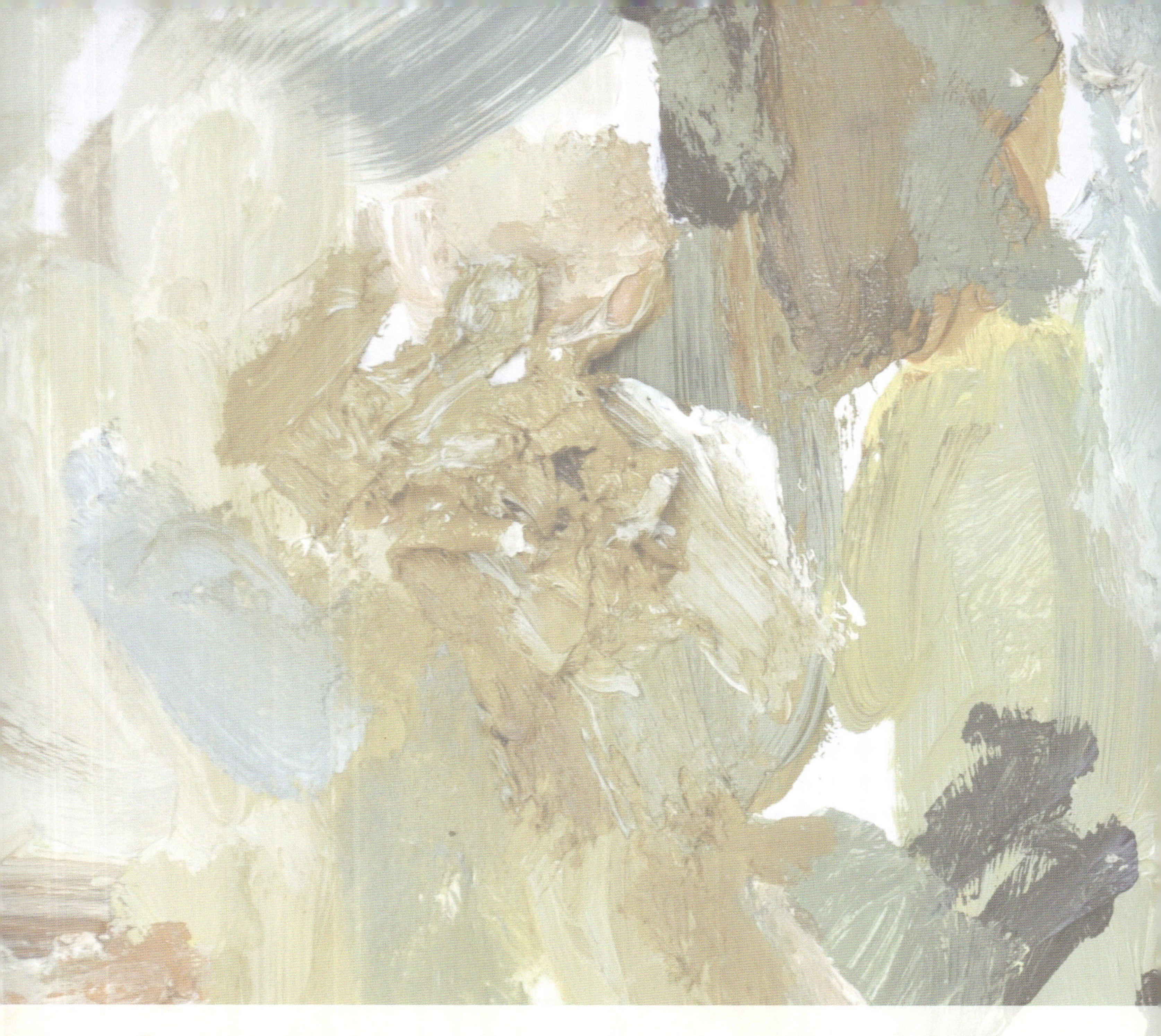

I HAVE TOLD YOU THESE THINGS, SO THAT
IN ME YOU MAY HAVE PEACE. IN THIS WORLD
YOU WILL HAVE TROUBLE. BUT TAKE HEART!
I HAVE OVERCOME THE WORLD.

John 16:33

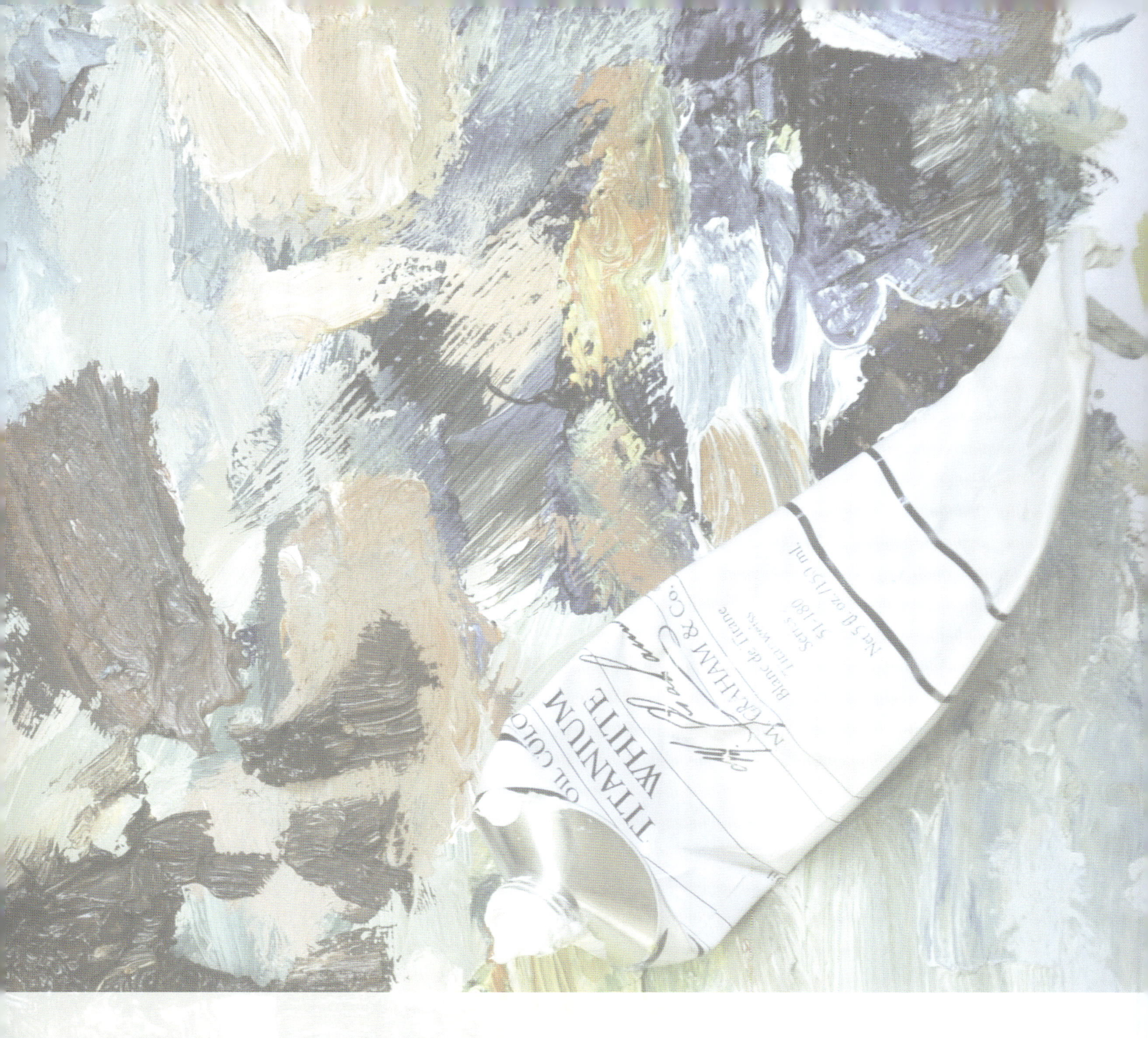

PEACE

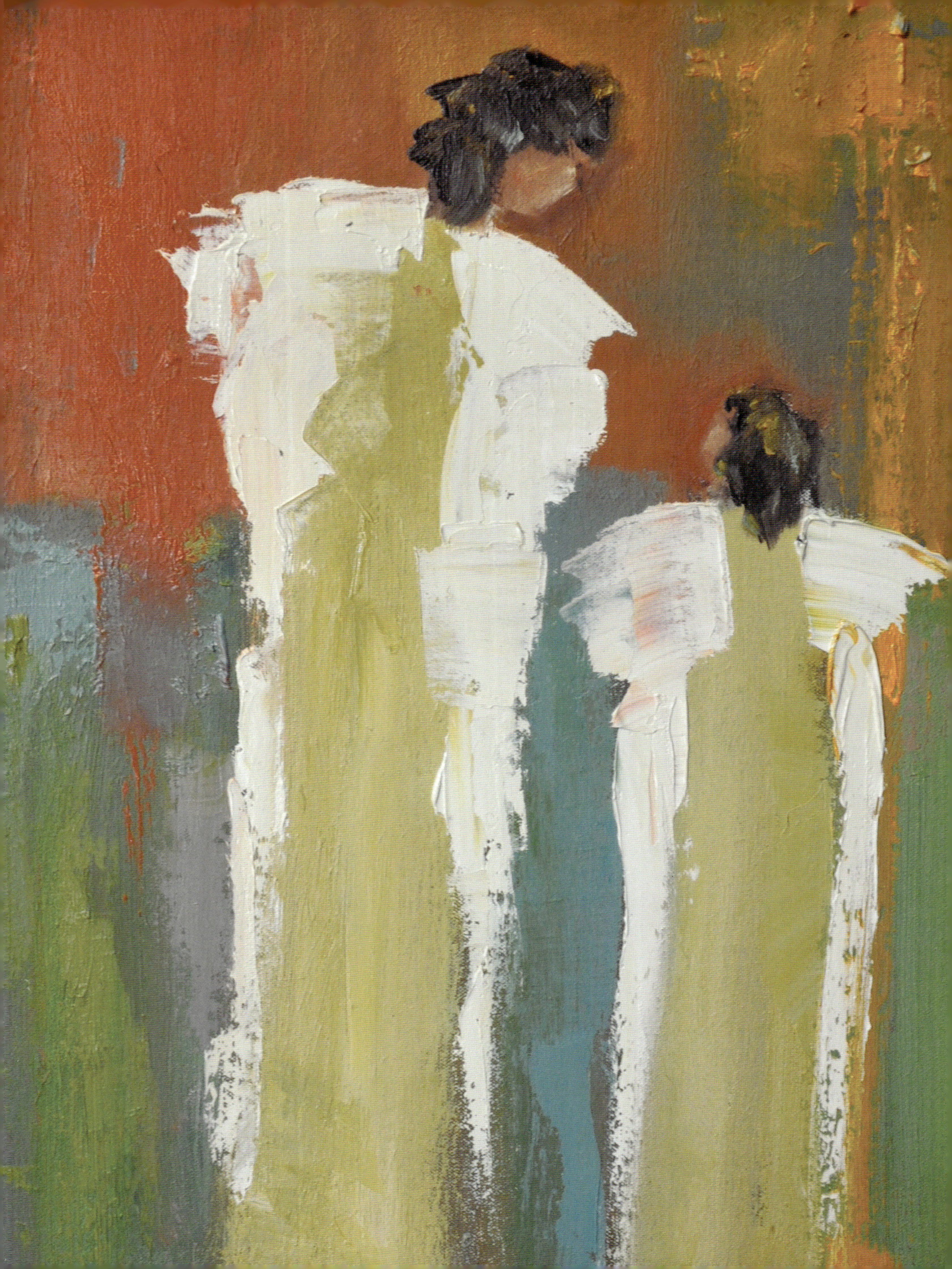

THEN YOU WILL EXPERIENCE GOD'S PEACE, WHICH
EXCEEDS ANYTHING WE CAN UNDERSTAND.
HIS PEACE WILL GUARD YOUR HEARTS AND
MINDS AS YOU LIVE IN JESUS CHRIST.

PHILIPPIANS 4:7

WORKS OF HEART

Levine Cardiac Kids
by Adrienne Mauntel

We found out that we were pregnant with our first child on Father's Day 2006 – how appropriate! My pregnancy was easy and I always felt great. When we had our ultrasound at 18 weeks, we assumed it would be like any other visit to the OB/GYN. Little did we know that our world as we knew it was about to change forever.

After several visits to a genetics specialist and two different pediatric cardiologists, our baby was diagnosed with hypoplastic right heart syndrome. Specifically, he had tricuspid atresia, which meant that the valve between the right atrium and right ventricle did not develop. As we learned, he was fine in utero, but shortly after birth he would struggle to breathe because there was no way for blood to get pumped out properly into his lungs. We were shocked, devastated and really scared.

We questioned what life would be like for our baby. Would he be able to walk, would he play sports, would he keep up with his friends? We were desperate to meet other families living in the same shoes that we would.

Ford was born on February 28, 2007 and to our wonderful surprise, he was able to come home with us immediately . . . just like any other child. Of course, we were to look for a number of signs that indicated heart failure, but we were thrilled to have our baby home!

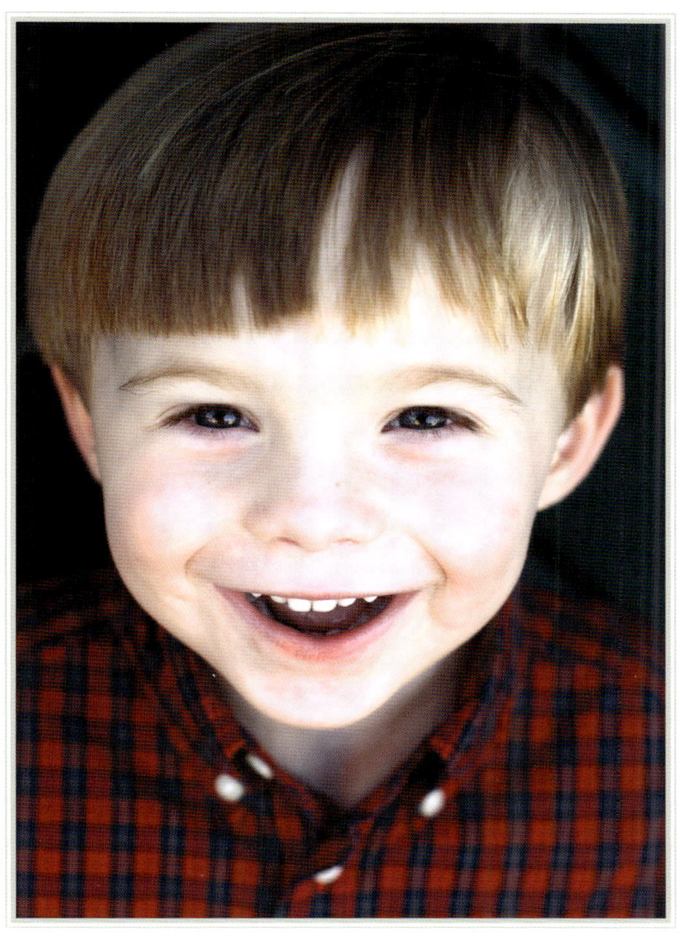

CHARLES "FORD" MAUNTEL

At 11 days old, Ford had his first open-heart surgery. He was struggling to breathe so it was time for the first of three surgeries he would ultimately undergo to repair his heart defect. The ten days he was in the hospital were extremely nerve-wracking. He had several set-backs, but he was a fighter. By day five, he was eating and gaining the strength he needed to get back on track.

We left the hospital and tried to get on with "normal" life (whatever that means with a newborn!). Ford progressed beautifully and was growing strong. We fell more and more in love with him each day. His personality is infectious and his charm, endearing. We had six months at home with him before he was ready for his next surgery. During this time, six families living with a child with a heart defect started Levine Cardiac Kids, a support group for families of children with Congenital Heart Defects (CHD). We immediately got involved and made several life-long friends who have provided so much guidance, support and love. Having friends who have walked in our shoes and experienced the same victories and set-backs in and out of the hospital is priceless. They truly understand our highs and lows and can provide real-life guidance to many medical situations.

Ford is now five years old. He swims, plays soccer, climbs across monkey bars and runs faster than his parents. He is truly a miracle of God and science. He's had three open-heart surgeries and two heart-catheterizations. And, although our medical journey is not over, we thank God every day for giving us Ford. He is an angel on Earth who blesses our lives everyday. I'll never understand where Ford gets his strength from. He has certainly been through more than most children or adults have been through in a lifetime, but, that does not phase him at all. He is the toughest person I have ever met. He always has a smile on his face and is very sweet and loving. He's made his father and I better people for knowing him, and taught us that there are miracles in life as FORD IS OUR MIRACLE!

Levine Cardiac Kids is a group that supports children who are being treated for, or have recently been diagnosed with CHD and their families. The goal is to provide a forum in which members: Support one another through the sharing of experience, educate ourselves on pertinent issues related to heart-health, diagnostic procedures, treatments, terminologies, financial/insurance considerations and coping strategies, spread awareness of congenital heart defects and the existence of our support group within the community, and seek to develop relationships with medical professional and hospitals that provide comprehensive pediatric cardiac care, such as Levine Children's Hospital, to provide our families with a direct link to the access of medical support, facilities, and advocation of quality pediatric medical care.

ABOVE ALL ELSE, GUARD YOUR HEART, FOR IT IS THE WELLSPRING OF LIFE.

Proverbs 4:23

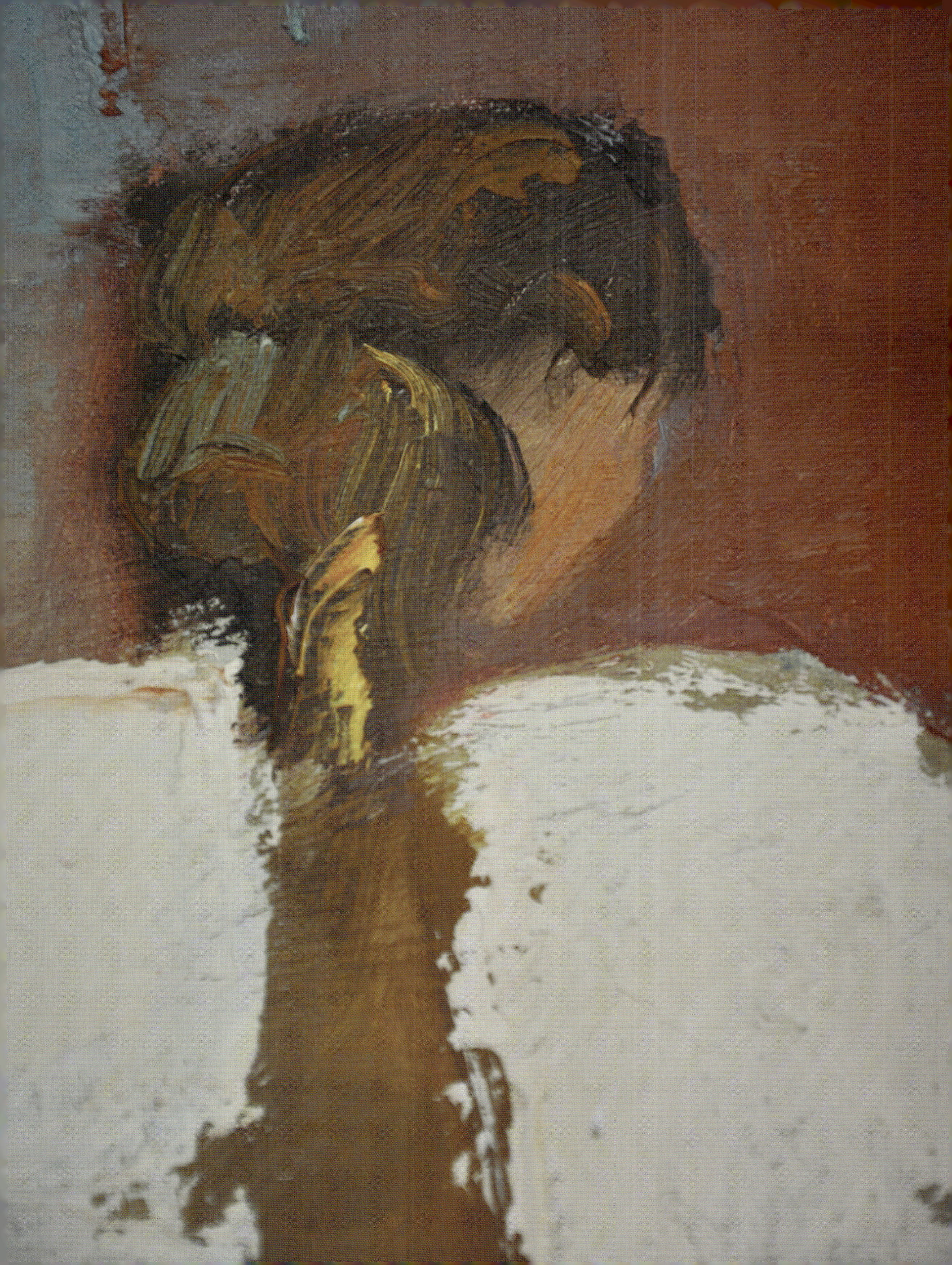

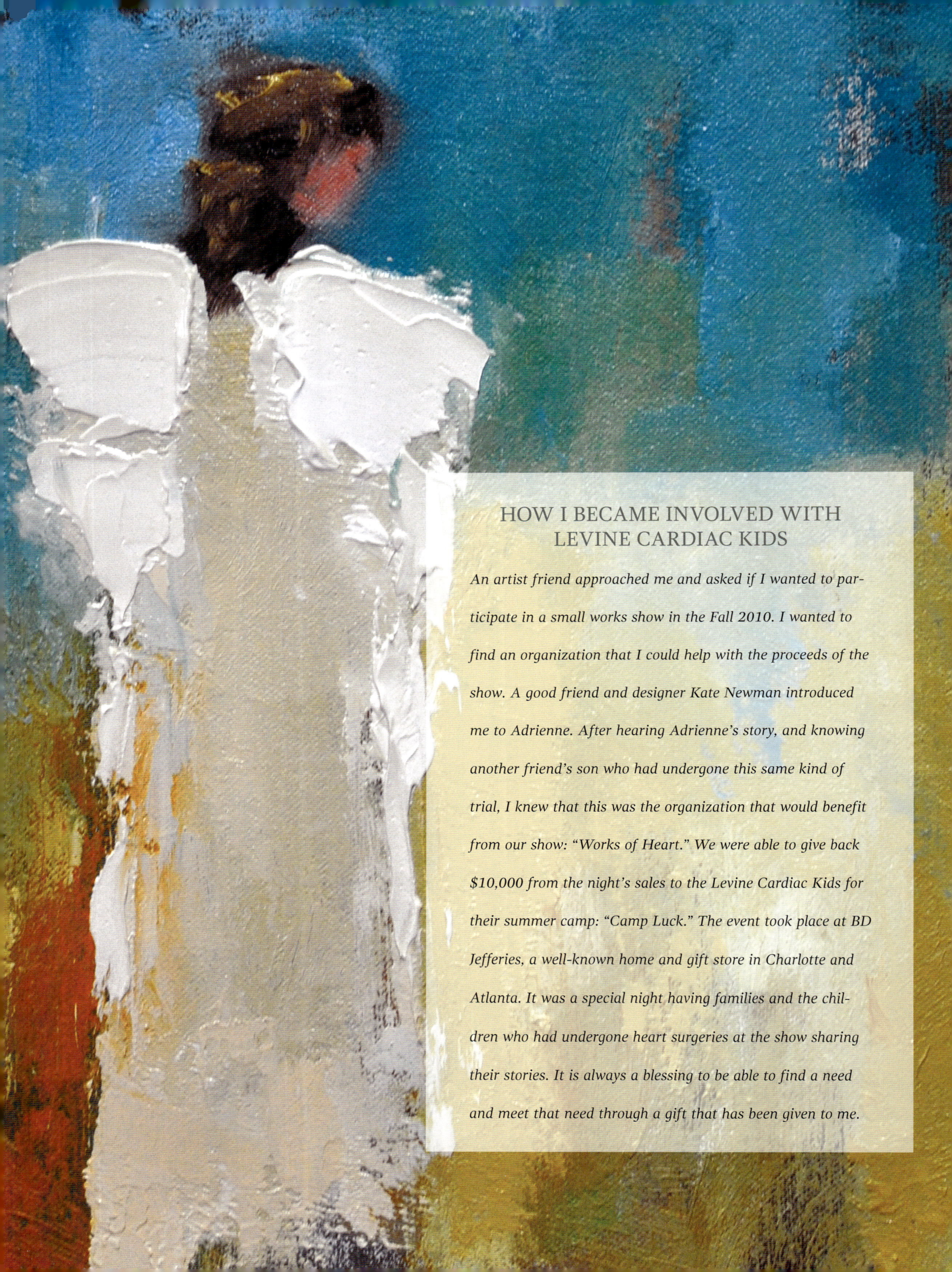

HOW I BECAME INVOLVED WITH LEVINE CARDIAC KIDS

An artist friend approached me and asked if I wanted to participate in a small works show in the Fall 2010. I wanted to find an organization that I could help with the proceeds of the show. A good friend and designer Kate Newman introduced me to Adrienne. After hearing Adrienne's story, and knowing another friend's son who had undergone this same kind of trial, I knew that this was the organization that would benefit from our show: "Works of Heart." We were able to give back $10,000 from the night's sales to the Levine Cardiac Kids for their summer camp: "Camp Luck." The event took place at BD Jefferies, a well-known home and gift store in Charlotte and Atlanta. It was a special night having families and the children who had undergone heart surgeries at the show sharing their stories. It is always a blessing to be able to find a need and meet that need through a gift that has been given to me.

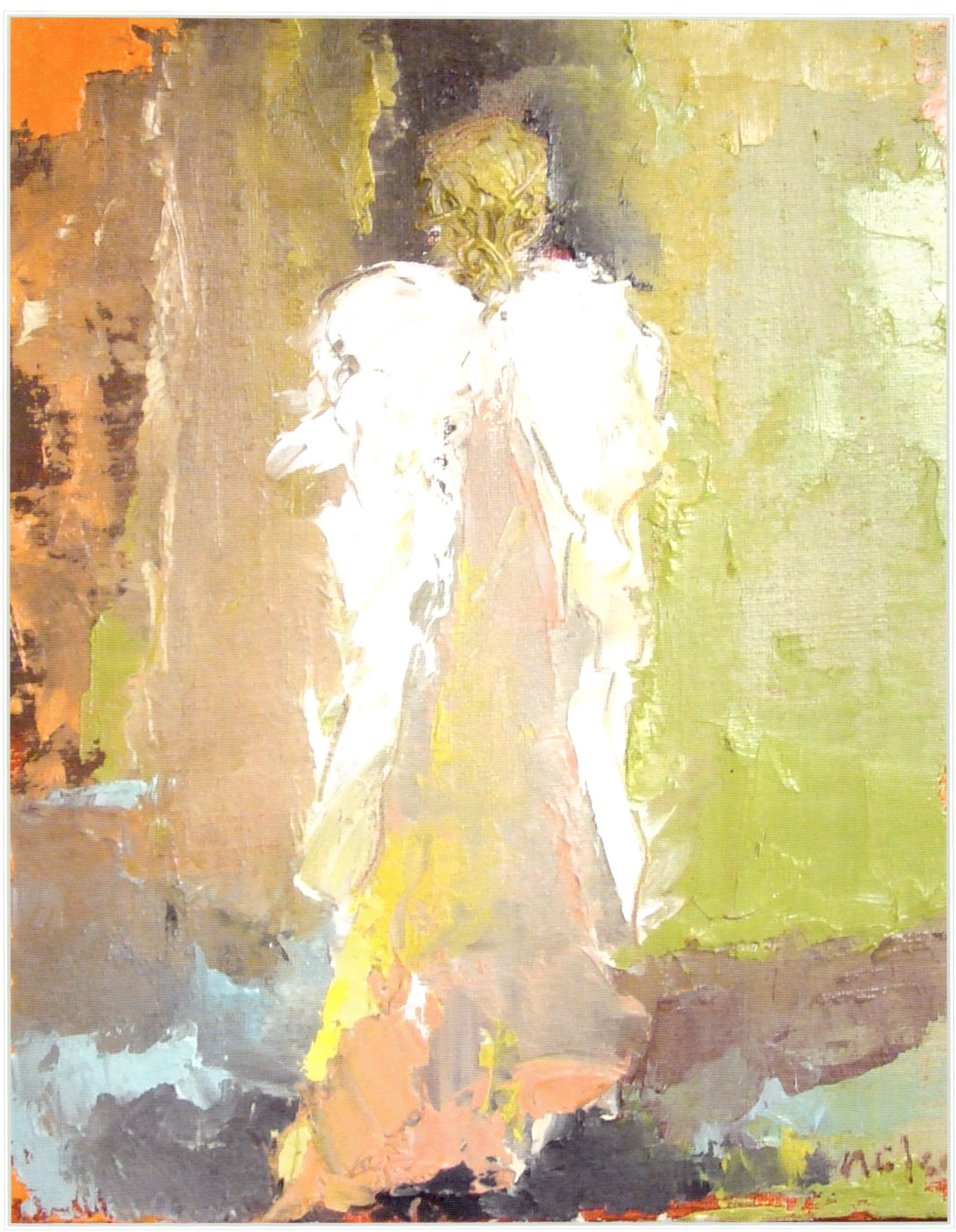

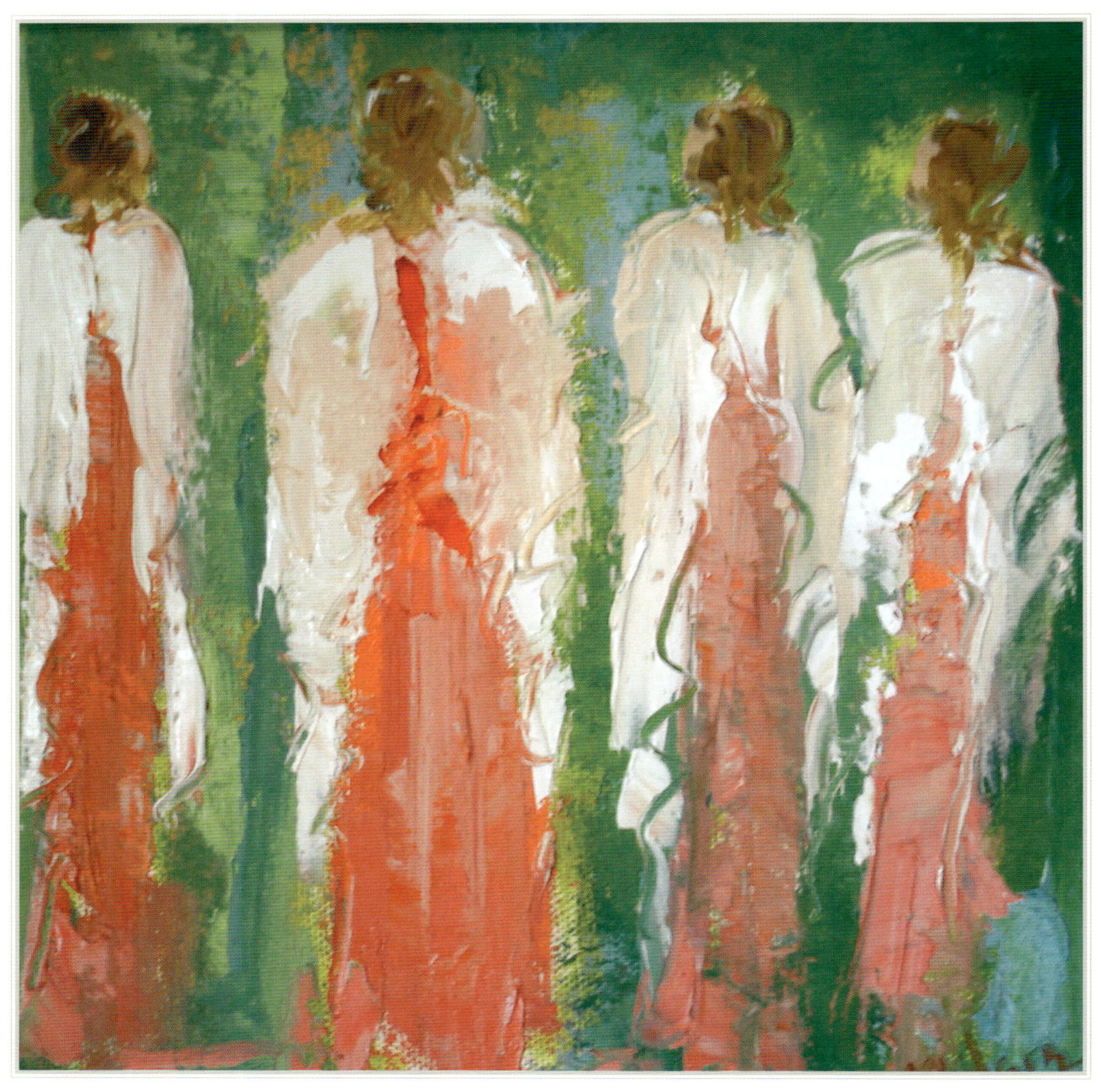

COME TO ME, ALL WHO LABOR AND ARE HEAVY LADEN, AND I WILL GIVE YOU REST. TAKE MY YOKE UPON YOU, AND LEARN FROM ME, FOR I AM GENTLE AND LOWLY IN HEART, AND YOU WILL FIND REST FOR YOUR SOULS. FOR MY YOKE IS EASY, AND MY BURDEN IS LIGHT.

MATTHEW 11:28-30

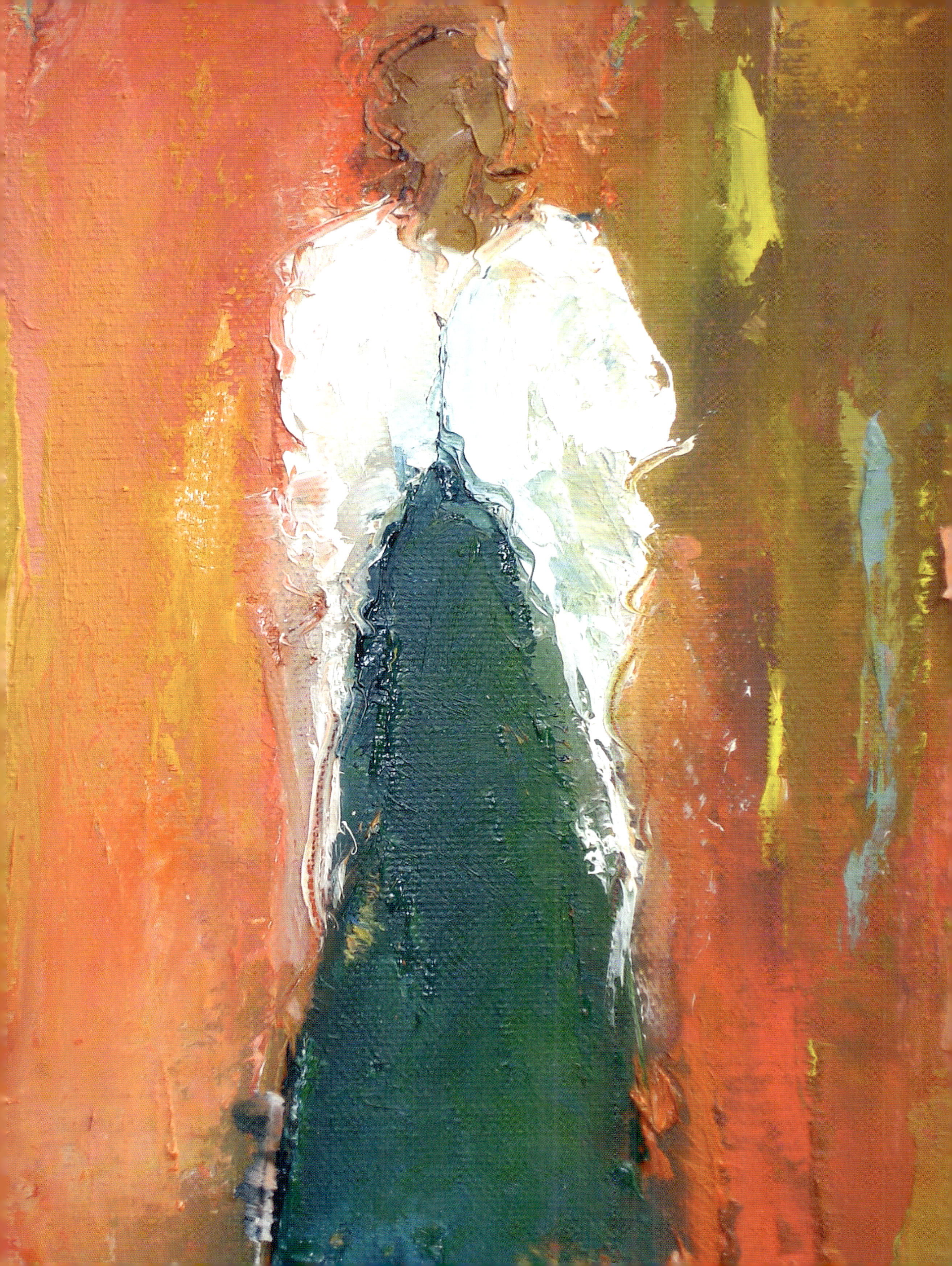

Anne Neilson's Angel paintings evoke a sense of deep peace inside of me. As a designer, I come across a lot of art, some I admire for clients, while others I covet for myself. My introduction to Anne's Angel Series was different. Years ago, I came across one of her small Angels on a visit to my hometown of Charlotte. I was perusing a great little gift boutique and was stopped in my tracks by this sweet, angelic painting hanging on the wall. The colors moved me and made me smile. The subject filled me up and I knew I had to take this Angel home with me. I returned a few days later and it was no longer available, sold the day before. I left Charlotte and could not stop thinking about it. Years later, I moved back to Charlotte and opened my design studio where by fate, I believe, Anne became my studio neighbor. I now own numerous Angels, and in each room where they hang, the paintings still make me smile and feel at peace. Anne has gone from an artist I admire to my neighbor, client, colleague and someone I now call a friend.

KATE NEWMAN

Owner, K. Interiors

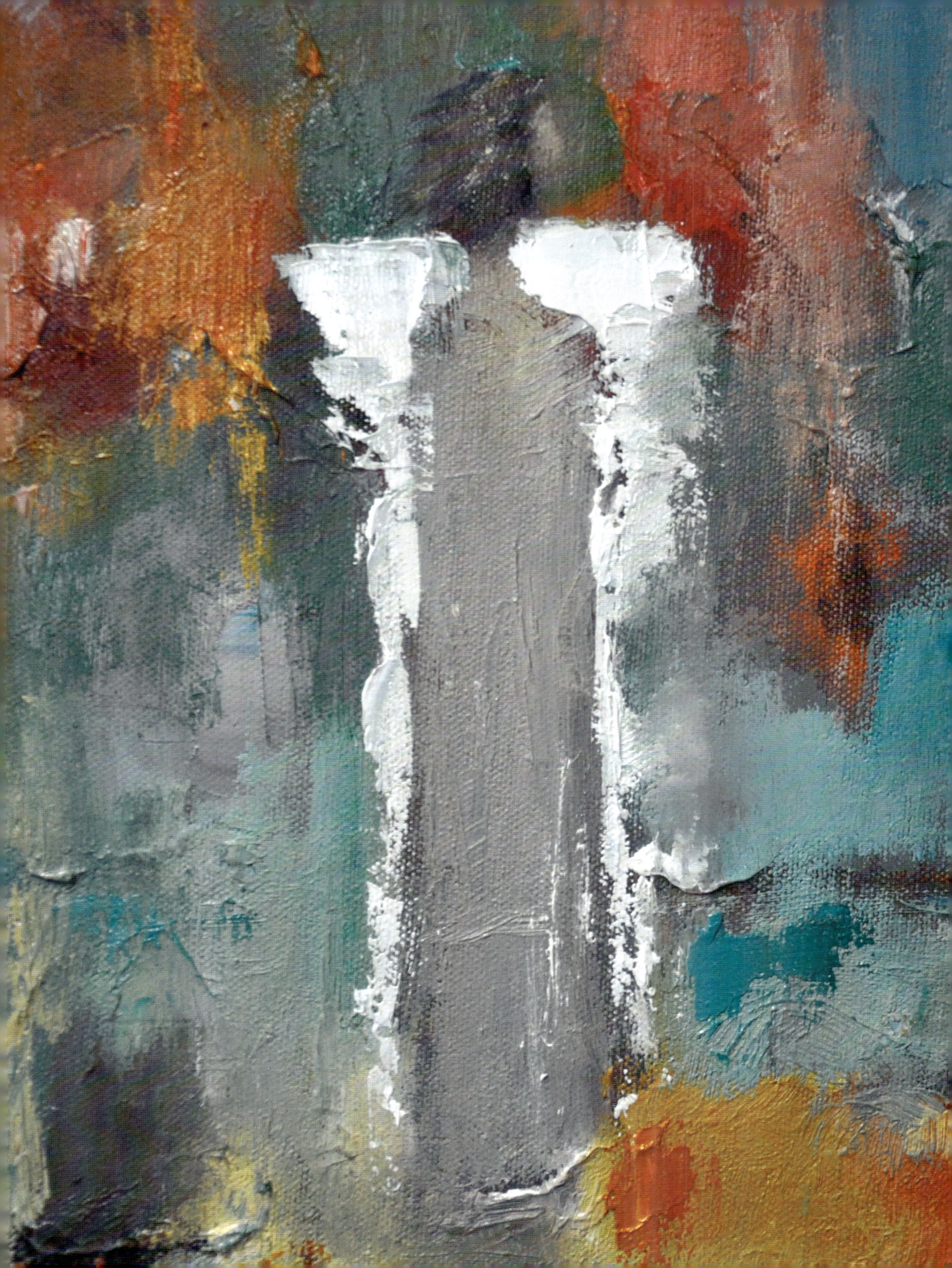

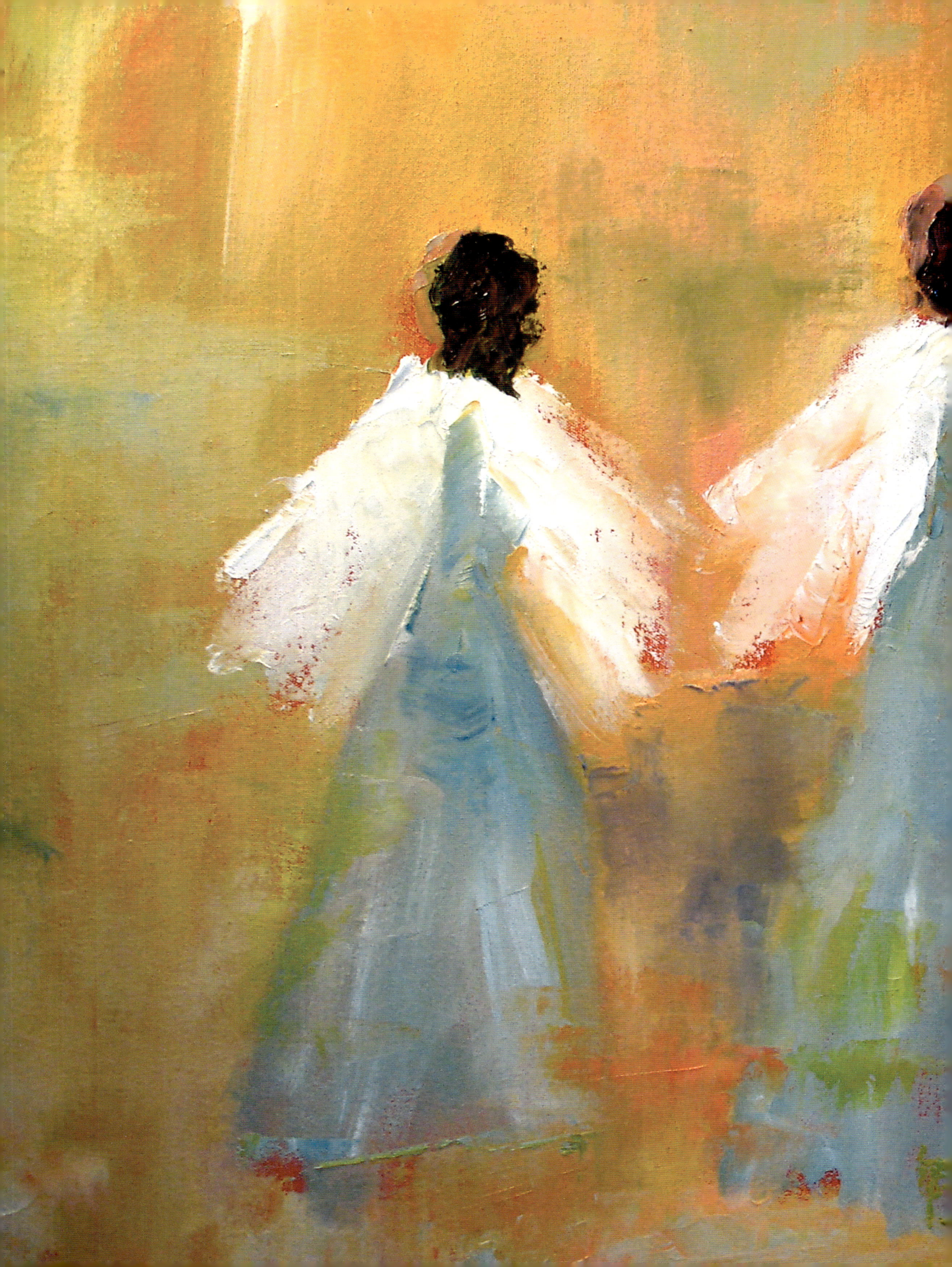

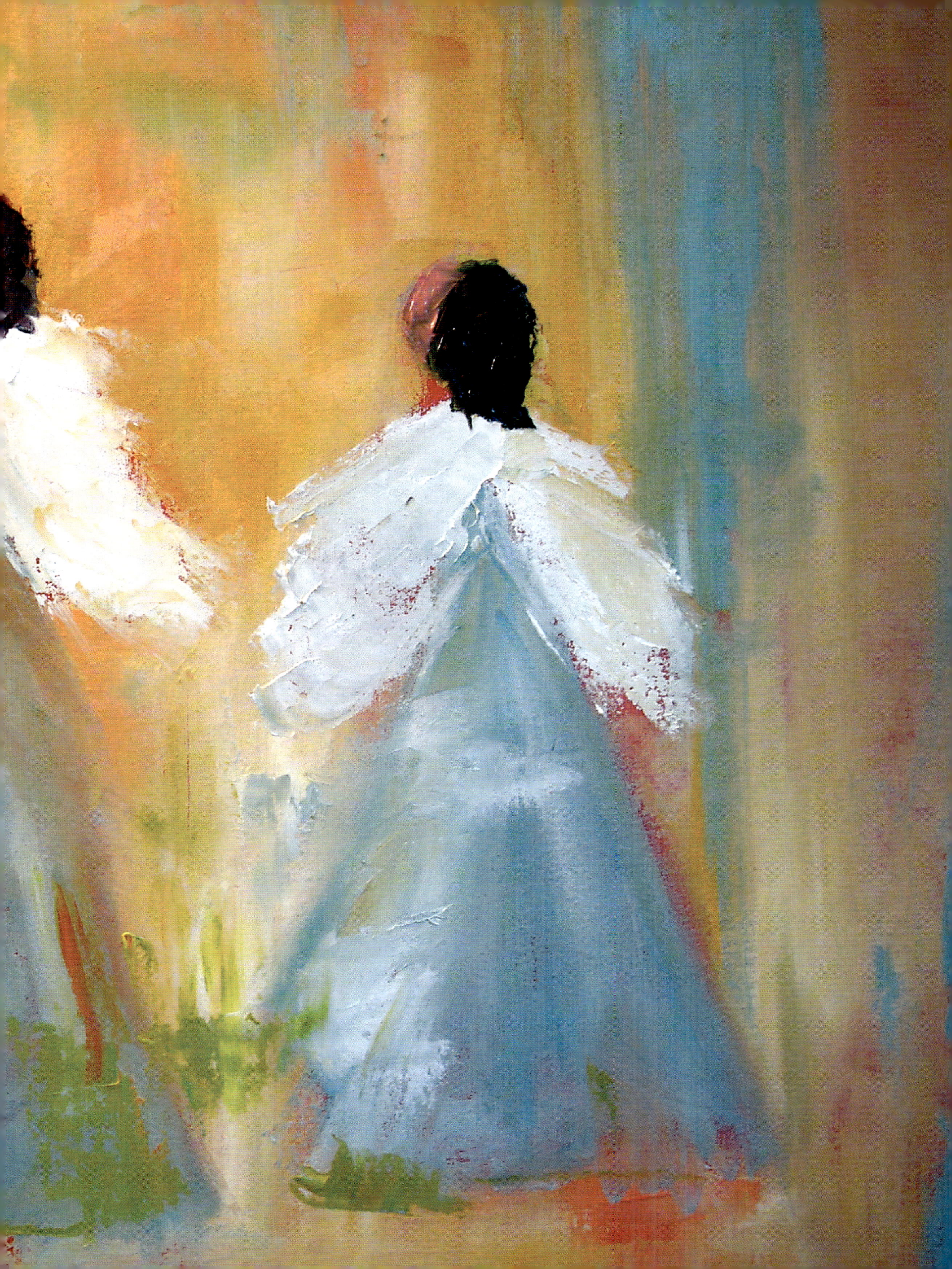

What a blessing it has been to know Anne Neilson and share her talent with our customers. A gifted technical artist, her work reflects a deep and abiding faith. Her love and passion flow through the Angels and mirror the peace, comfort, and serenity of that faith.

ABBIE BOGGS and PAM MISLE

3 French Hens, Charlotte, NC

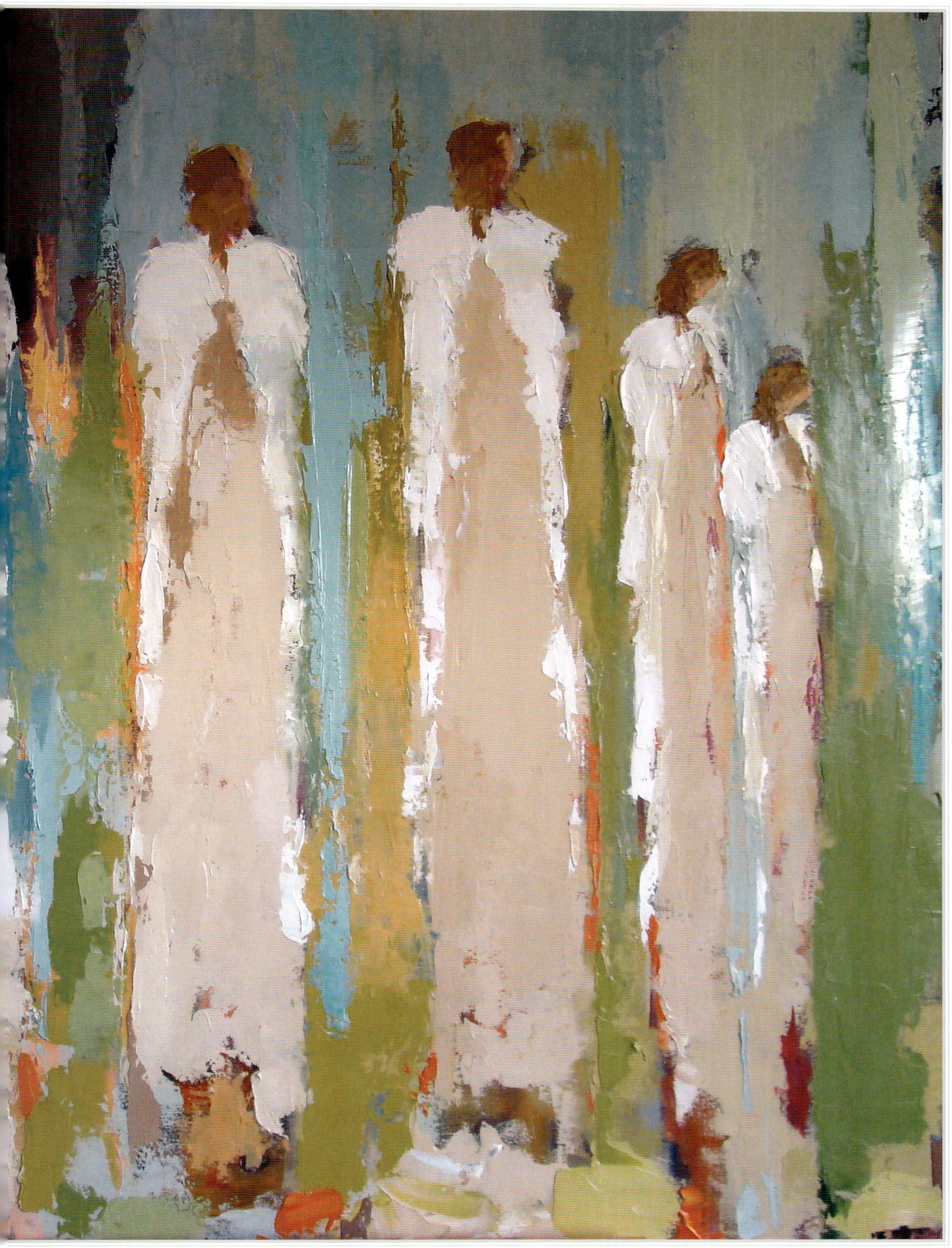

PEACE I LEAVE WITH YOU; MY PEACE I GIVE TO YOU. NOT AS THE WORLD GIVES DO I GIVE TO YOU. LET NOT YOUR HEARTS BE TROUBLED, NEITHER LET THEM BE AFRAID.

John 14:27

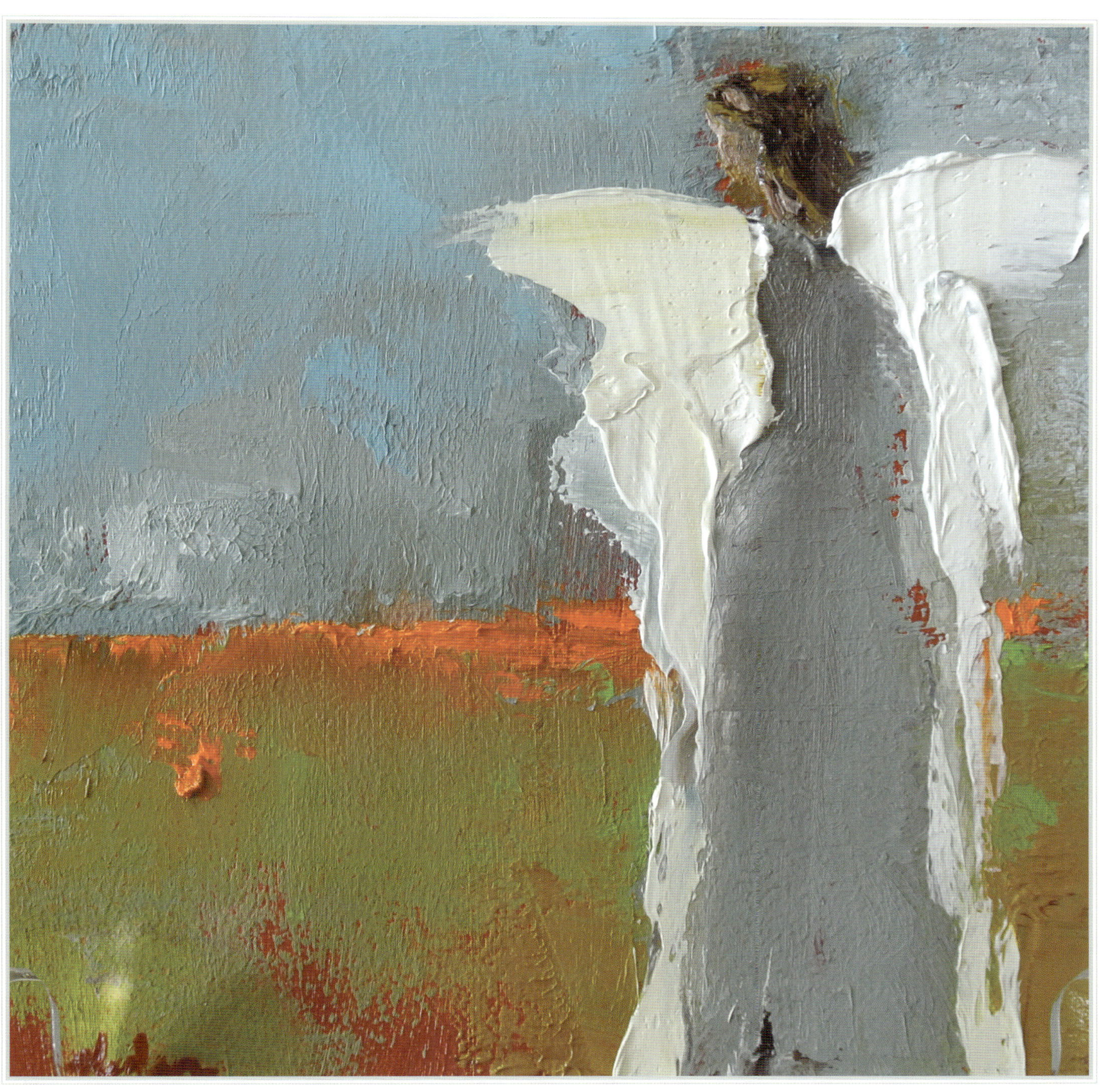

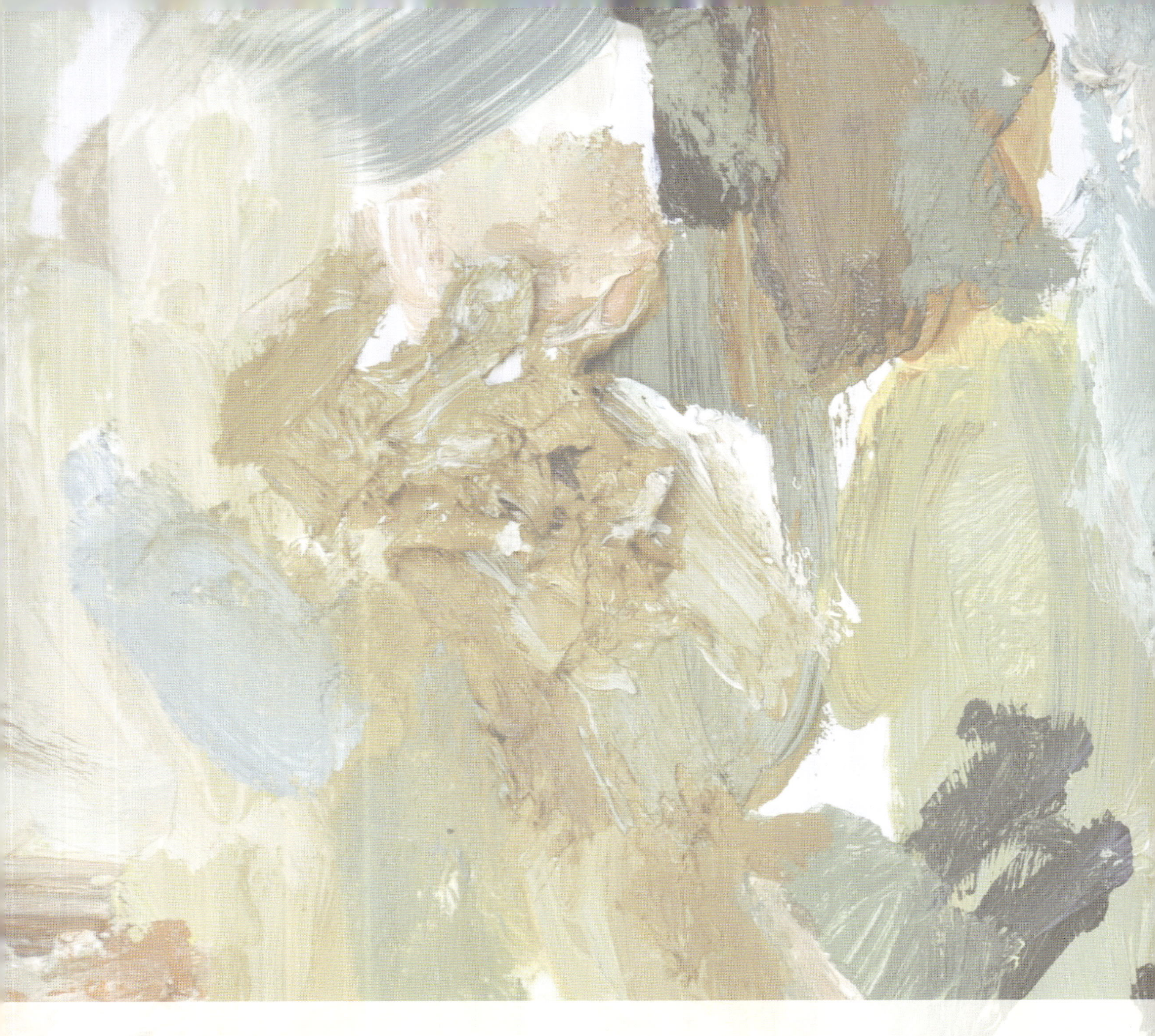

THERE IS A TIME FOR EVERYTHING,
AND A SEASON FOR EVERY ACTIVITY
UNDER THE HEAVENS.

Ecclesiastes 3:1

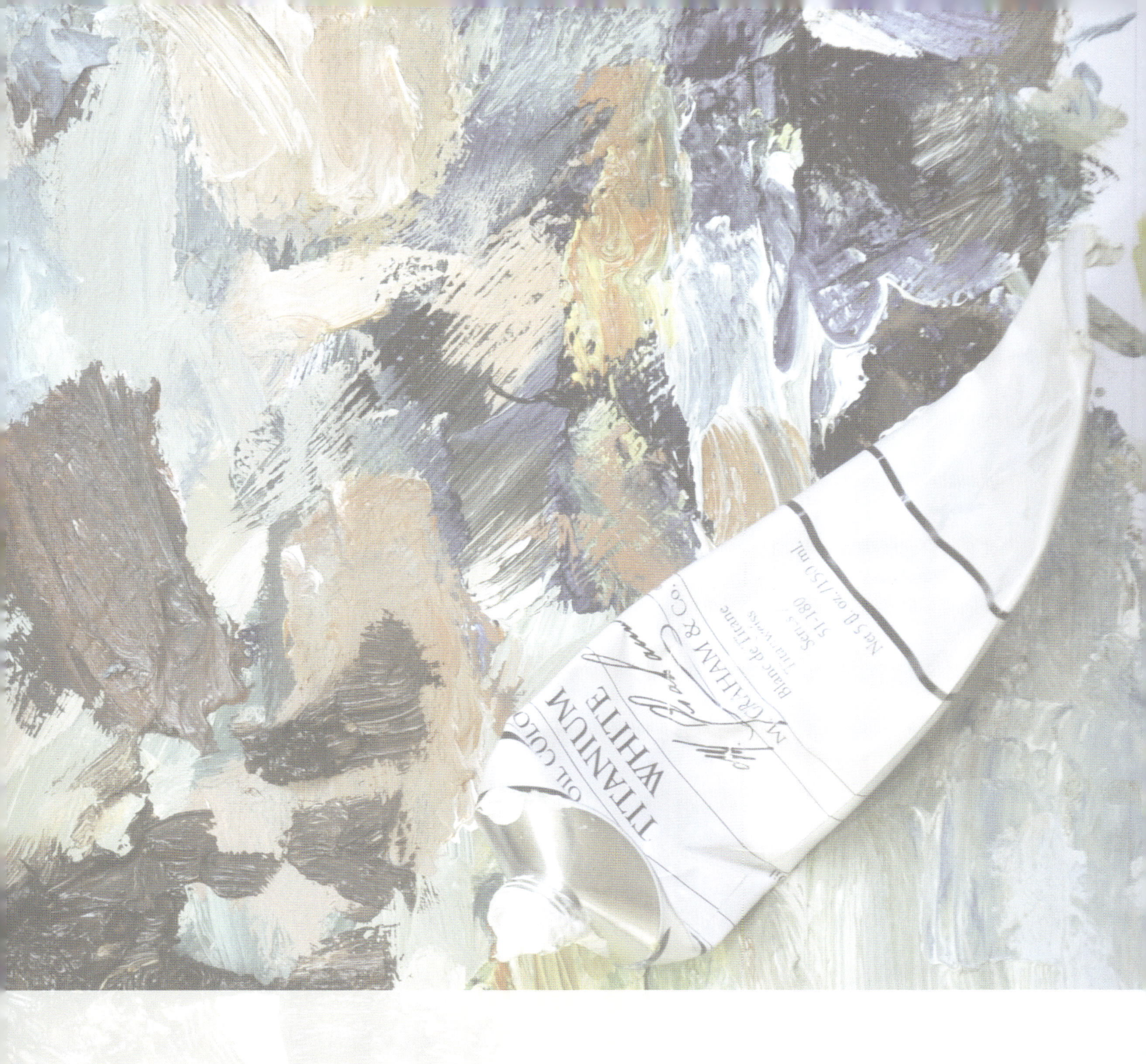

PATIENCE

LET US NOT BECOME WEARY IN DOING GOOD, FOR AT THE PROPER TIME WE WILL REAP A HARVEST IF WE DO NOT GIVE UP.

Galatians 6:9

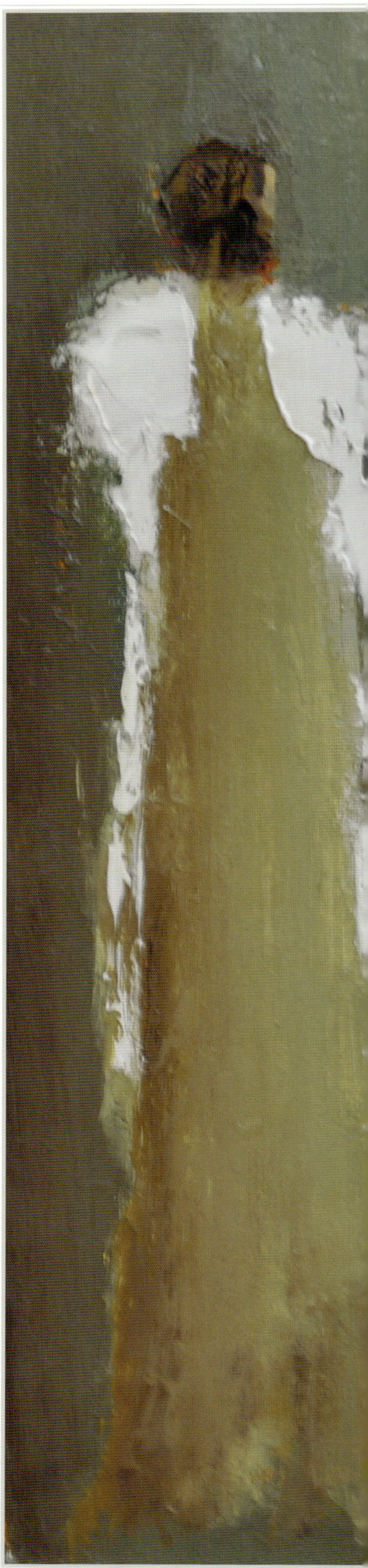

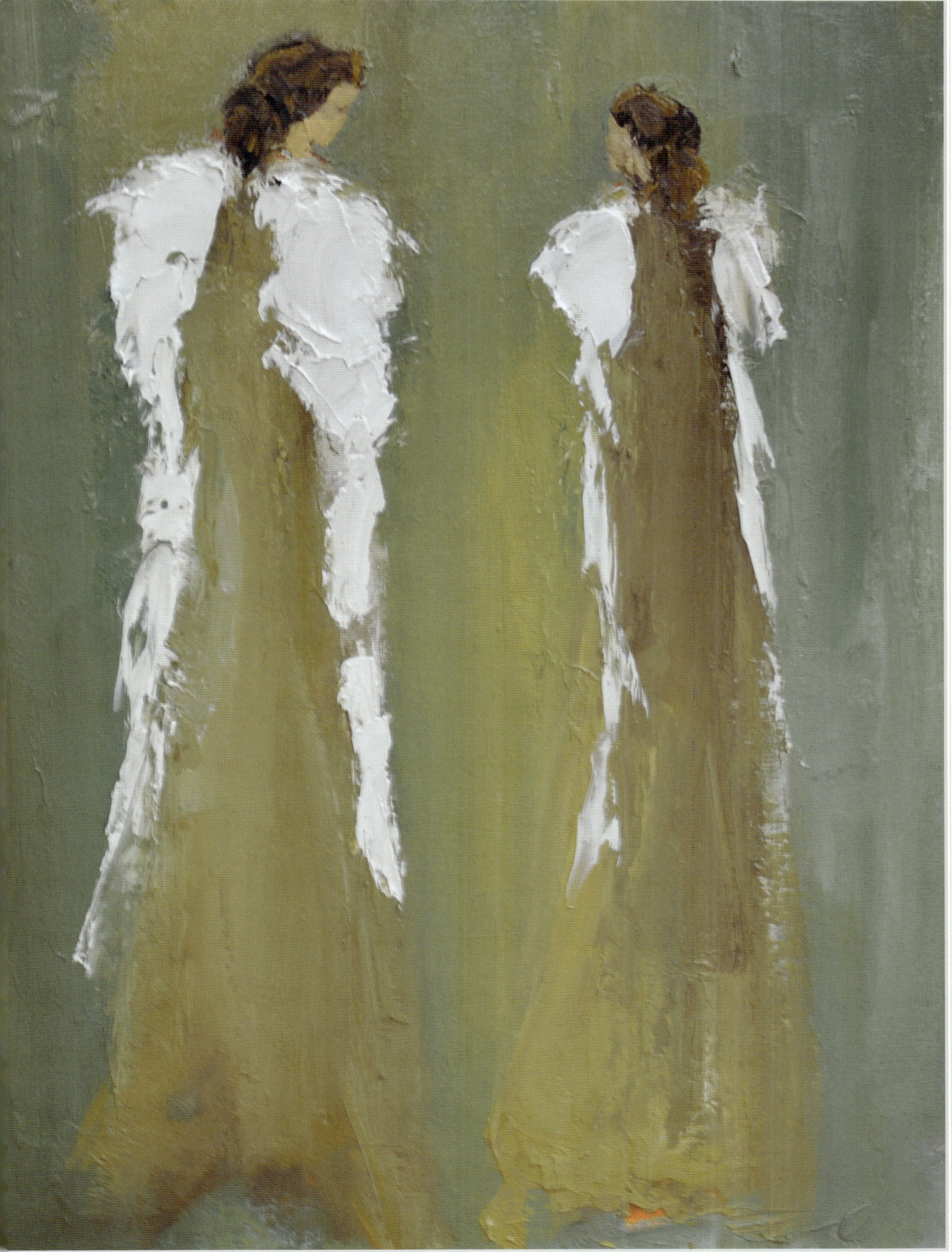

BUT THOSE WHO HOPE IN THE LORD
WILL RENEW THEIR STRENGTH.
THEY WILL SOAR ON WINGS LIKE EAGLES;
THEY WILL RUN AND NOT GROW WEARY,
THEY WILL WALK AND NOT BE FAINT.

Isaiah 40:31

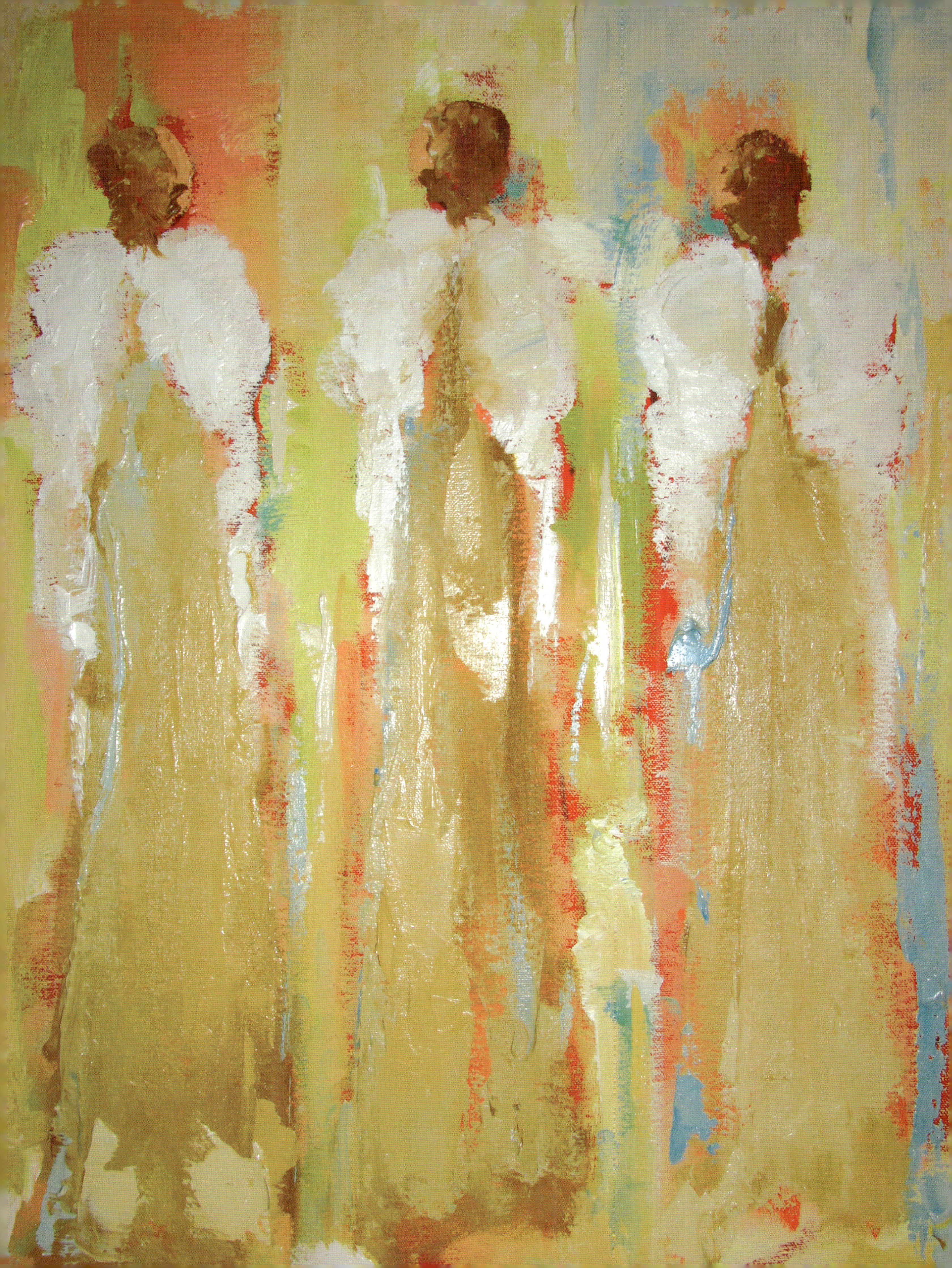

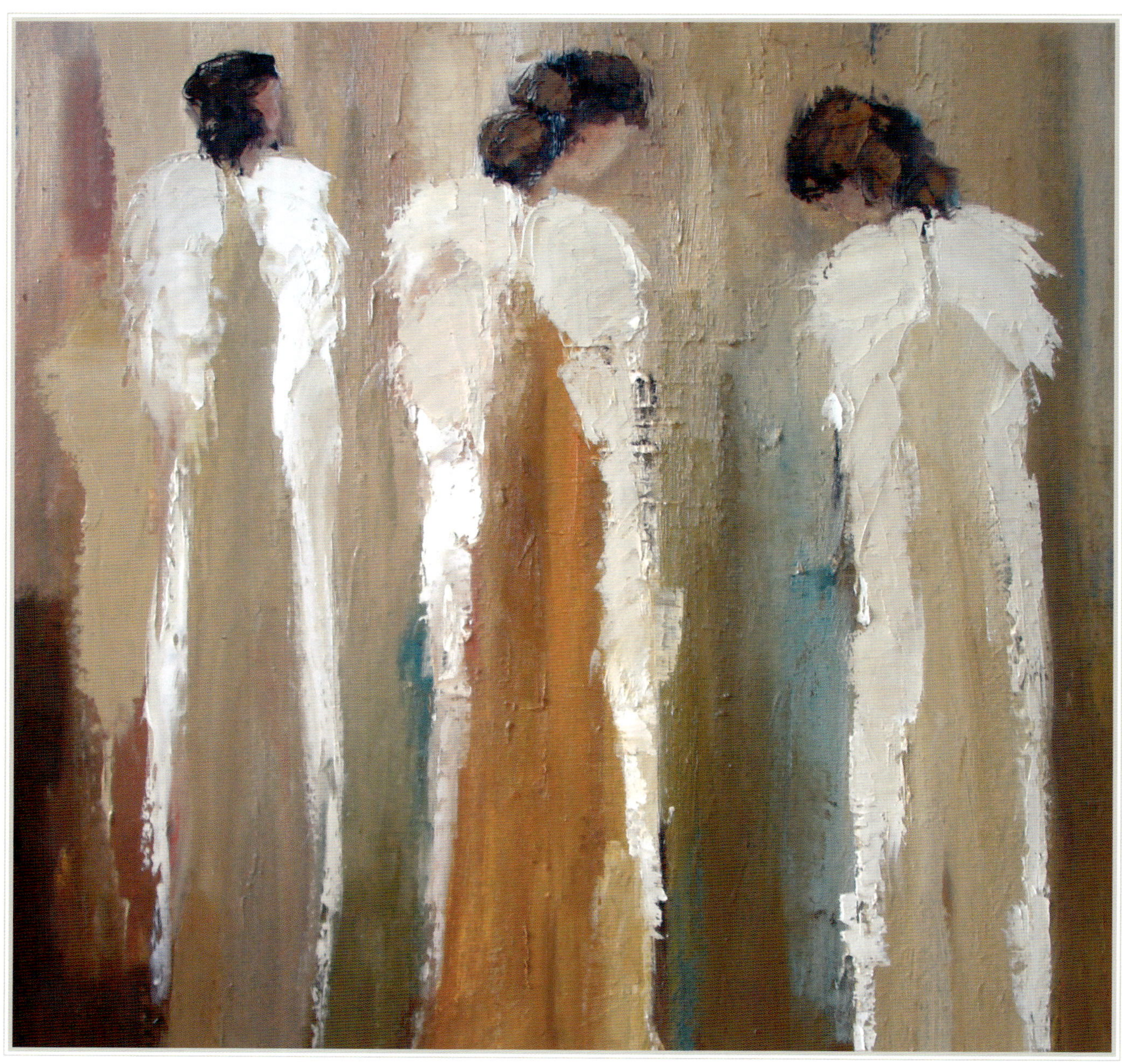

As with most art, words cannot convey the feeling that these Angels evoke in the beholder. It's as if these beautiful beings are about to fly off the canvas at any minute, with your heart neatly in hand.

KARSEN PRICE

Editor, *Today's Charlotte Woman*

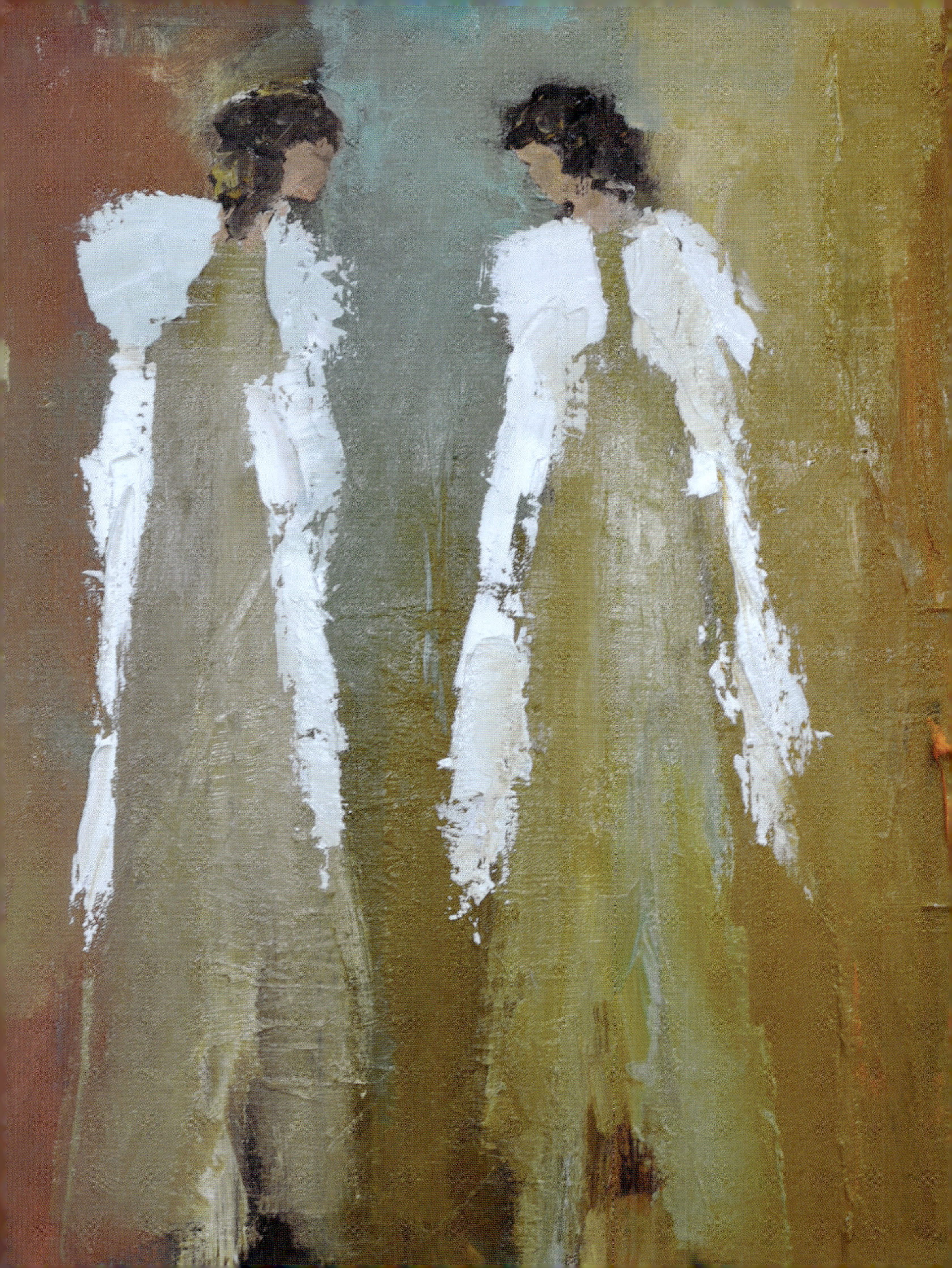

A PAINTING FOR OPRAH

God's Perfect Timing

Ever since I started painting Angels, I knew I was supposed to send one to Oprah Winfrey. I was captivated by how she gives back to the community and how she truly gives from her heart. I watched her show when she went to Africa and gave gifts to children who had nothing. The love and joy witnessed there was truly overwhelming. One day, when I was standing at my easel, with praise music playing, a painting developed and God whispered in my heart: "This one is for Oprah."

I began a painting of three African American Angels – the center angel a little larger, with the other two angels flanked on either side reaching the shoulder of the center angel, both very similar to one another in size, color and hair. I finished the painting, yet I never did send it to her; the three angels did not make sense to me. Who did they represent? Why three angels? I kept it in the studio for about a year. Several people inquired about purchasing the painting, yet I hung onto it, knowing that it somehow belonged to Ms. Winfrey.

On January 9th, 2011, our Pastor Steven Furtick at Elevation Church was preaching about how we need to believe God for the big things in our lives. All I could think about was the angel painting for Ms. Winfrey and that it was time to reach out to her. A few days later, I wrote in my journal that I was trusting and believing that God

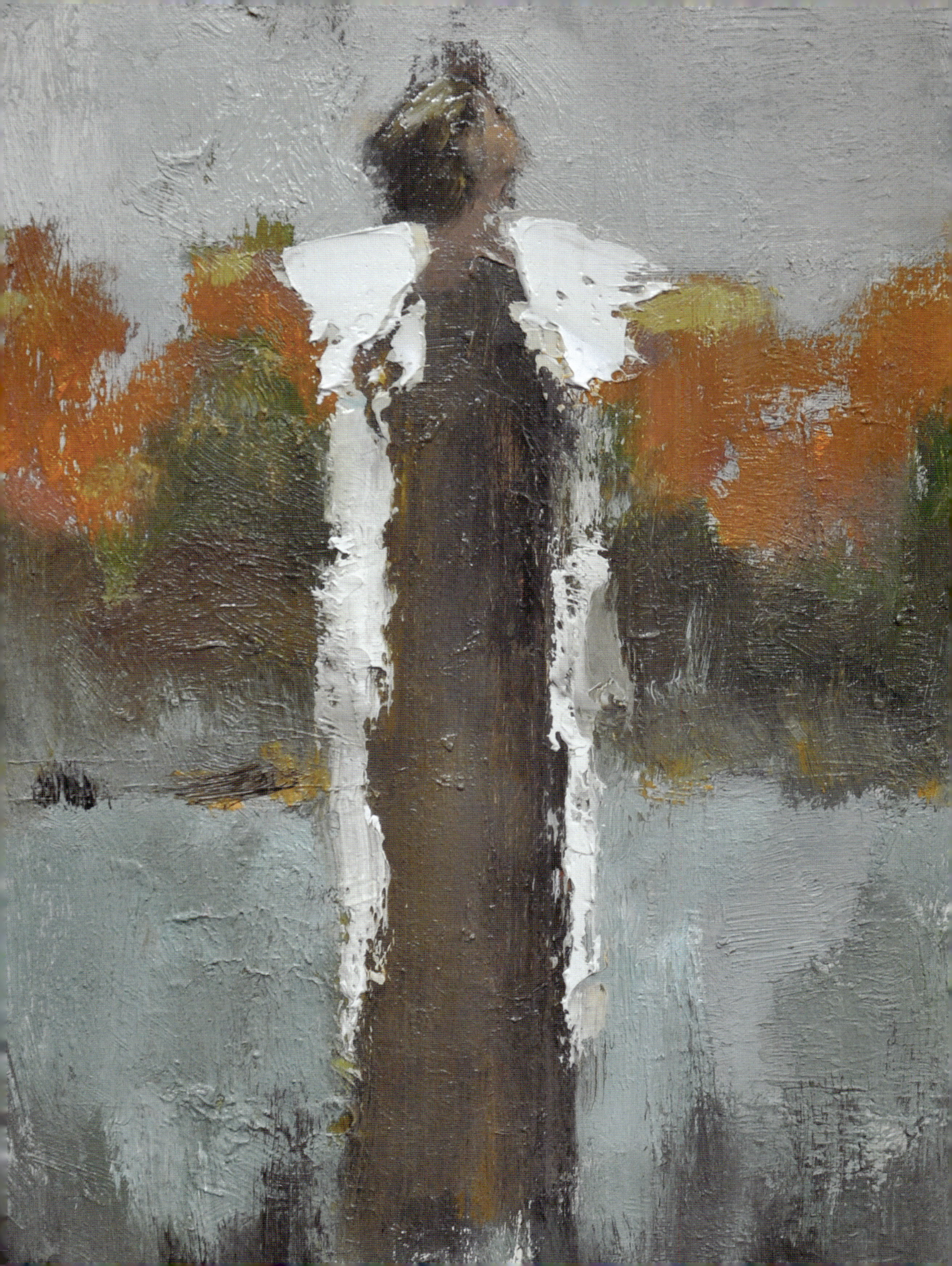

BUT THOU, O LORD, ART A GOD FULL OF COMPASSION, AND GRACIOUS, LONG SUFFERING, AND PLENTEOUS IN MERCY AND TRUTH.

PSALM 86:15

would show Himself big for my marriage, my children, and my art. I even wrote about Ms. Winfrey and the chance to talk to her about Jesus. After that, I made up my mind that I would one day repaint for her a smaller angel. But that never happened.

At the end of January 2011, there was breaking news out about Oprah and her newly-found half-sister. I tuned into the *Oprah* show and saw that most amazing story: Oprah had a half-sister Patricia and a half-brother Anthony, who had both passed away. Then there was another half-sister whom she did not know about, who was given up for adoption back in 1963. Her name was Patricia as well. Both Patricias looked so similar in photos shared on air. When Patricia came

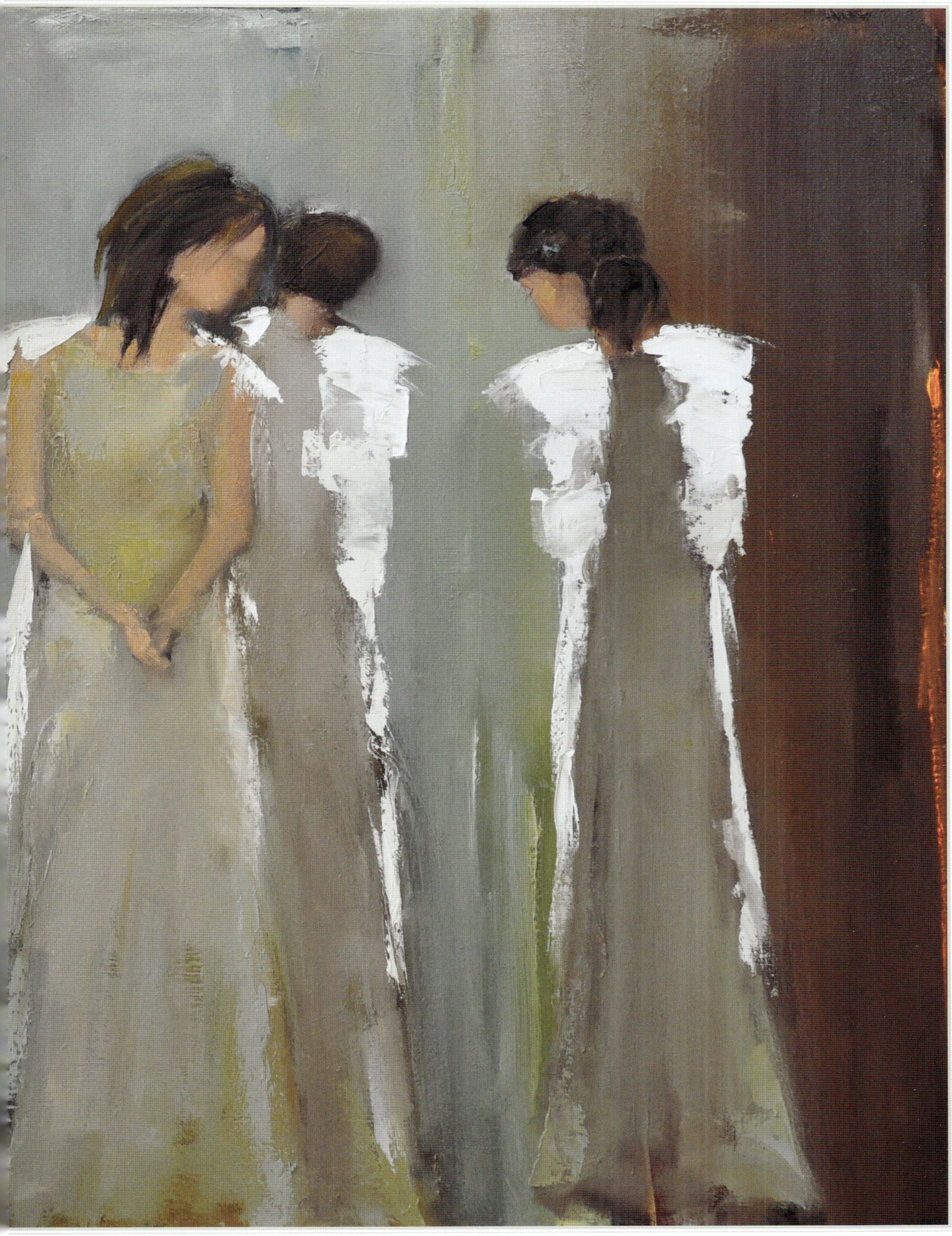

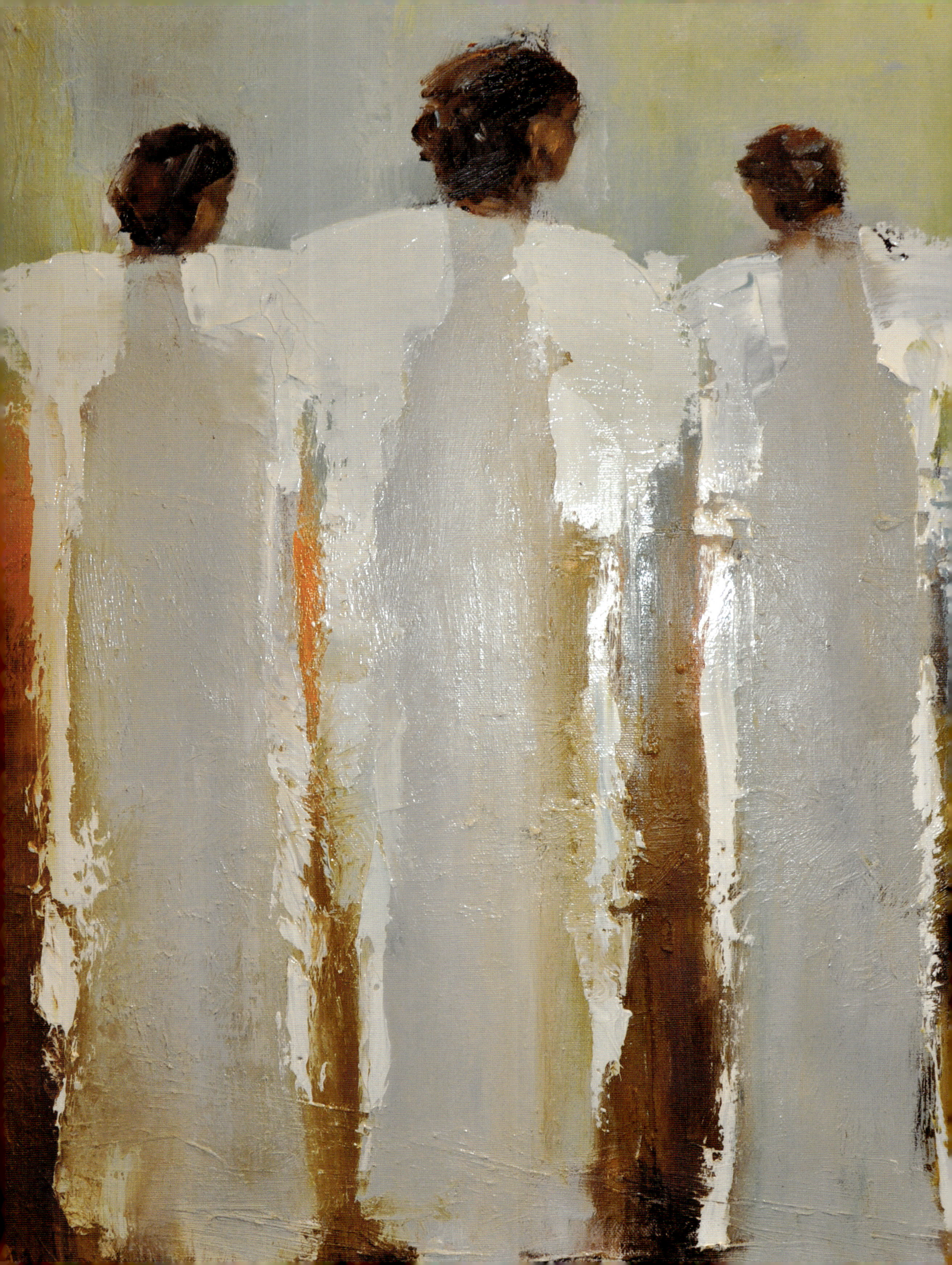

out on stage during the show, she hugged Oprah. Patricia was much shorter than Oprah - she came up to her shoulders. I looked at my husband and said: "That is my painting." It all made sense then that I had held onto that painting for over a year. The next day, I packaged the painting up and wrote a note telling Ms. Winfrey that I had always thought she was the one who was supposed to have an Angel painting, but after seeing the show, I knew that this painting was for her to give to her newfound sister Patricia. It was overwhelming to me. But God knew all along that this was a painting that held special meaning for those sisters.

About three weeks later, I received a personal phone call from Ms. Winfrey herself thanking me for the painting. I was in shock, but honored and giddy with delight that when we are patient stepping out in faith, trusting and obeying God – He can do amazing things.

Anne Neilson is probably one of the most energetic people I know. She keeps me on my toes. I suspect that she is very driven, as are all accomplished artists. Although Anne is a master in many genres, it is her Angels that garner the most attention. Using a palette knife to create an impasto look, each painting depicts a very interesting dimension. I have actually had clients walk into the gallery and make a beeline to these faceless graceful figures. Clients seem to be drawn to their strength.

ANNE IRWIN

Gallery Owner, Anne Irwin Fine Art, Atlanta, GA

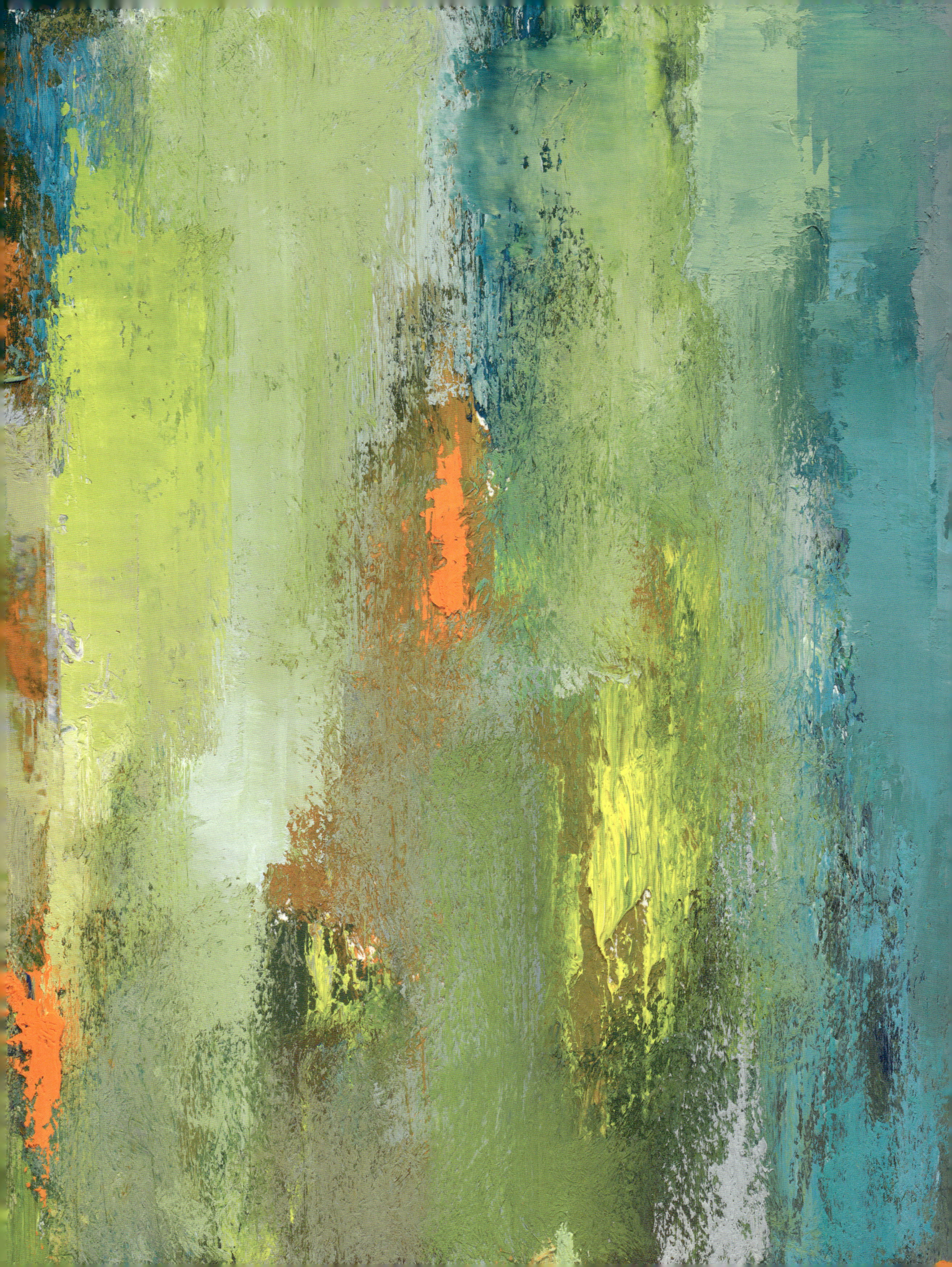

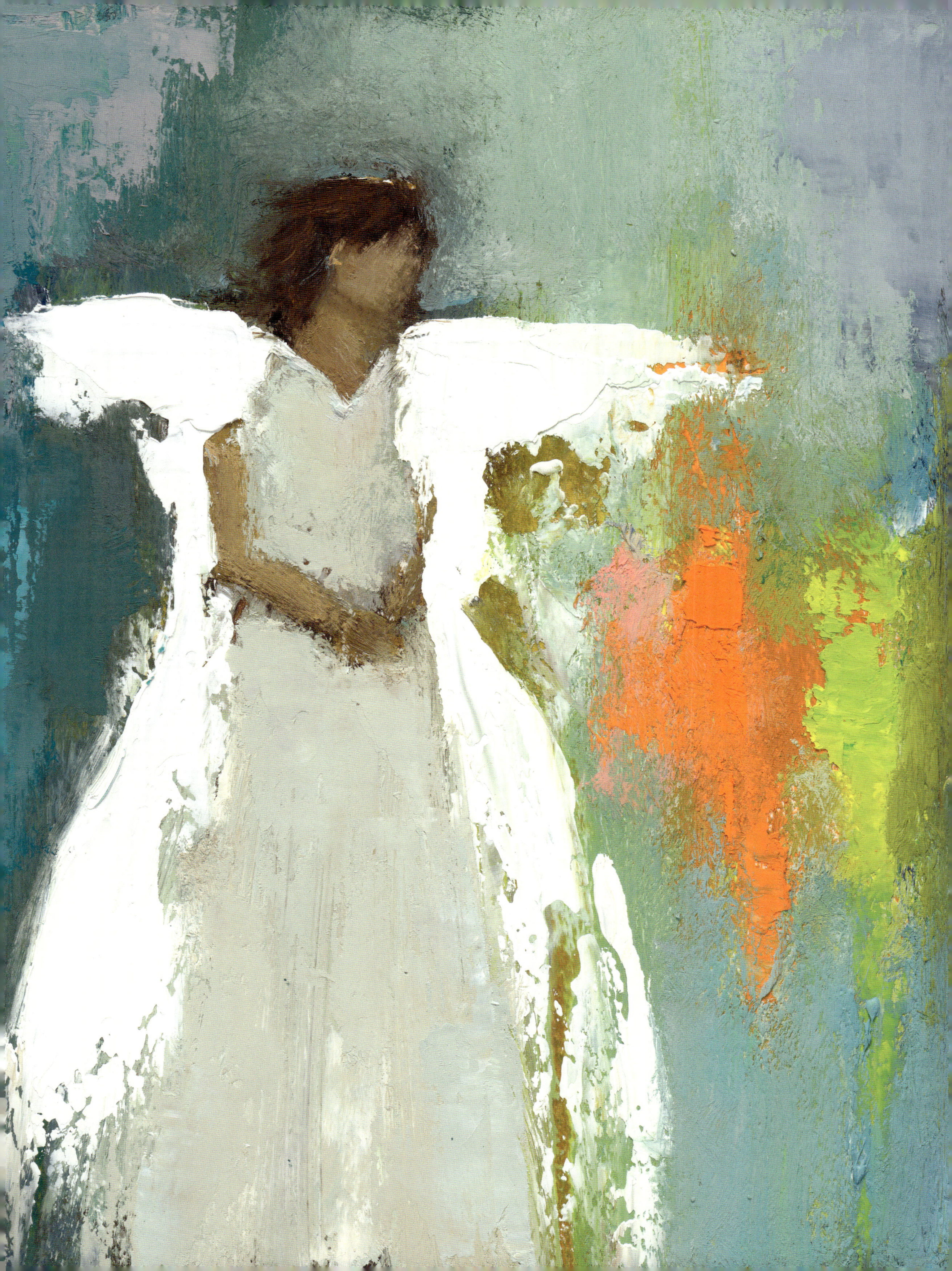

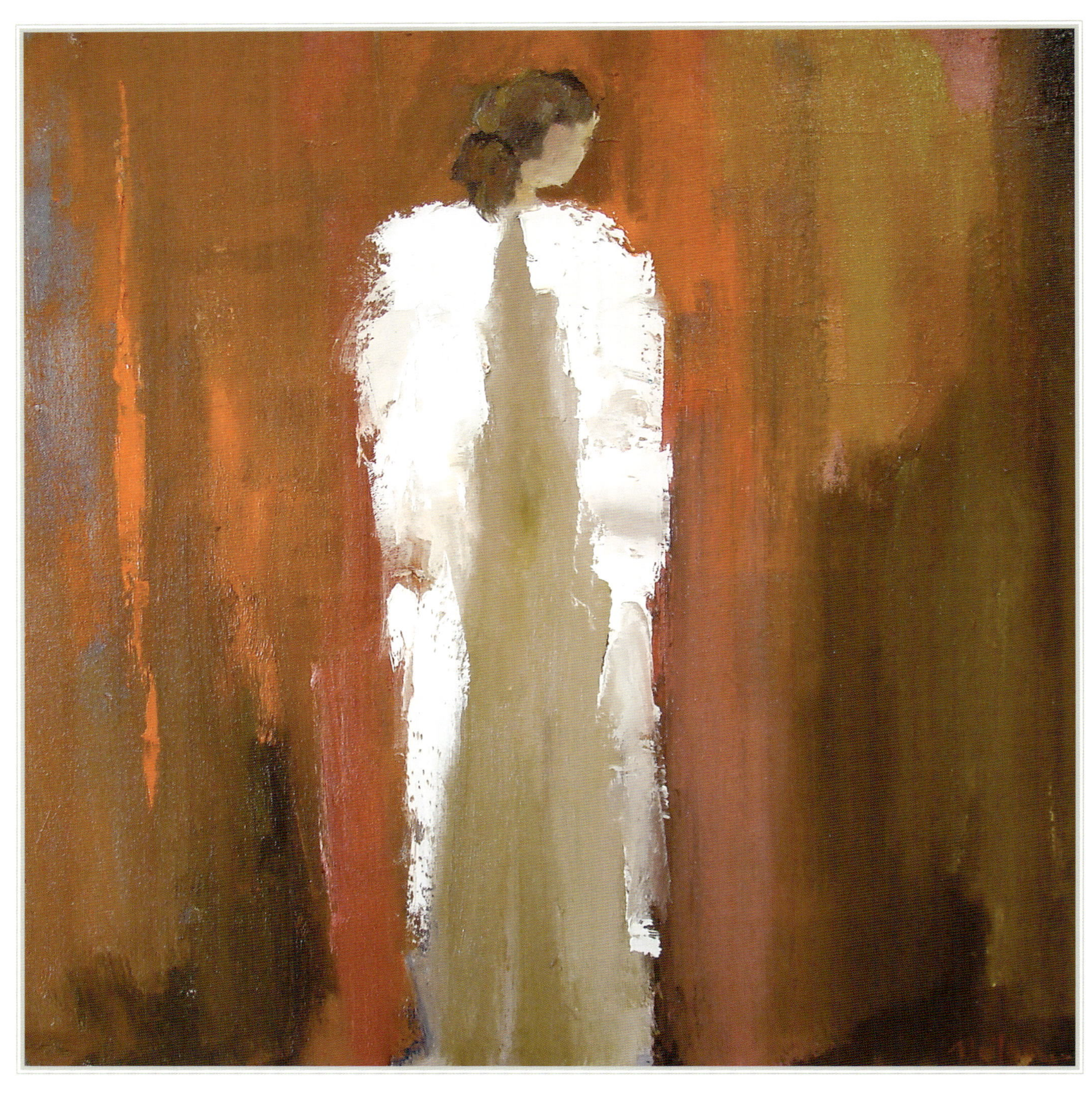

ART WASHES AWAY FROM THE SOUL THE DUST OF EVERYDAY LIFE.

—PABLO PICASSO

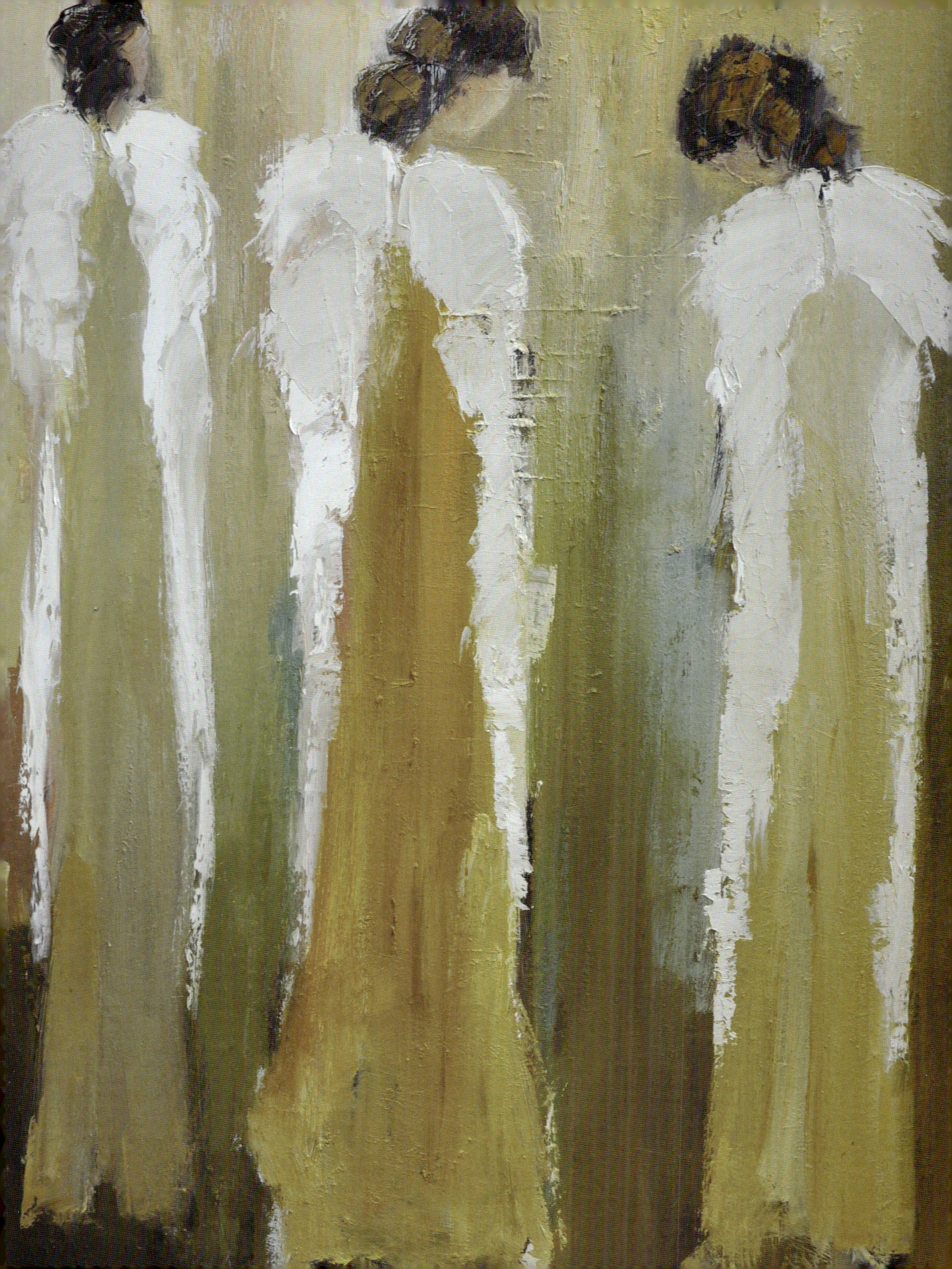

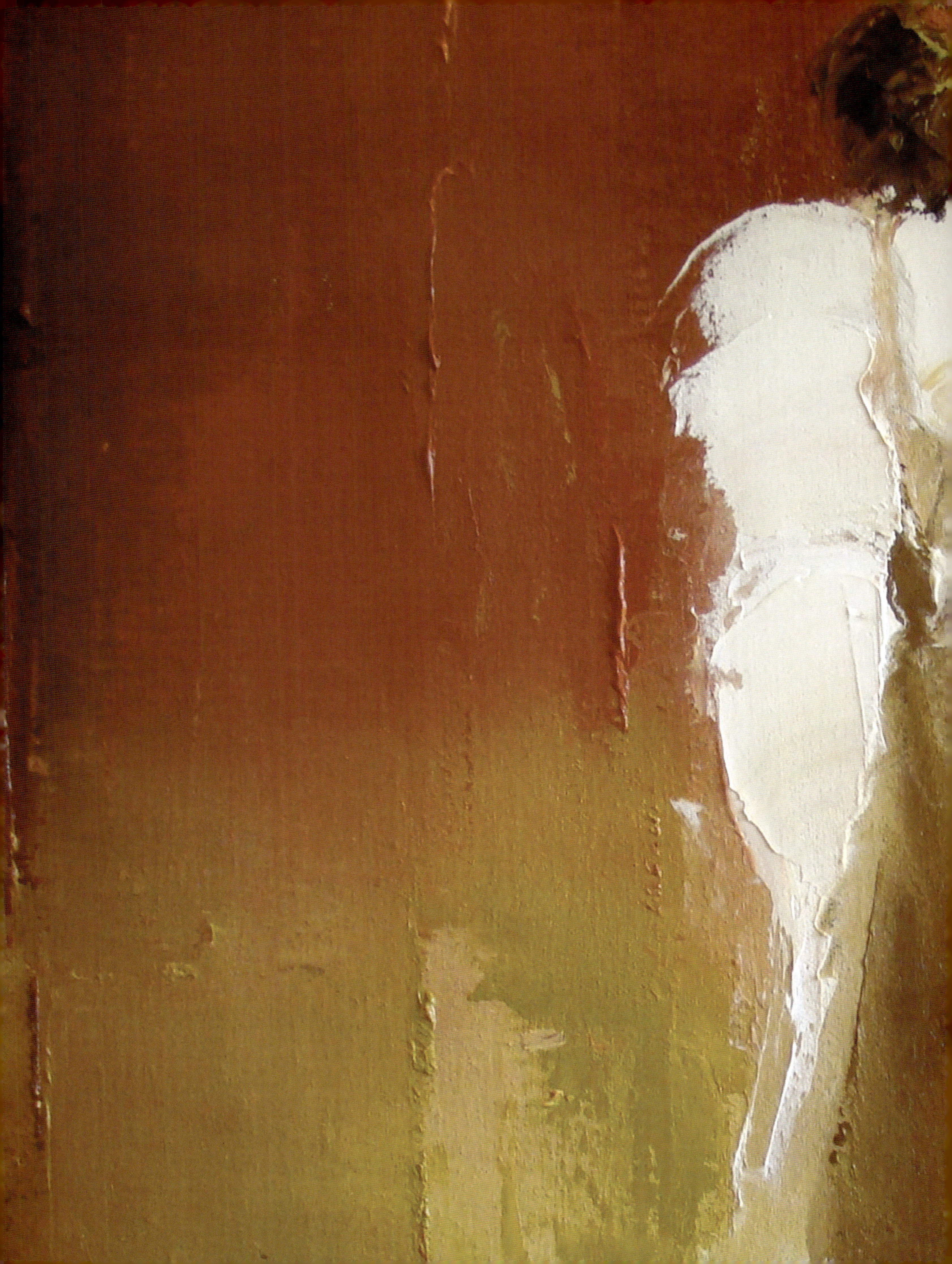

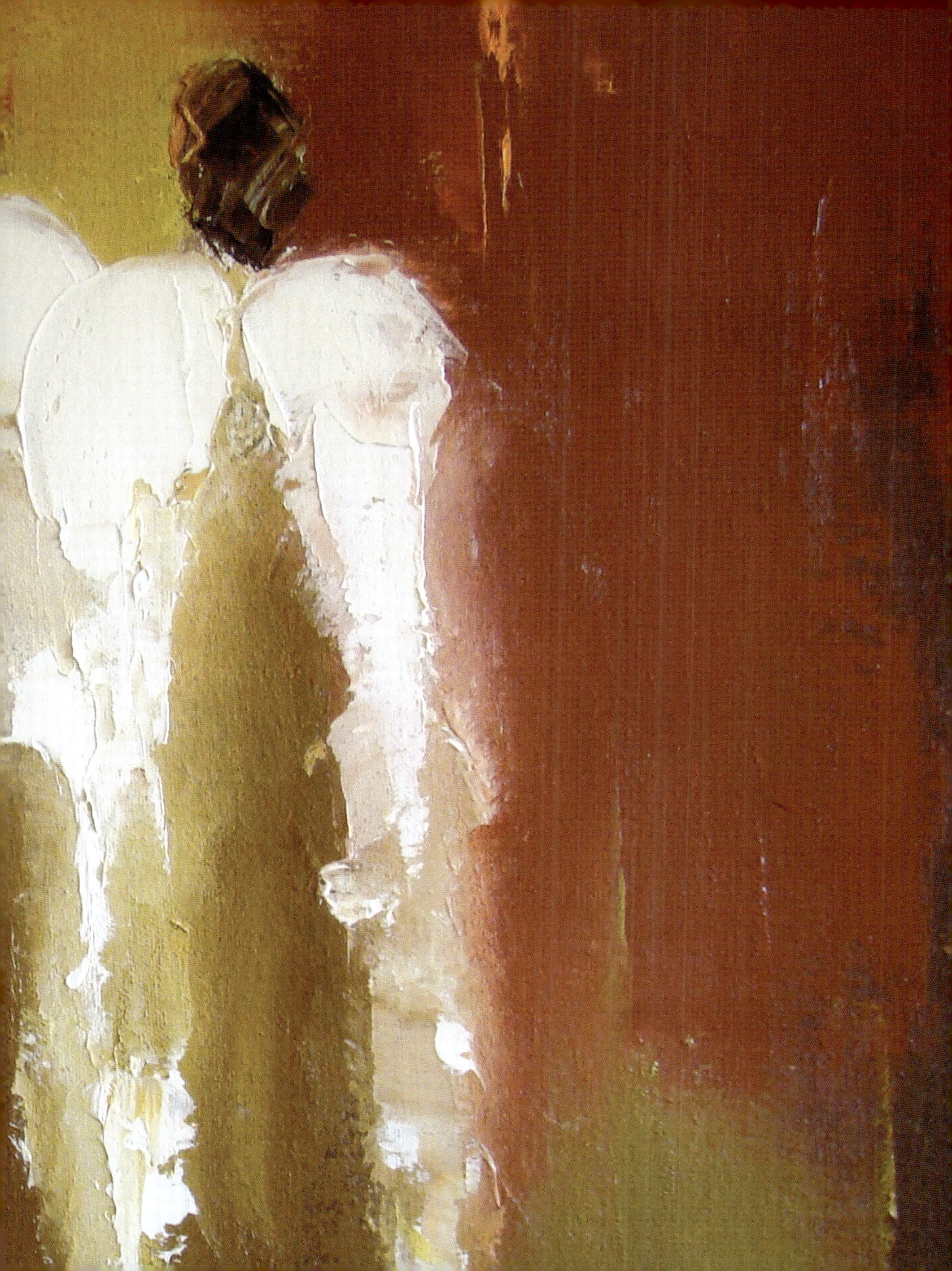

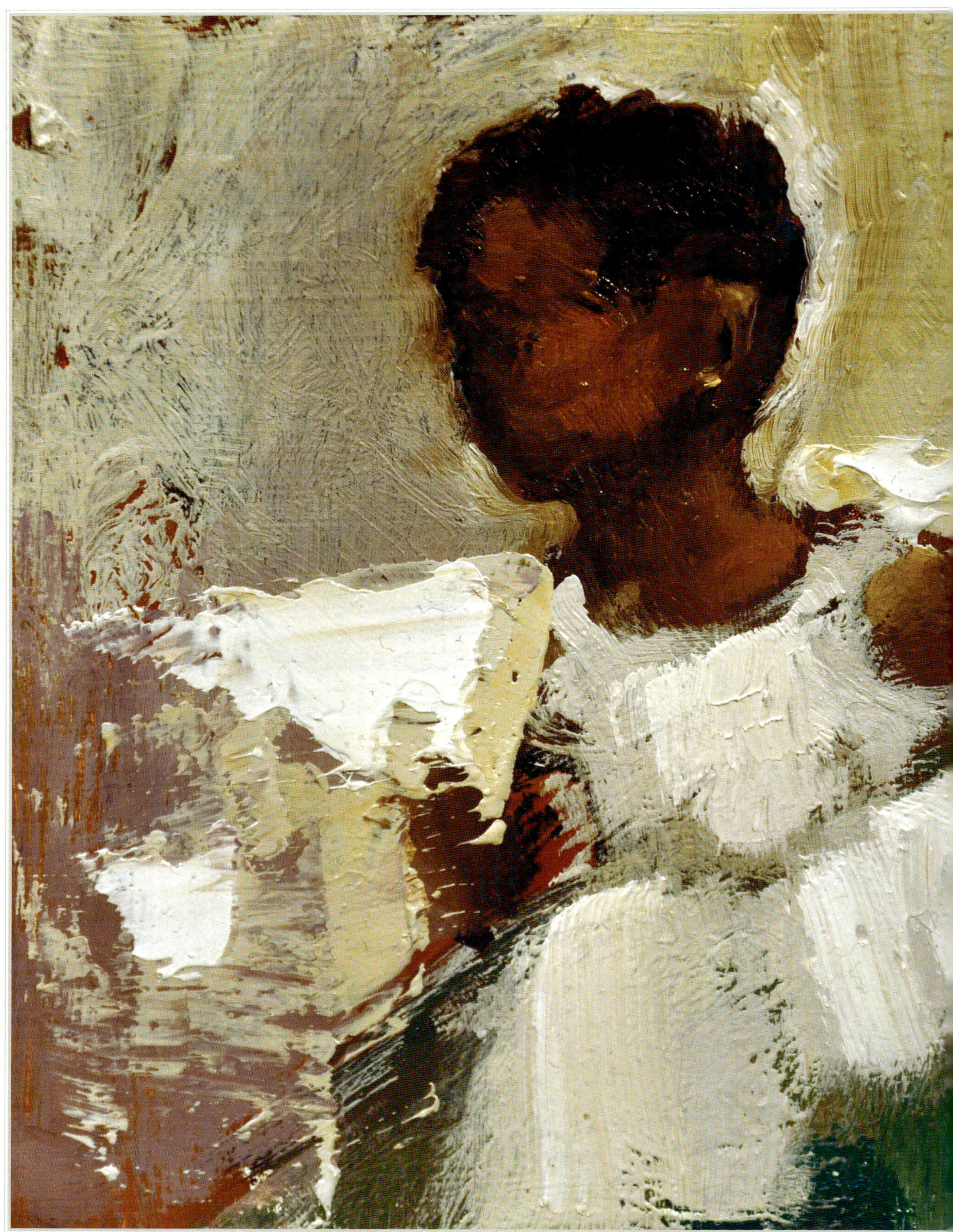

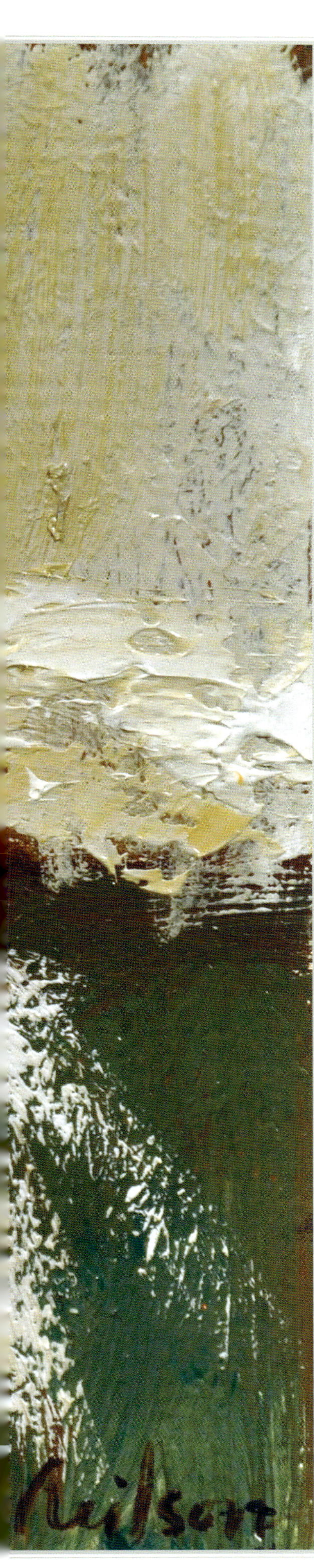

YOU NEED TO PERSEVERE SO THAT WHEN YOU HAVE DONE THE WILL OF GOD, YOU WILL RECEIVE WHAT HE HAS PROMISED.

HEBREWS 10:36

We are so honored to have Angels in our shop. The soft colors along with Anne's style of applying texture through many layers of paint is extraordinary. It really does feel like the Angels are real. They evoke such emotion in the customer. Many times they put a name on one of the faces because it reminds them of a loved one and becomes so personal to them. Anne's talent is an inspiration and we are thankful for it!

PATTY SIMPSON

Owner, Granville Antiques, Charlotte, NC

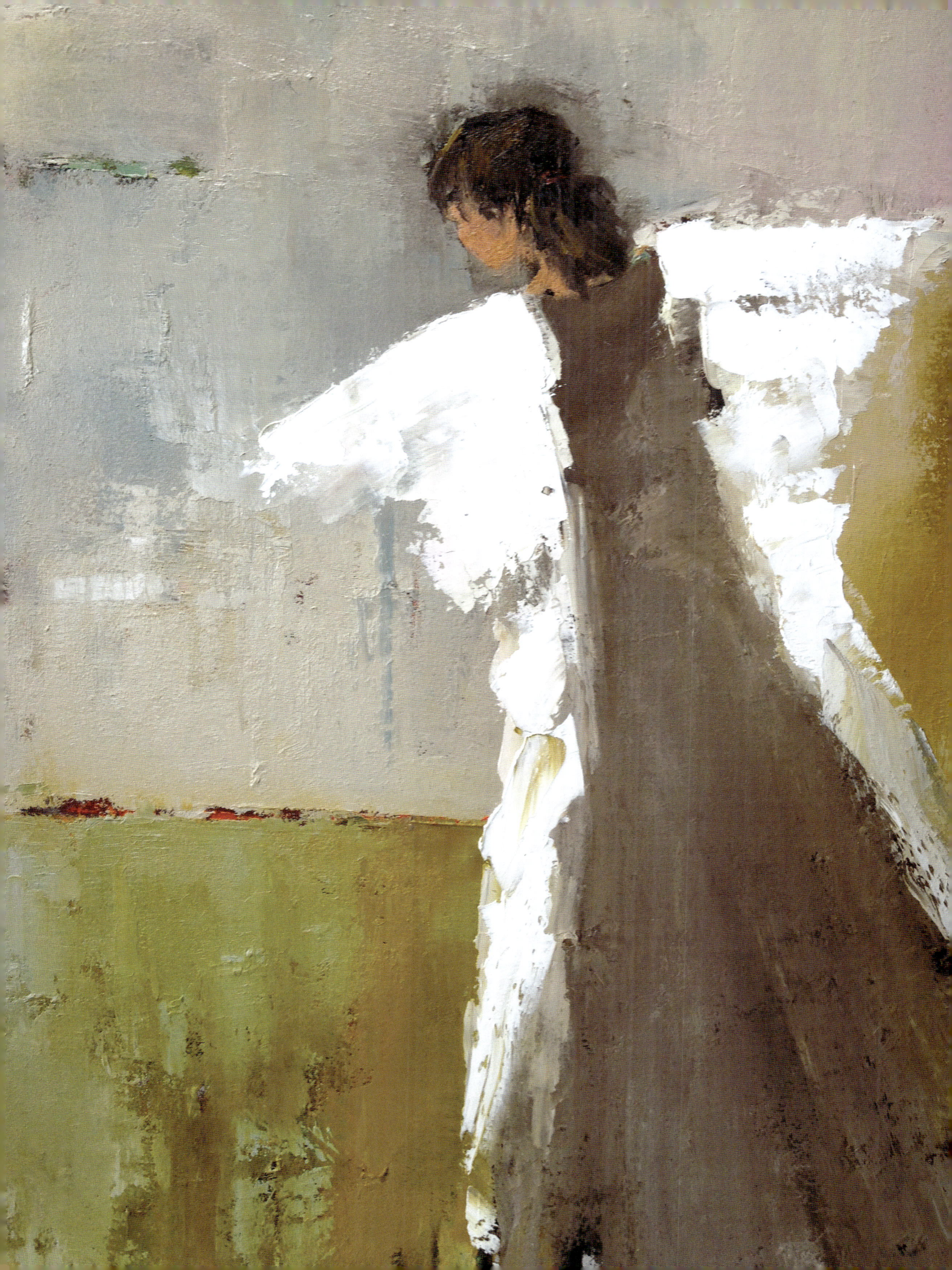

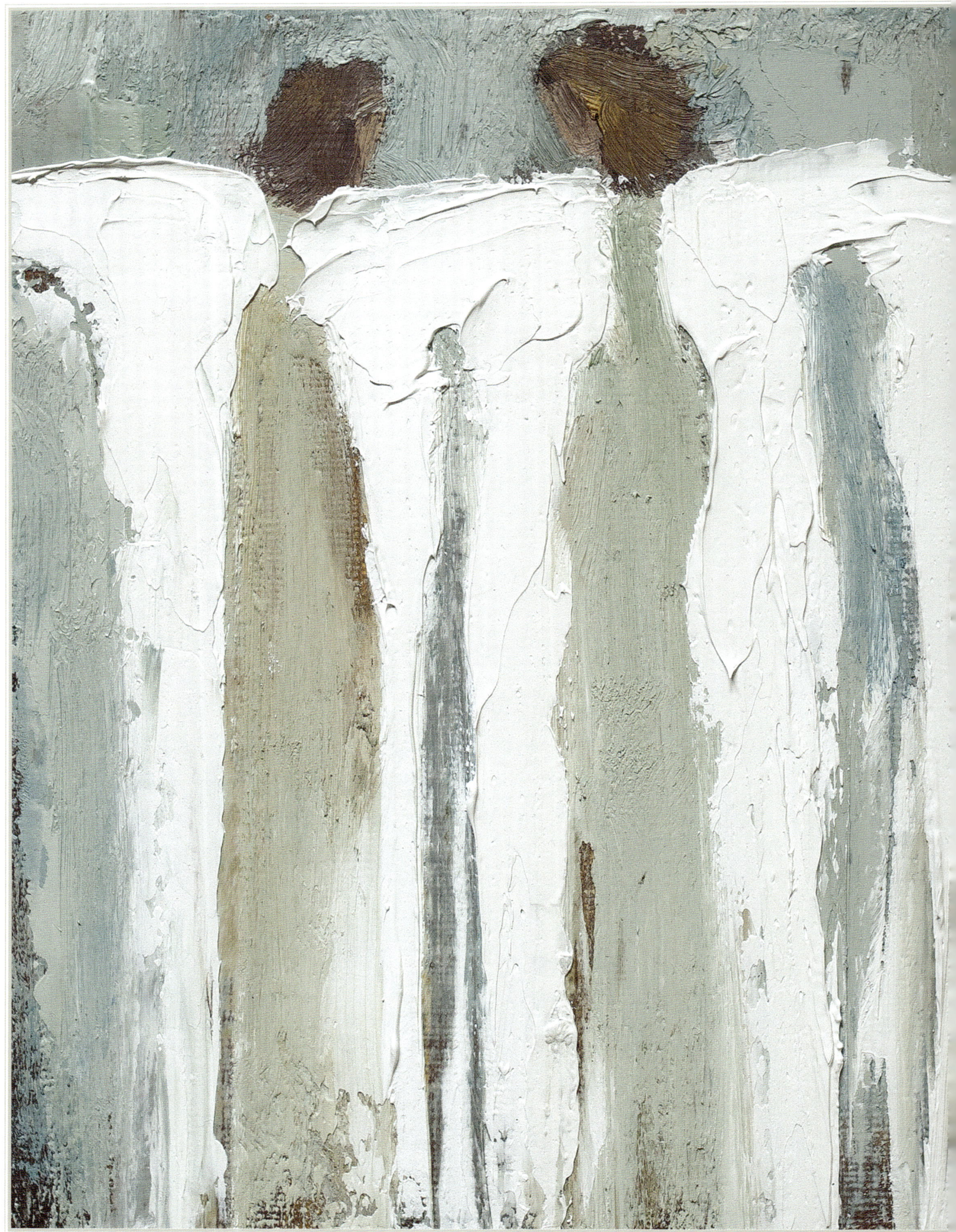

Anne Neilson is passionate about her faith, her family and her painting; but it is her passion for giving that impacts so many lives in our community and around the world. Anne is a truly gifted artist, and her paintings transcend and touch your soul. I am always drawn to her work at charity events throughout the year. Her beautiful Angels remind me of their presence in our midst, and I am humbled by God's love. Anne's sweet and generous spirit is a blessing and inspiration to me and all who have the privilege to know her.

KATHY BUCKLEY

Editor-in-Chief, *Charlotte Living*

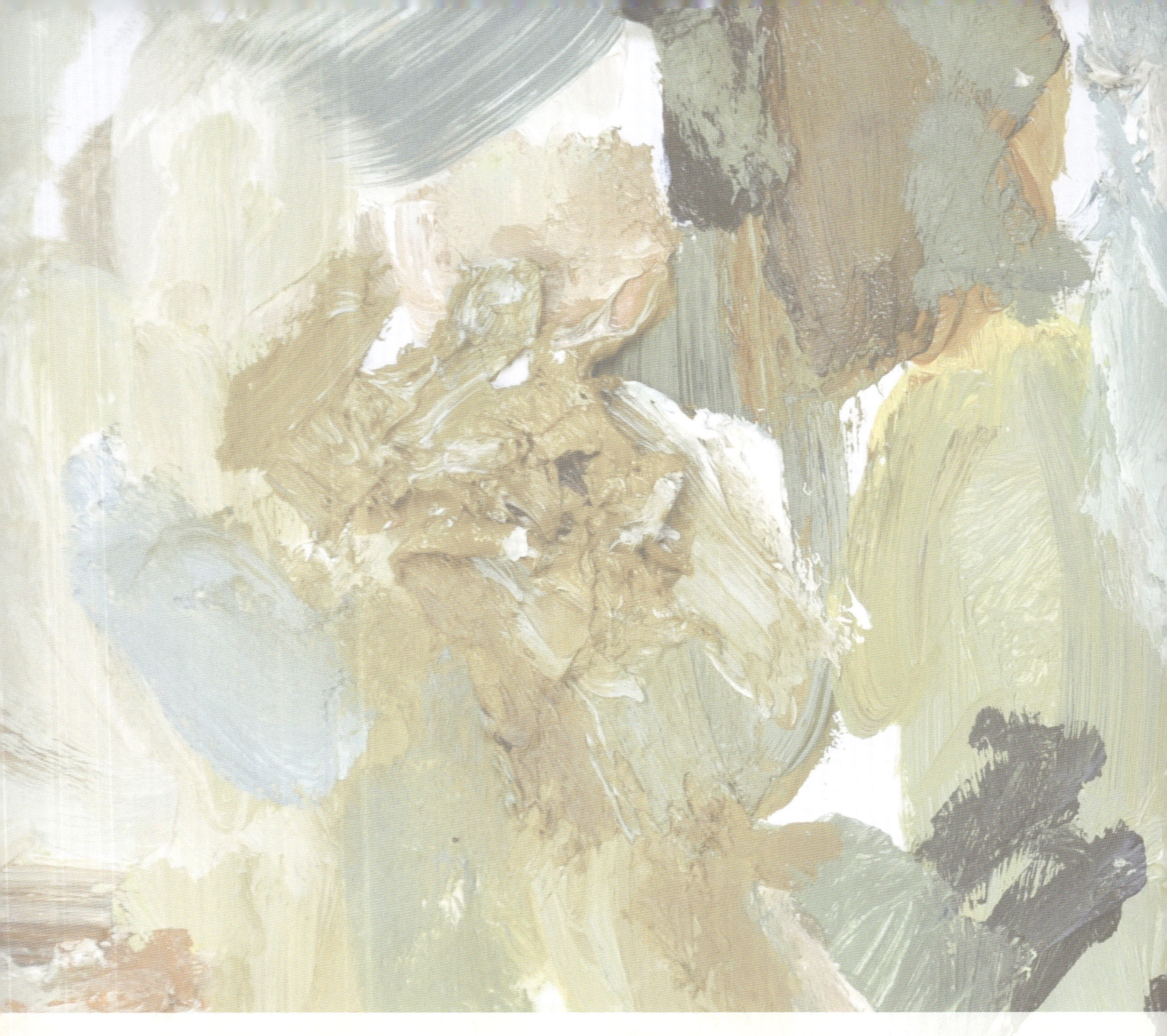

AND WHATEVER YOU DO, WHETHER IN WORD OR DEED, DO IT ALL IN THE NAME OF THE LORD JESUS, GIVING THANKS TO GOD THE FATHER THROUGH HIM.

Colossians 3:17

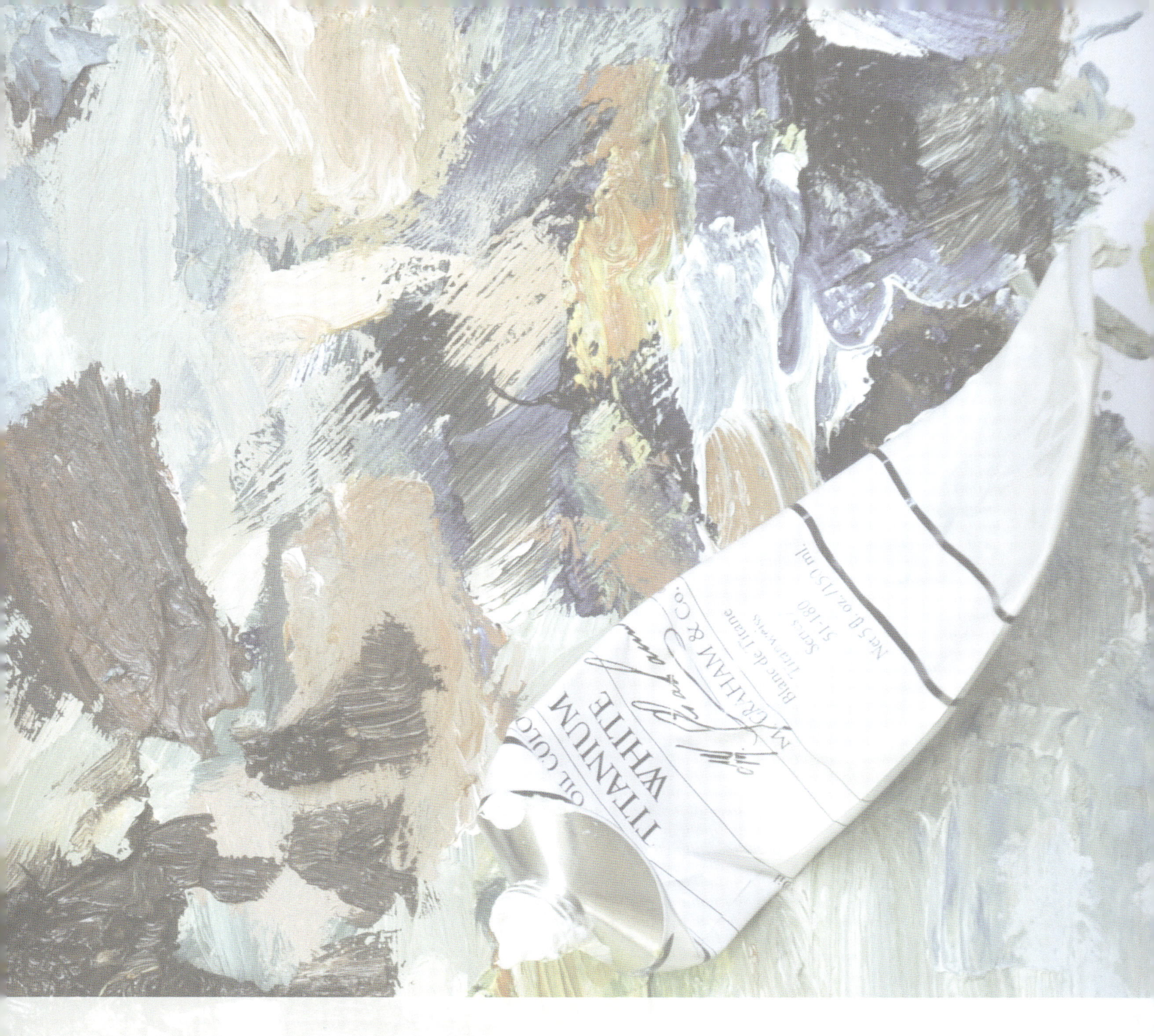

KINDNESS

IN HIS KINDNESS GOD CALLED YOU TO SHARE IN HIS ETERNAL GLORY BY MEANS OF CHRIST JESUS. SO AFTER YOU HAVE SUFFERED A LITTLE WHILE, HE WILL RESTORE, SUPPORT, AND STRENGTHEN YOU, AND HE WILL PLACE YOU ON A FIRM FOUNDATION.

1 PETER 5:10

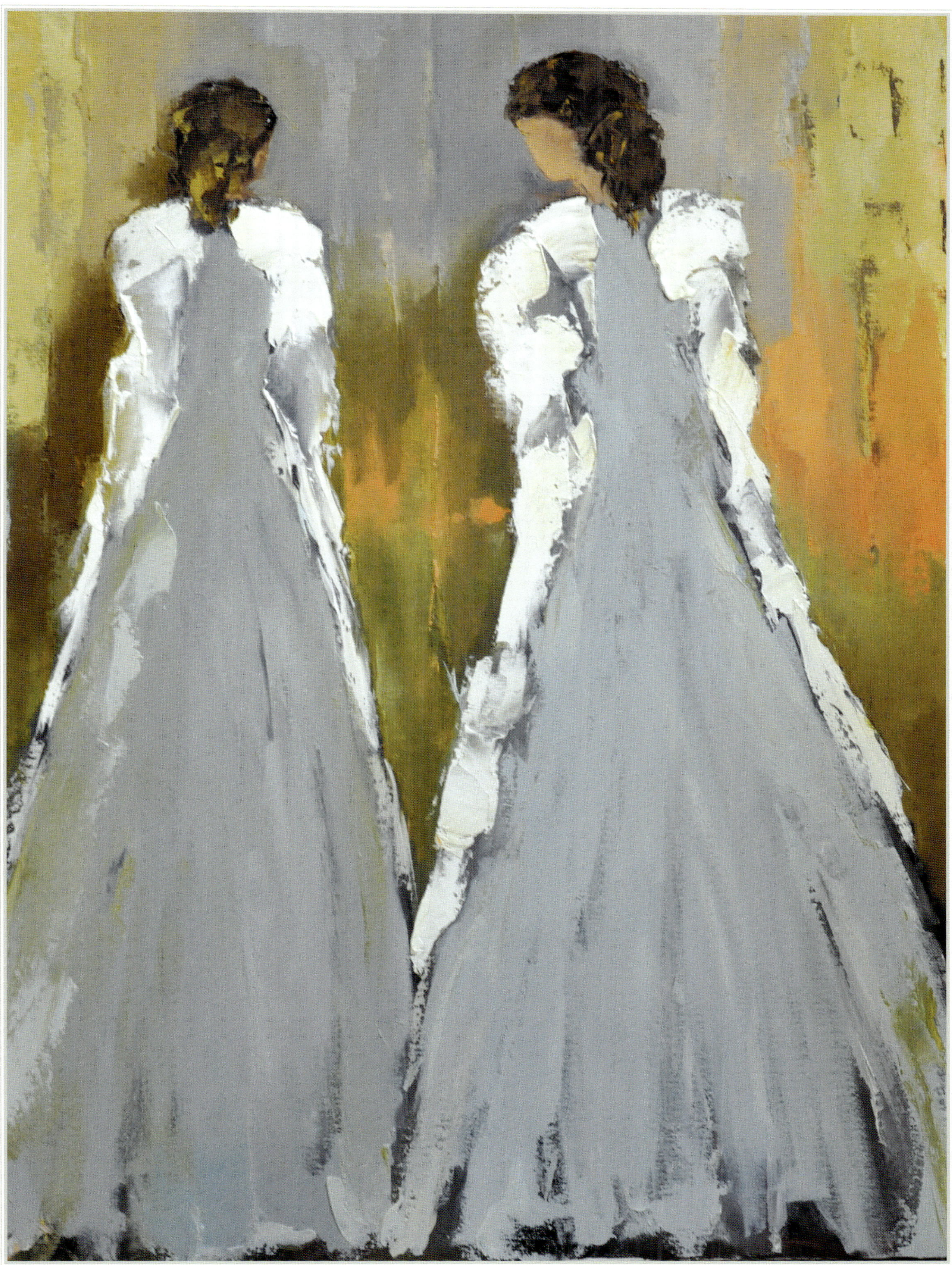

The paintings have a life of their own. They give you a glimpse of Heaven that will encourage those who doubt and thrill those who believe.

TERESA BINDEL

Gallery Owner, Gallery Elite, Carmel, CA

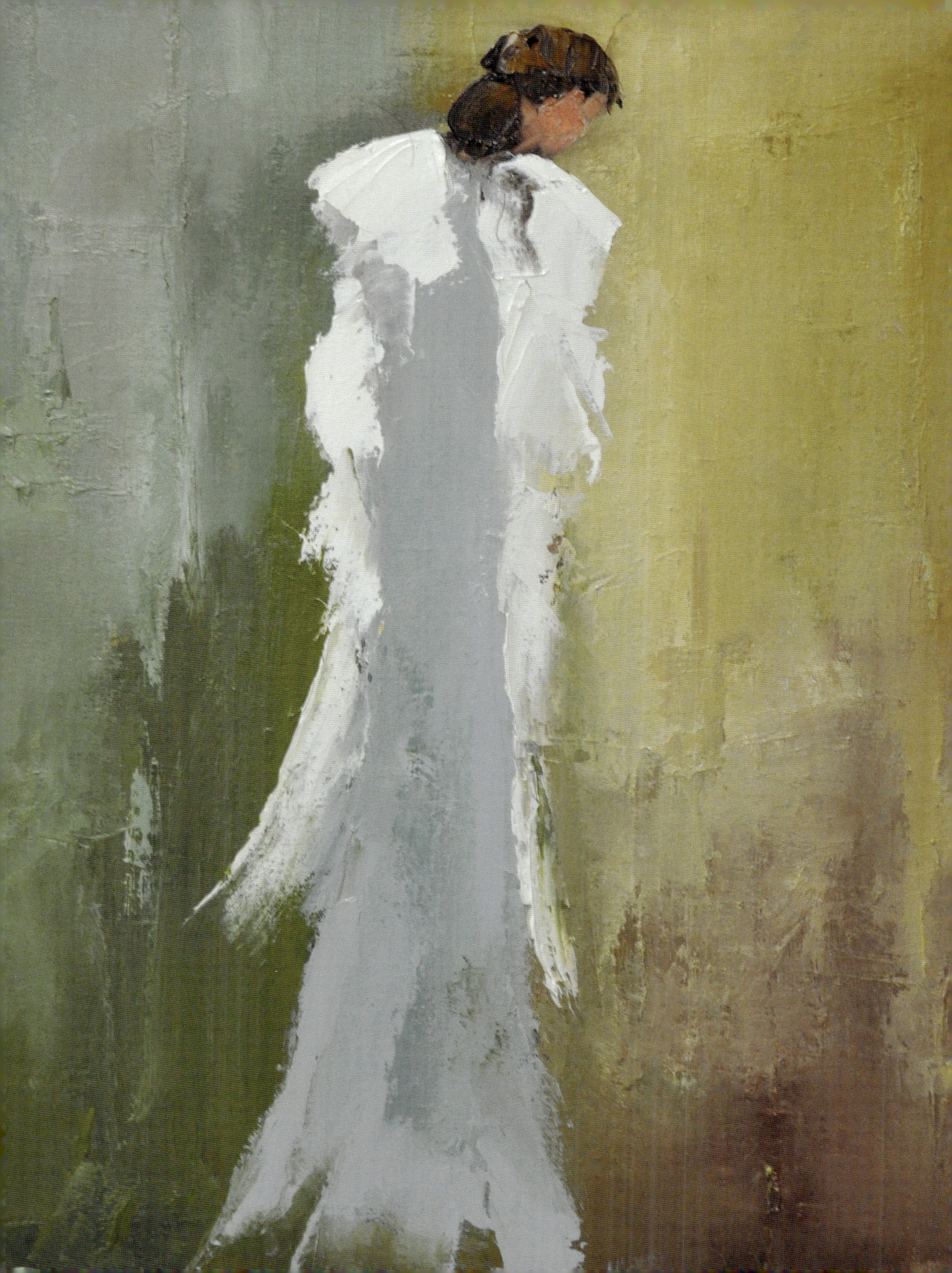

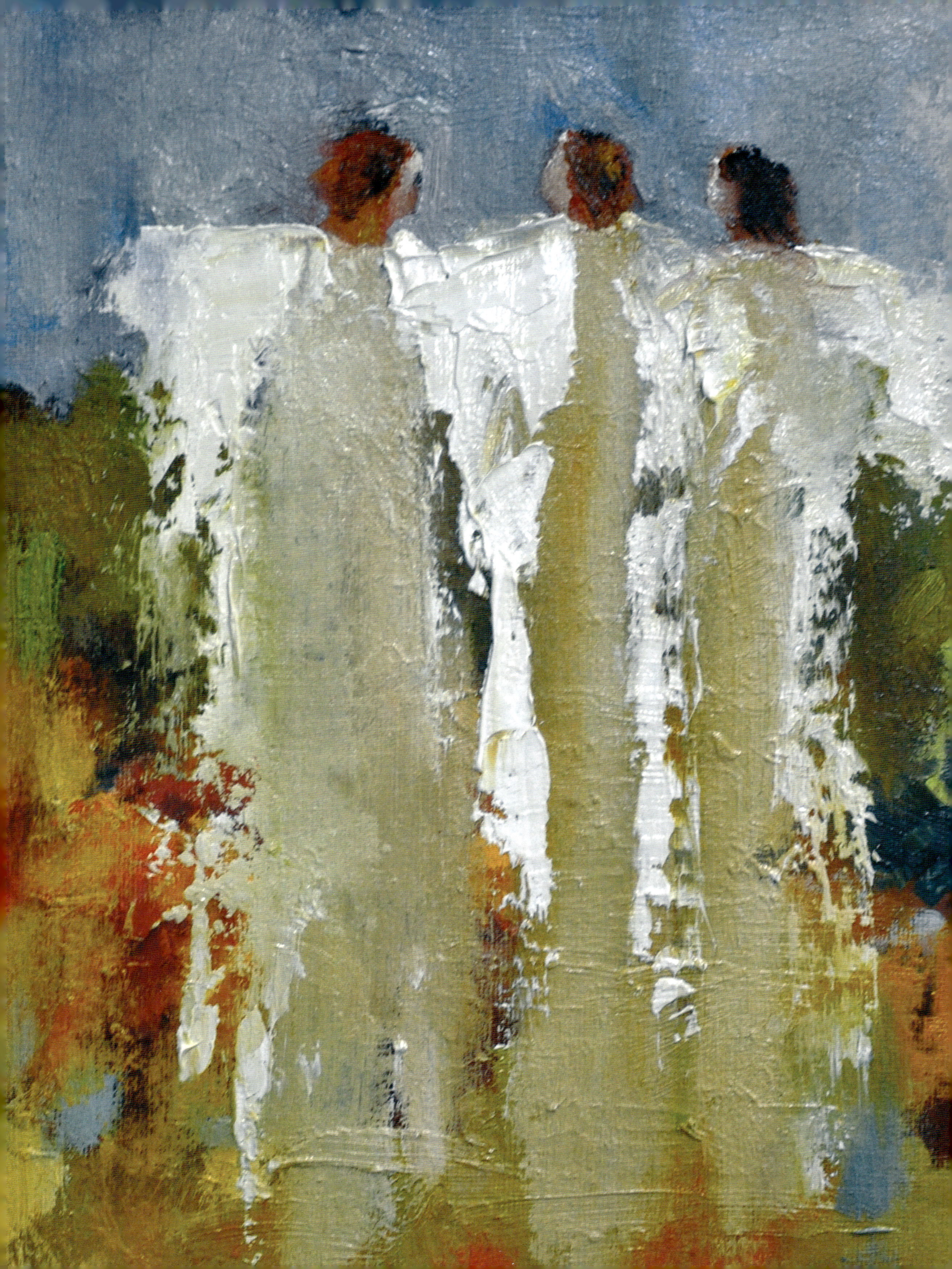

OPEN THE EYES OF MY HEART

The Story of James Harrison and With Open Eyes
by Jan Harrison

With Open Eyes did not begin as a vision or a plan to make a great impact. It was not birthed out of the foresight and planning process of great intellectual minds, or students of politics and power. With Open Eyes began with the life of one individual with an uncertain future and a curiosity piqued by challenges to see and experience the unconventional. At 22 years of age, James Harrison left the comfort and ease of Charlotte, North Carolina, in search of himself. He was intrigued with the unknown, the dangerous, and risk. The invitation to join relief efforts in the war-torn country of Sudan was enthusiastically accepted.

Within a short period of time after arriving in Lui, South Sudan, James began to discover and share in the suffering and the tremendous loss experienced by the people there. As he traveled with the local evangelists and pastors he visited hospitals, TB wards, burned out villages, met sole survivors of brutal attacks, and experienced the overwhelming need for basic survival. Yet in all of those circumstances, his heart was encouraged and strengthened by the dedication of those pastors to take the Good News of the Gospel to their own people. He made a commitment and was moved to respond in a tangible way.

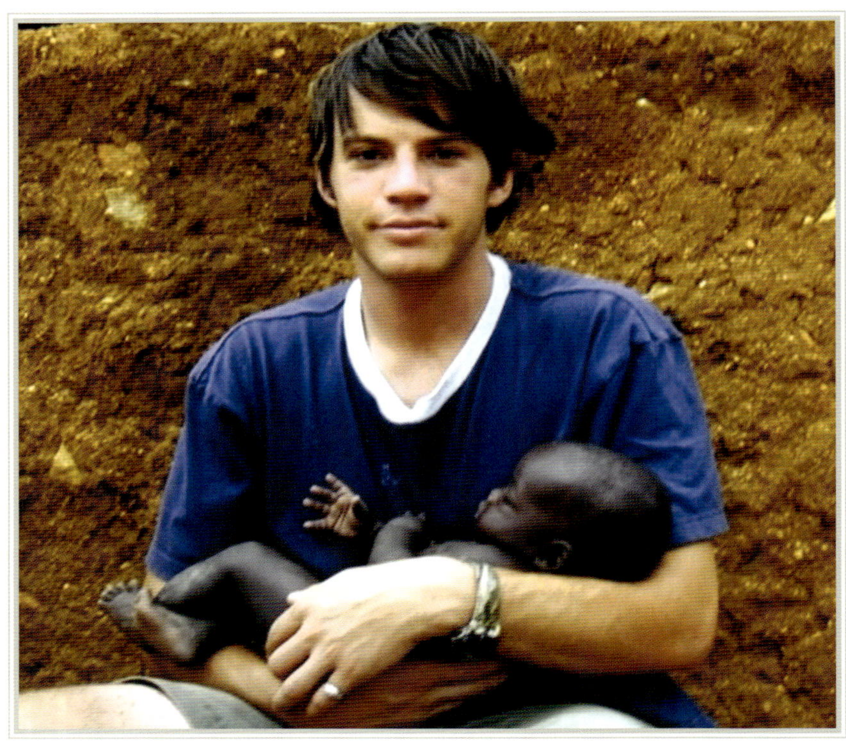

Always in touch with those back home, he shared the desperate situation of the people with passion and conviction. James relayed his experiences, and it was evident that his own heart was being stretched and strengthened while he challenged his family, and especially his father, Frank Harrison, Chairman and CEO of Coca Cola Consolidated, to "help these people." James saw individuals in the crowd, the multitude, the village, and the church. His heart was moved by their faith in Jesus providing strength and joy. He was one young man who glimpsed the eternal in the midst of sorrow and suffering. He was compelled to help empower these pastors to be effective in their work.

In 2008, the Mobile Messenger program was launched to provide motorcycles and other forms of transportation to accelerate sharing the message of God's love and deliver hope to remote areas hard to reach on foot. These pastors could now bring the Good News and practical relief to those who were previously beyond their reach.

From his initial trip to Sudan in 2005, James returned to Africa many times to serve alongside these godly men who had become respected friends and mentors in his life. It was here the young man who left initially in

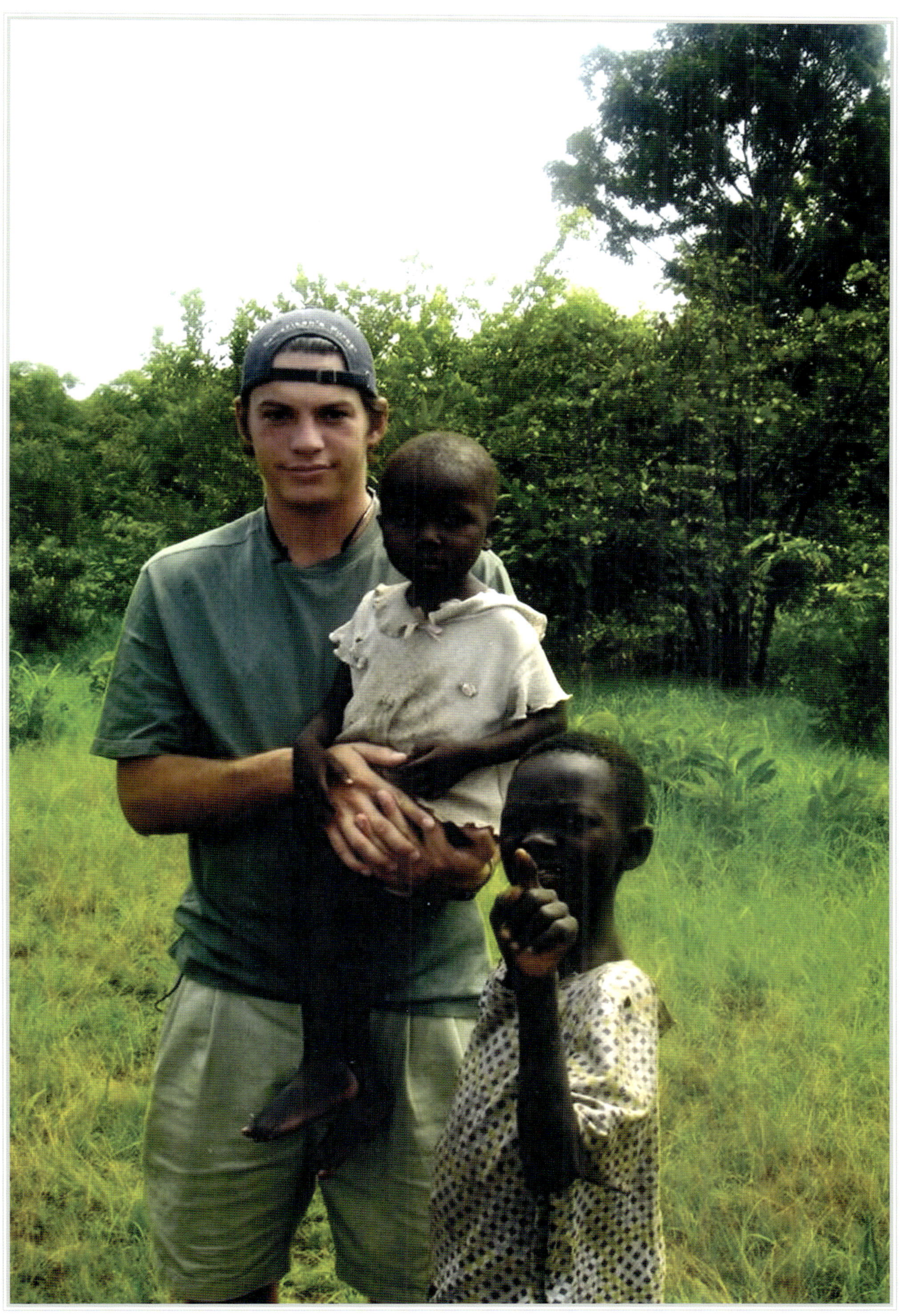

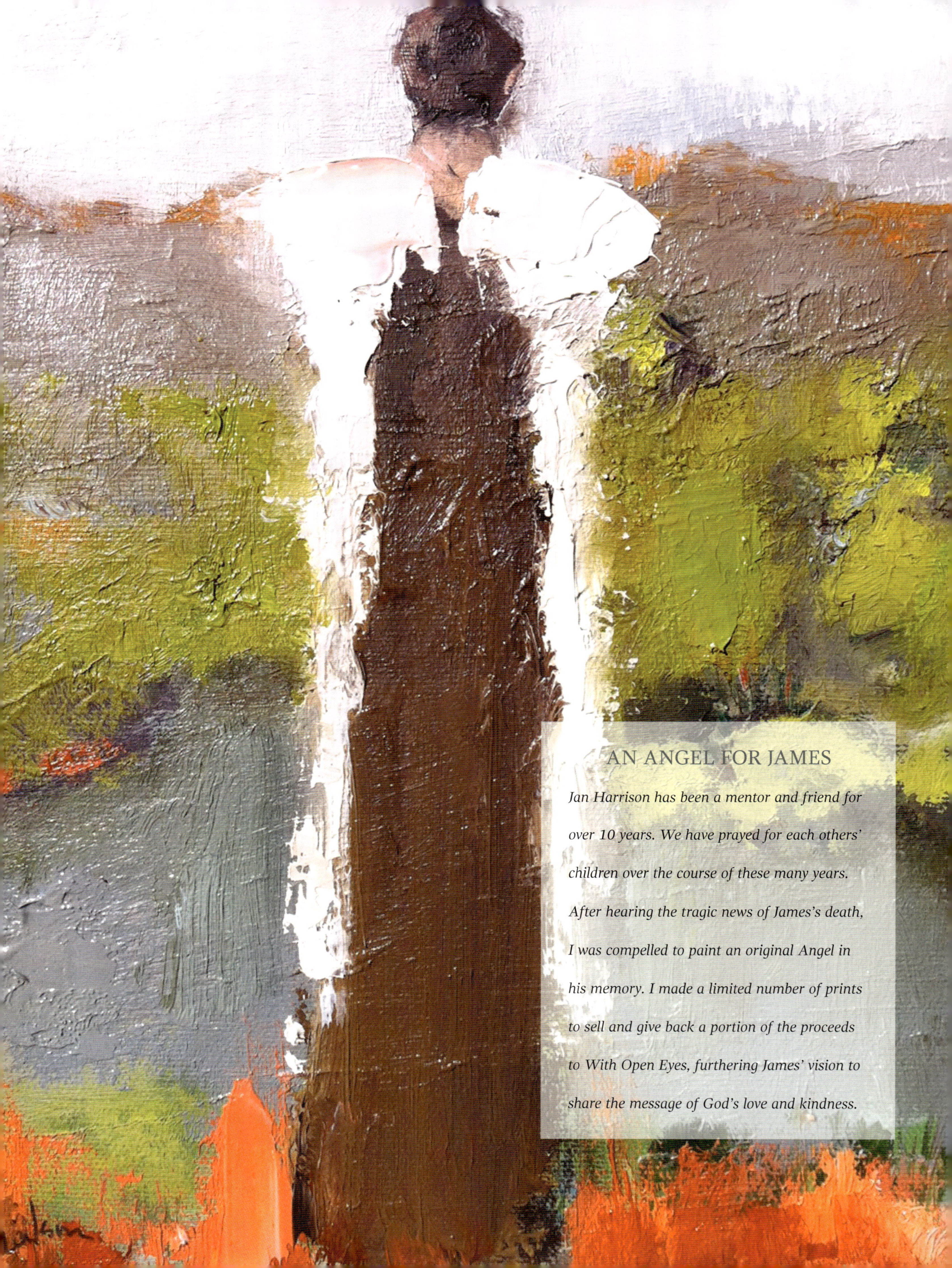

AN ANGEL FOR JAMES

Jan Harrison has been a mentor and friend for over 10 years. We have prayed for each others' children over the course of these many years. After hearing the tragic news of James's death, I was compelled to paint an original Angel in his memory. I made a limited number of prints to sell and give back a portion of the proceeds to With Open Eyes, furthering James' vision to share the message of God's love and kindness.

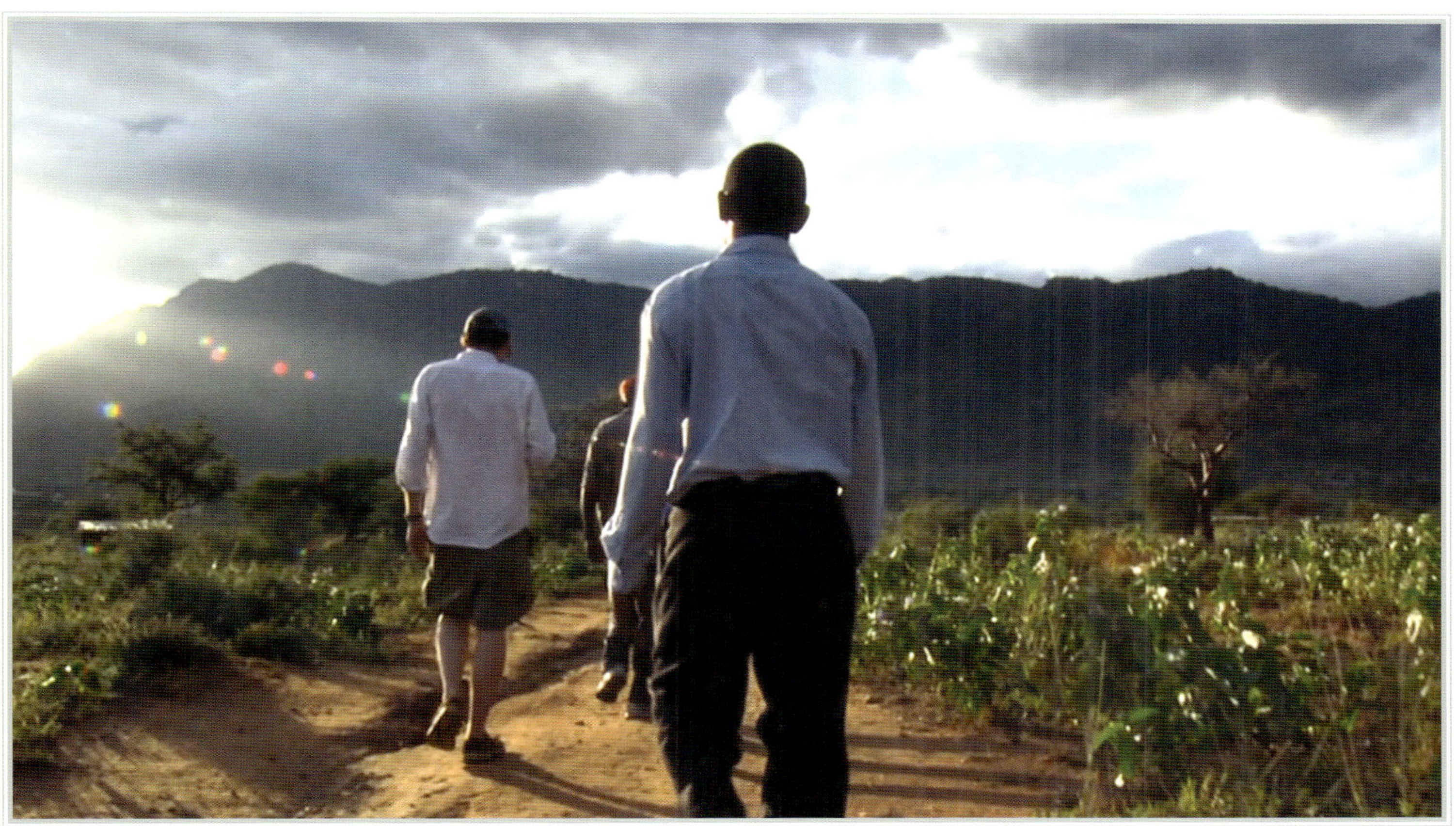

search of adventure and challenge found a genuine sense of purpose in serving the poor and providing help to the needy.

On October 5, 2010, James Harrison died in Nairobi, Kenya. His many acts of kindness and selfless service will continue to inspire many, but his greatest gift, compassion that moves to action, will be carried on through With Open Eyes as they continue to accelerate the message of Jesus Christ to the unreached and underserved peoples of the world. James was truly an Angel In Our Midst.

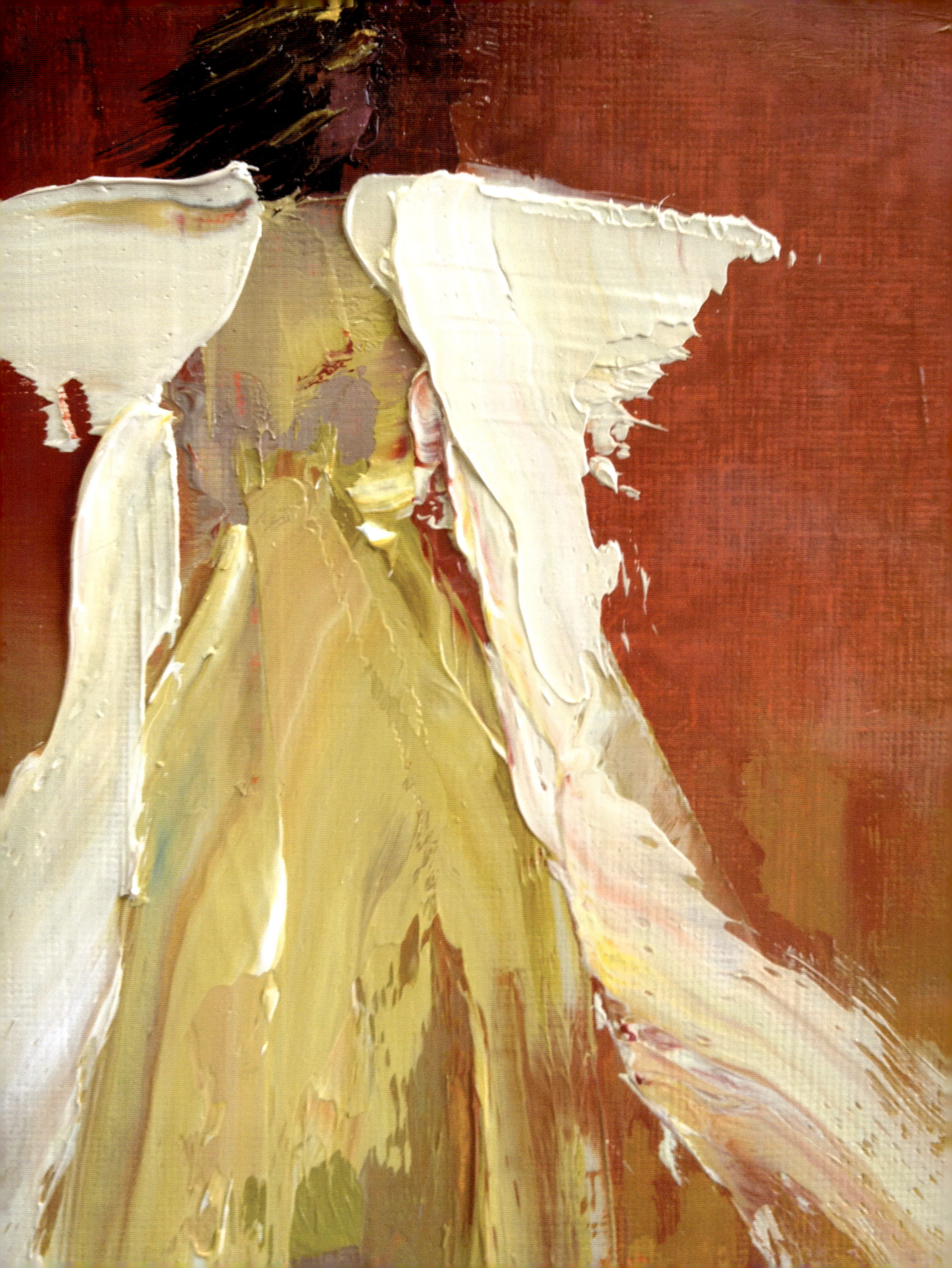

HE IS SO RICH IN KINDNESS AND GRACE THAT HE PURCHASED OUR FREEDOM WITH THE BLOOD OF HIS SON AND FORGAVE OUR SINS. HE HAS SHOWERED HIS KINDNESS ON US, ALONG WITH ALL WISDOM AND UNDERSTANDING.

EPHESIANS 1:7-8

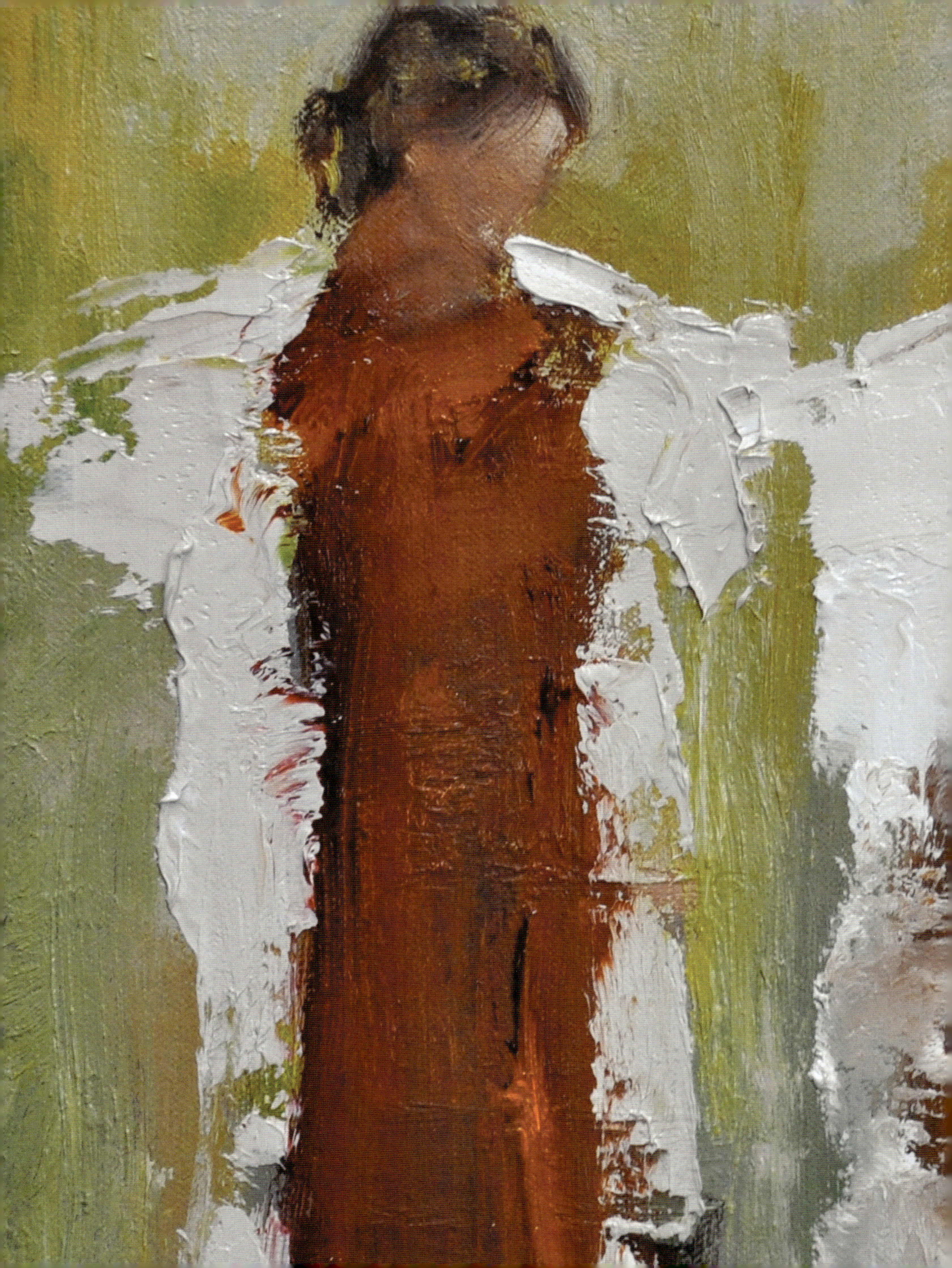

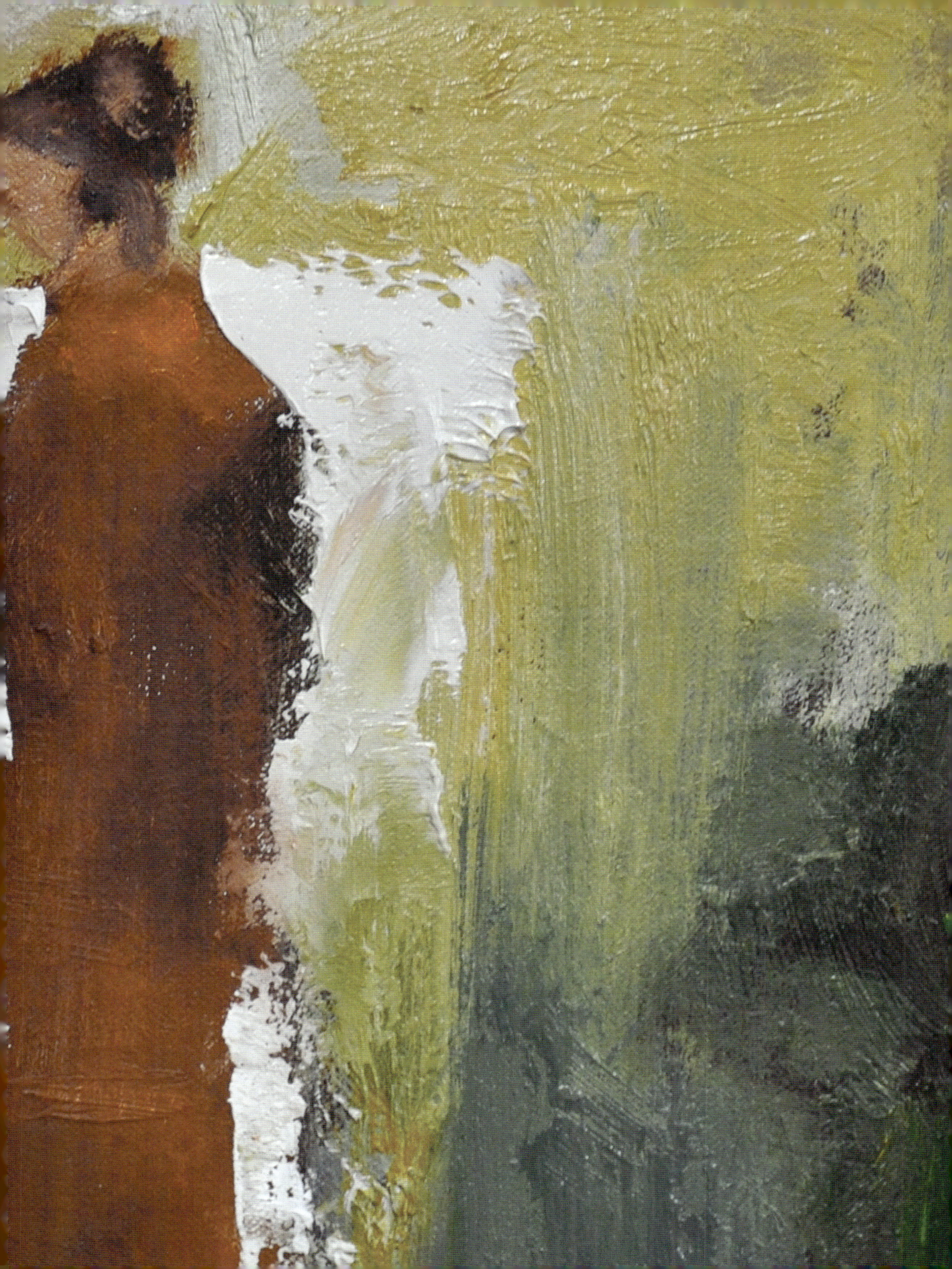

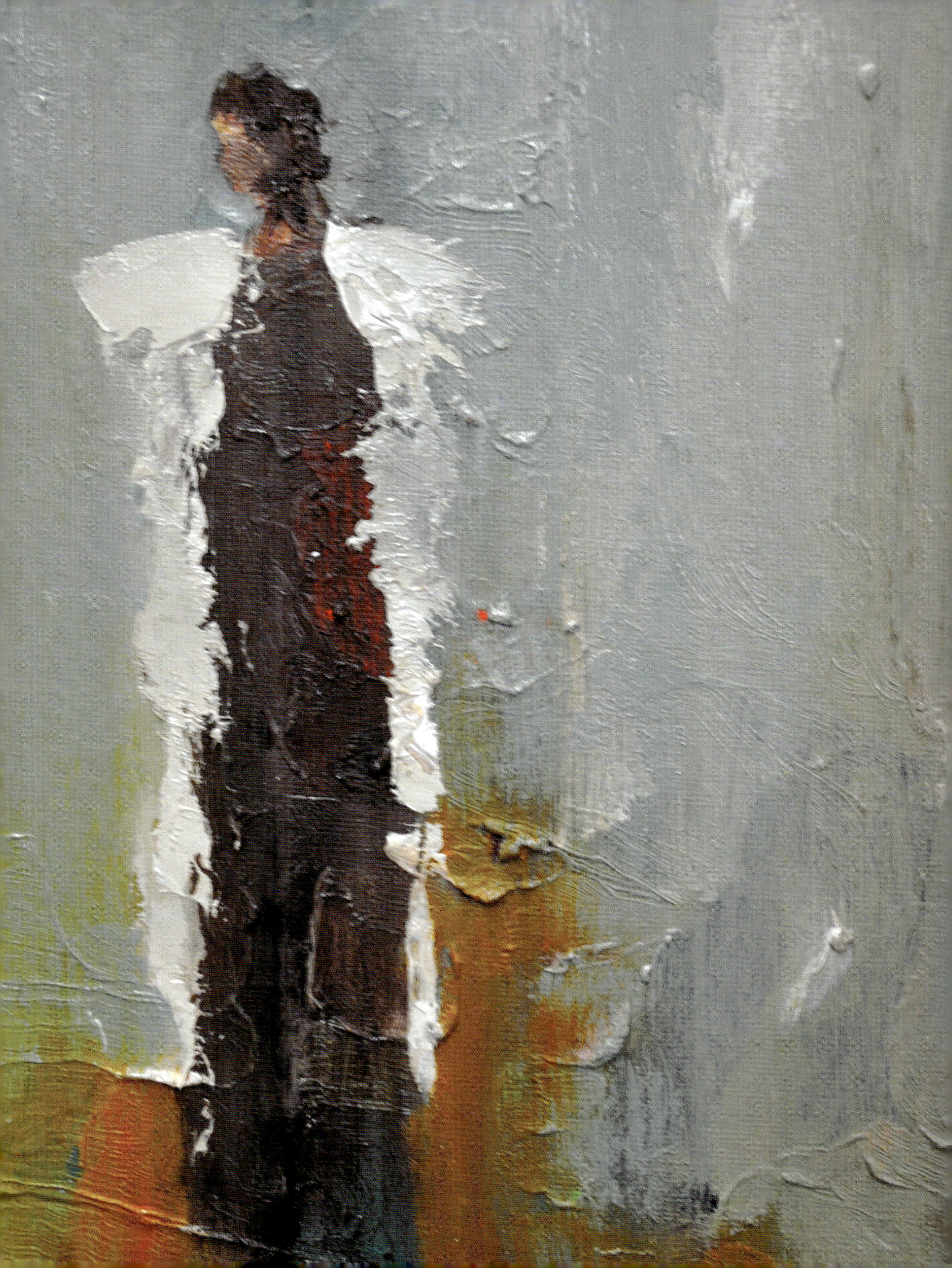

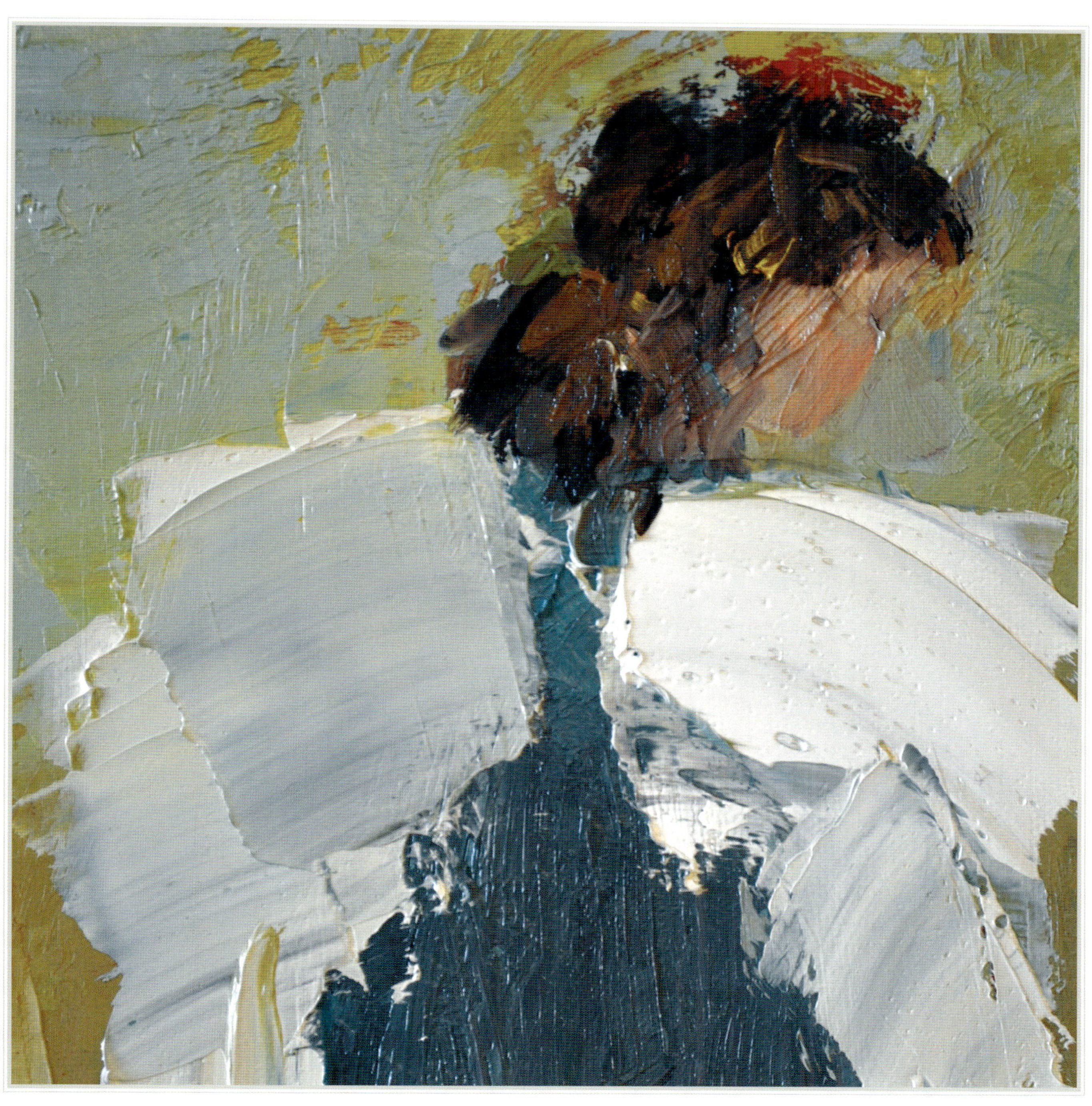

THE LORD IS RIGHTEOUS IN EVERYTHING HE DOES;
HE IS FILLED WITH KINDNESS.

Psalm 145:17

HOW PRECIOUS IS YOUR LOVING KINDNESS, O GOD! AND THE CHILDREN OF MEN TAKE REFUGE IN THE SHADOW OF YOUR WINGS.

Psalm 36:7

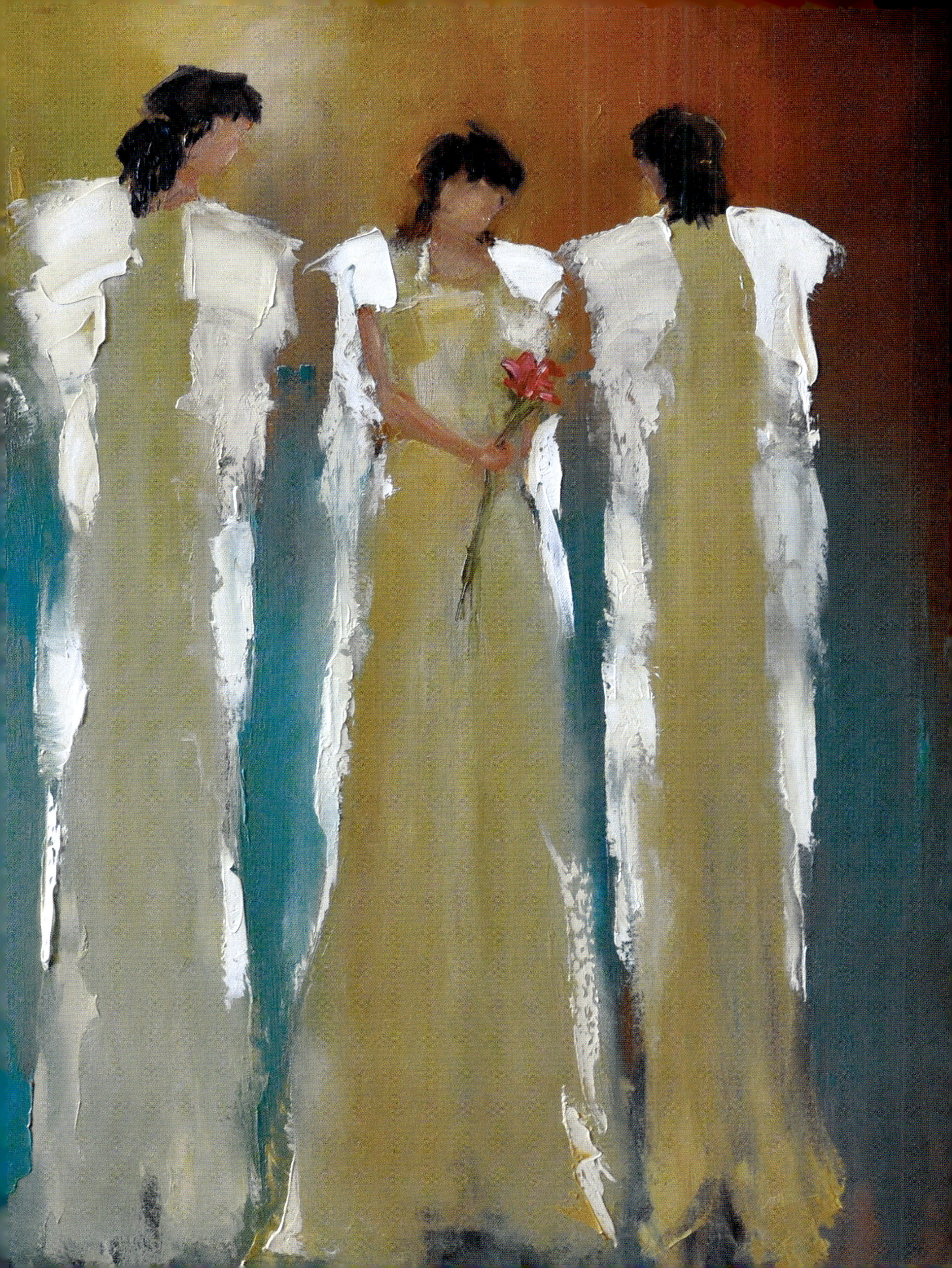

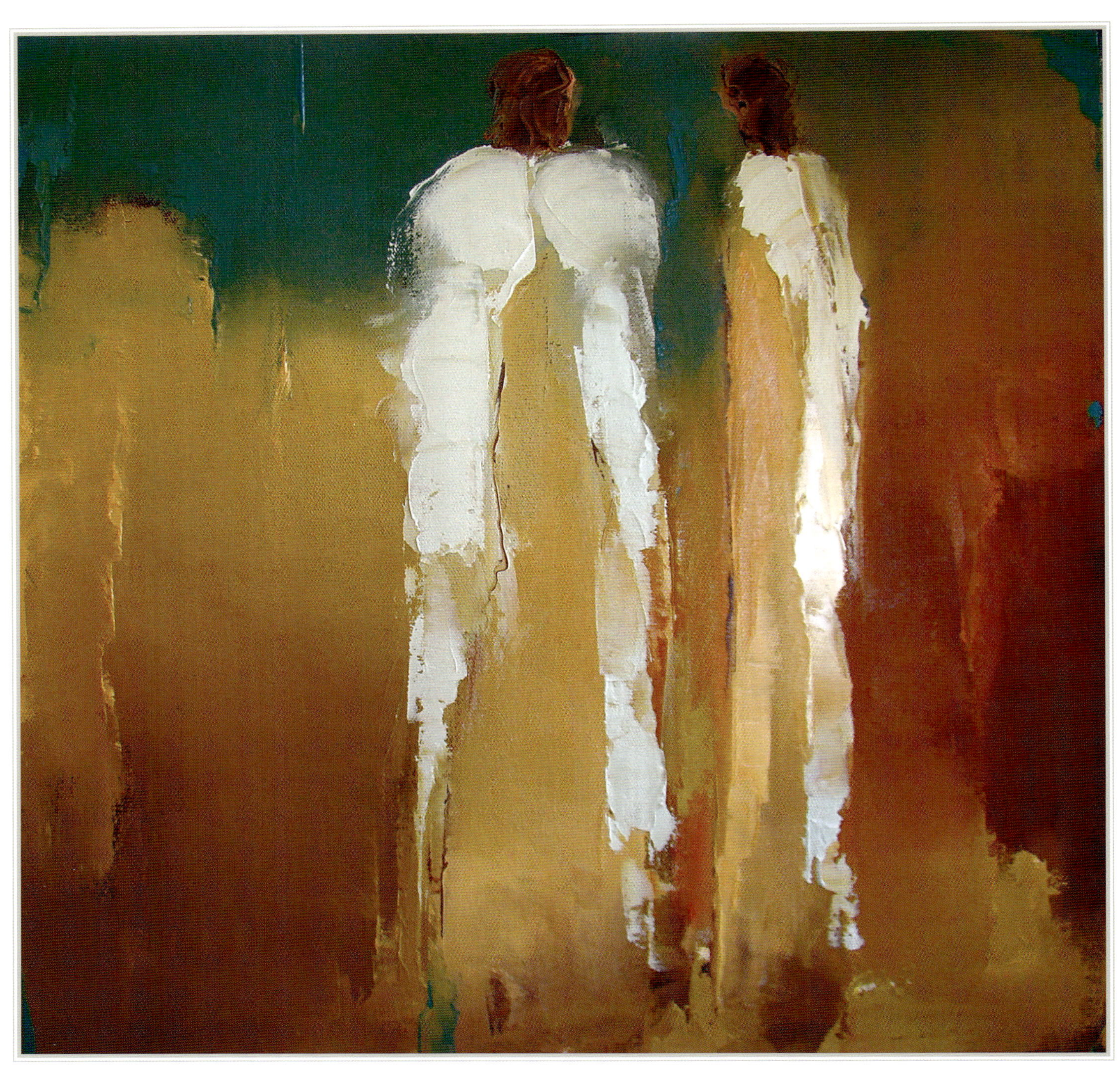

I WANT TO TOUCH PEOPLE WITH MY ART.
I WANT THEM TO SAY 'HE FEELS DEEPLY, HE FEELS TENDERLY.'

—VINCENT VAN GOGH

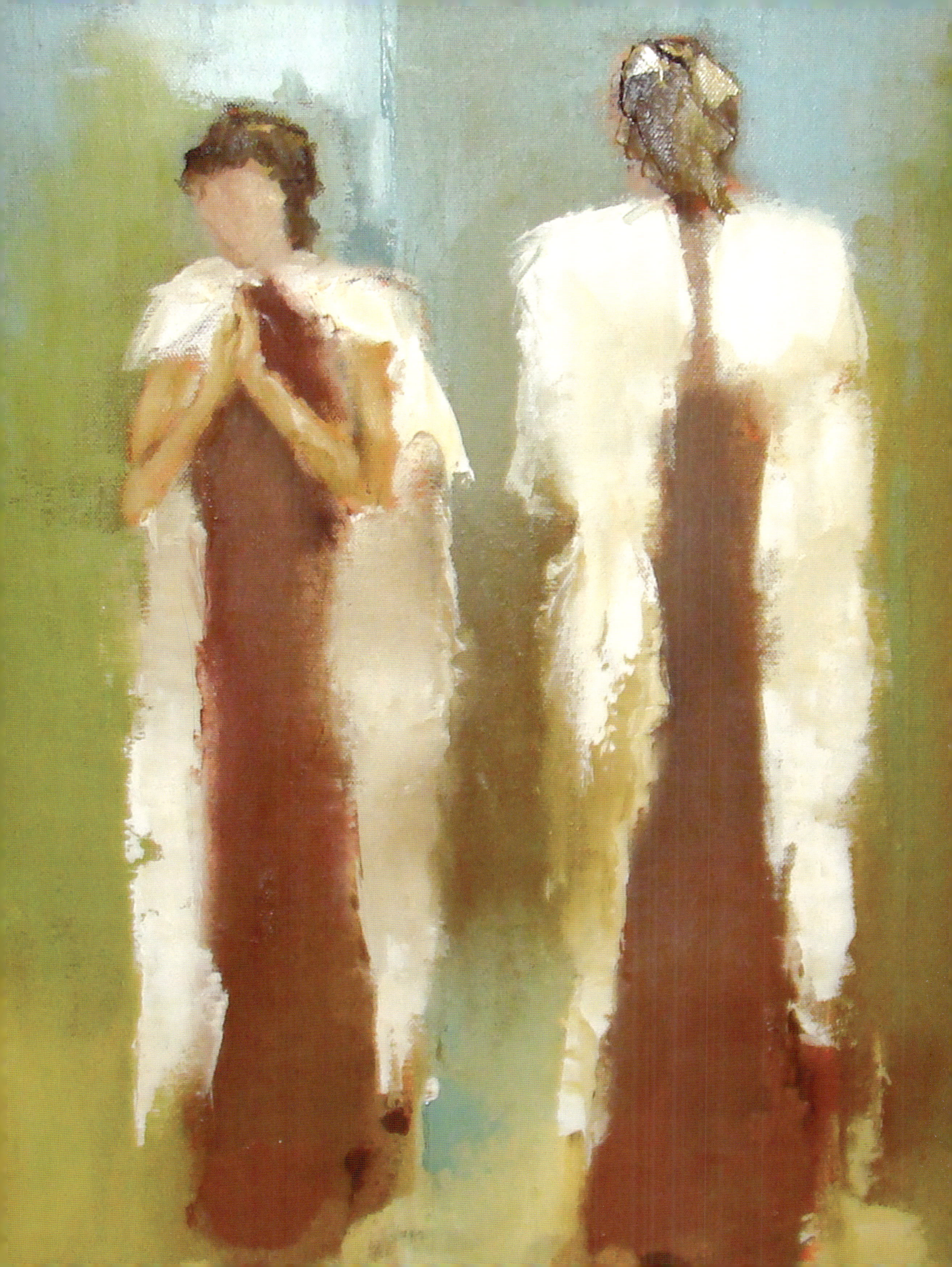

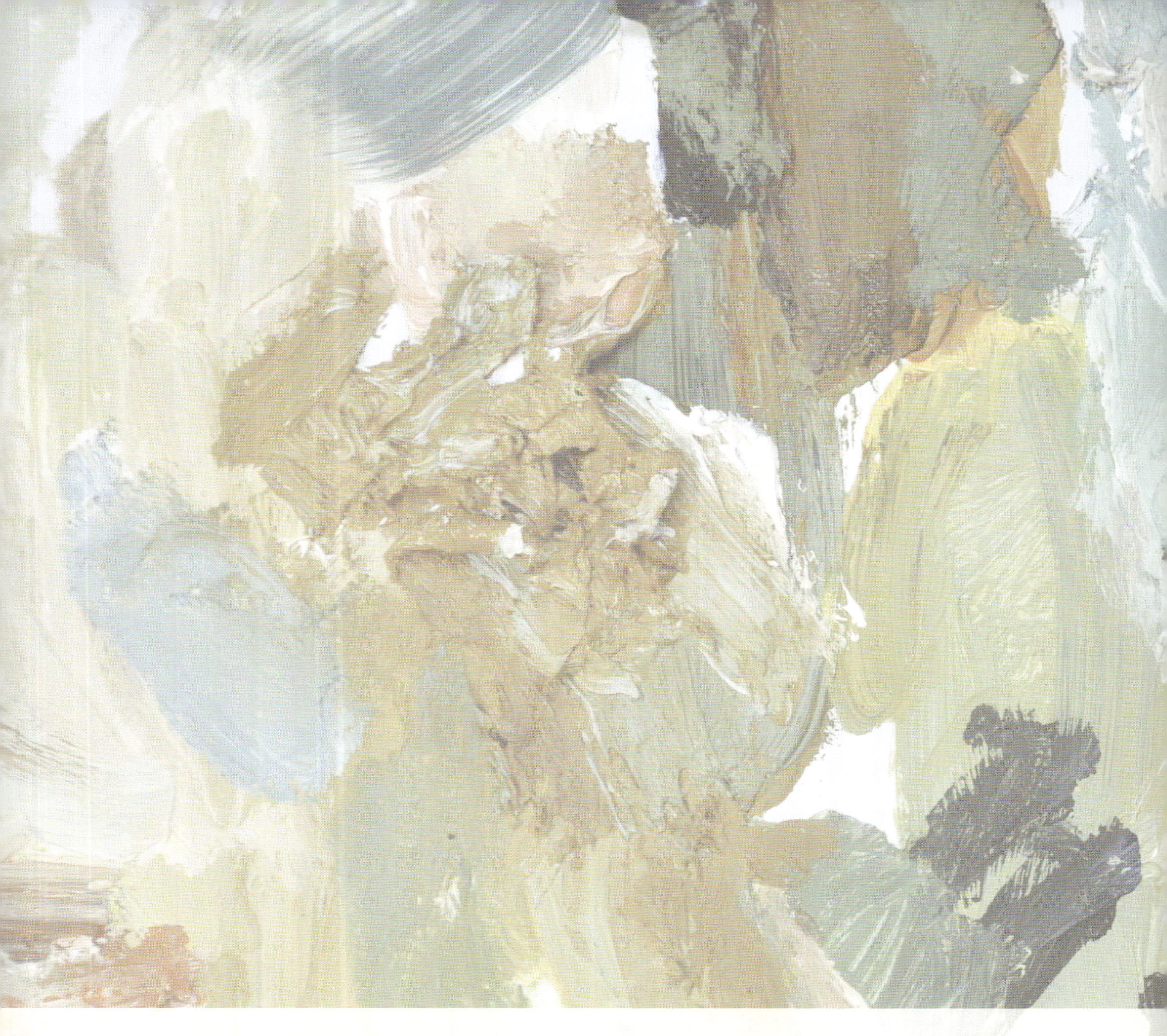

AND WE KNOW THAT IN ALL THINGS GOD WORKS FOR THE GOOD OF THOSE WHO LOVE HIM, WHO HAVE BEEN CALLED ACCORDING TO HIS PURPOSE.

Romans 8:28

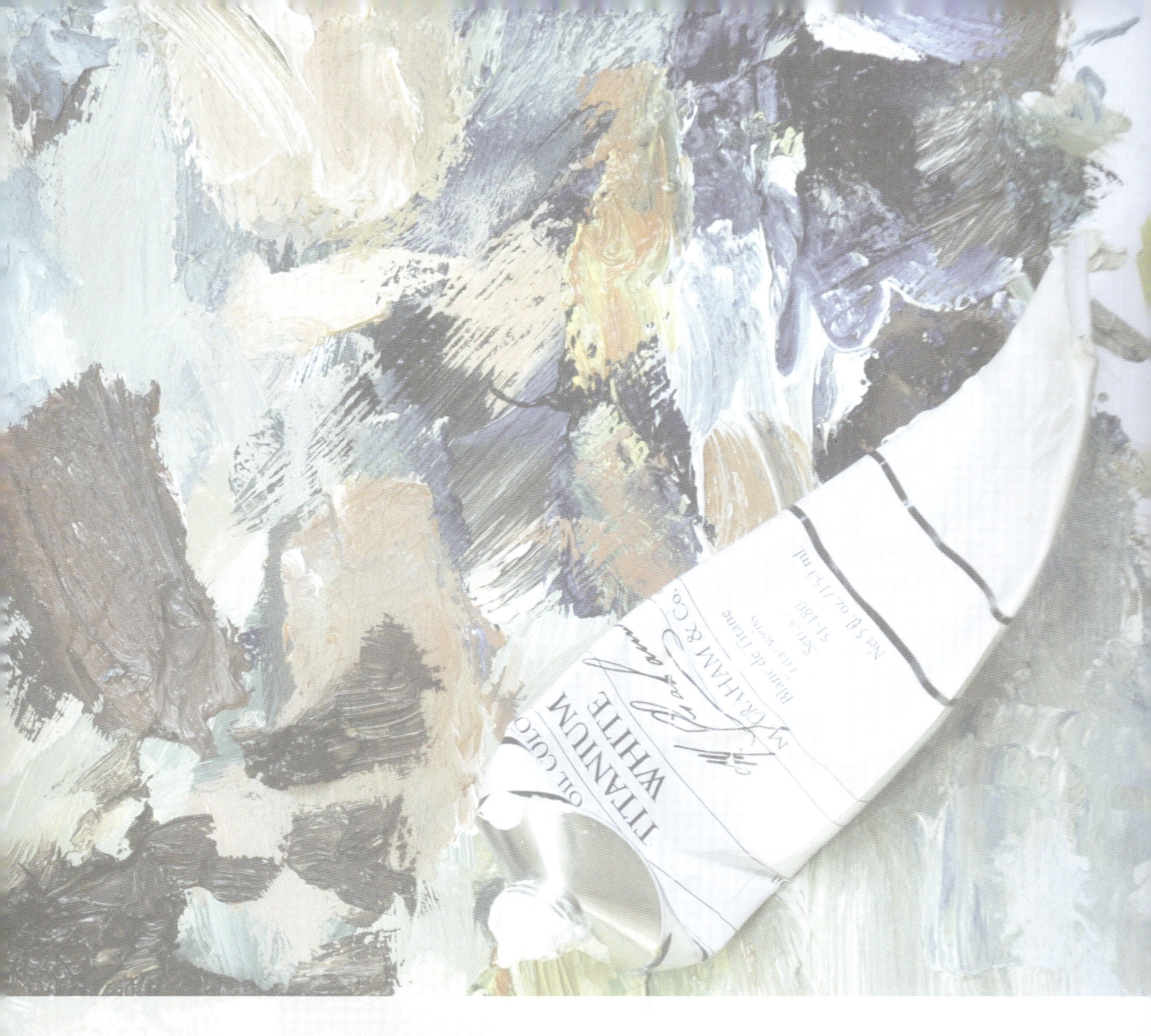

GOODNESS

STROKES OF COMPASSION

A Show Benefiting Presbyterian Hospice and Palliative Care

Several years ago, I started hosting solo shows through the galleries that represent my work, calling them: "Angels in Our Midst." After the galleries took their share of the sales, I was able to give a portion of the proceeds back to organizations that hold a special place in my heart. Four years ago, I started hosting these shows on my own, once a year, to give back 50% of the art proceeds to different organizations. But I wanted to do more, so last year, I changed the name of the show from Angels in Our Midst to "Strokes of Compassion," allowing me to invite other artists to participate.

I met Kathy Brown of Presbyterian Hospice and Palliative Care several years ago and we stayed in touch over the years. She invited me to an event that they were hosting about "Angels." We had originally wanted to auction off an angel painting at the event, but eventually decided that a show with a great body of works would be the best way to raise money for Hospice. We teamed up and before you knew it we had a large part of the Charlotte community supporting the event. Individuals from several restaurants, caterers, and a party rental company

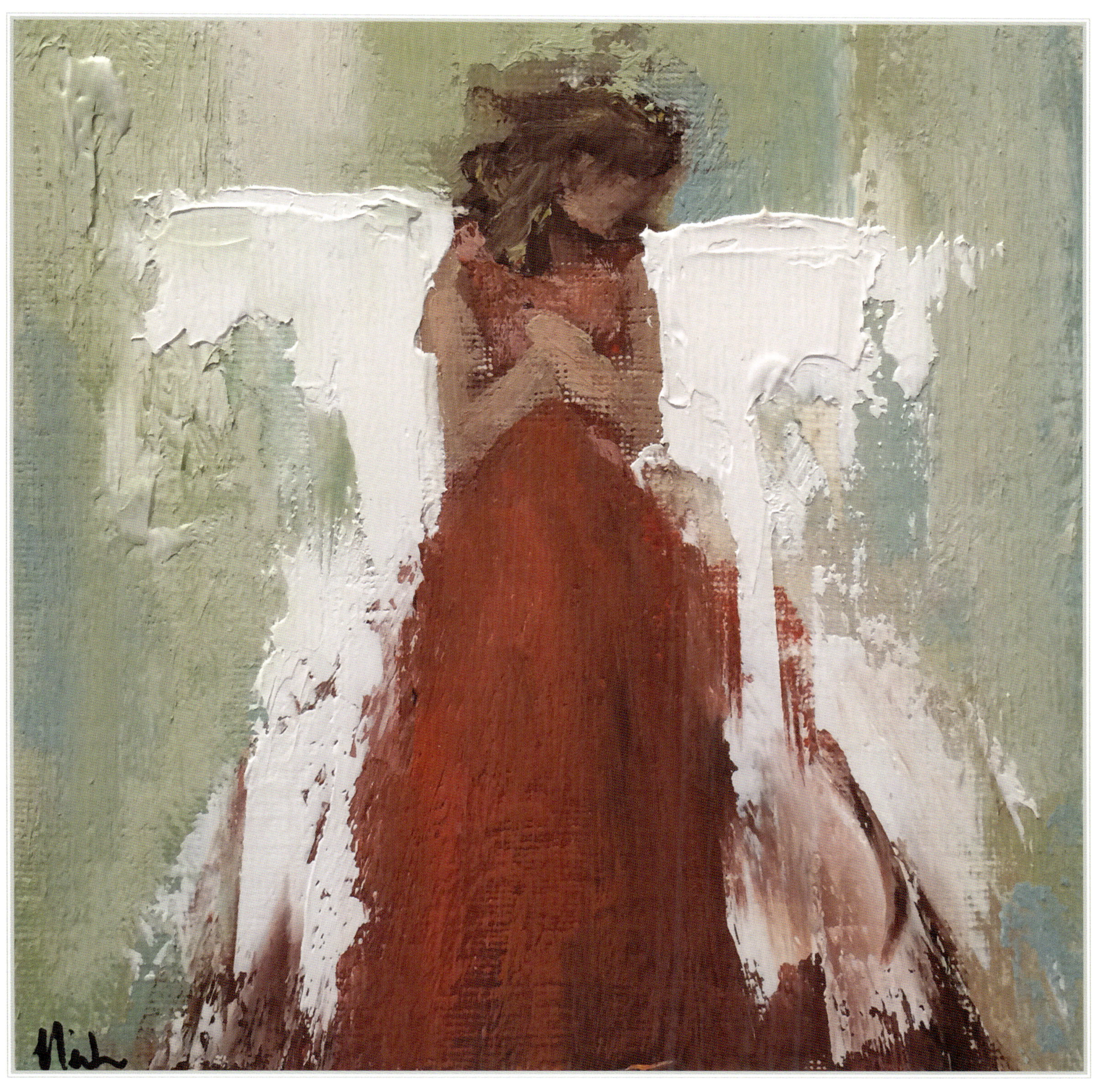

THE JOB OF AN ARTIST IS TO ALWAYS DEEPEN THE MYSTERY.

—FRANCIS BACON

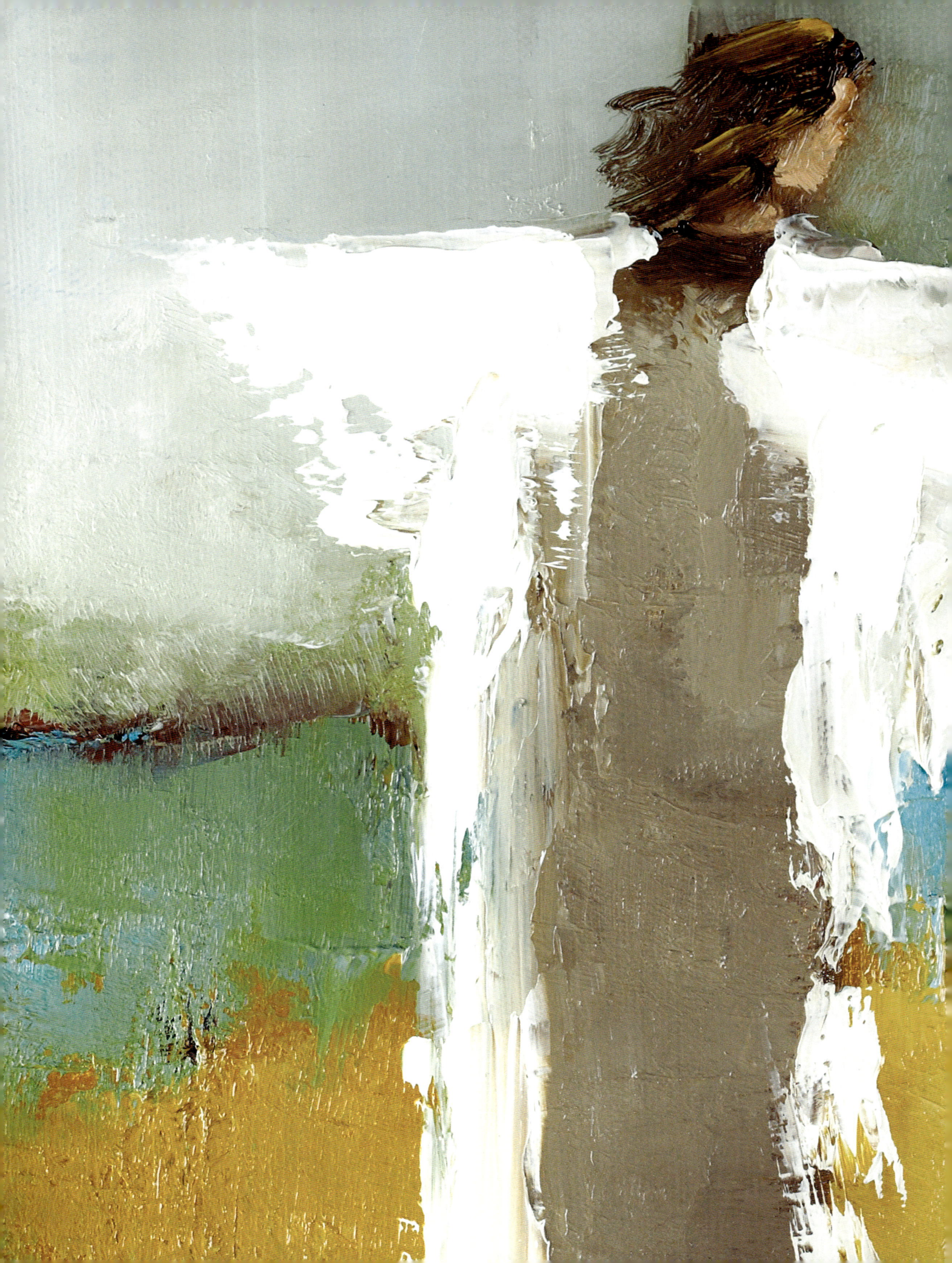

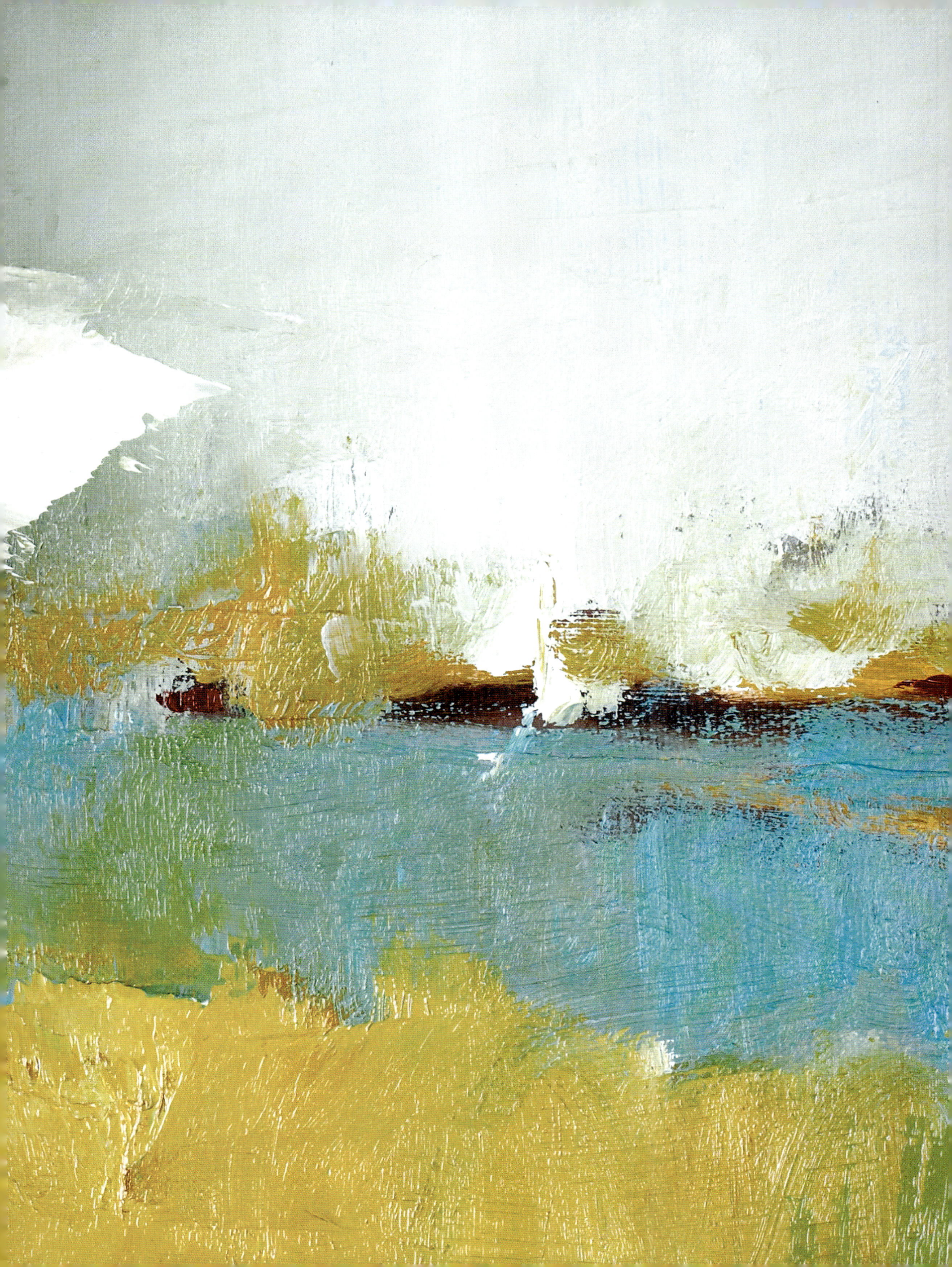

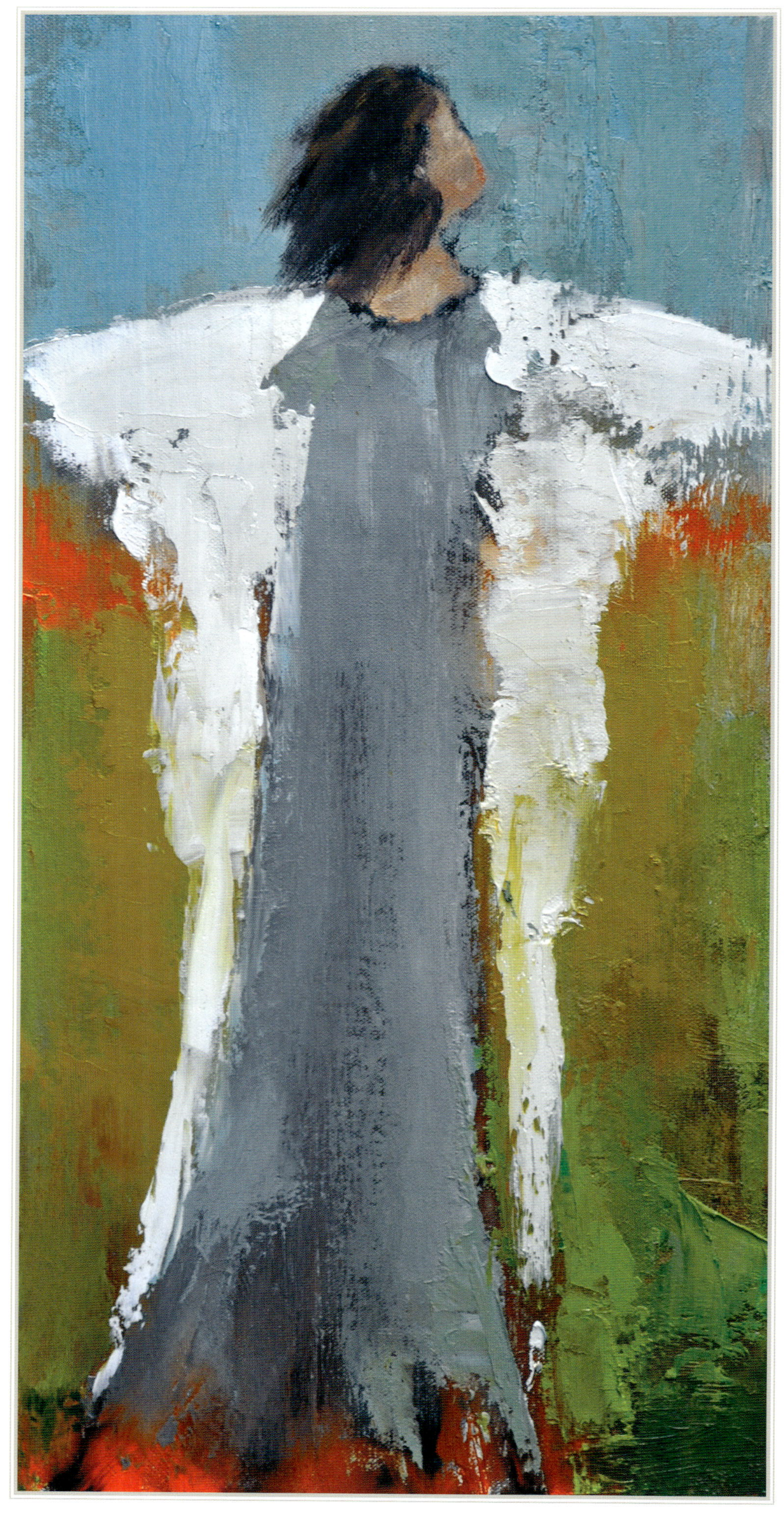

were honored and touched to be a part of this night. The Hospice team stepped up to make this event a memorable one. Everyone who participated helped make the evening a huge success raising $10,000 for Hospice.

From hospice to the homeless, domestic violence shelters to disadvantaged children, I will continue to use my creative gift to reach across the community and impact thousands of people both locally and internationally. Going forward, I pray that every brushstroke would be an expression of compassion for others.

On November 10, 2011, Anne was hosting an art show, *Strokes of Compassion*, to benefit Presbyterian Hospice & Palliative Care. As PHPC's marketing/development & volunteer manager, I was very involved in the event; yet my mind was more focused on a personal issue, surgery scheduled for the next morning, November 11. Anne knew about the surgery and prayed with me before the show. The same faith and compassion Anne showed me through prayer, I also see in her work. During the evening's event, I was drawn to one of Anne's paintings titled *Renewed Strength*. As I looked at the painting, I heard Matthew 9:22 in my heart. God can change what seems unchangeable, giving new purpose and hope—renewed strength! I bought the painting as a reminder to keep my faith, heart and eyes focused upward on God—plus I helped to support a very worthy cause, Presbyterian Hospice & Palliative Care.

KATHY BROWN

Presbyterian Hospice & Palliative Care Manager

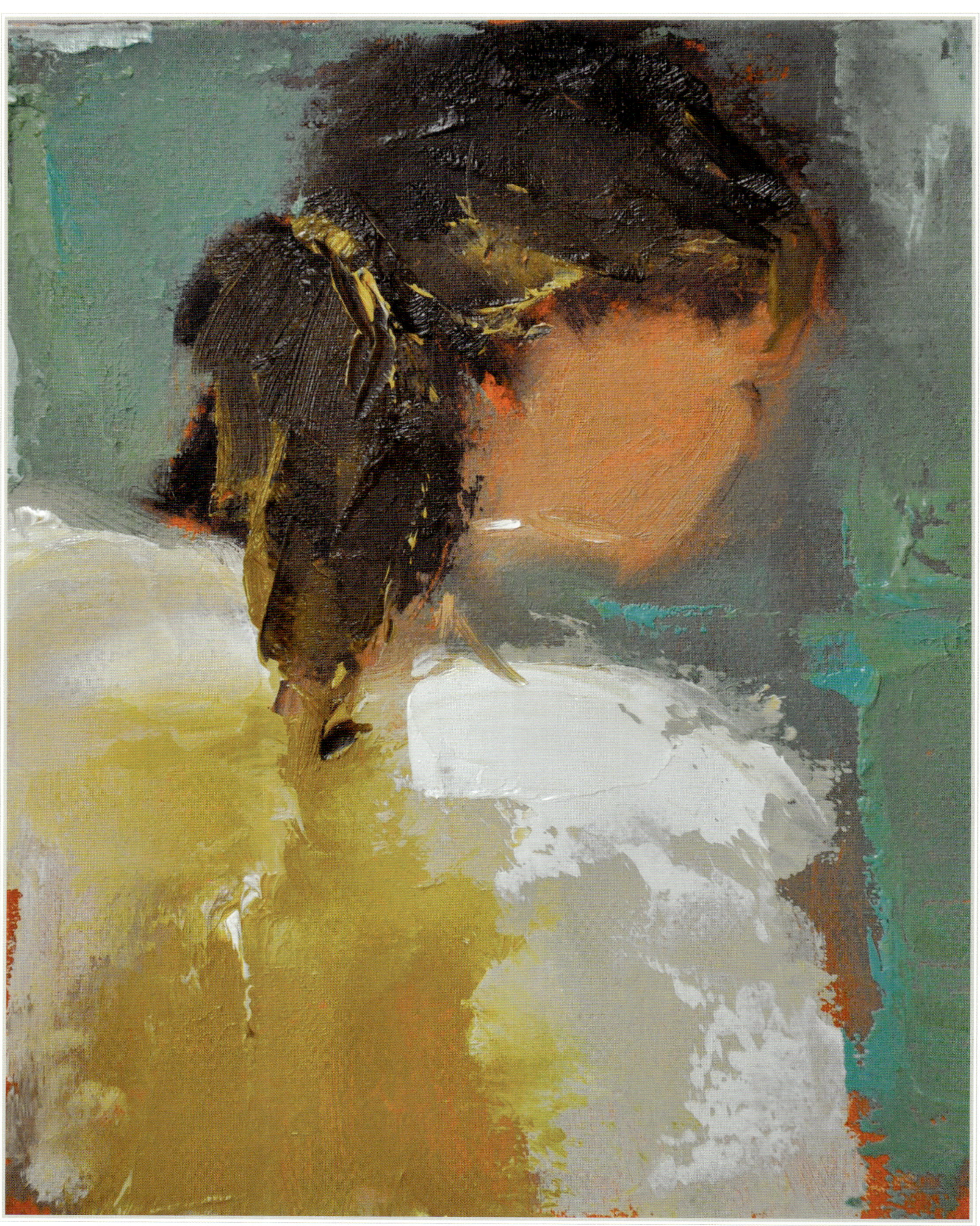

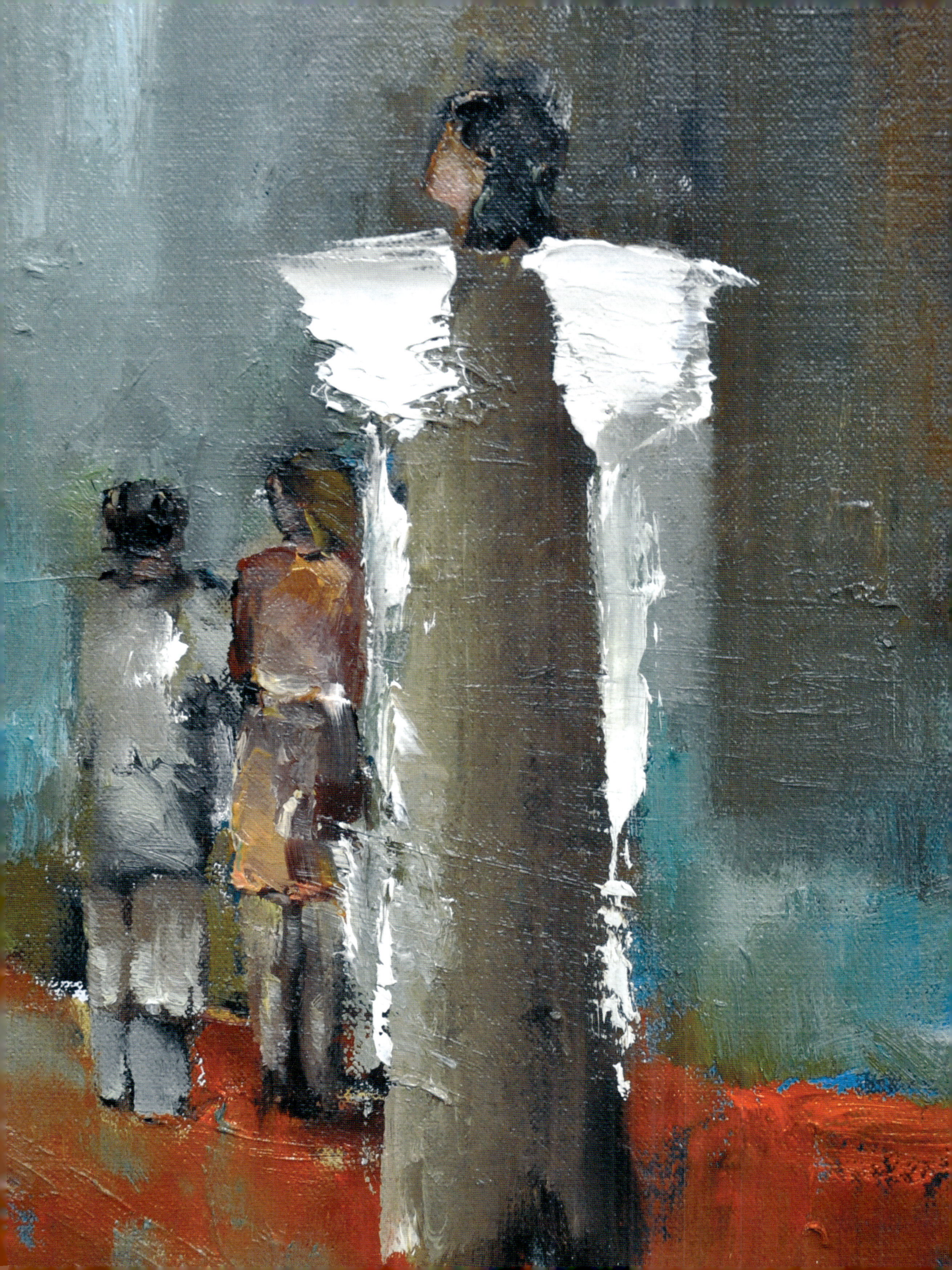

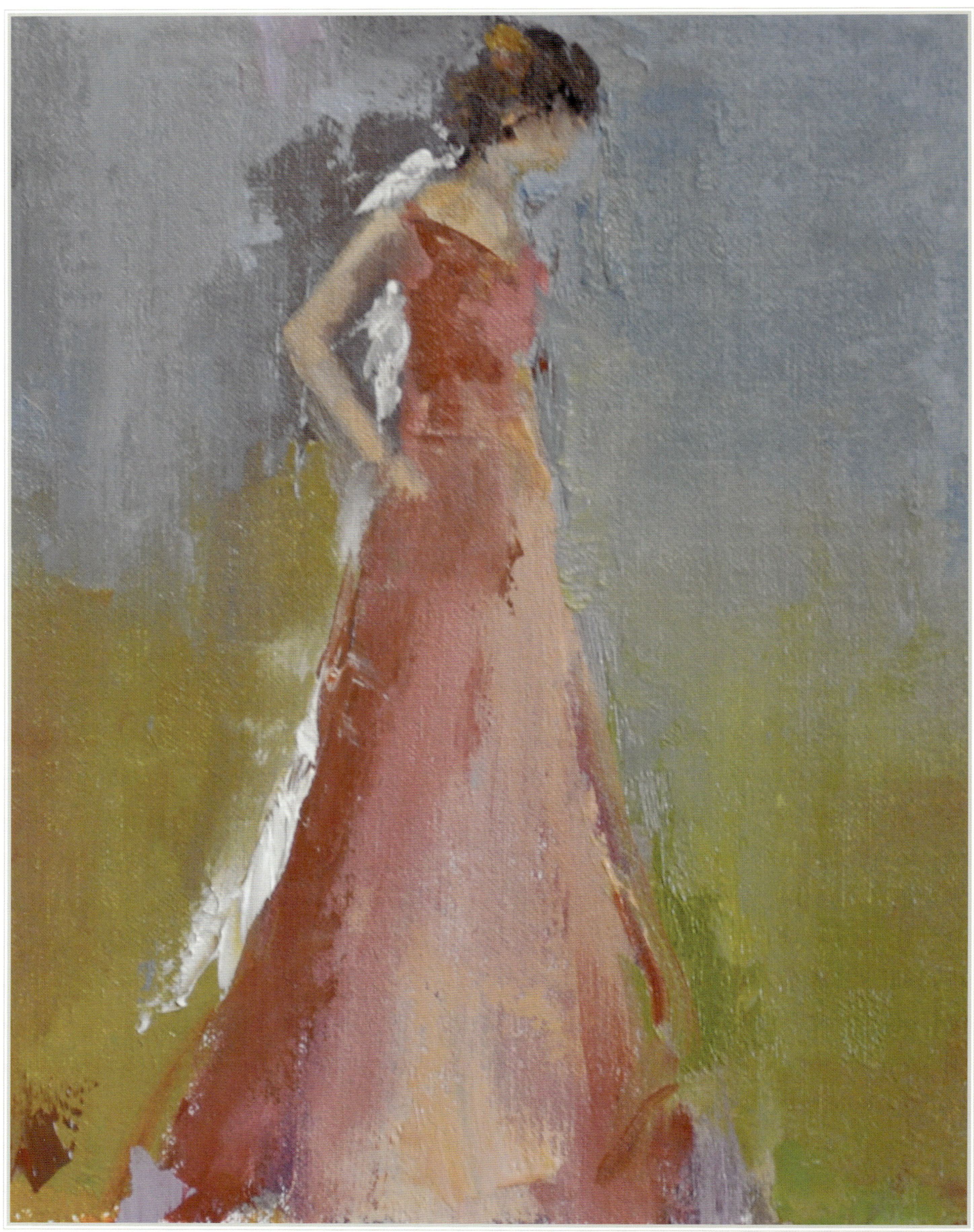

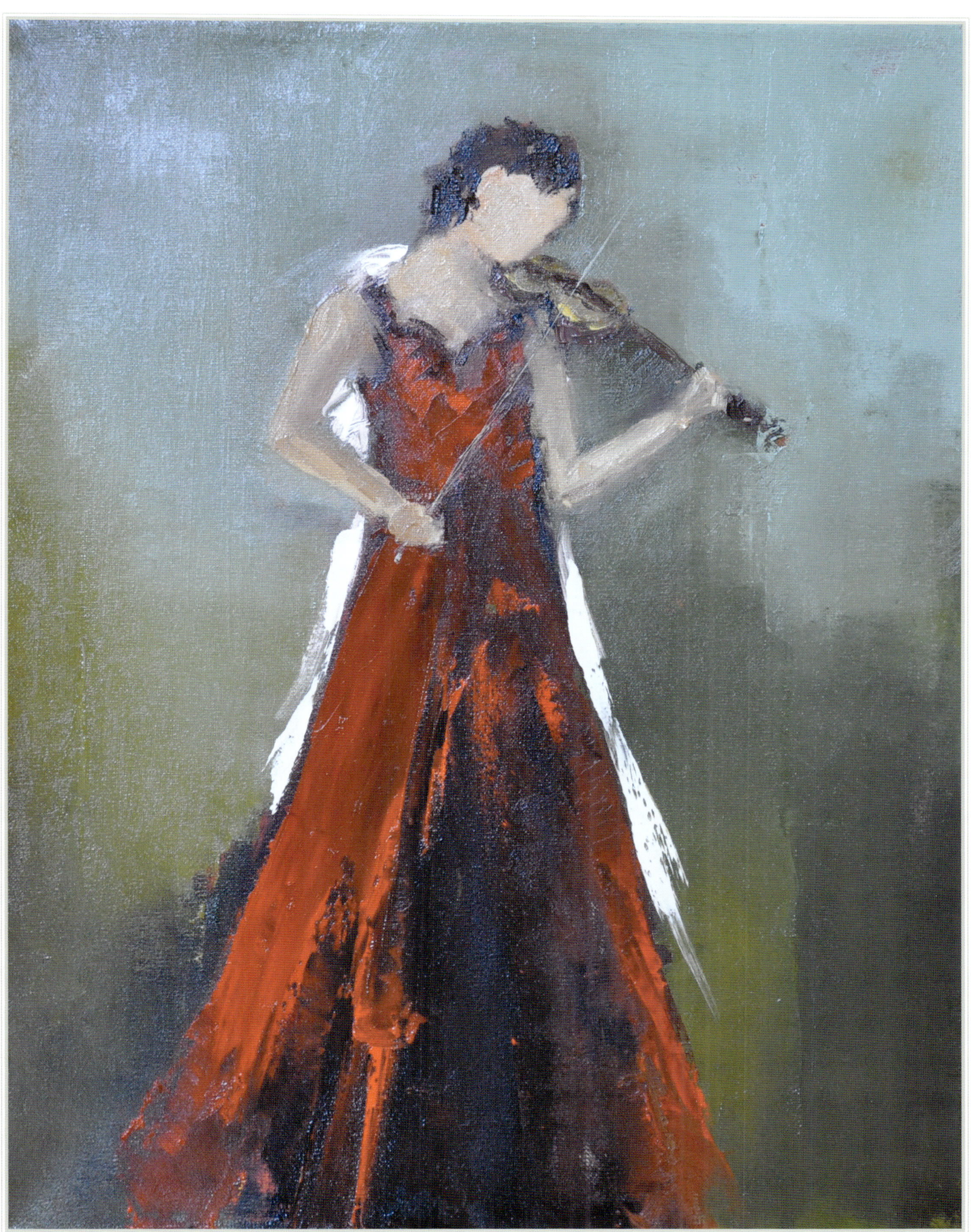

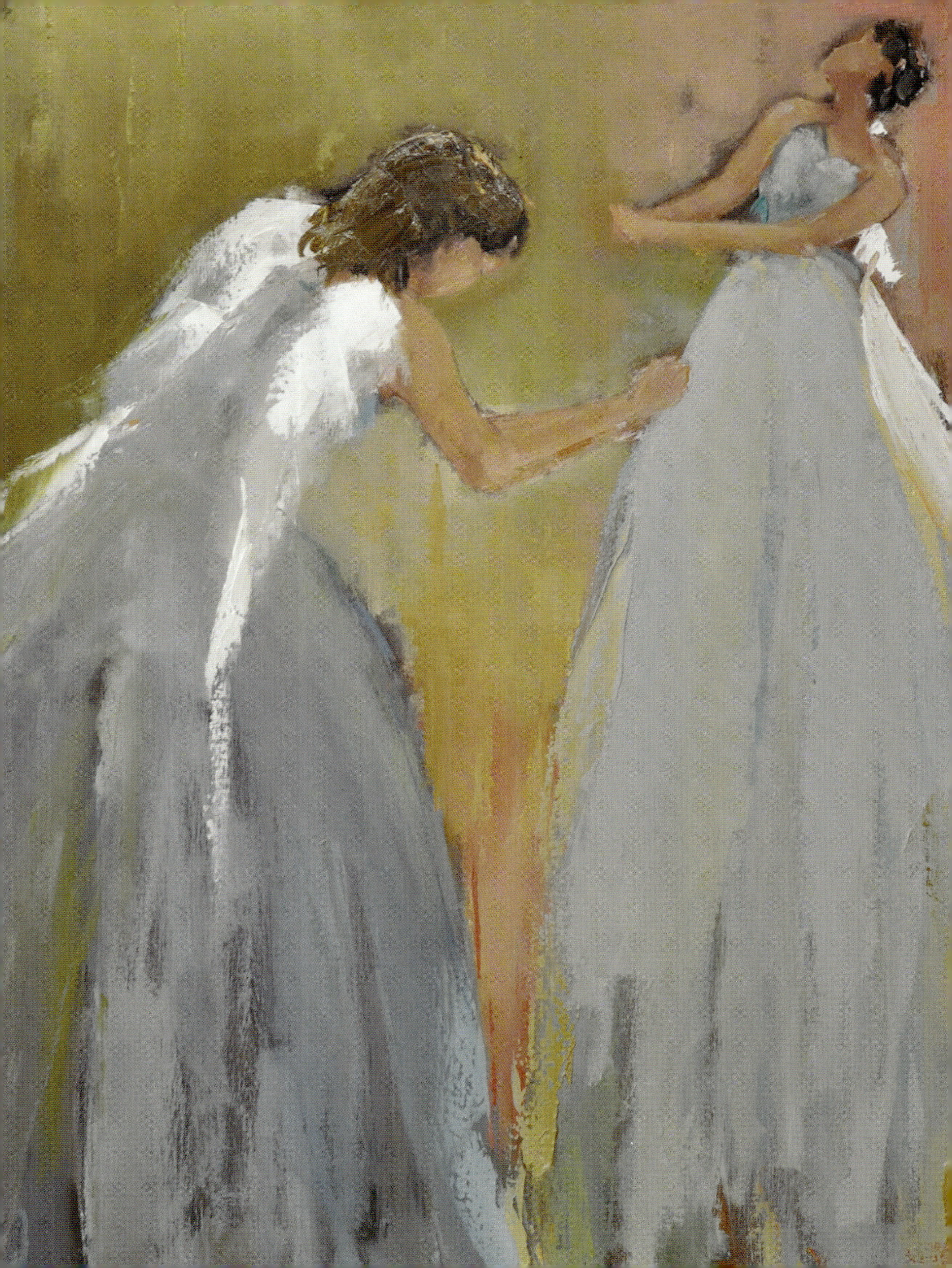

DO NOTHING FROM SELFISHNESS OR EMPTY CONCEIT, BUT WITH HUMILITY OF MIND LET EACH OF YOU REGARD ONE ANOTHER AS MORE IMPORTANT THAN HIMSELF; DO NOT MERELY LOOK OUT FOR YOUR OWN PERSONAL INTERESTS, BUT ALSO FOR THE INTERESTS OF OTHERS. HAVE THIS ATTITUDE IN YOURSELVES WHICH WAS ALSO IN CHRIST JESUS, WHO, ALTHOUGH HE EXISTED IN THE FORM OF GOD, DID NOT REGARD EQUALITY WITH GOD A THING TO BE GRASPED, BUT EMPTIED HIMSELF, TAKING THE FORM OF A BOND-SERVANT, AND BEING MADE IN THE LIKENESS OF MEN.

PHILIPPIANS 2:3-7

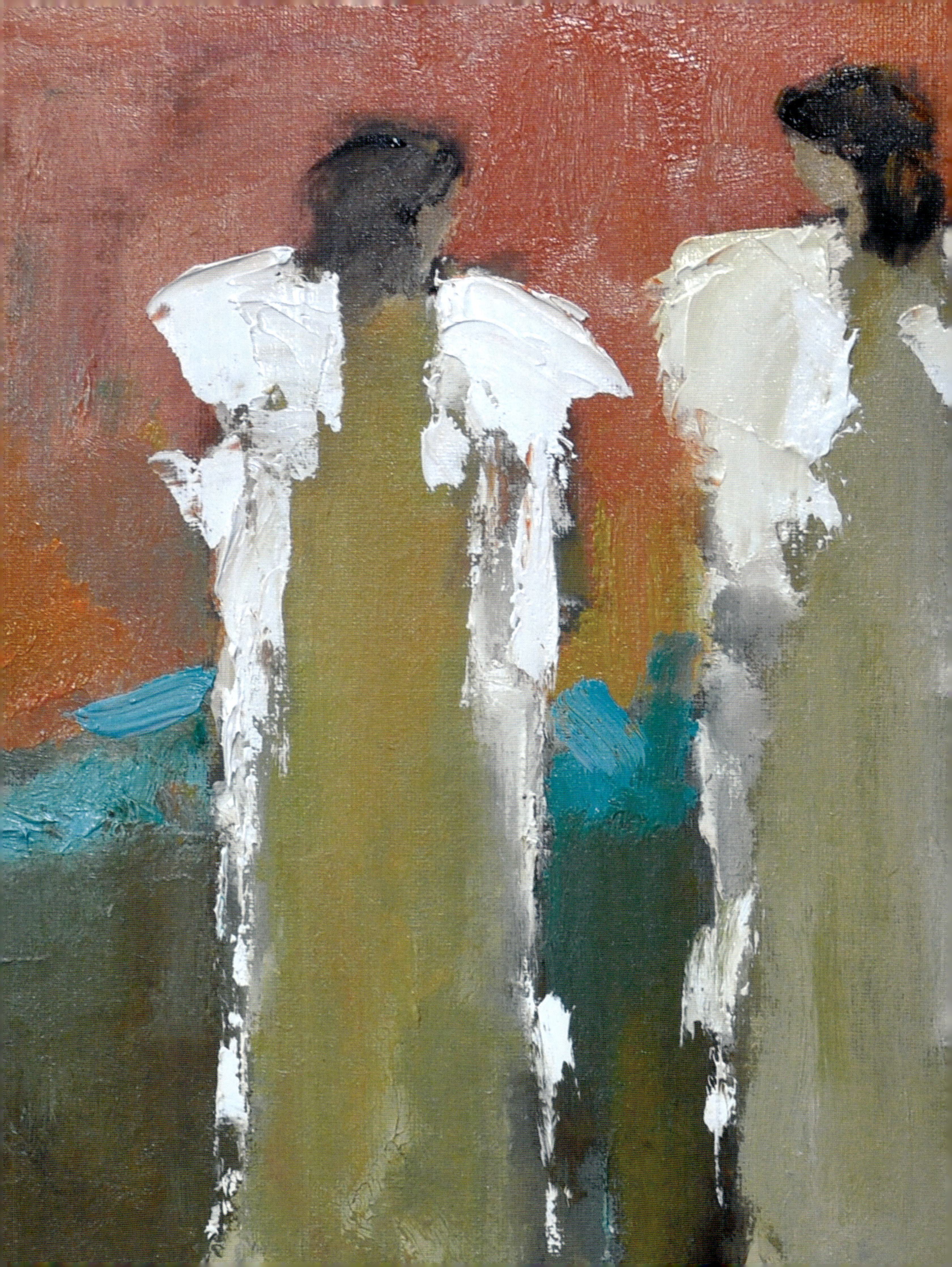

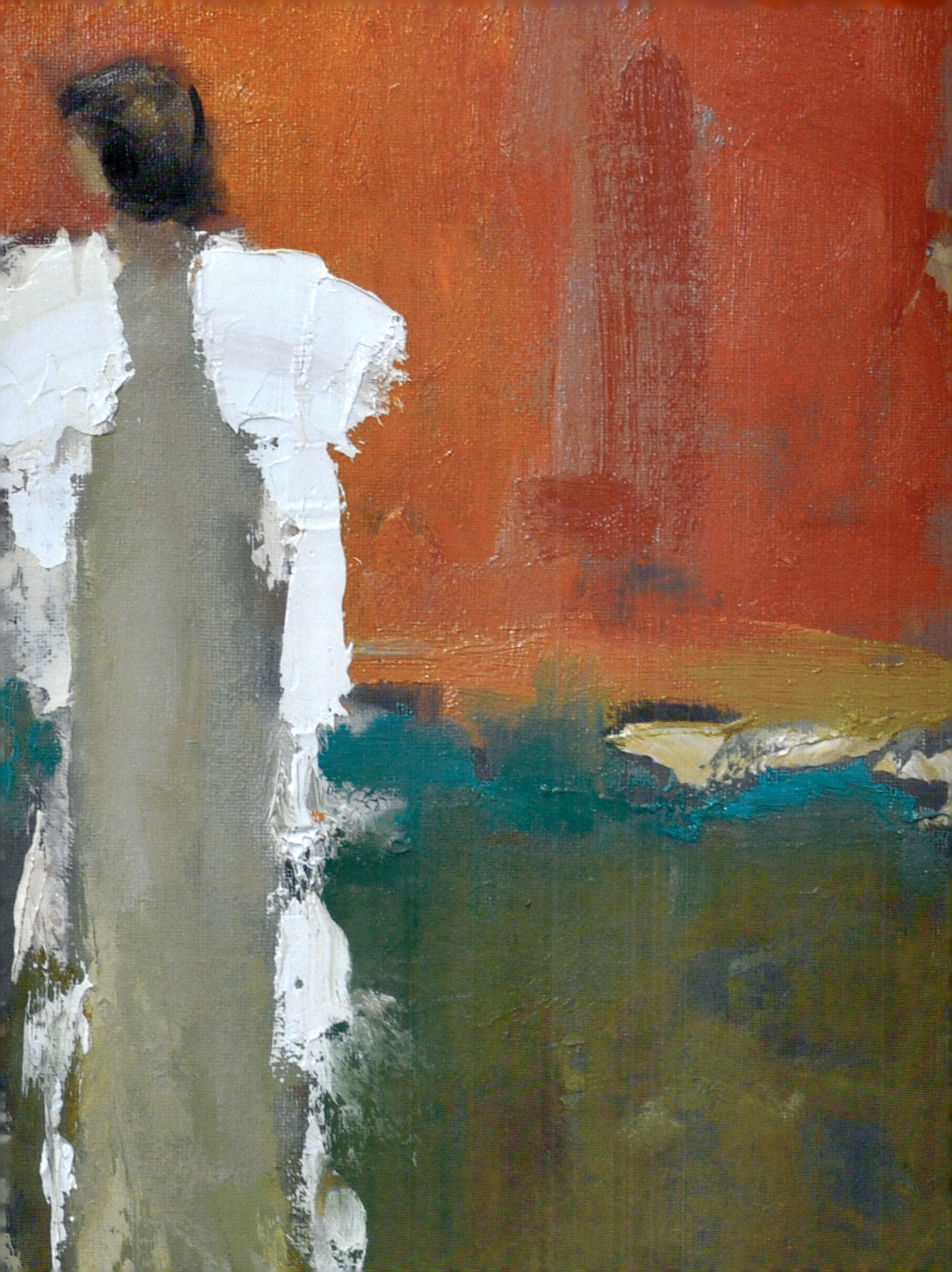

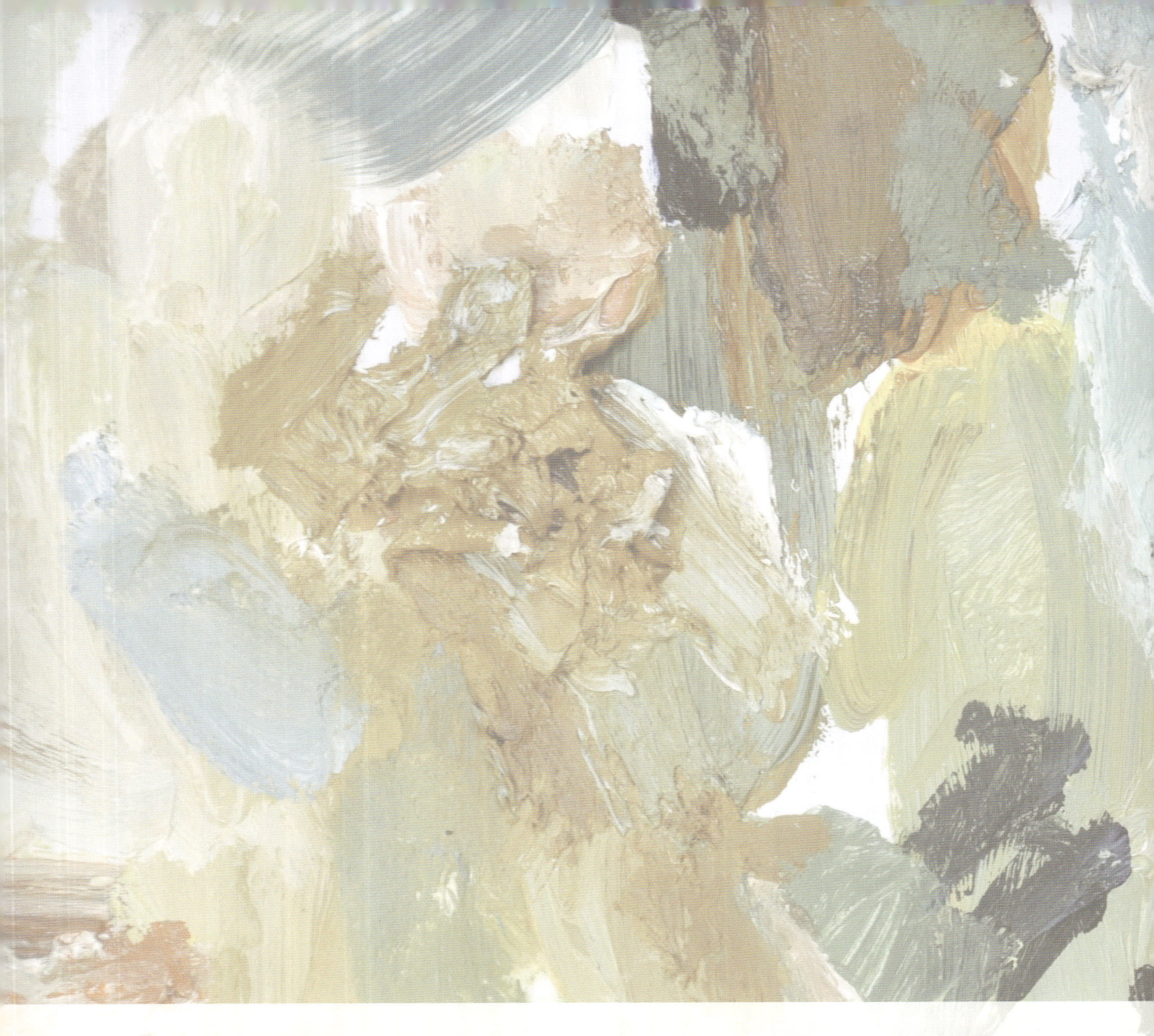

BECAUSE OF THE LORD'S GREAT LOVE
WE ARE NOT CONSUMED,
FOR HIS COMPASSIONS NEVER FAIL.
THEY ARE NEW EVERY MORNING;
GREAT IS YOUR FAITHFULNESS.

Lamentations 3:22-23

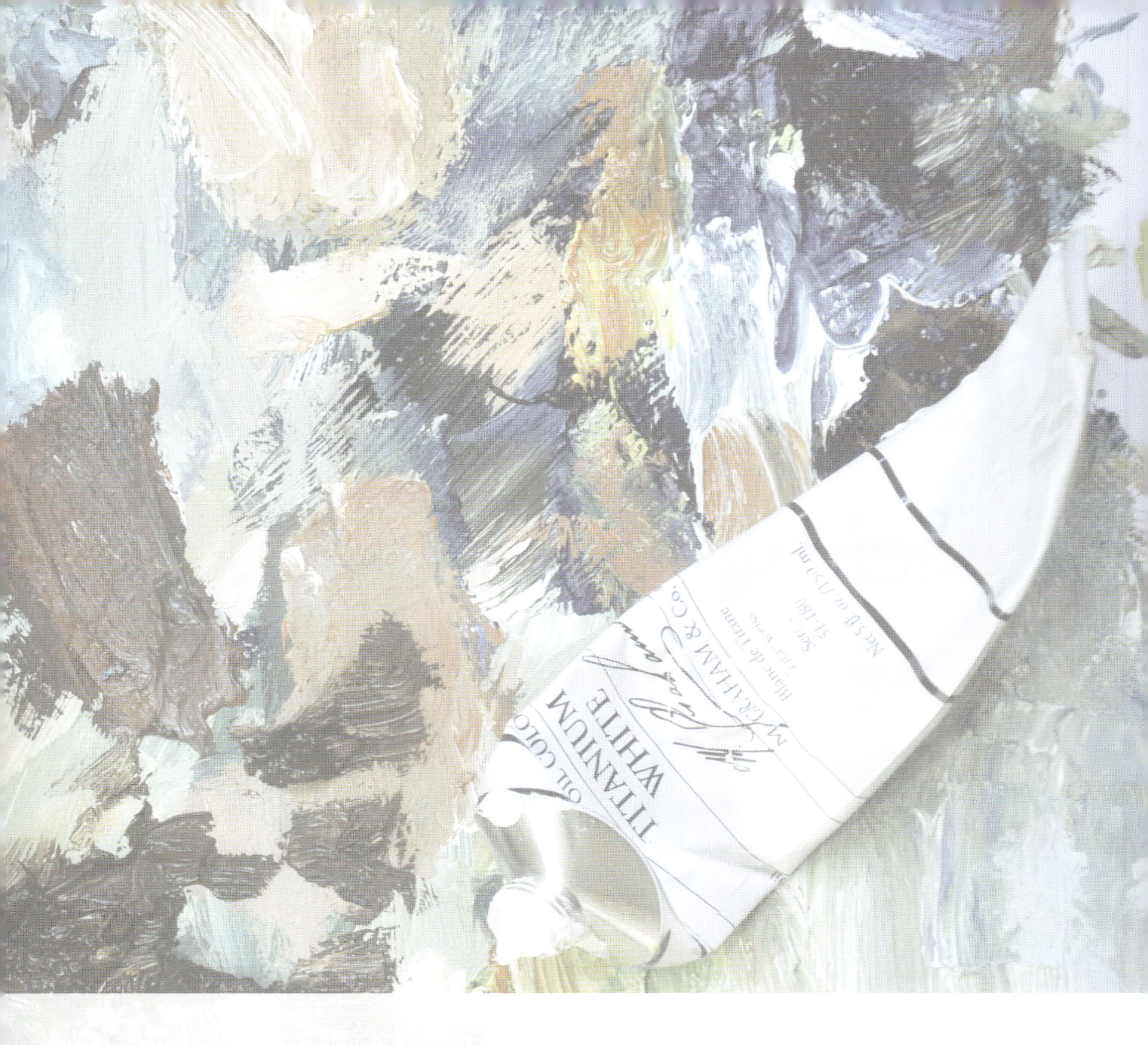

FAITHFULNESS

STORIES BEHIND THE MUSIC

A Painting for the Chapman Family

My studio is my sanctuary. . . . It is my place of peace and comfort. When I come into the studio each day, I experience a unique and intimate worship time as I paint. As I listen to Christian music and the words from each song wash over me, they reach right down to the heart of God and speak volumes of truth and life. That experience goes straight from my heart and onto the canvas. With an emphasis on intimacy and prayer, the worship songs capture my heart, and leaves me with an enduring sense of His presence.

One of my favorite Christian artists is Steven Curtis Chapman. As a contemporary Christian singer and songwriter, his music and life have been centered around his faith and family. I have listened to his music for years, attended several concerts, and have been inspired by his work with orphans.

After raising their three children, the Chapmans were encouraged by their oldest daughter, Emily, to adopt a baby. Over the course of several years, they adopted three beautiful girls from China. In 2003, Steven Curtis and Mary Beth Chapman founded Show Hope ministry, enabling individuals and communities the opportunity to serve orphans in China. Show Hope was named for their first adopted daughter, Shoahannah Hope, and addresses orphaned children's needs for food, shelter, care, spiritual nourishment and the love of a family.

On May 21, 2008 I was heartbroken to hear the tragic news that their youngest adopted daughter, Maria Sue Chapman, had died after being accidentally hit by a car in the family's driveway. Although I have never met the Chapman family personally, I cried for days over their loss. Even as I write this portion of the book, tears fill my eyes at the thought of that great loss. I spent days in the studio listening to Steven Curtis Chapman and was moved to paint an Angel for the Chapman family. Tears flowing, from the heart to the canvas, a small angel appeared with her hair tousled, fastened in a red pony-tail holder. The colors were not my 'typical' pallet colors. They were pale yellows and pinks and greens.

The painting remained in my studio for weeks, and I debated whether or not to send it due to the fact that I had just recently read an article describing the Chapman's home and I was unsure if the colors of the painting would fit in with their style as described in the article. But as always, I felt the nudge of God leading me to send the painting. I contacted a dear friend Barbara Cash, whose son Ed was in the music business in Nashville, and asked if she would contact him to see if he would be willing to somehow get the painting to the Chapmans. A few days later I sent the painting to Ed Cash, knowing that this painting was not from me but a gift from God. I never expected anything but just wanted to be obedient in the gift that HE has given me.

Fast forward several months later. It was a Tuesday morning, a few weeks before Thanksgiving and I was struggling over what to do with my art career and asking GOD to show me a sign if I should continue painting. Being a mother of four and bible study leader and more, I was feeling overwhelmed. I drove into my studio that morning and received an email from Barbara relaying a conversation that Ed had with Mary Beth Chapman. It read something like this . . . "Oh my, let me tell you about the painting that came our way . . . we about dropped it when we opened it . . . the colors were the same colors as our home and our little Maria Sue always wore her hair tousled in a ponytail. . . . " Tears filled my eyes, and I knew that God had a purpose for that painting. As long as I seek HIM first . . . he will lead the way.

LET US NOT LOSE HEART IN DOING GOOD.

Galatians 6:9

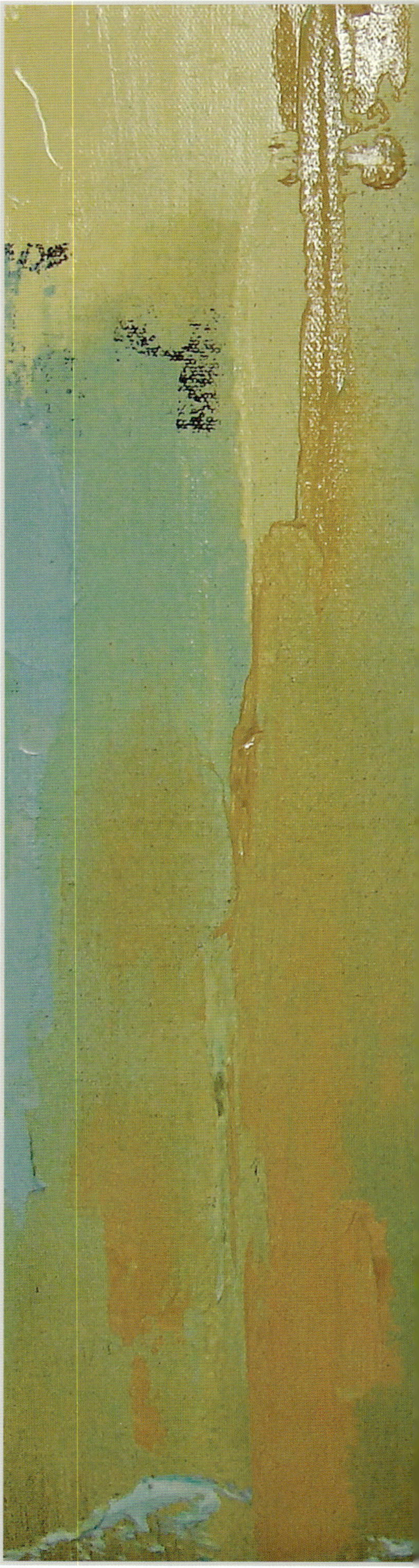

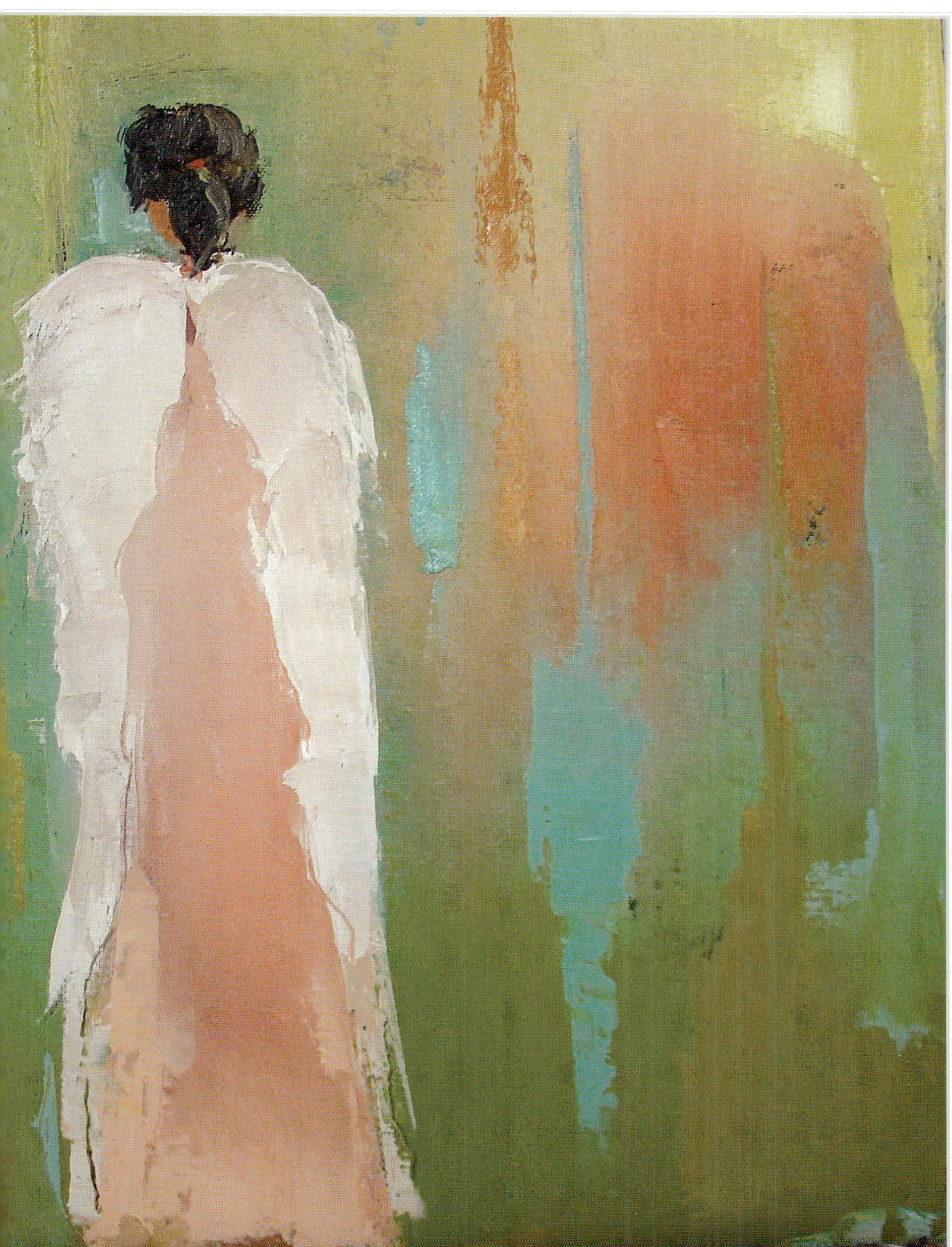

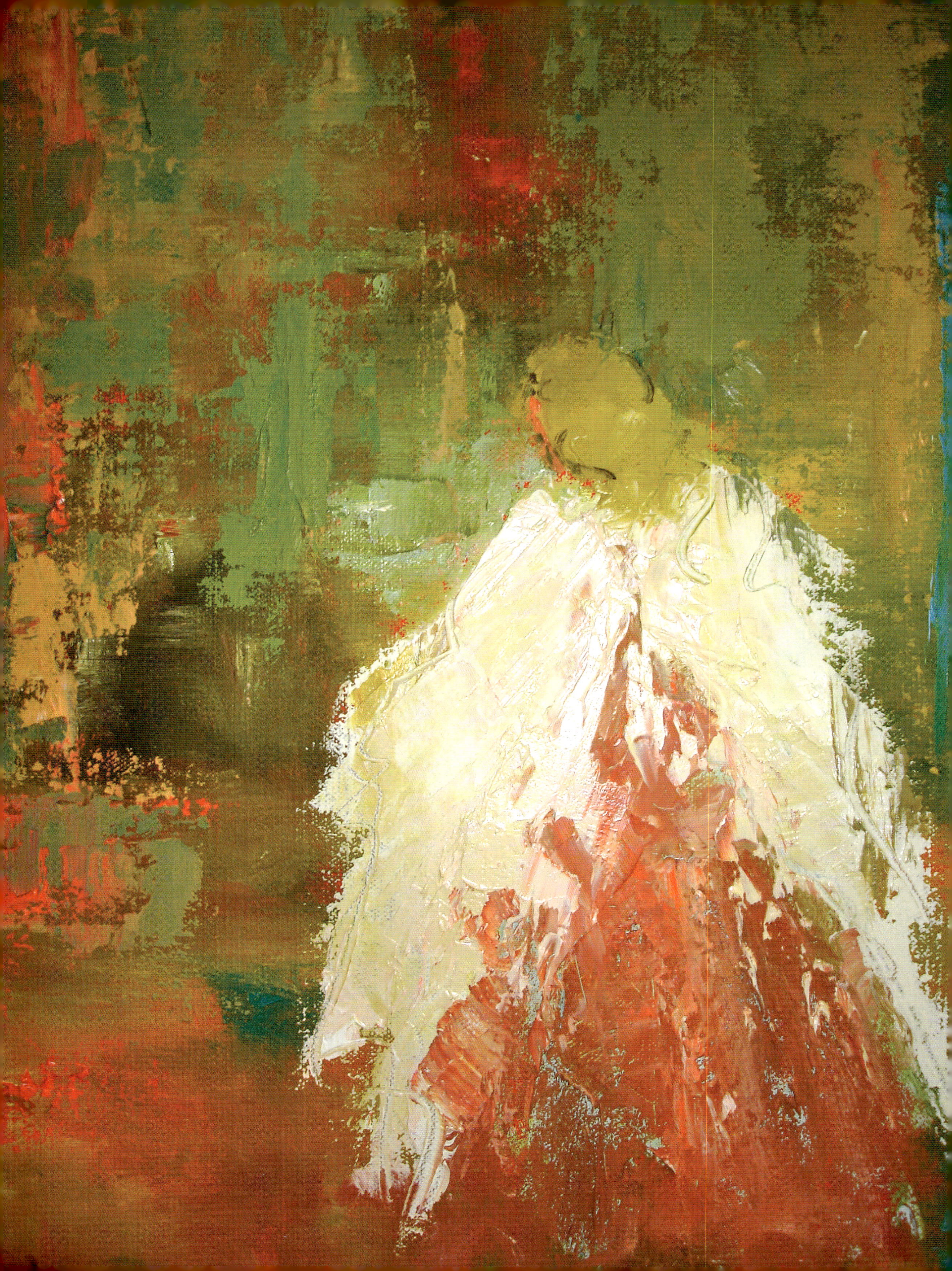

PUT ON THEN, AS GOD'S CHOSEN ONES, HOLY AND BELOVED,
COMPASSIONATE HEARTS, KINDNESS, HUMILITY, MEEKNESS, AND
PATIENCE, BEARING WITH ONE ANOTHER AND, IF ONE HAS A
COMPLAINT AGAINST ANOTHER, FORGIVING EACH OTHER;
AS THE LORD HAS FORGIVEN YOU, SO YOU ALSO MUST FORGIVE.

Colossians 3:12-13

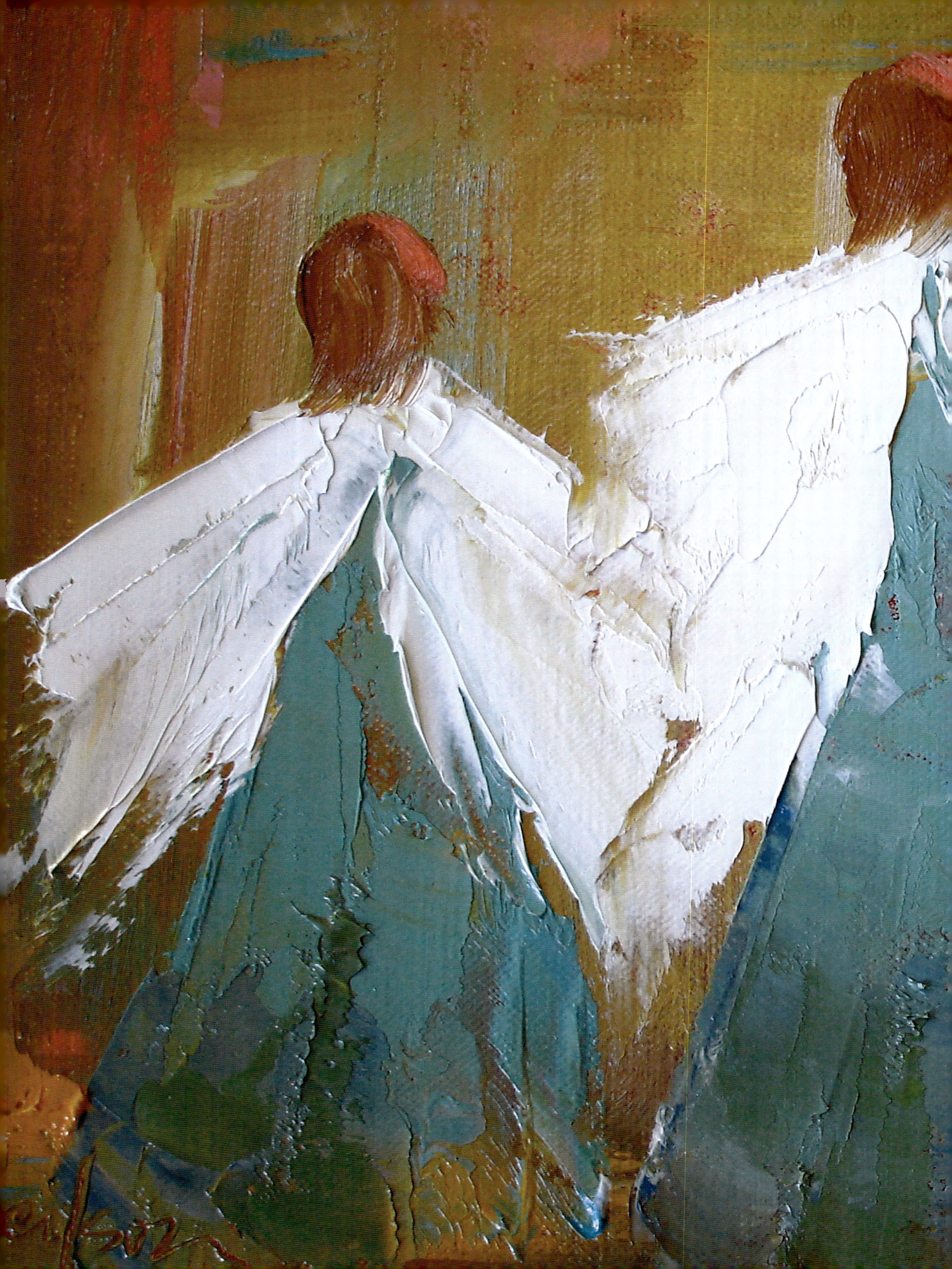

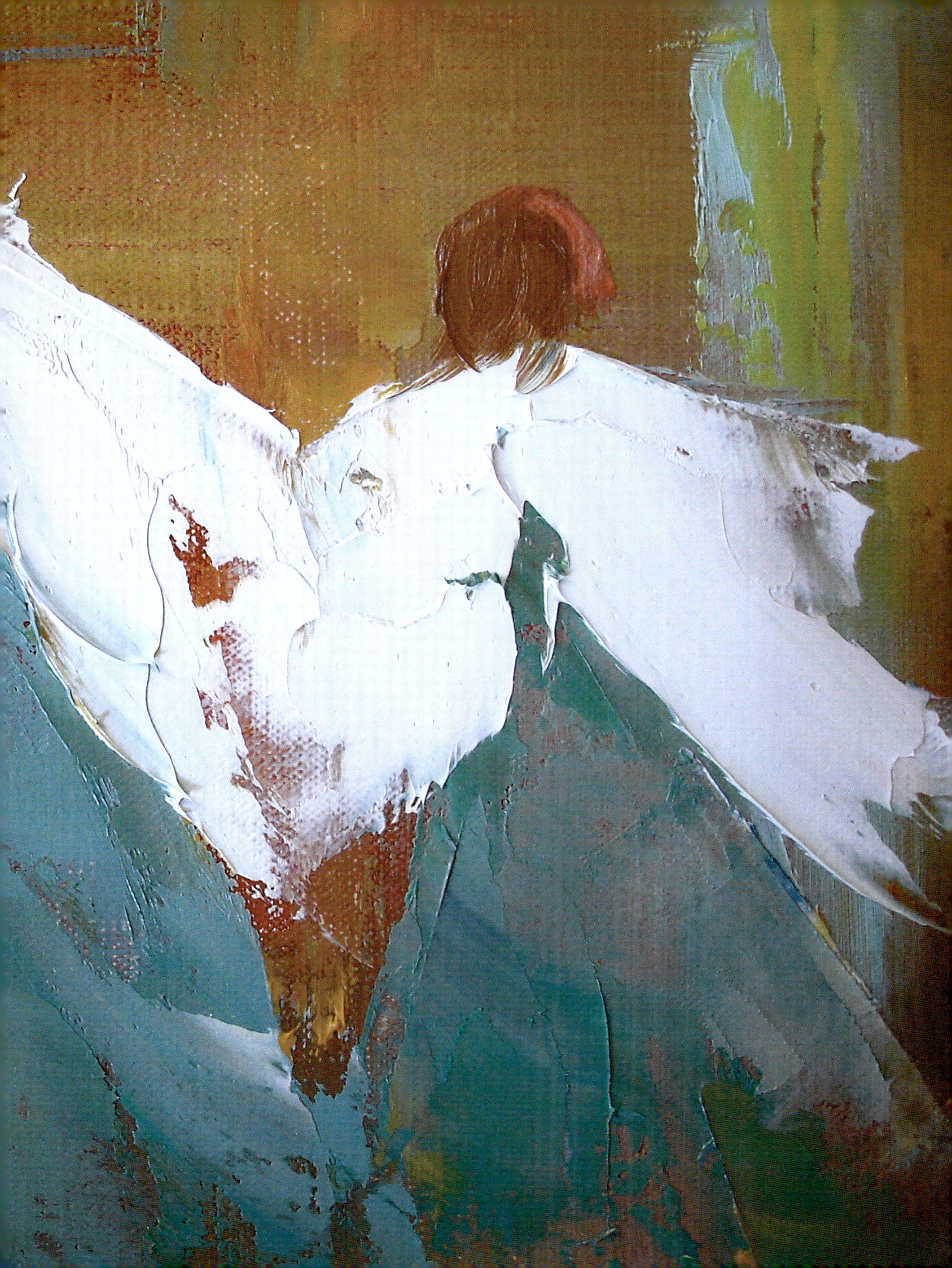

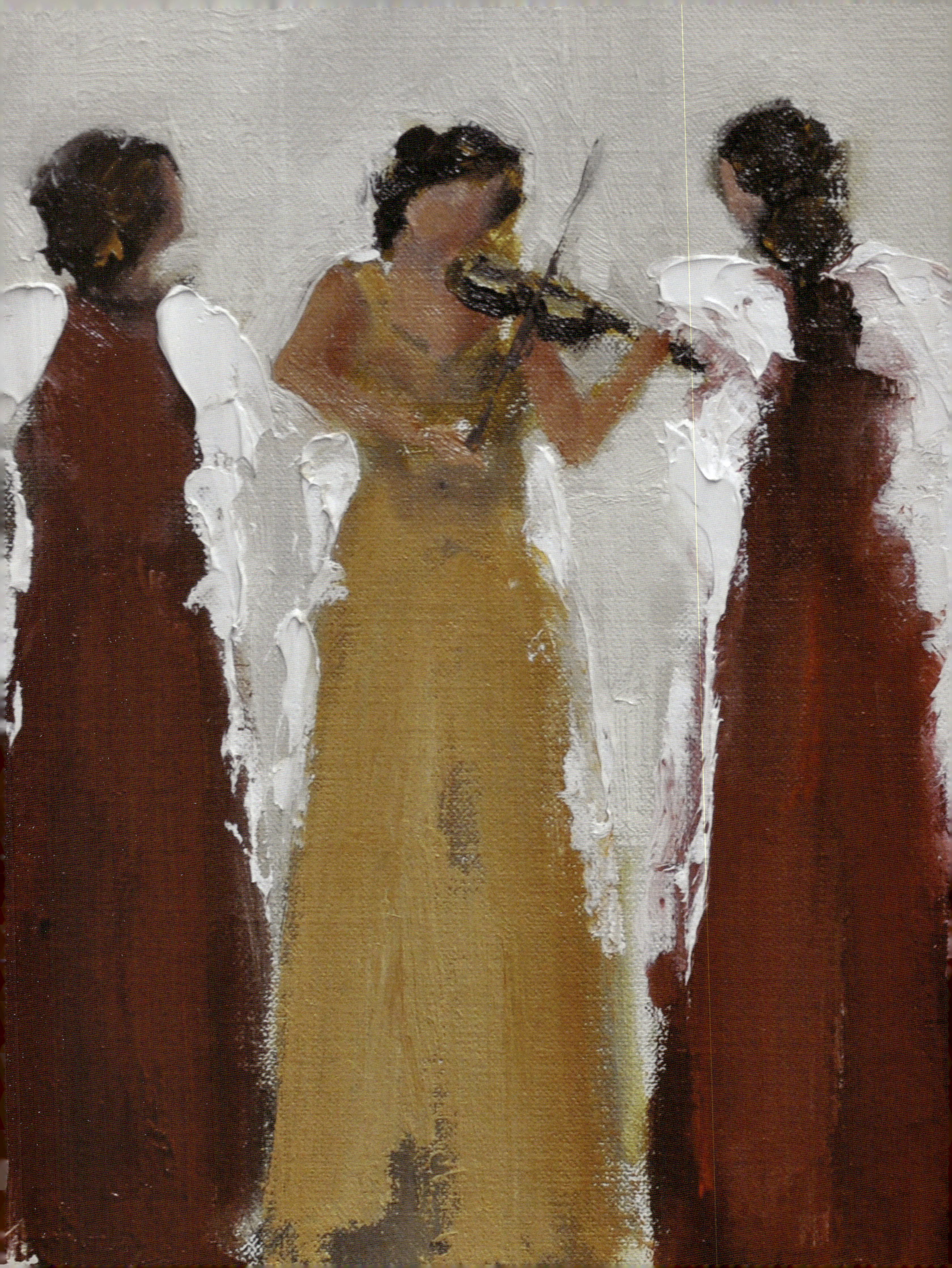

STORIES BEHIND THE MUSIC

K-Love and Air 1

This past Spring, my family and I had the privilege of touring a Christian Radio station out in California. K-Love and Air 1 are two stations (operating out of Rocklin, California) that are 501(c)(3) non-profit radio stations using contemporary Christian music to spread the Gospel. The tour of the facility was incredible. Spread out over several acres, these stations feed more than 700 separate signals across the US, reaching more than seven million people per week. We were honored to start the tour with a visit with Mike Novak, President/CEO of K-Love and Air 1.

We sat and told stories about how this work was not about 'us,' but about us being the vessels for God's ministry here on earth. K-Love and Air 1 have seven pastors on staff for the listeners and receive 40,000 prayer requests a month. We ended our tour of the facility in a large room known as the Chapel. The staff, which consists of 320 in Rocklin and another 45 around the US, gather in chapel to pray for these requests each day.

It was such a blessing to see the behind the scenes of what is such an important process of my painting. I spoke with Mike and asked if he would share a few stories about how God has used music to touch the lives of many. Here are just a few.

Stories from Mike Novak

I walked in my office one morning and there was a package on my desk. A plain, brown paper wrapped package about the size of a box of Kleenex. It was addressed to me, in care of K-LOVE. I noticed how the package had been wrapped with great care, to protect whatever was inside. Once I was able to free the contents, a 12-gauge shotgun shell fell out, landing in my lap. “What’s up with this?” I thought. Looking inside of the box for more clues, I found a note that had been wrapped around the shell. It simply said: “I won’t need this anymore.”

It came from a man who had lost his wife, his home and his entire way of life. He decided to take his own life. This guy even planned where to ‘do it,’ in a storage locker. As he was going out the door, 12-gauge shotgun in hand, a song came on the radio. It was a Newsboys song; the exact title he never shared. God’s message to him, right then and there, made him stop in his tracks. He put the 12-gauge in the closet and said “tomorrow.” Tomorrow came with the same result. Same door, same song, same outcome. Thank God! After the third time, he knew God was trying to tell him something about love, grace and having a true relationship with Christ. He fell to his knees and asked God to come into his life, again, and rededicated his heart to the Lord. After more prayers and counsel, he sent me the shotgun shell wrapped in a note. God never lets us go.

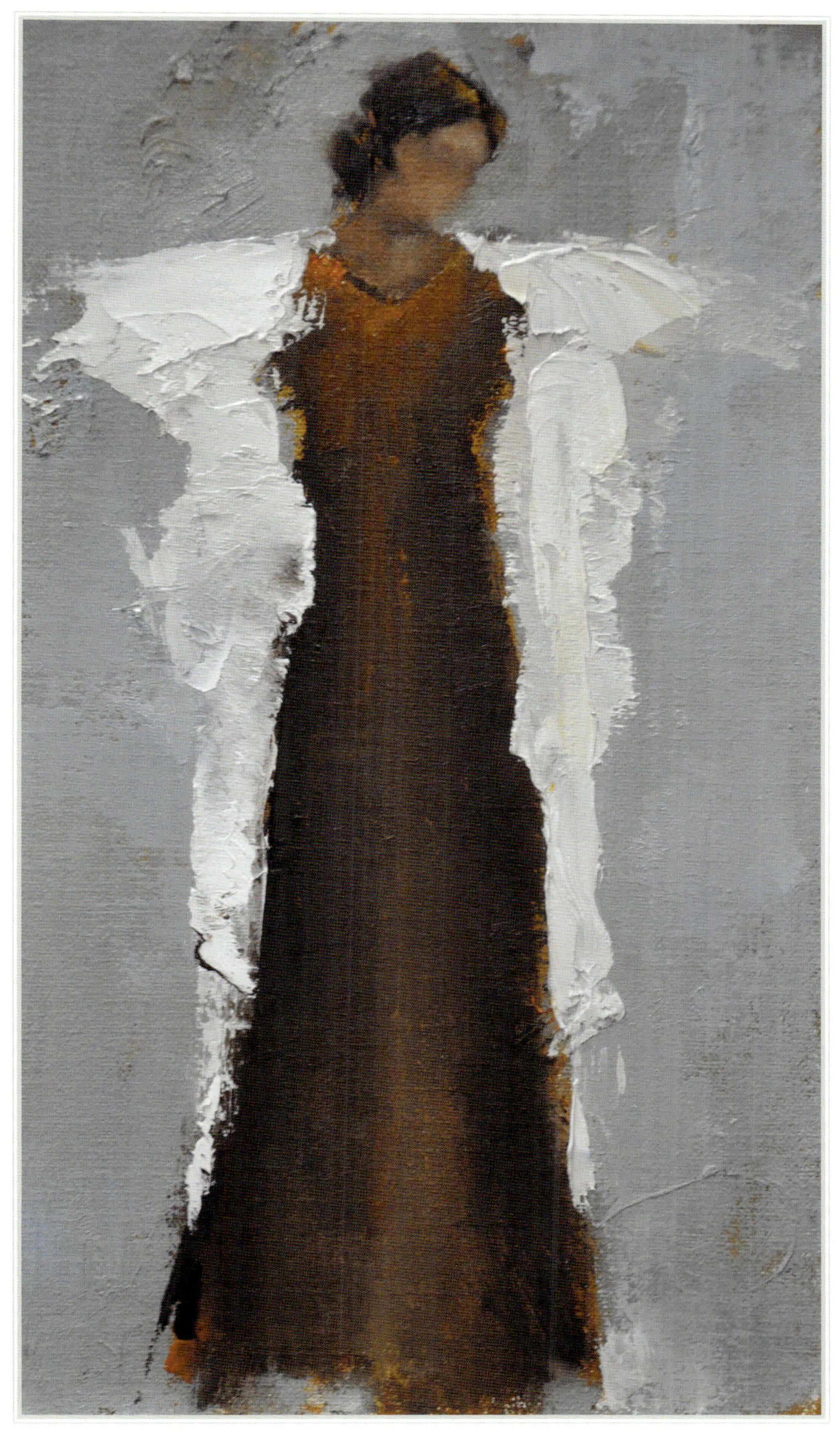

A WORK OF ART WHICH DID NOT BEGIN IN EMOTION IS NOT ART.

—PAUL CEZANNE

During the last K-LOVE Pledge Drive I took a call from a lady in Texas. She wanted to give $10. I thanked her for her gift and asked where could I send the statement. She replied: "I do not have an address. I live out of my car. I lost my job and what money I had is being held by the bank." I asked: "Are you sure this is the best use of your $10? Maybe if you prayed for us, that would be a tremendous gift to the ministry." Her answer took me by surprise: "No. I want and need to give." It was then I realized that I was robbing her of the joy of giving to something far greater than herself: God's work here on Earth, and the resultant blessings from God to her. I took a neighbor's address, prayed for her right then and there and thanked her for making my day. I shared to her that it's examples like this that show me that it's not about equal gifts, it is about equal sacrifice.

These stories, to me, point out clearly that this is NOT about K-LOVE or Air 1. Does He need us? No. Is He using us for His Kingdom? Yes. Our responsibility is to show up and be available, to do whatever we do with excellence, and get out of His way!

—MIKE NOVAK, Past President/CEO K-Love & Air 1 Radio Station Rocklin, CA

FOR IN THIS HOPE WE WERE SAVED. NOW HOPE THAT IS SEEN IS NOT HOPE. FOR WHO HOPES FOR WHAT HE SEES? BUT IF WE HOPE FOR WHAT WE DO NOT SEE, WE WAIT FOR IT WITH PATIENCE.

ROMANS 8:24-25

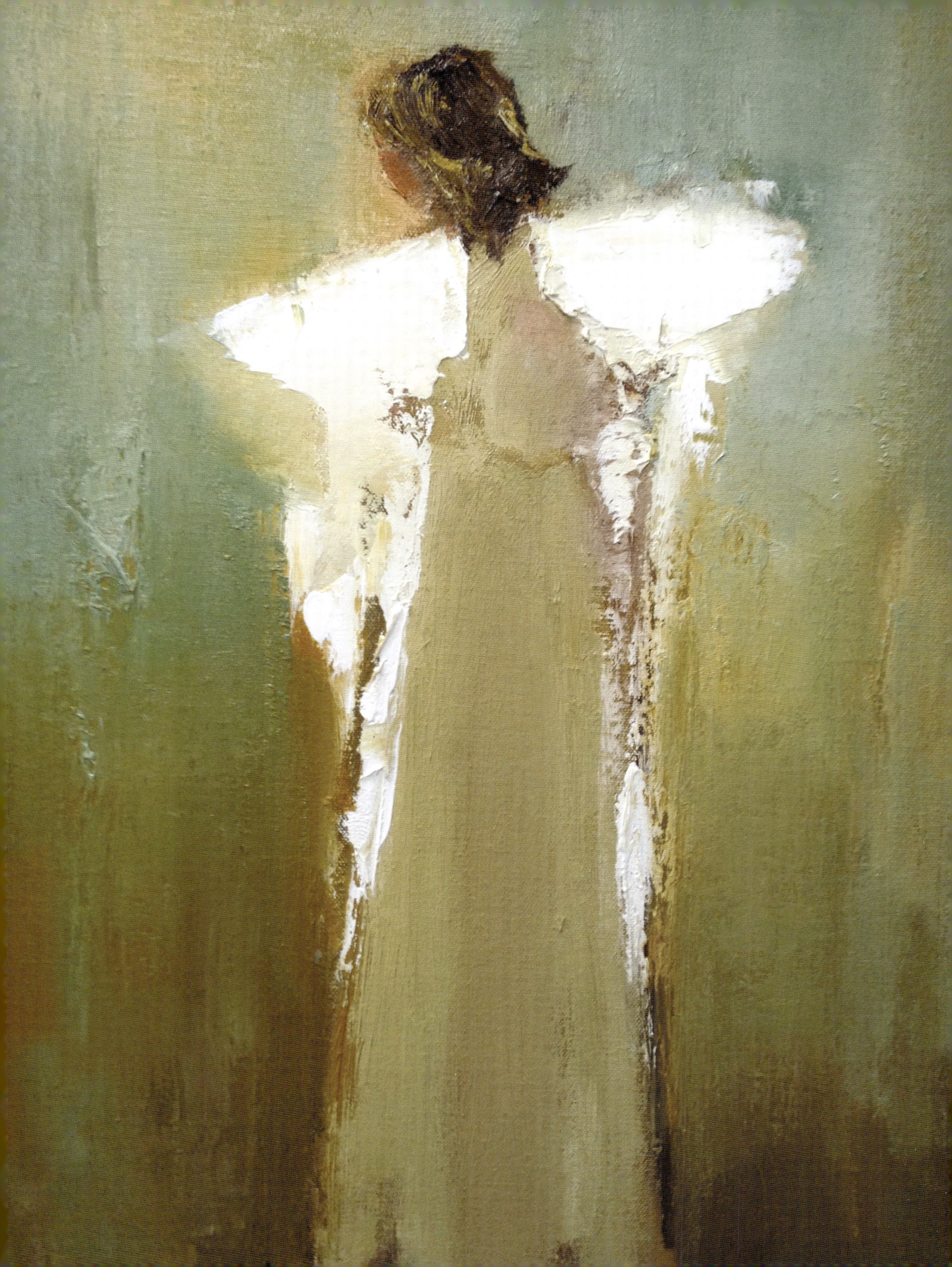

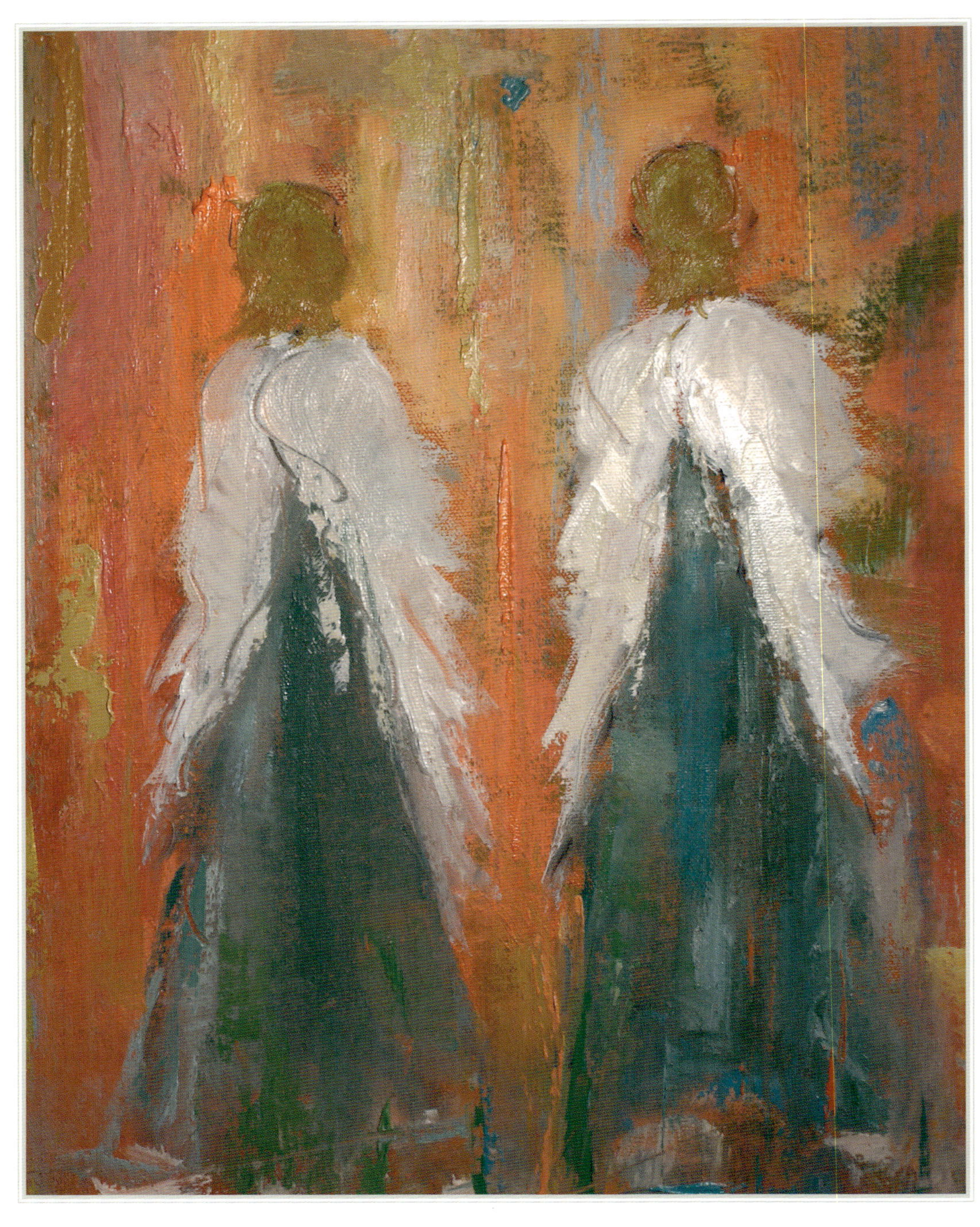

BUT SEEK FIRST HIS KINGDOM AND HIS RIGHTEOUSNESS,
AND ALL THESE THINGS WILL BE GIVEN TO YOU AS WELL.

MATTHEW 6:33

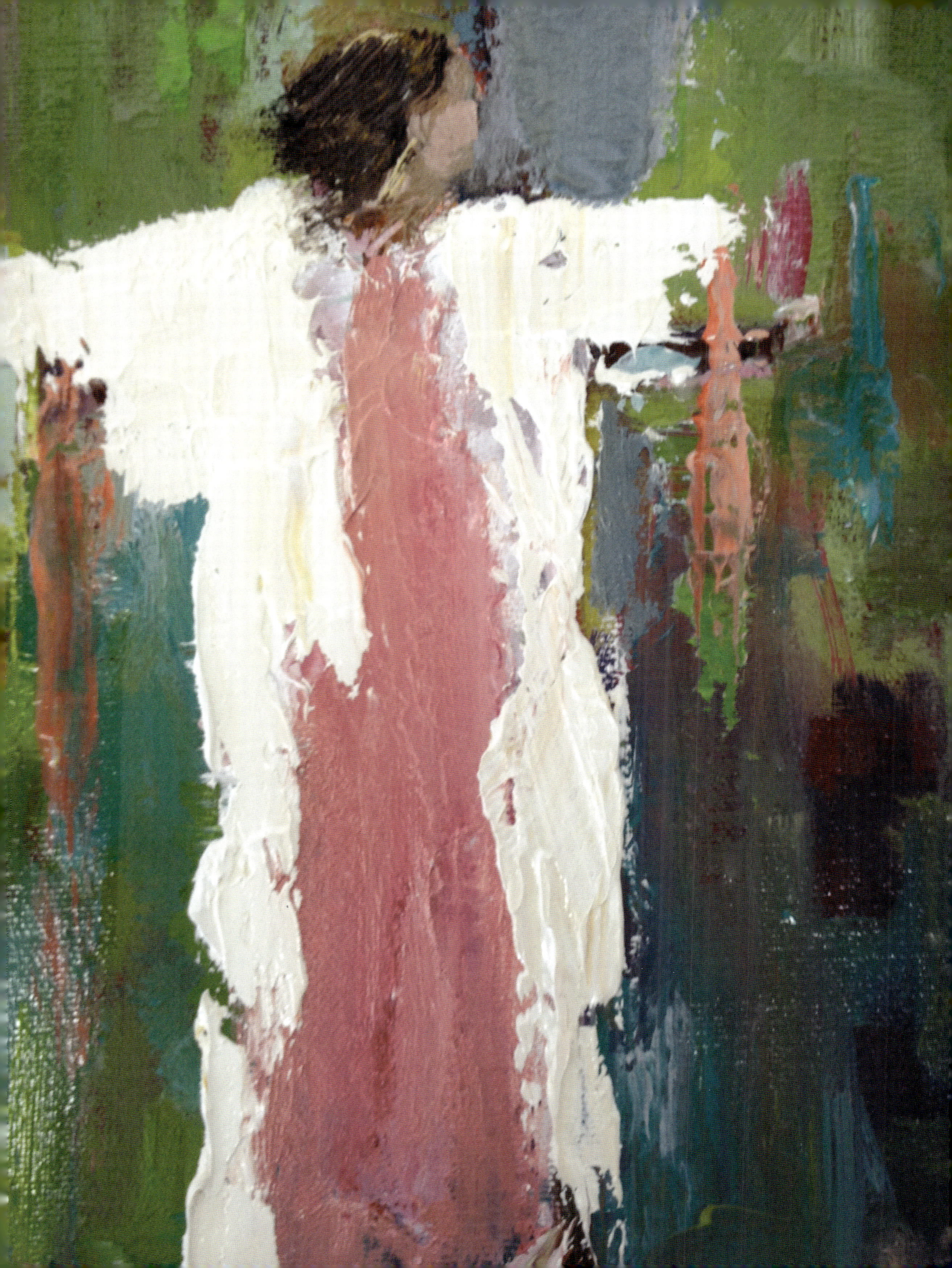

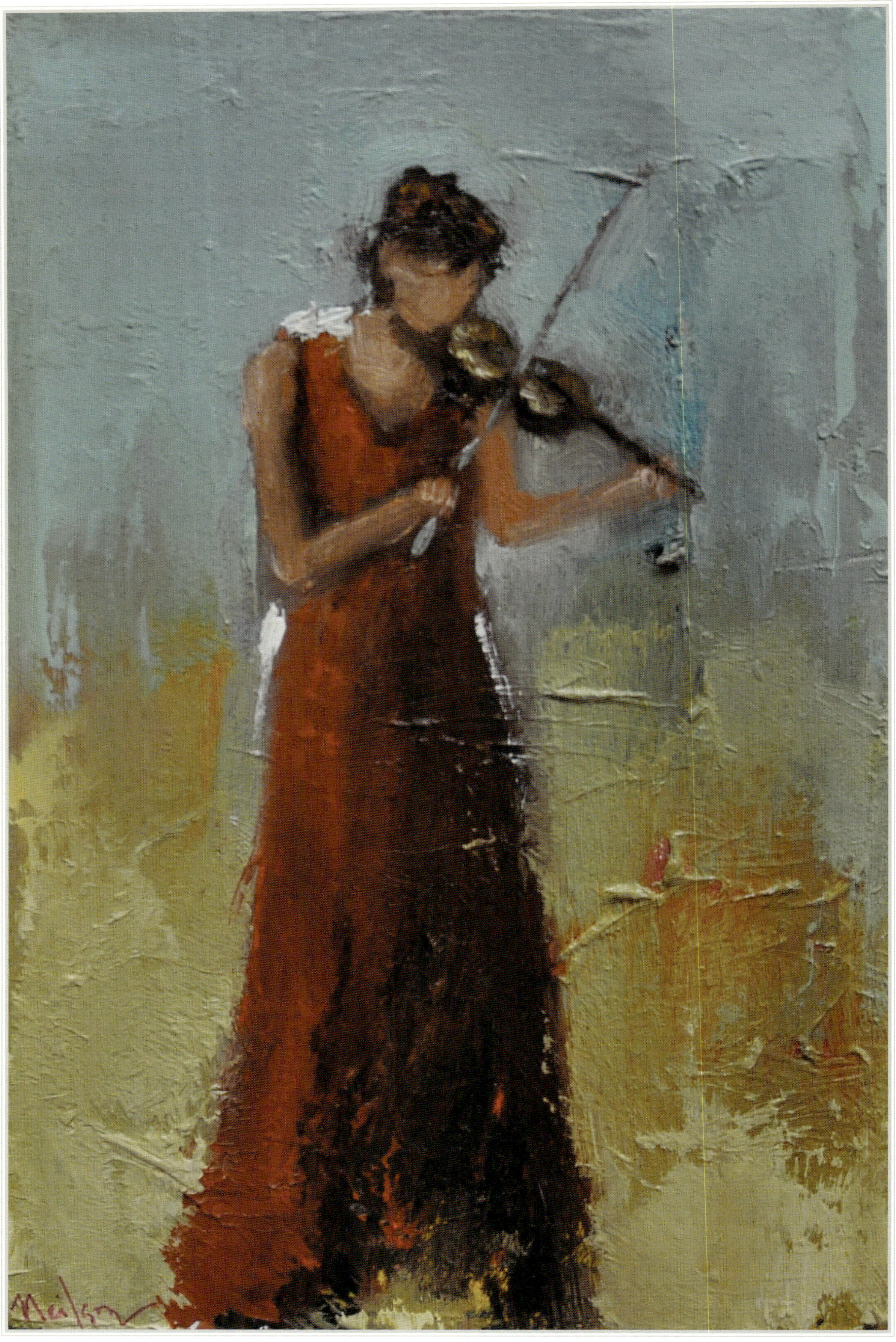

Anne has the God-given talent to paint. Although she is creative in many ways, her ability to hear God's Voice and display on the canvas what He inspires causes an anointing to be released on each painting she paints. I will never forget seeing a piece she did of an Angel in a long flowing red dress holding a violin. There is a supernatural presence of God that is captured in that painting and I found myself drawn in as I looked at it. Her works continue to inspire, bless and reveal a view of the heavenly realm. I am blessed to know her and call her my friend.

ANNE COCHRAN

Author of *The Mustard Seed Chronicles*

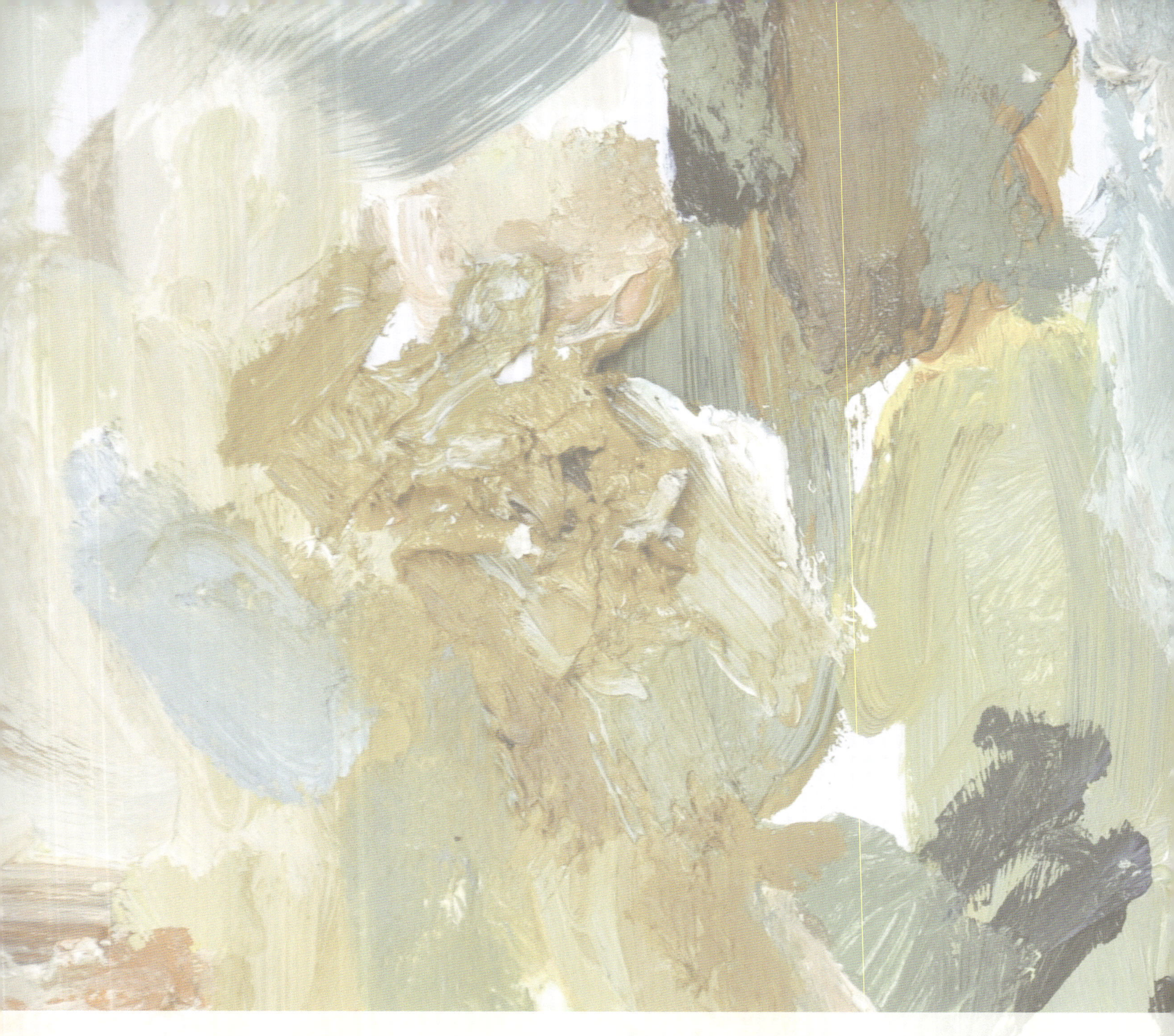

COME TO ME, ALL YOU WHO ARE WEARY AND BURDENED, AND I WILL GIVE YOU REST. TAKE MY YOKE UPON YOU AND LEARN FROM ME, FOR I AM GENTLE AND HUMBLE IN HEART, AND YOU WILL FIND REST FOR YOUR SOULS. FOR MY YOKE IS EASY AND MY BURDEN IS LIGHT.

MATTHEW 11:28-30

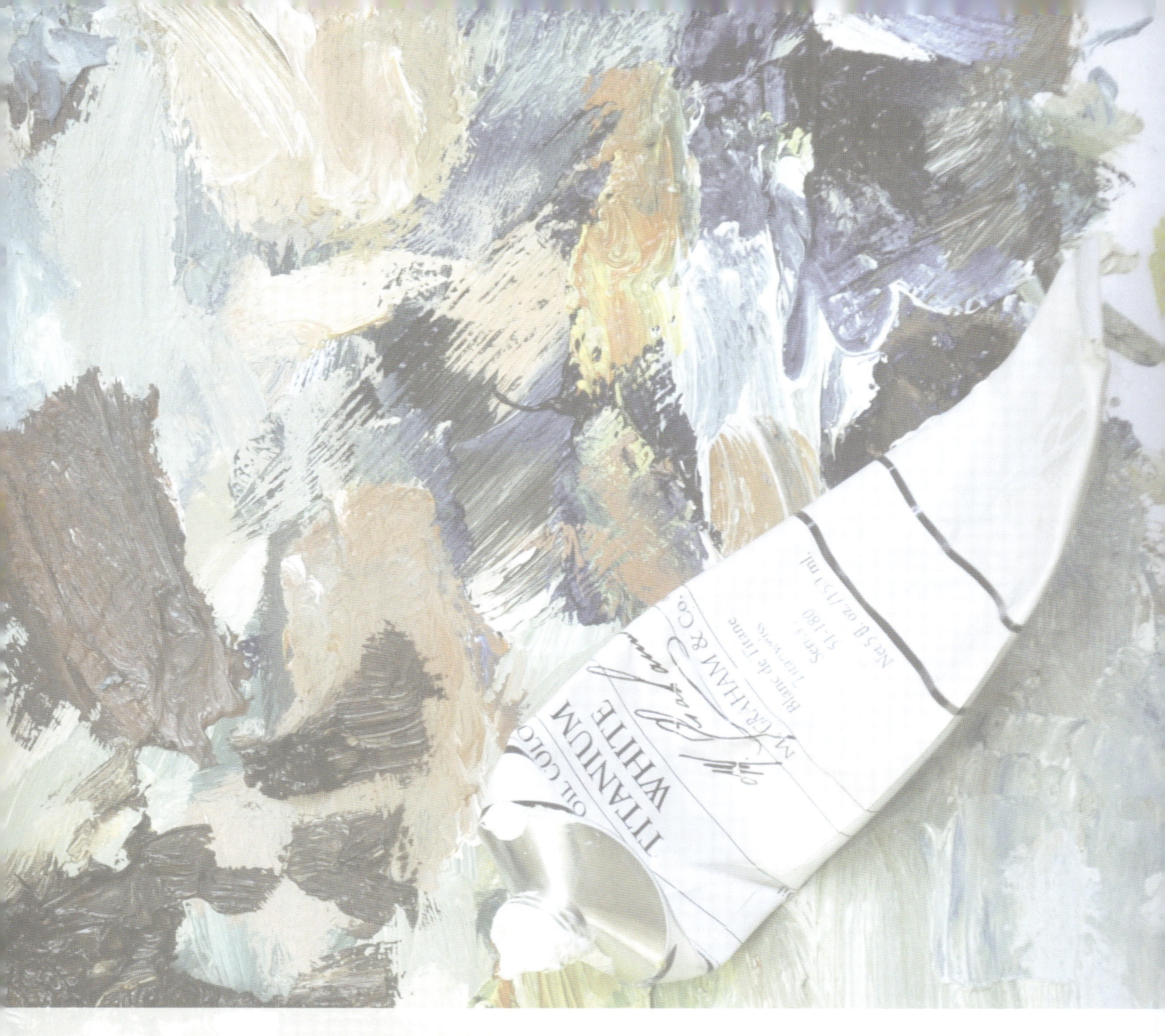

GENTLENESS

BUT THE WISDOM FROM ABOVE IS FIRST PURE, THEN PEACEABLE, GENTLE, OPEN TO REASON, FULL OF MERCY AND GOOD FRUITS, IMPARTIAL AND SINCERE.

JAMES 3:17

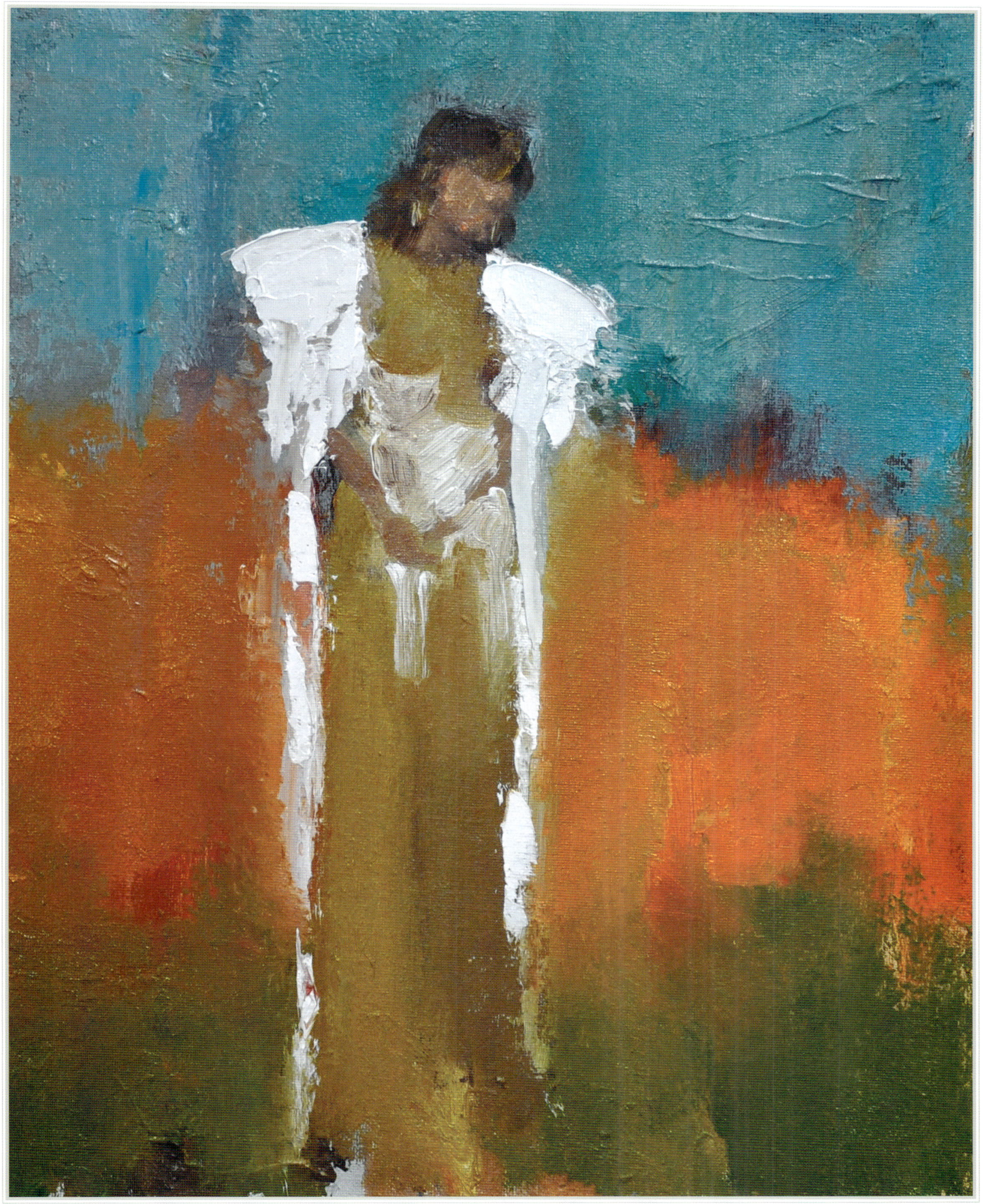

ANGELS AMONG US

An Angel in the Room

Throughout this journey of painting angels, I have come across some pretty awesome stories. Most of them come from other people, but I've had a few of my own. I remember a lady who came to the studio to see the Angels. She proceeded to tell me a story about when she was born. Her mother, after leaving the hospital, stopped into the chapel to lift up a prayer of protection for her new daughter. She asked that Angels would surround her daughter all the days of her life. The grown daughter in my studio told me that she had surgery a few years back, and the nurses told her as she was coming out of surgery there were angels surrounding her in that operating room. When she was in recovery she mentioned what the nurses said about the angels to her mother. Her mother then explained what she had done at the hospital. Fast-forward a few years later and this woman was moving to Charlotte. She and the real estate agent were looking at a home and as they were wandering through the house a little girl who lived there sat in the kitchen drawing a picture. When the lady was about to leave the little girl came up to her and handed her the picture. It was a picture of the lady with angels surrounding her and in quotes on the page were "Angels surround you."

She pulled out a picture to show me and we both sat there speechless.

I know that angels do surround us. I witnessed this last summer. My precious step-father of 28 years,

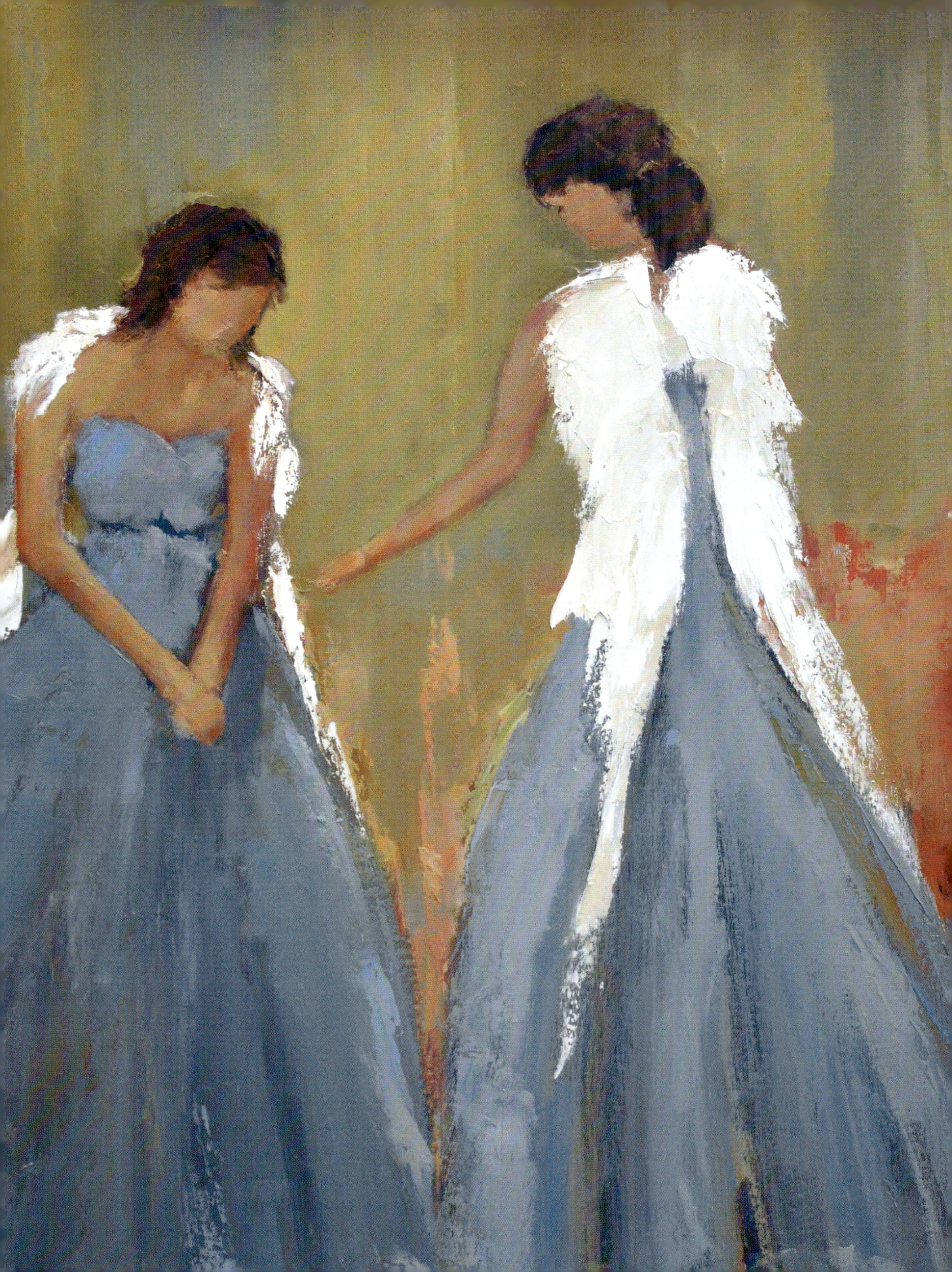

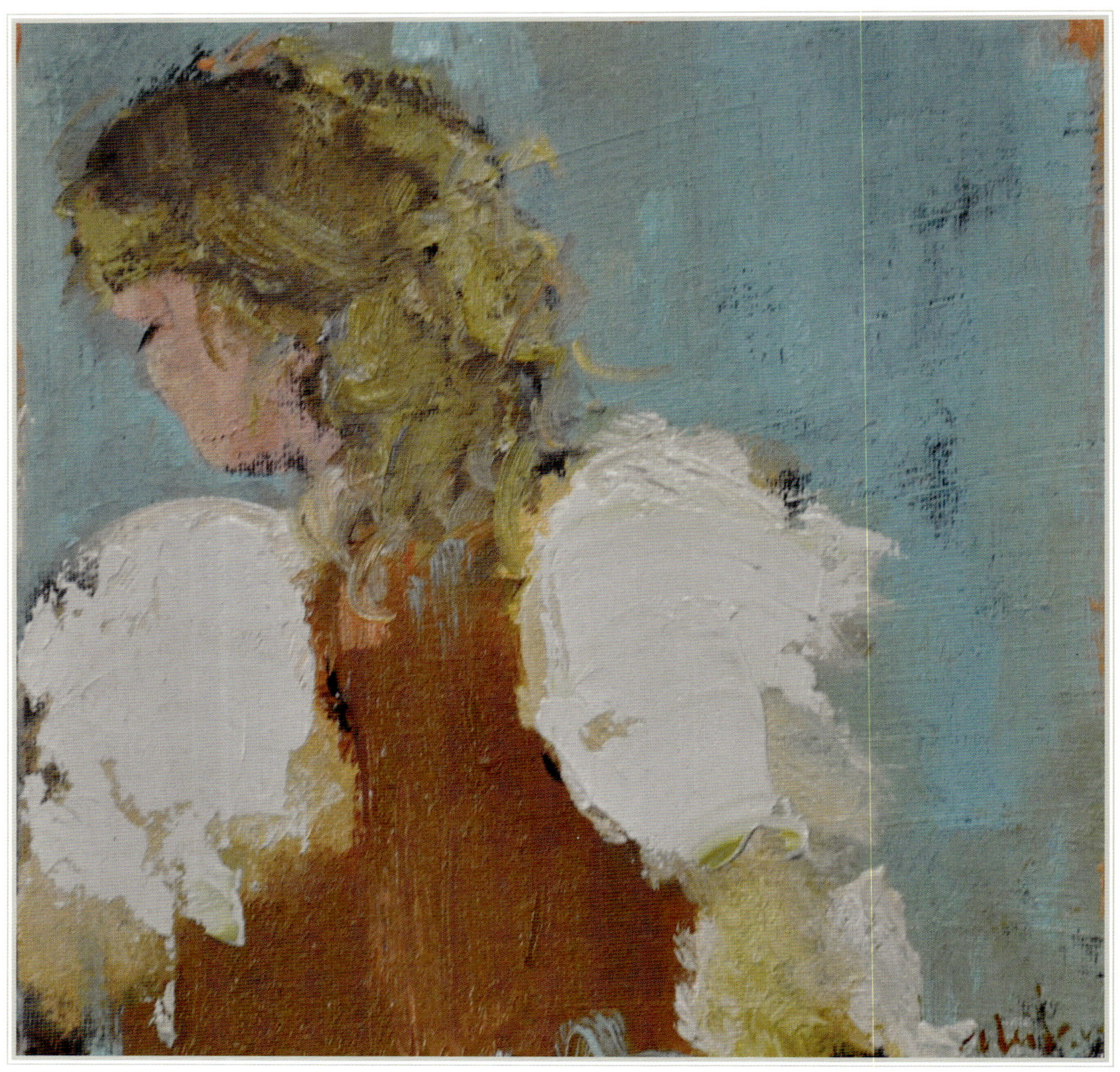

Bronson, went into the hospital for heart surgery. He was the most gentle soul and loved my mom dearly. The day he went into the hospital (which was their 28th anniversary), we were told that the surgery would be long but they hoped for the best. We all thought he was in pretty good shape for an 84-year-old man. He had a young soul, and was kind, gentle, loving and the most giving person I have known. The surgery was grueling and the entire family sat waiting patiently for news. Finally, the doctor came out to tell us that the surgery did not go as smoothly as they had hoped. Bronson was weak and we just had to wait and see.

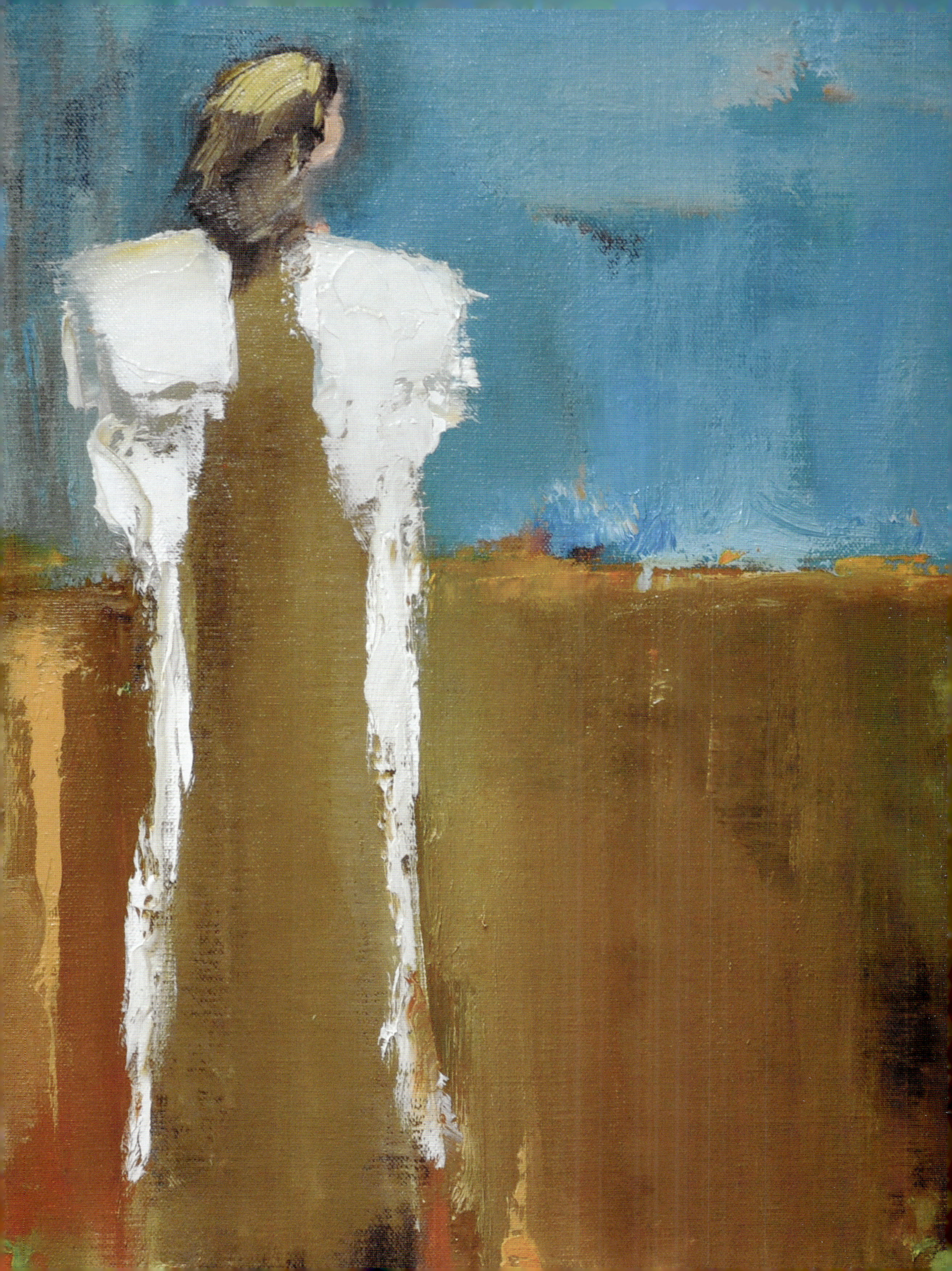

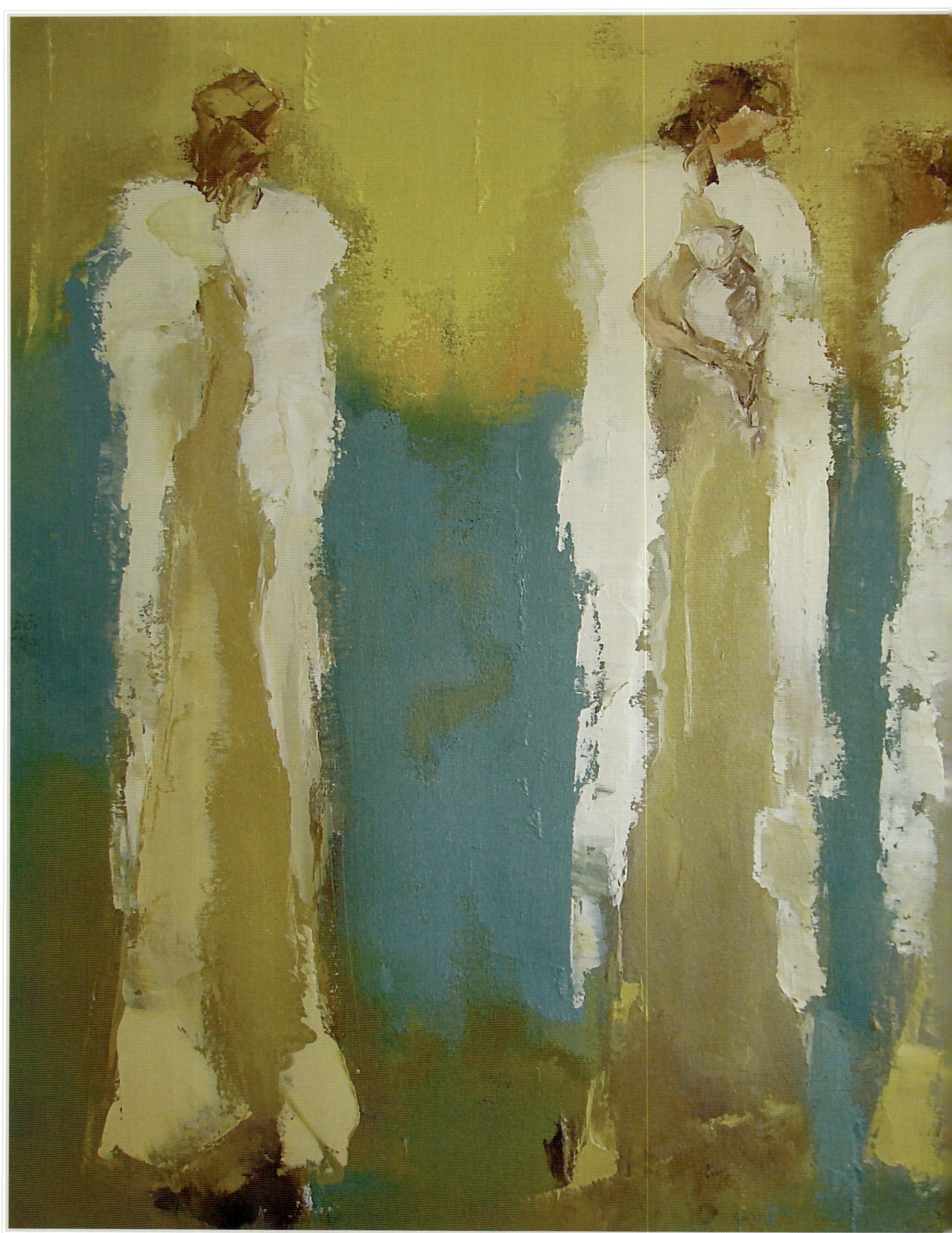

Six days later, my step-sister and I went for an early morning walk and ended up at the hospital to check on Bronson. The nurses had just taken out his breathing tube, which we all thought was a good sign. As we entered the room, Bronson began to open his eyes and point furiously at something over towards me. We would ask all kinds of questions: "Do you need this? Do you want the TV on? Do you want Mom?" But he shook his head furiously no, and continued to point and try to tell us something. I left to come home for a night or two, thinking that the signs were good and he was coming out of the woods.

I got a call the next day to head back: we all needed to be there. I was in Charlotte, NC traveling to Charleston, SC. It was the longest drive I think I have ever taken. I was shaking and tears were streaming down my face as I would get updates from family members of his condition; I just wanted him to hang on until I got there to tell him goodbye. All of a sudden, still an hour away from Charleston, this amazing peace overcame me. I felt like the Lord was telling me: "He was pointing to Angels - Angels were surrounding him yesterday and he was trying to tell you everything is OK."

That peace, the peace that passes all understanding overtook my entire body. The uncontrollable shaking disappeared. The tears for the moment ceased. And a calming presence permeated throughout the rest of the trip. I got to the hospital just as he flew to Heaven into Jesus's arms. He died on June 23, 2011.

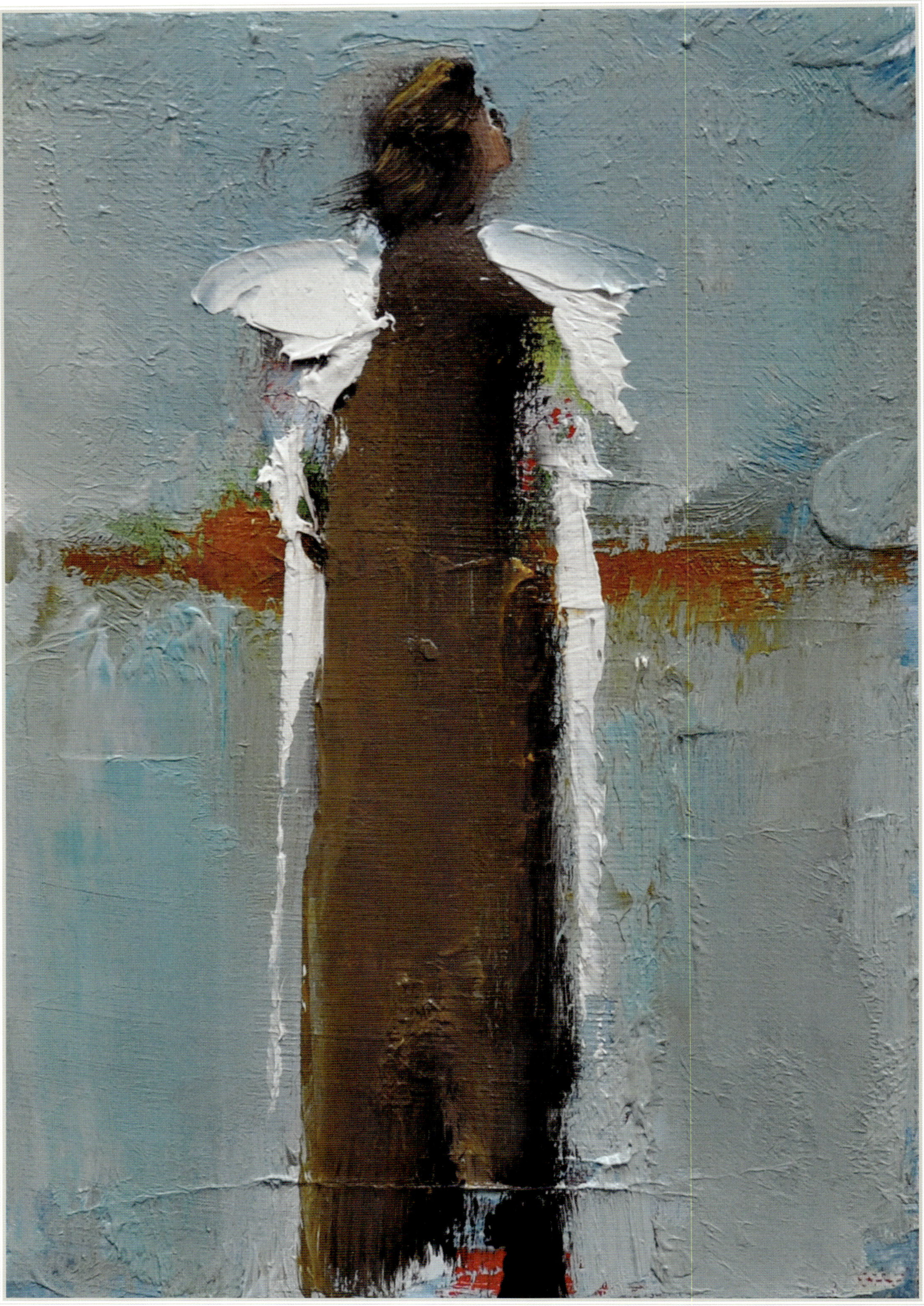

LET NOT YOUR HEARTS BE TROUBLED. BELIEVE IN GOD; BELIEVE ALSO IN ME. IN MY FATHER'S HOUSE ARE MANY ROOMS. IF IT WERE NOT SO, WOULD I HAVE TOLD YOU THAT I GO TO PREPARE A PLACE FOR YOU? AND IF I GO AND PREPARE A PLACE FOR YOU, I WILL COME AGAIN AND WILL TAKE YOU TO MYSELF, THAT WHERE I AM YOU MAY BE ALSO. AND YOU KNOW THE WAY TO WHERE I AM GOING.

JOHN 14: 1-4

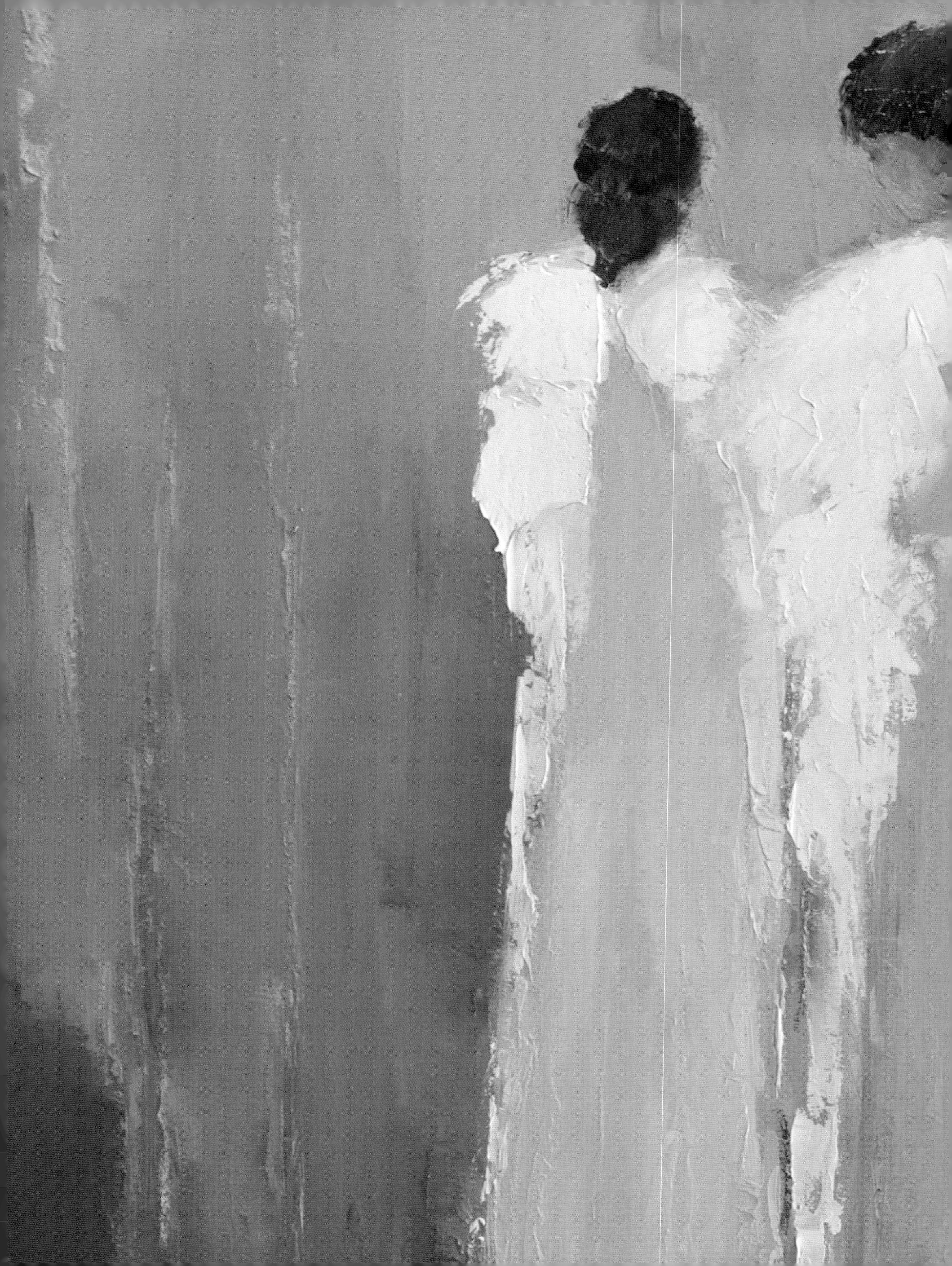

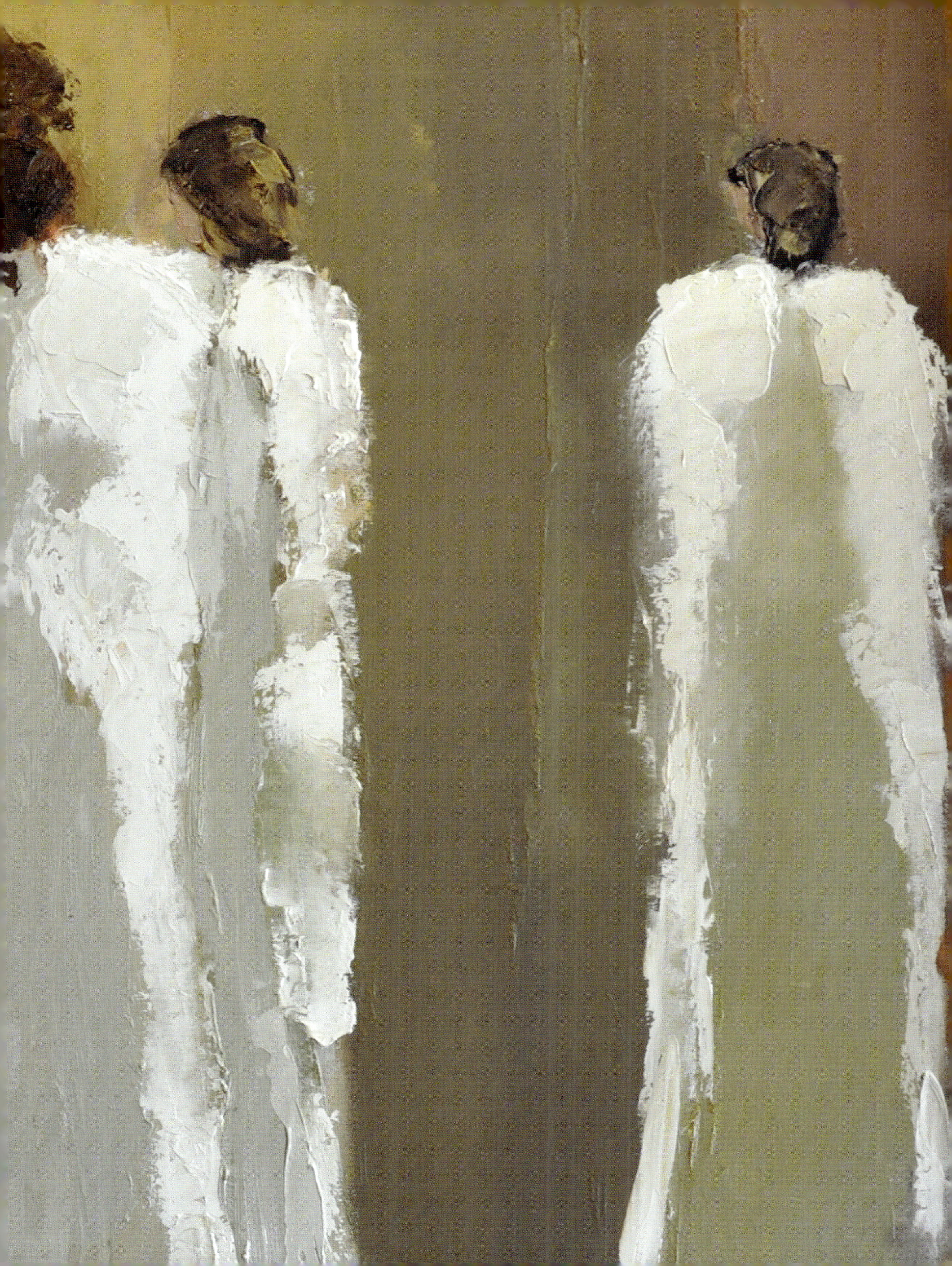

HE WILL TEND HIS FLOCK LIKE A SHEPHERD; HE WILL GATHER THE LAMBS IN HIS ARMS; HE WILL CARRY THEM IN HIS BOSOM AND GENTLY LEAD THOSE THAT ARE WITH YOUNG.

Isaiah 40:11

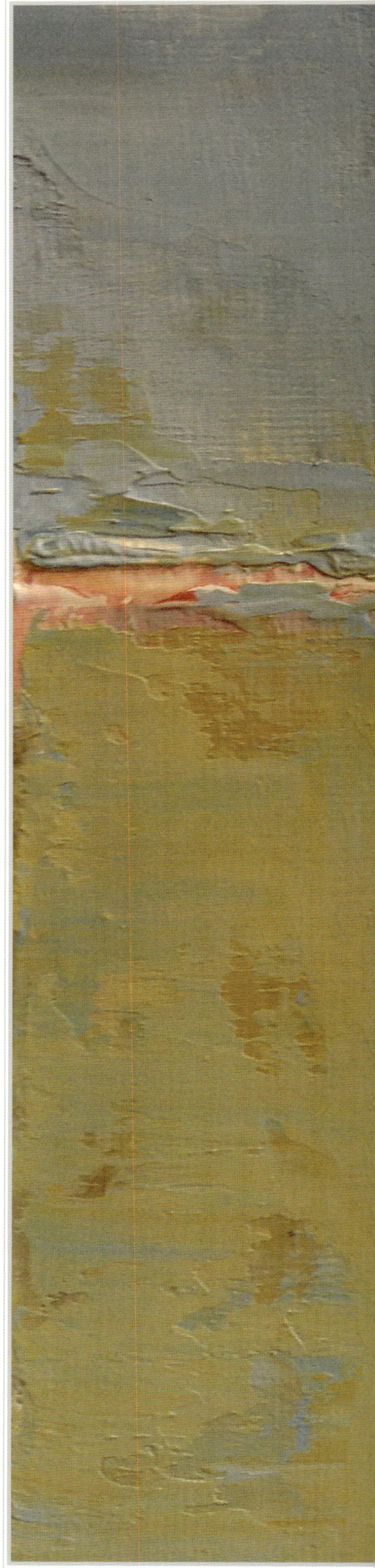

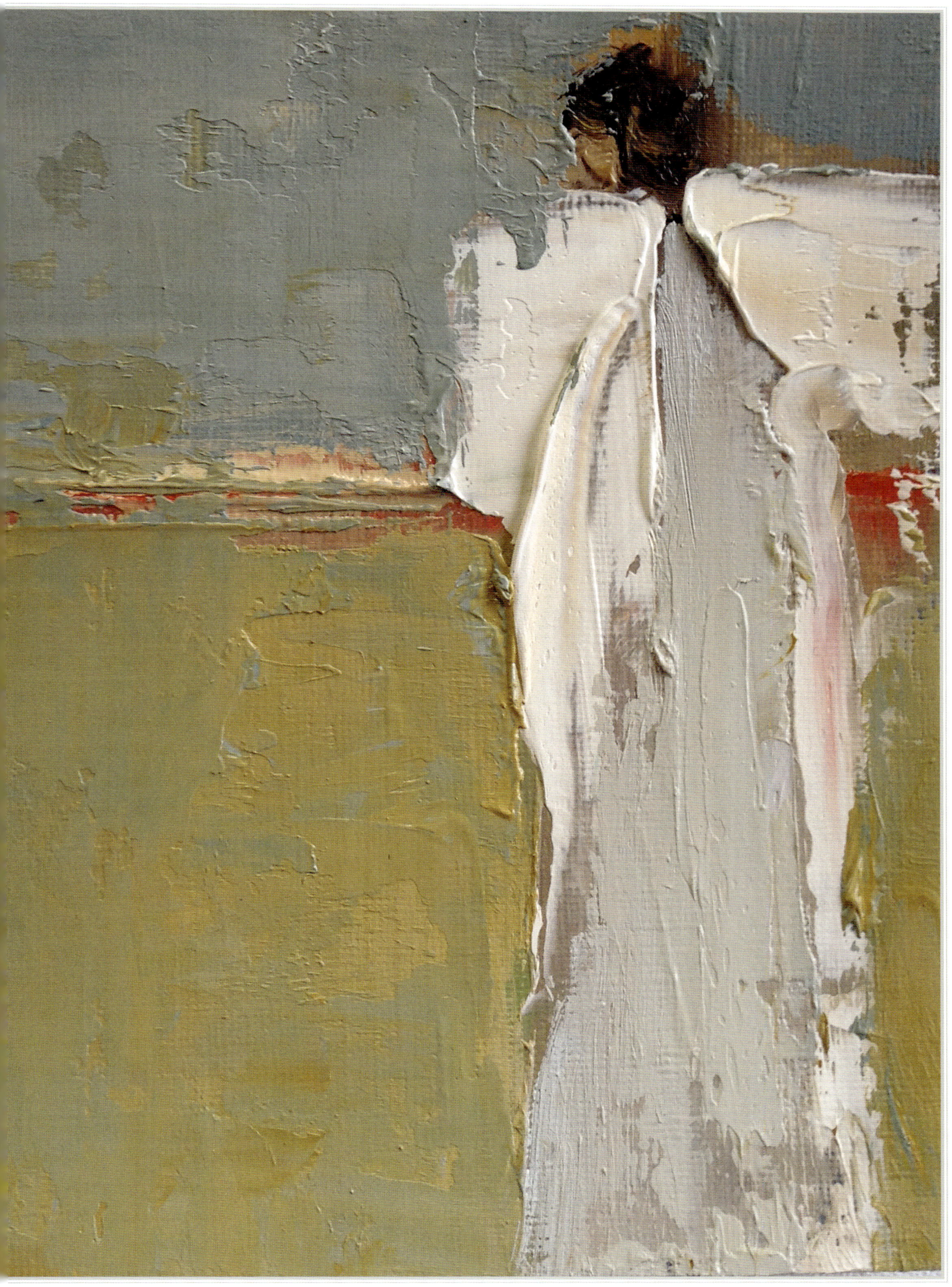

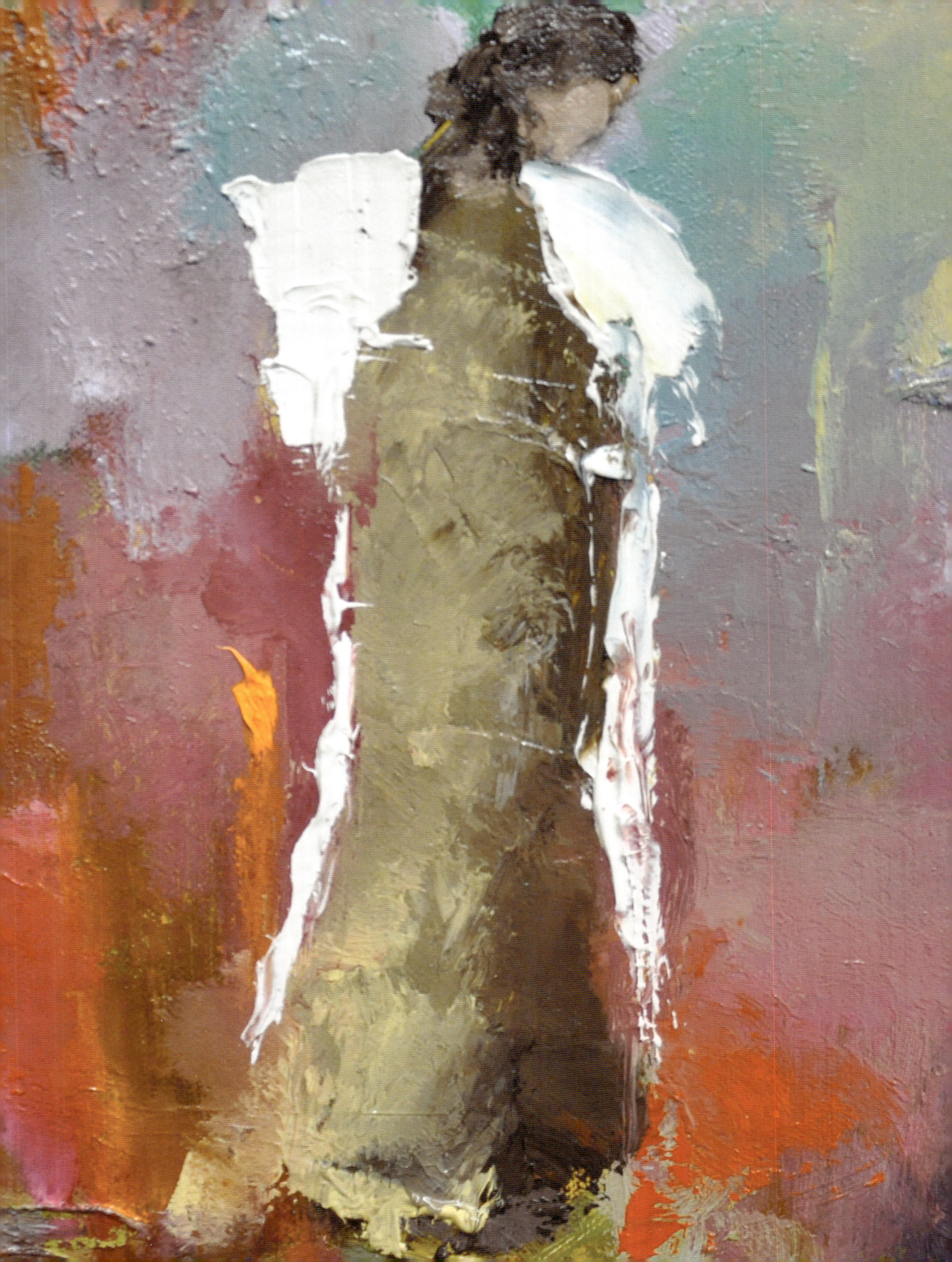

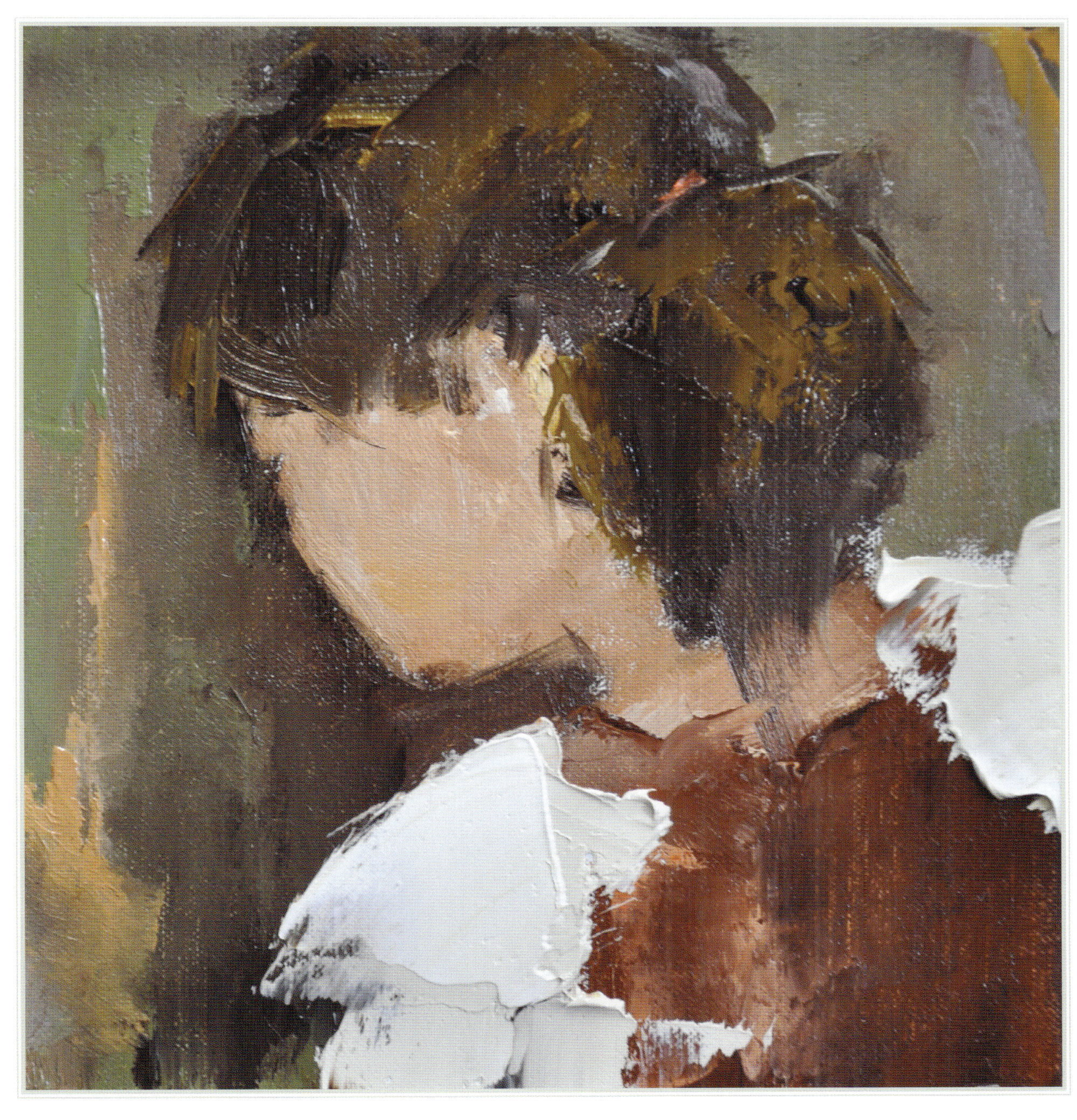

IT'S NOT WHAT YOU LOOK AT THAT MATTERS, IT'S WHAT YOU SEE.

— HENRY DAVID THOREAU

PEACE I LEAVE WITH YOU; MY PEACE I GIVE TO YOU. NOT AS THE WORLD GIVES DO I GIVE TO YOU. LET NOT YOUR HEARTS BE TROUBLED, NEITHER LET THEM BE AFRAID.

JOHN 14:27

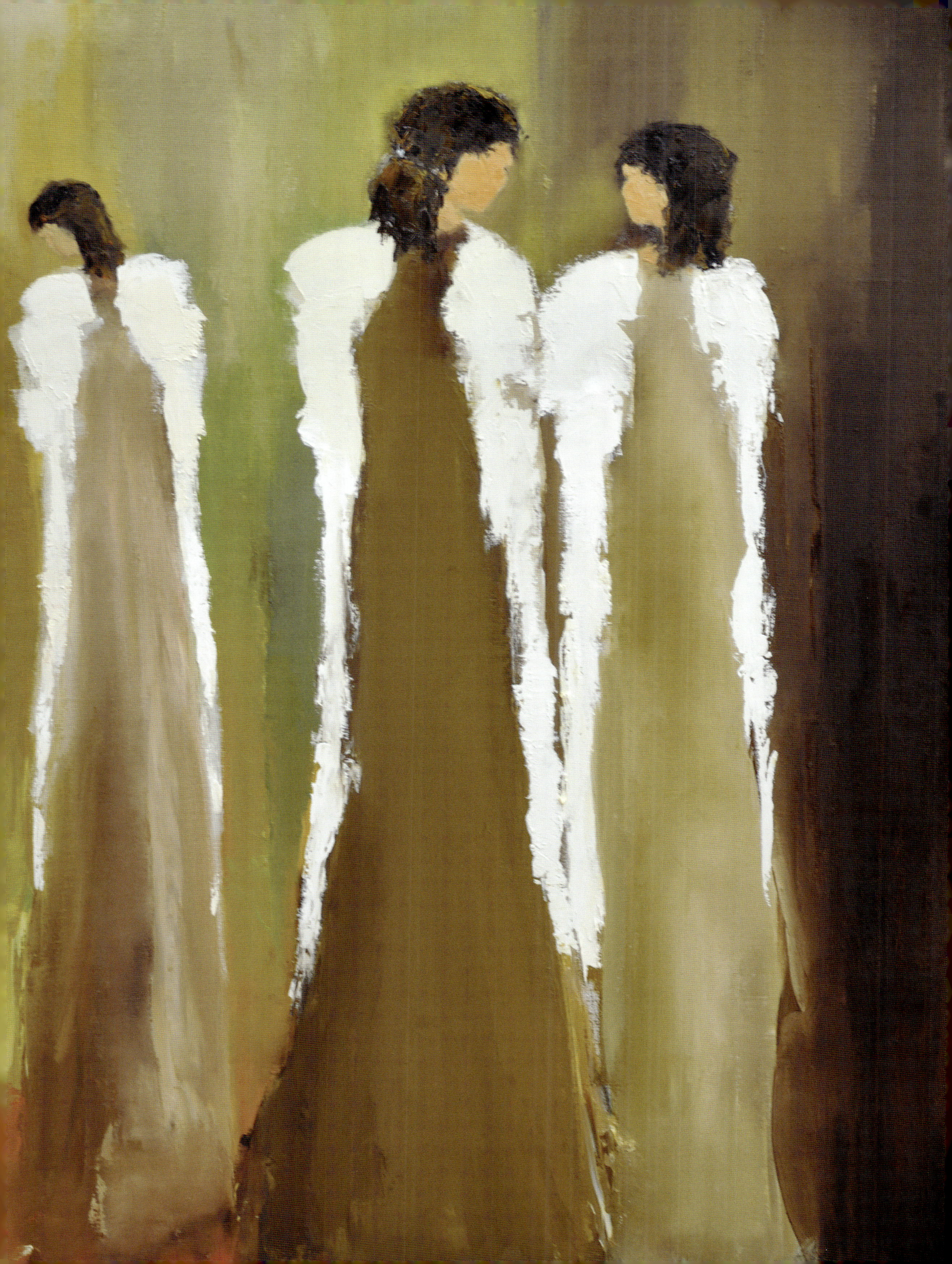

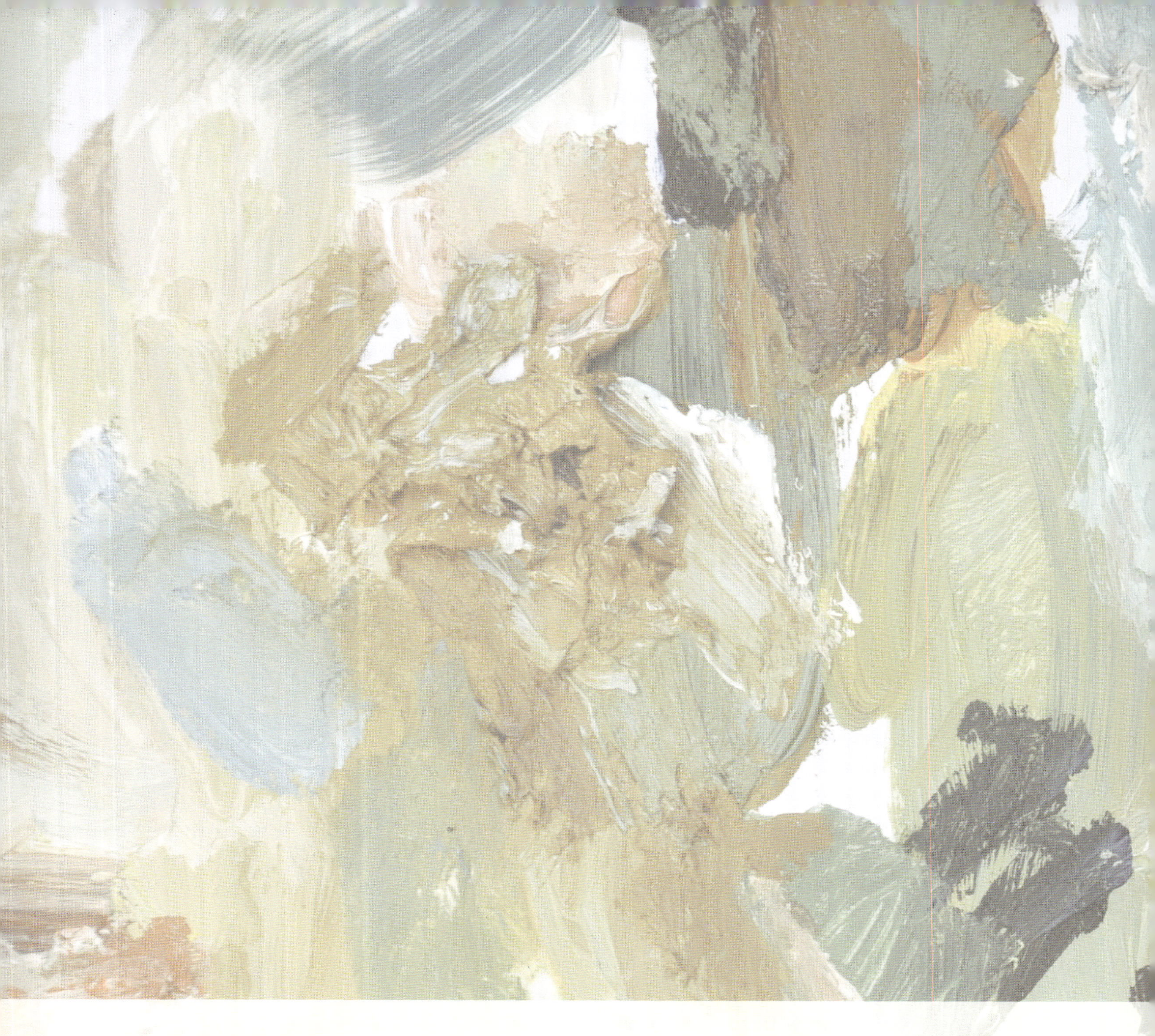

FOR WE ARE GOD'S HANDIWORK, CREATED IN CHRIST JESUS TO DO GOOD WORKS, WHICH GOD PREPARED IN ADVANCE FOR US TO DO.

EPHESIANS 2:10

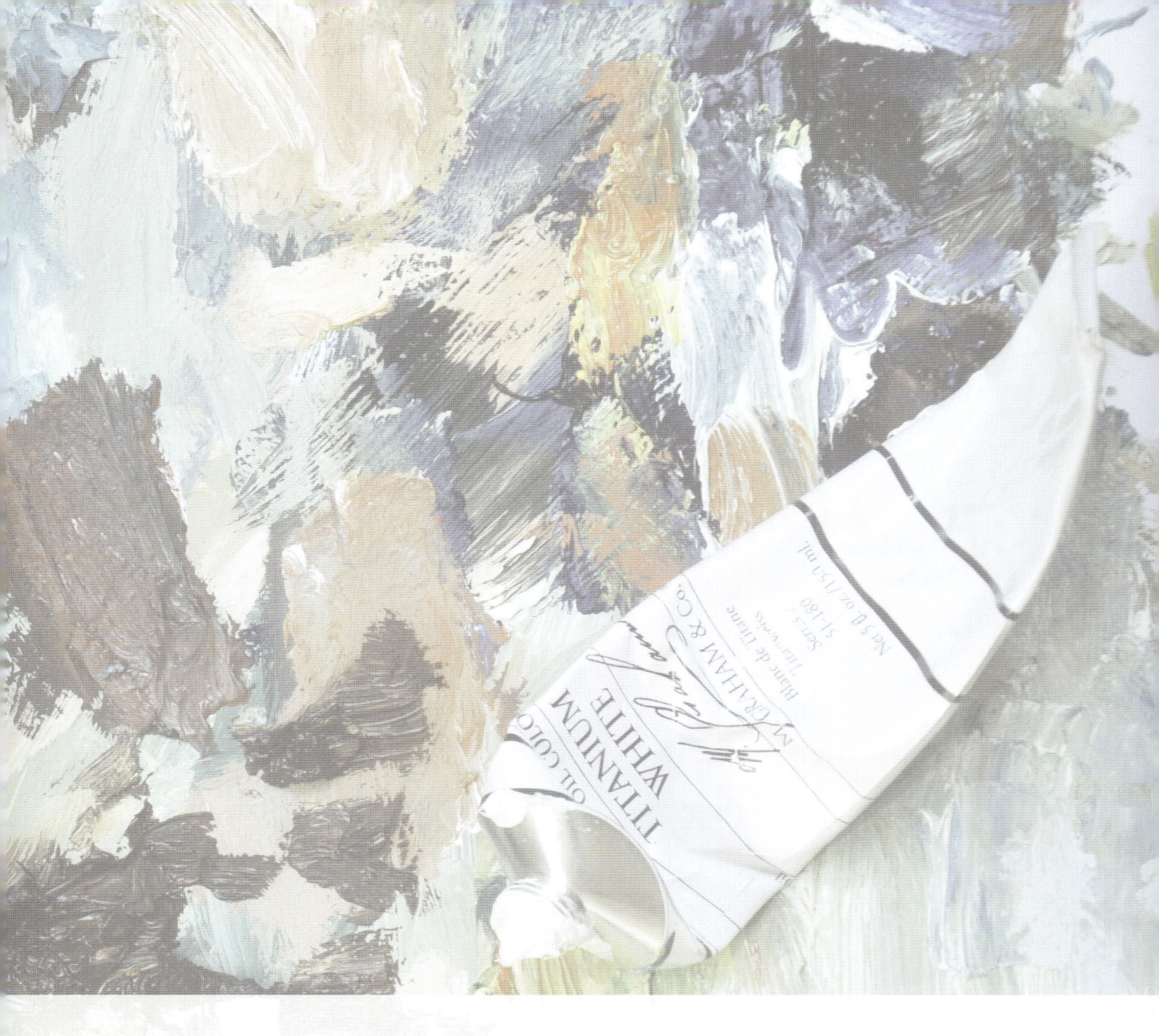

DEVOTIONS

LANDSCAPES

The Narrow Path

I recently completed a meaningful bible study on the names of God. I believe that all His names are powerful and should be called upon daily. During the study, I had a vivid image of Jehovah Rohi –which translated means: The Lord Our Shepherd. As we studied about the Lord as our shepherd, I had an image of God guiding us along HIS path, and it is not your typical path.

A few years ago our family hiked the towns of Cinque Terre (Five Lands) in Italy, which is the rugged portion of coastline on the Italian Riveria. It is comprised of five villages. We were ambitious as a family, and set out early one morning to hike all five lands. The hotel manager took one look at us (especially me wearing sandals that were not made for hiking) and told us to take the train to the first two towns, skipping the hardest part and then hiking the rest. We all agreed that we could do this and set out on our way.

The beginning of the hike was steep and rocky. My husband and I did not think that we were going to make it, and that was only five minutes into this journey! We finally rallied our spirits, got our act together, and said: We can do this!

When the path leveled, it also narrowed. The kids led the way in front, but it was pretty scary because there

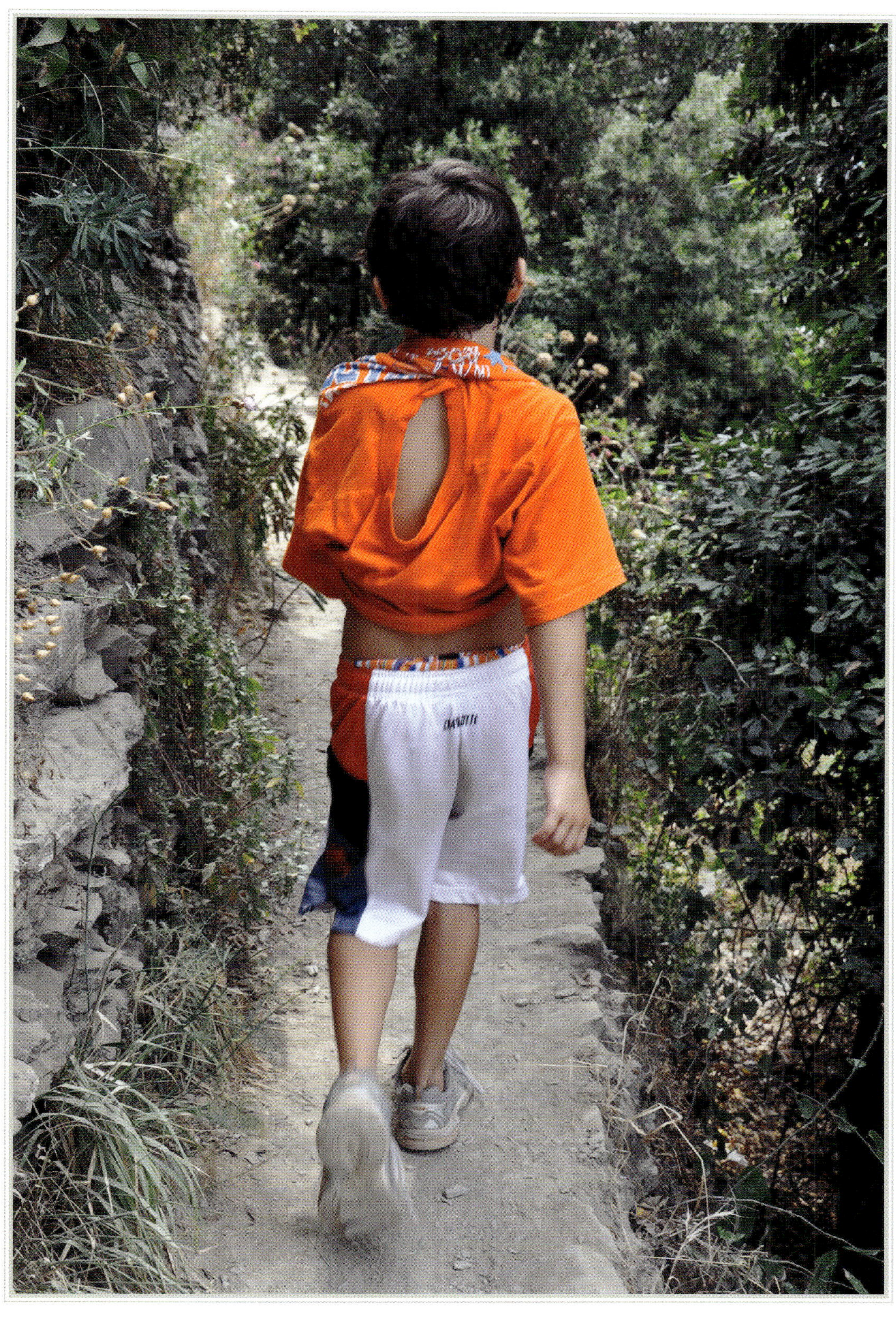

DO NOT GO WHERE THE PATH MAY LEAD, GO INSTEAD WHERE THERE IS NO PATH AND LEAVE A TRAIL.

—RALPH WALDO EMERSON

was a steep drop-off on the side. There was not much to see in front of us because of the green brush surrounding the path, but we kept moving: putting one foot in front of the other, no matter what.

I think that is much like our walk with the Lord as He guides us through life. Sometimes is may be steep and hard and rocky, and you are not sure you can make it. Most always the path is narrow, for God's Word tells us in Matthew 7:13-14: "*Enter through the narrow gate. For wide is the gate and broad is the road that leads to destruction and many enter through it. But small is the gate and narrow the road that leads to life and only a few find it.*"

Being on the hike with the steep rocky parts and the narrow path, putting one foot in front of the other, we eventually rounded the bend to see the most breathtaking view that you can imagine.

We need to know that we have a God who loves us and will guide us through anything that life brings our way. Life may be hard, steep and rocky, whether it is with your marriage, your finances, your children, or your health. But hold fast to God's word and His Character - the Good Shepherd - putting one foot in front of the other that is faith. Faith is the substance of things hoped for, the evidence of things not yet seen.

God is the Good Shepherd and He will guide you through all the paths in our lives and the best is yet to come.

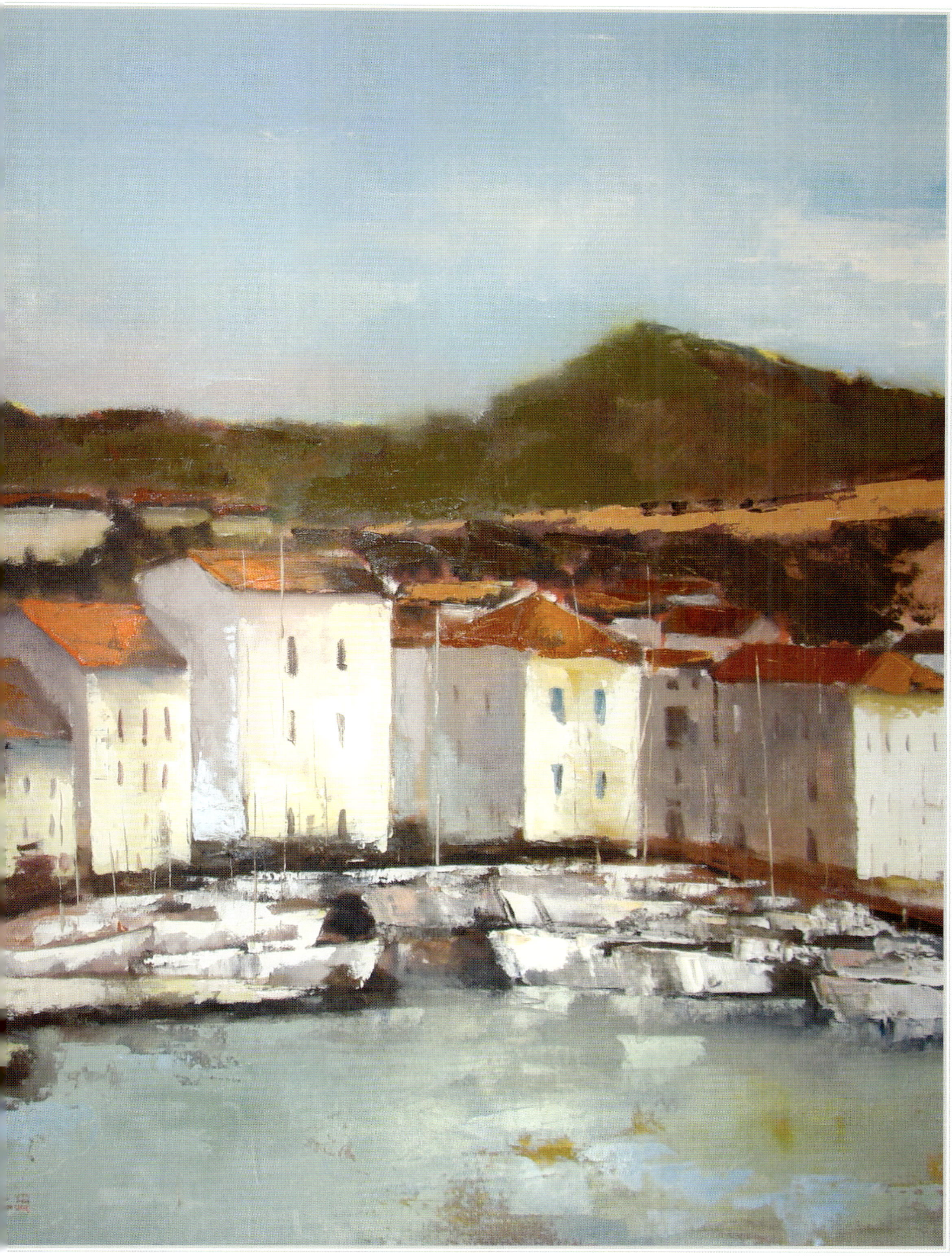

ENTER THROUGH THE NARROW GATE. FOR WIDE IS THE GATE AND BROAD IS THE ROAD THAT LEADS TO DESTRUCTION, AND MANY ENTER THROUGH IT. BUT SMALL IS THE GATE AND NARROW THE ROAD THAT LEADS TO LIFE, AND ONLY A FEW FIND IT.

MATTHEW 7:13-14

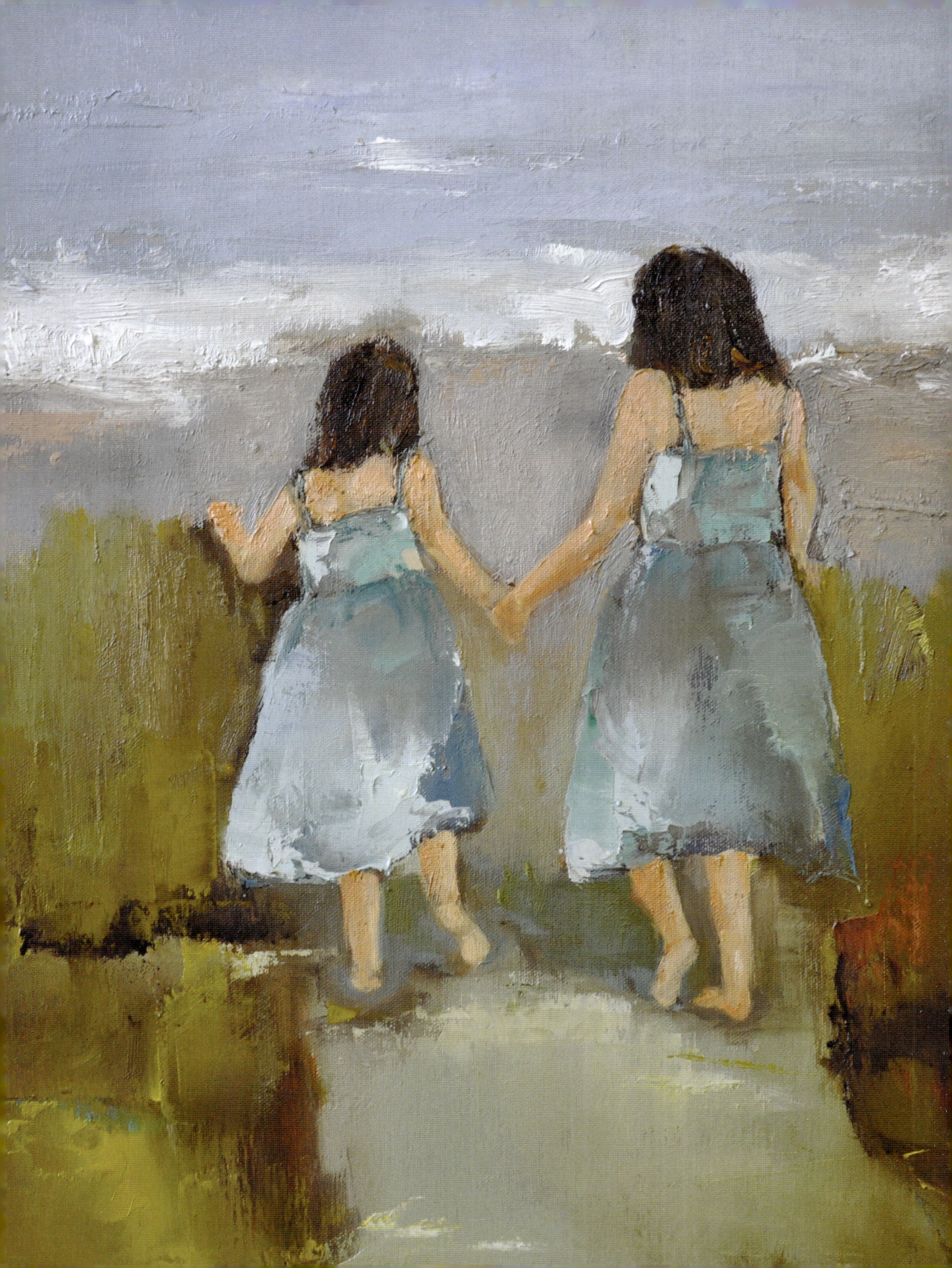

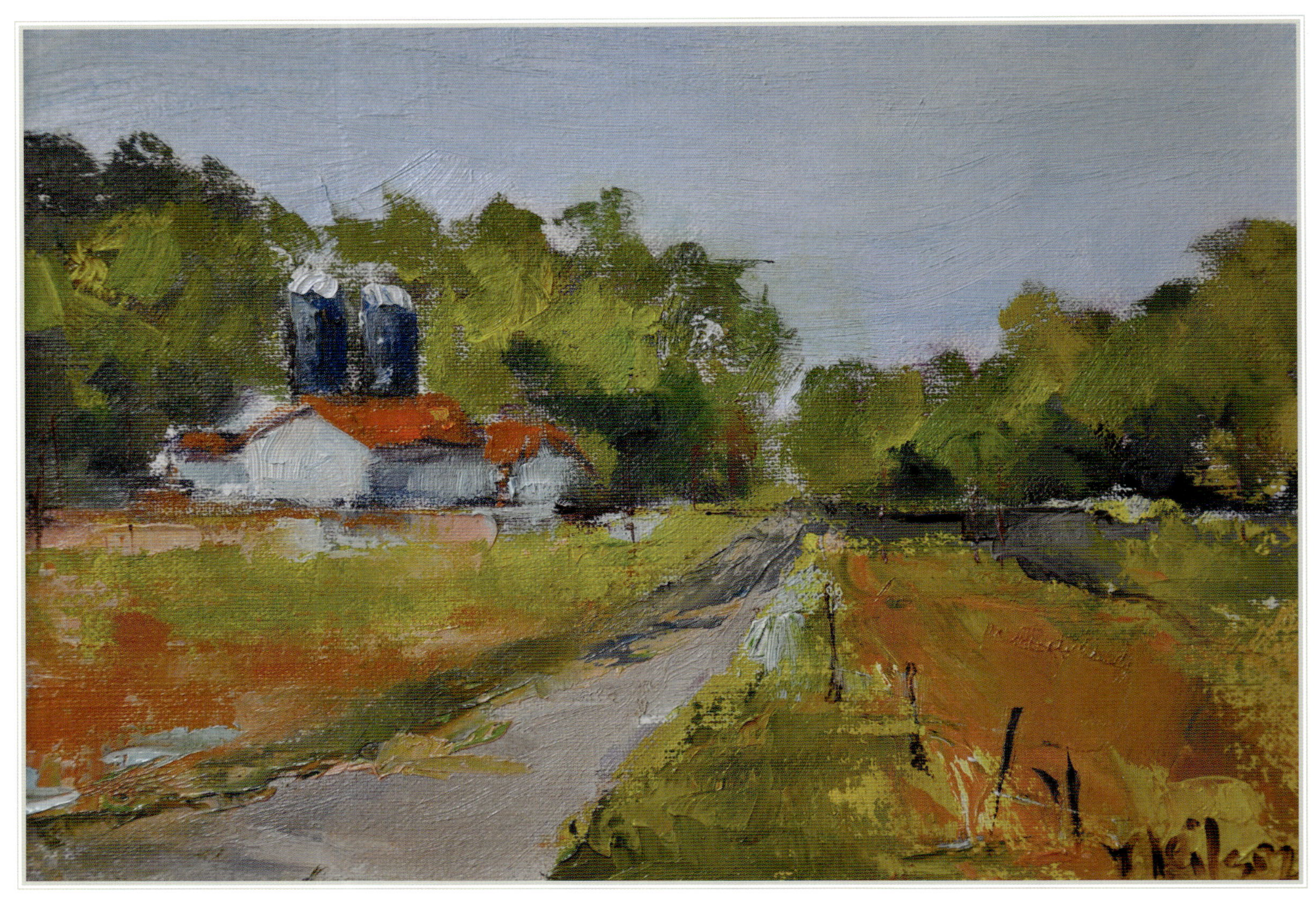

GREAT ART PICKS UP WHERE NATURE ENDS.

—MARC CHAGALL

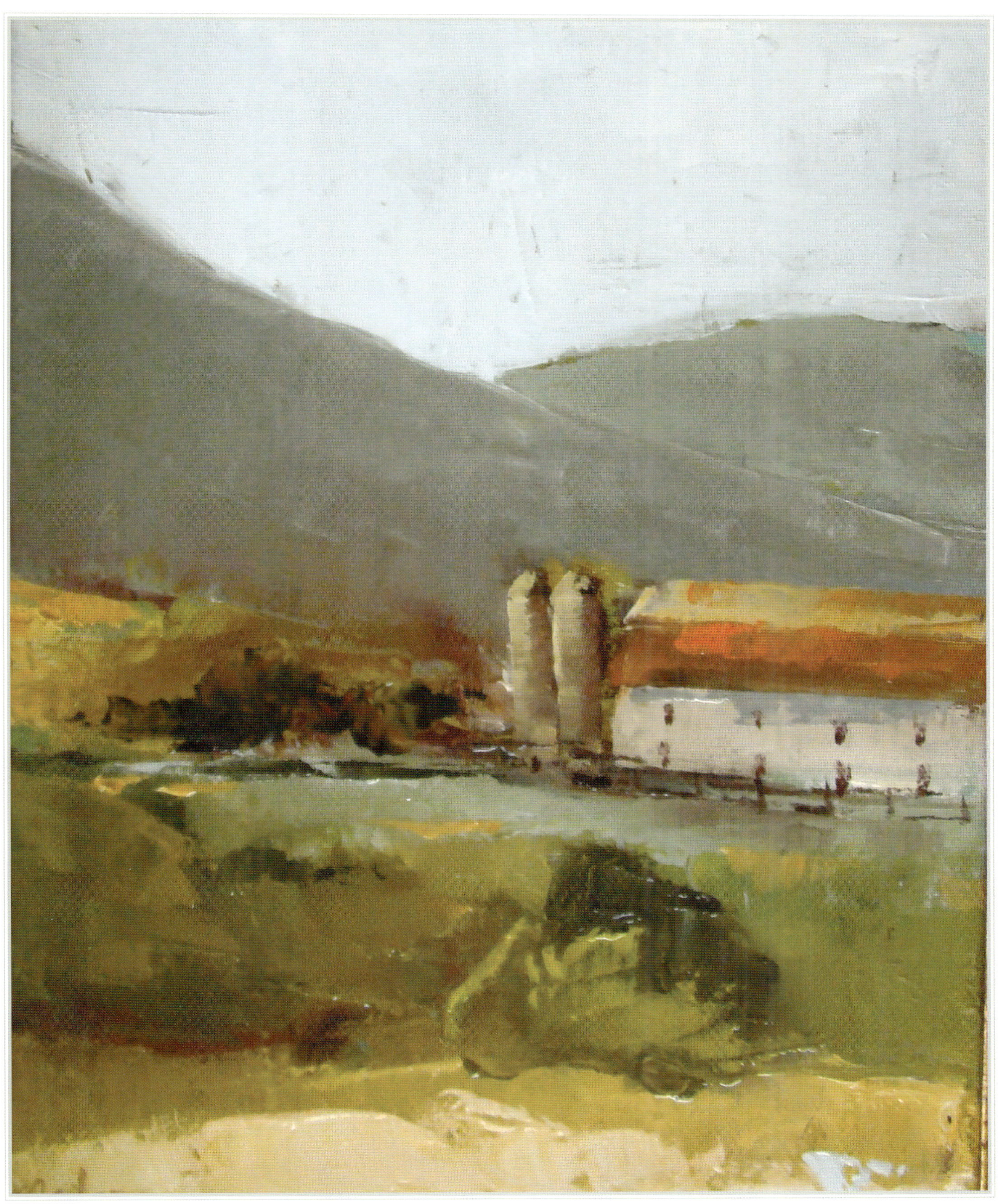

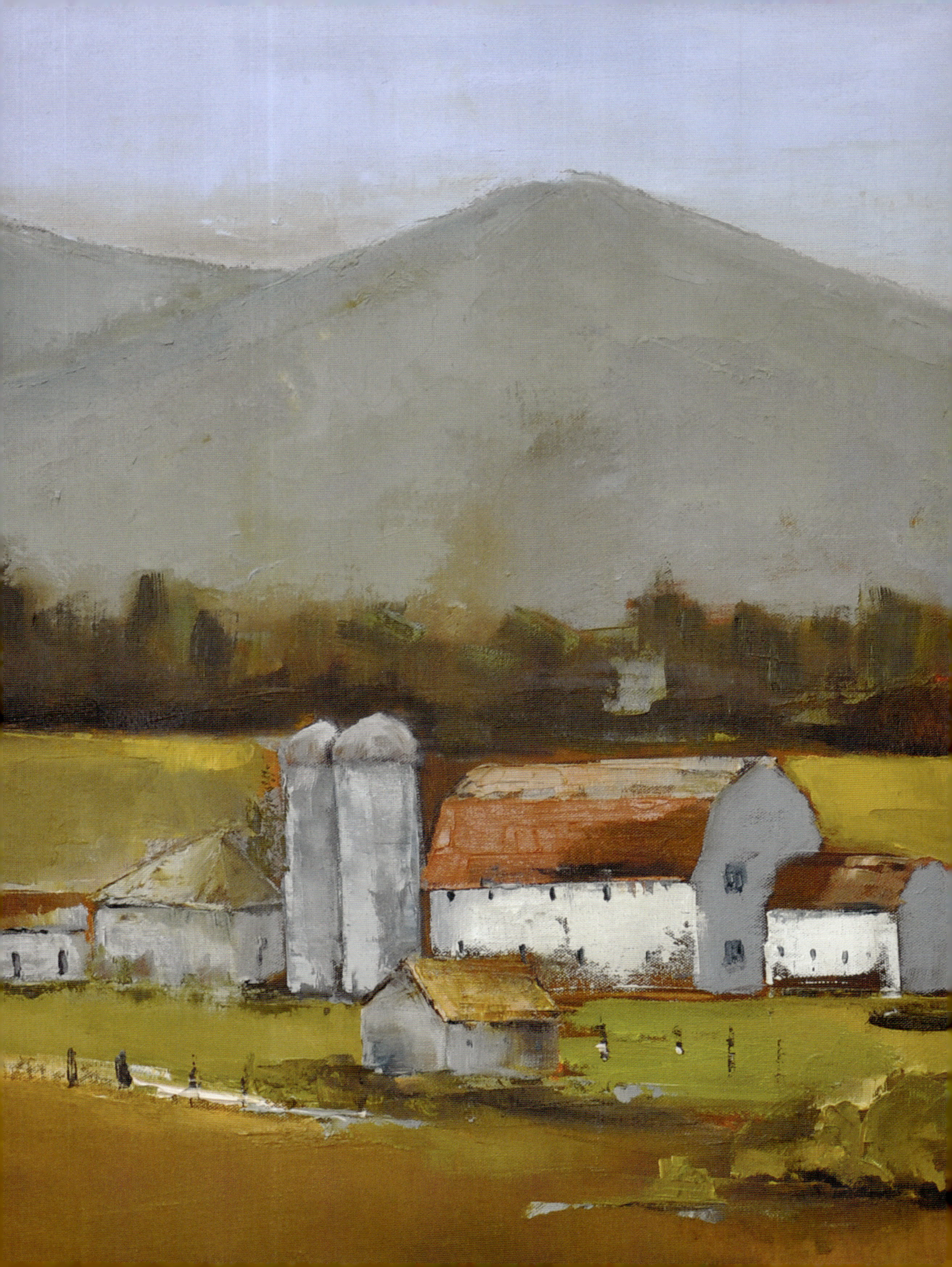

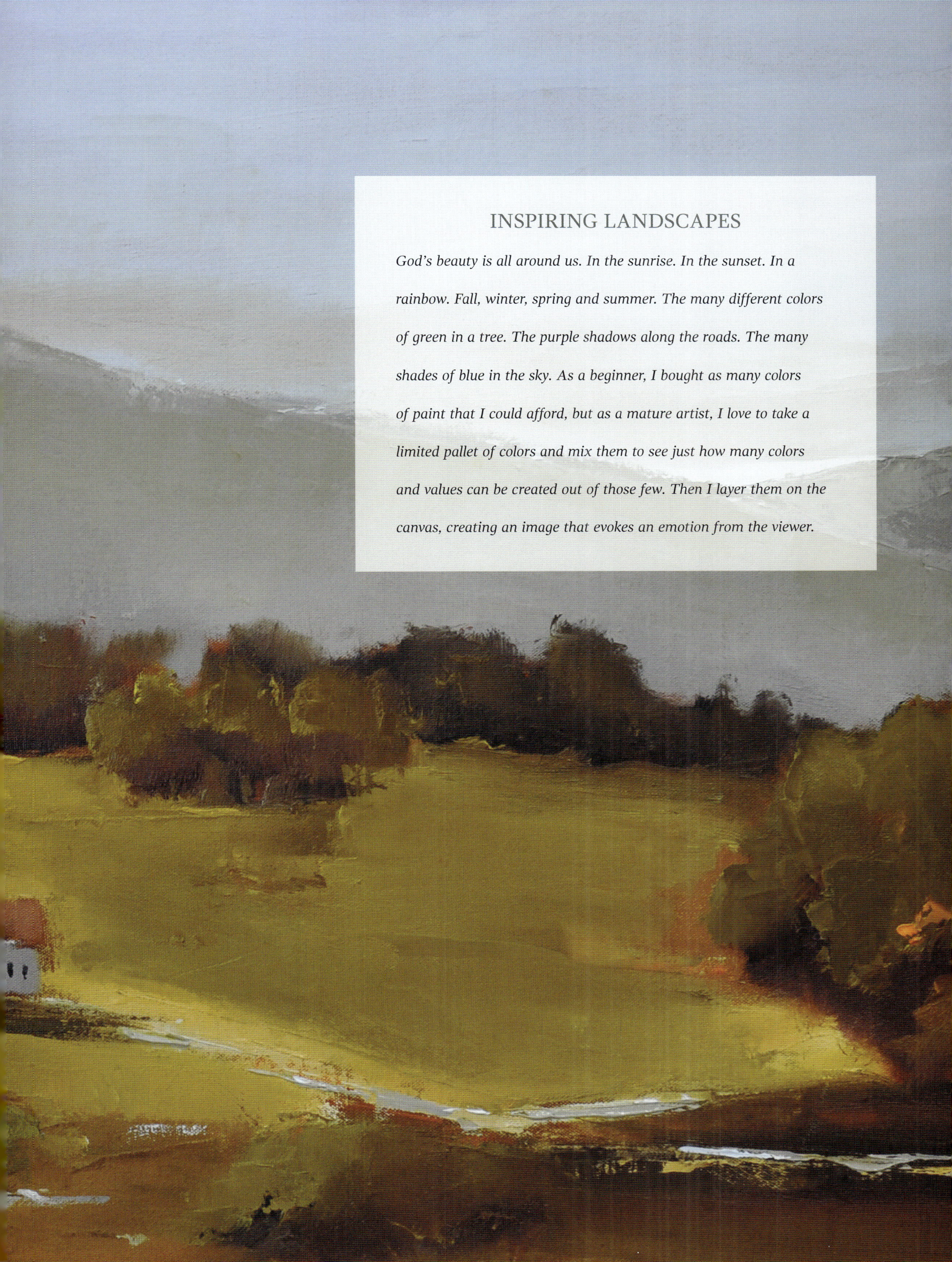

INSPIRING LANDSCAPES

God's beauty is all around us. In the sunrise. In the sunset. In a rainbow. Fall, winter, spring and summer. The many different colors of green in a tree. The purple shadows along the roads. The many shades of blue in the sky. As a beginner, I bought as many colors of paint that I could afford, but as a mature artist, I love to take a limited pallet of colors and mix them to see just how many colors and values can be created out of those few. Then I layer them on the canvas, creating an image that evokes an emotion from the viewer.

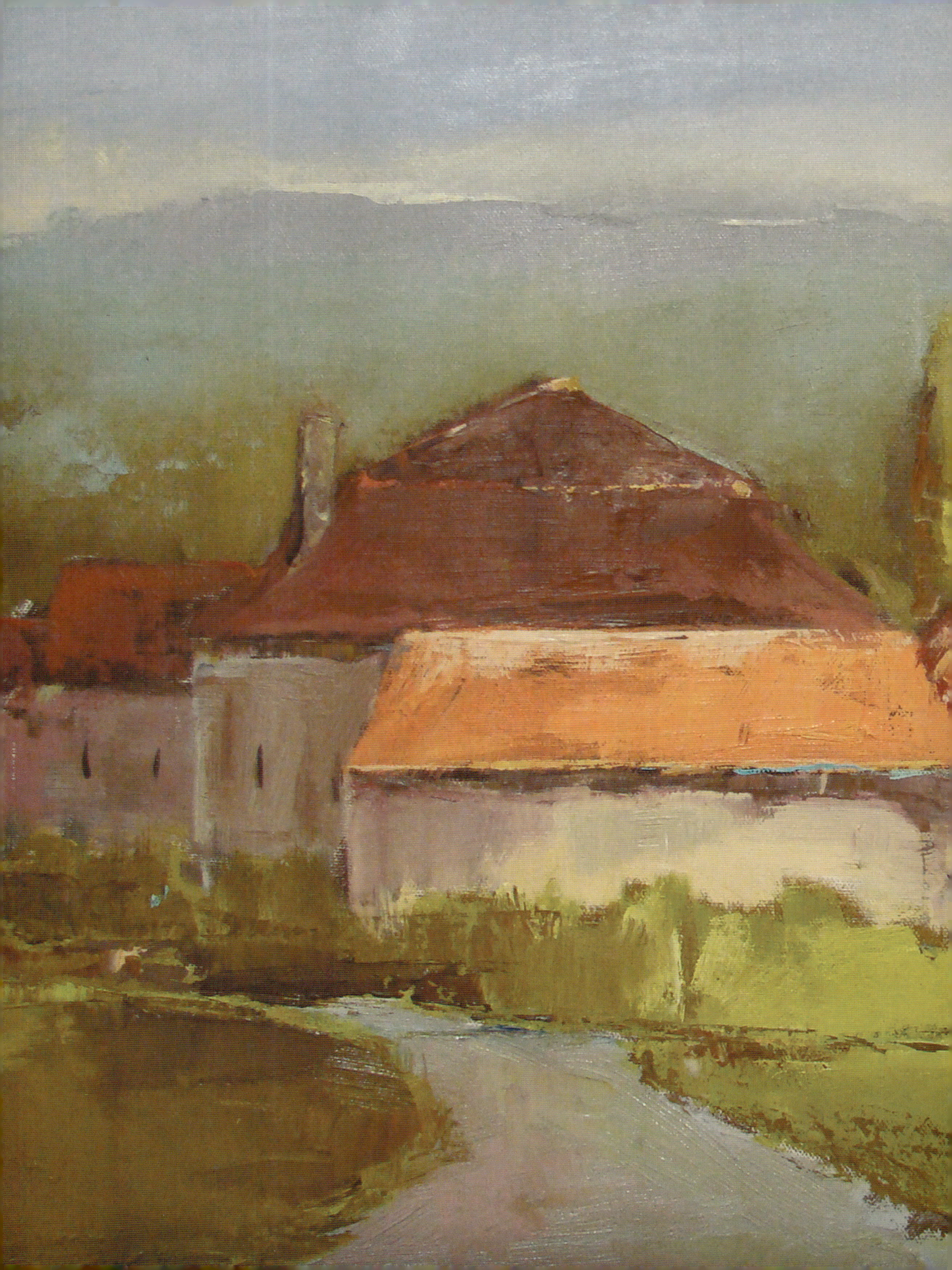

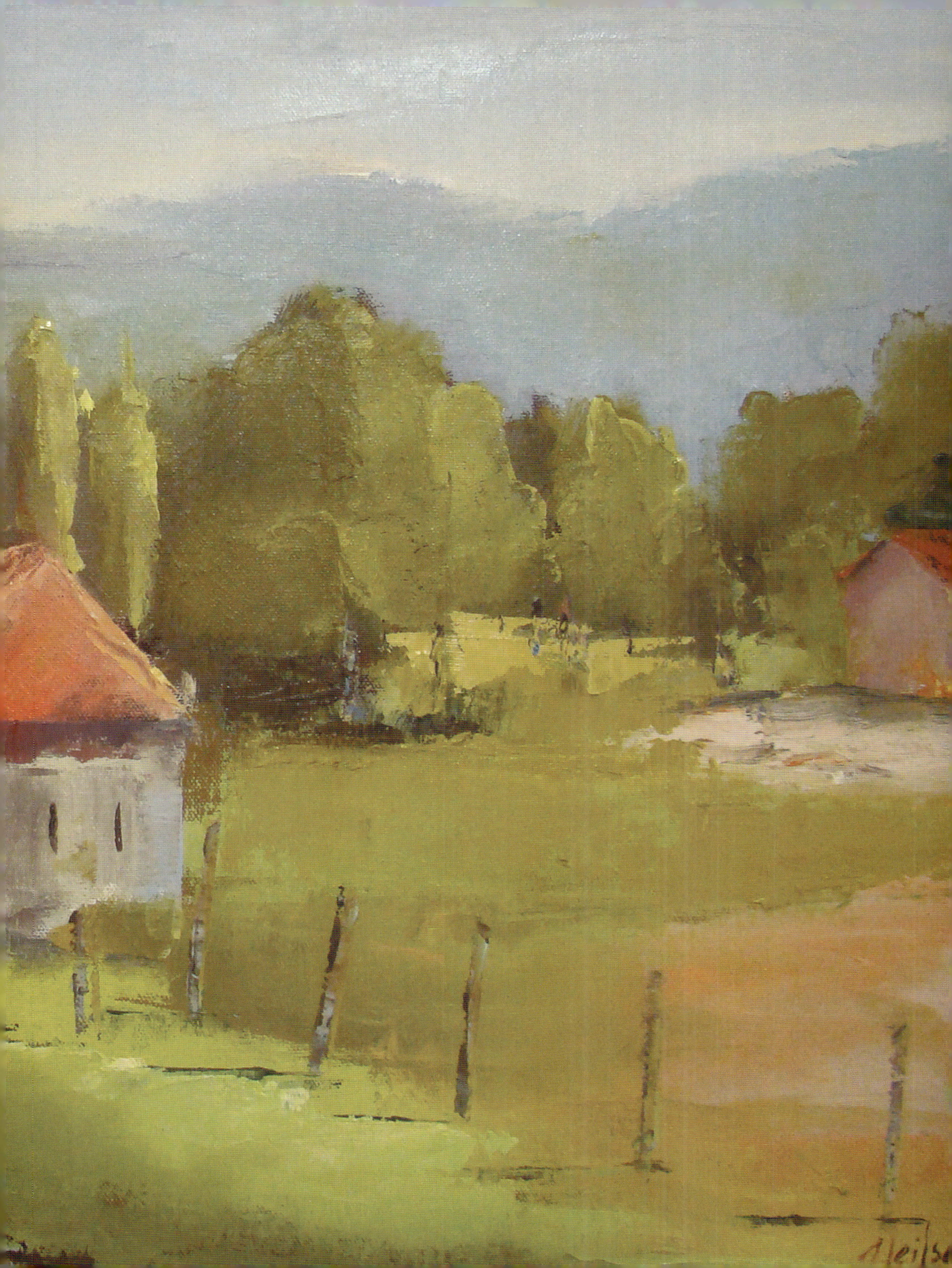

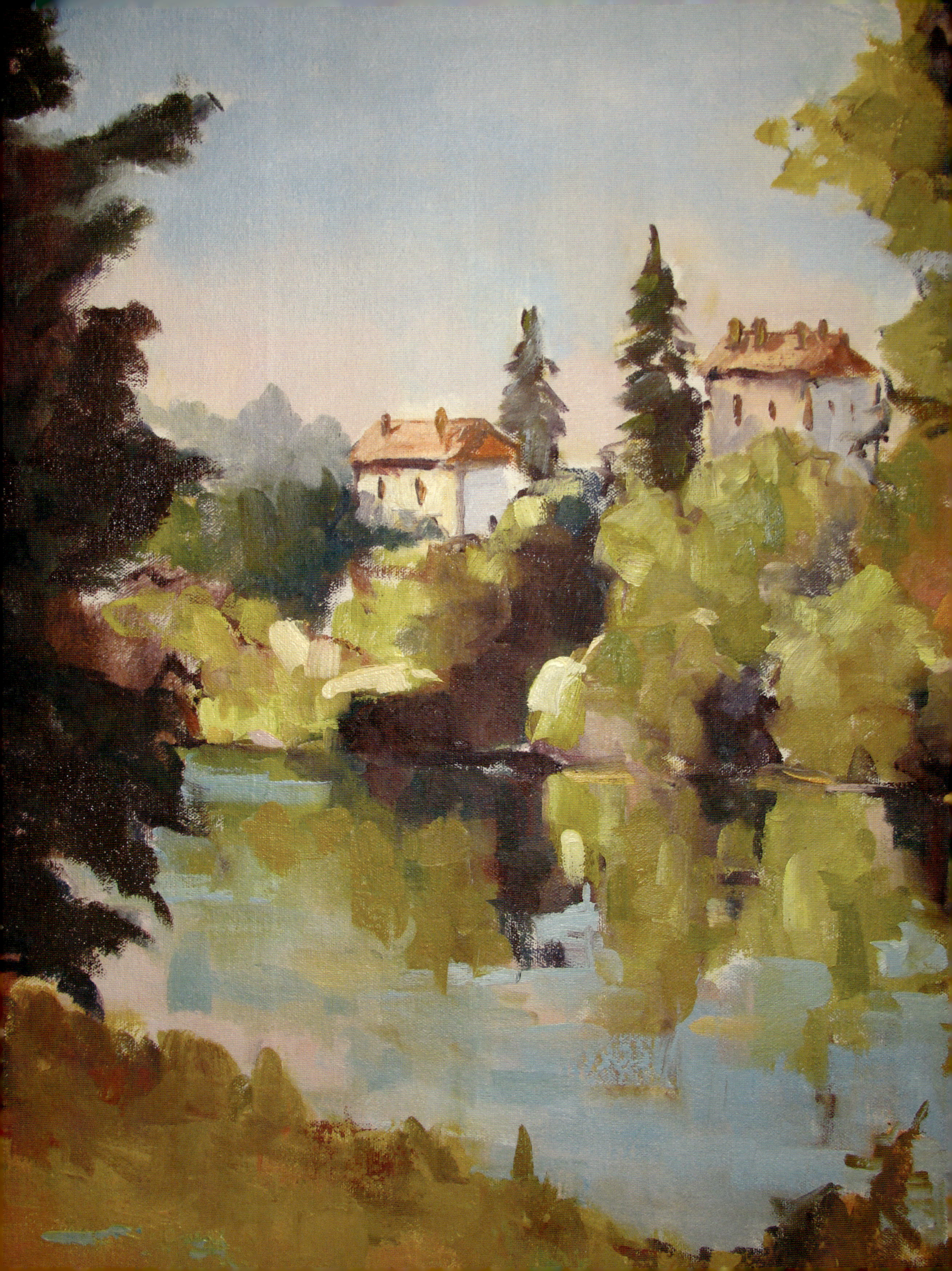

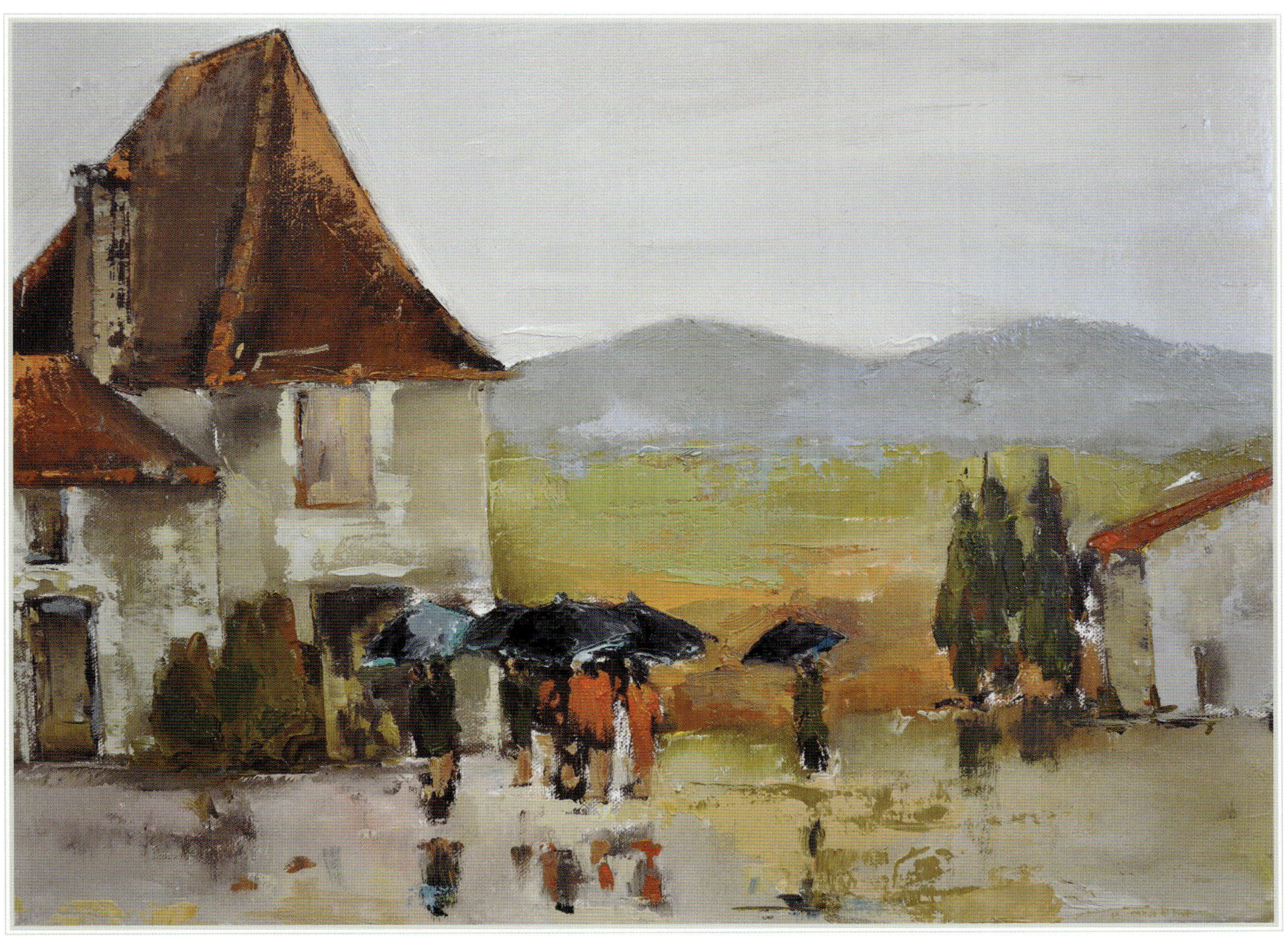

Anne's landscapes, like the rest of her work, are colorful. They employ unique palettes that rely heavily on the interplay of soft color relationships and beautiful grays (chromatic neutrals). The delightful results deliver us to a calmer, simpler, more bucolic state that allows us to feel a peaceful personal revelry.

ANDY BRAITMAN

Artist, Andy Braitman Studios

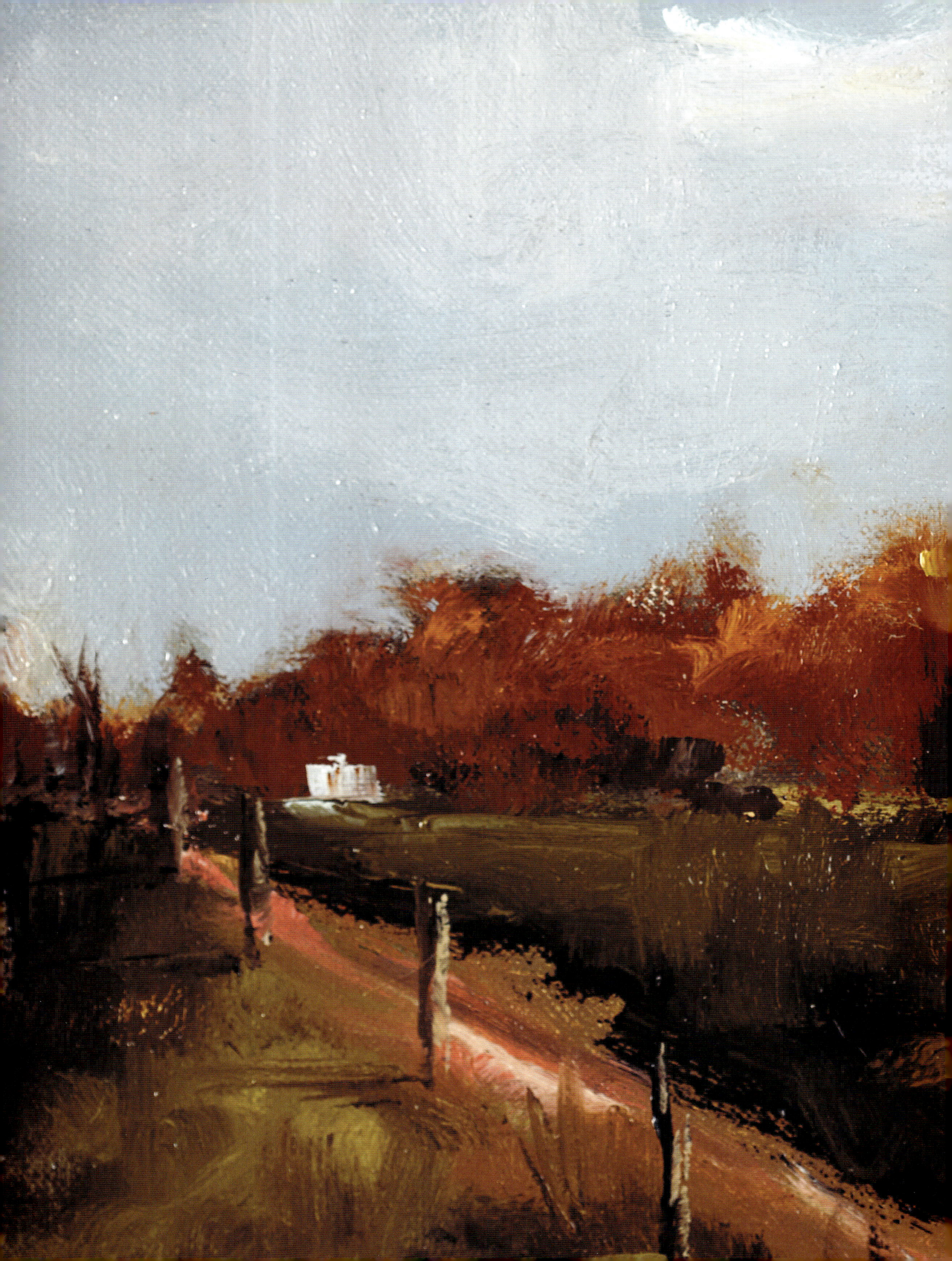

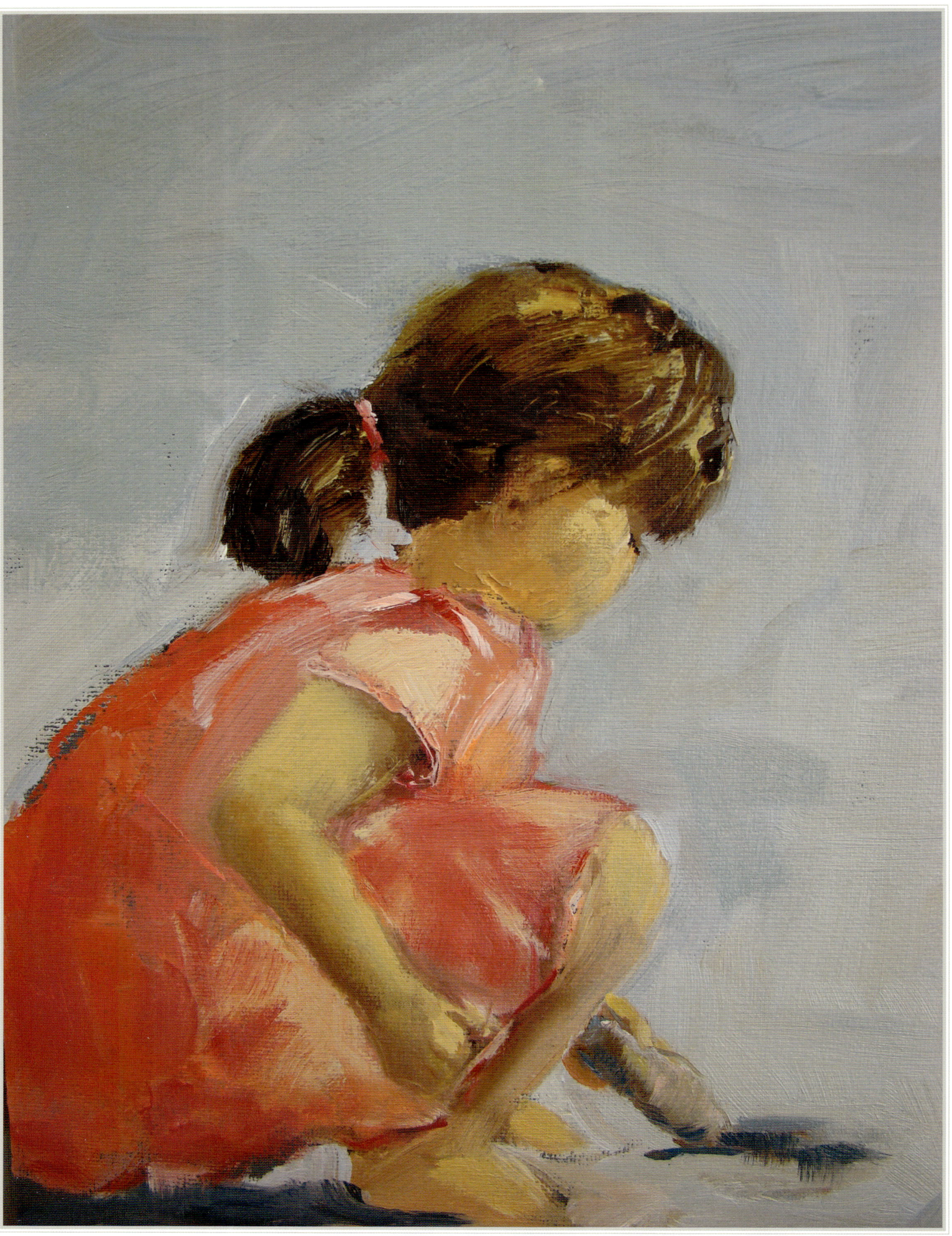

FIGURES

Seashells

It was a beautiful day at the beach. We were there for a girls' trip: my mom, my sister and three step-sisters. I had young children that I left back home with my husband, and promised them I would bring back a large cup of sharks' teeth. I love the beach. I love walking along the beach praising God for his mighty creation. There is such a calmness about hearing the ocean waves crash along the shore.

One morning I was walking ahead of the group praying, talking to God and cleaning up the sharks' teeth. I was a little greedy and giddy with delight of all the sharks' teeth found - I heard a still small voice: "Can you release these sharks' teeth that you have found?" I walked on and pretended I did not hear what I just heard, but it grew louder and louder in my heart. "Can you release these?" After much arguing in my spirit, I knelt down and laid all the sharks' teeth in a neat little pile. I was a little disappointed knowing that my sister would come up behind me and think she hit the jackpot with all the "teeth," and as I looked up I saw the most incredible conch shell about a foot ahead of me. You do not see these kinds of shells at Ponte Vedra Beach, only small crushed shells and lots of sharks' teeth. I was stunned. When I picked it up I heard that still small voice speaking to my heart. "See when you surrender . . . when you TRUST me...when you are obedient to me - see what I can do?"

That shell became a great reminder that when we let go and let God work in our life . . . HE can do so much more than we ever could imagine. The conch shell stayed next to my kitchen sink. It was a daily reminder to always listen to His still small voice, to trust and obey and watch what God can do in our lives.

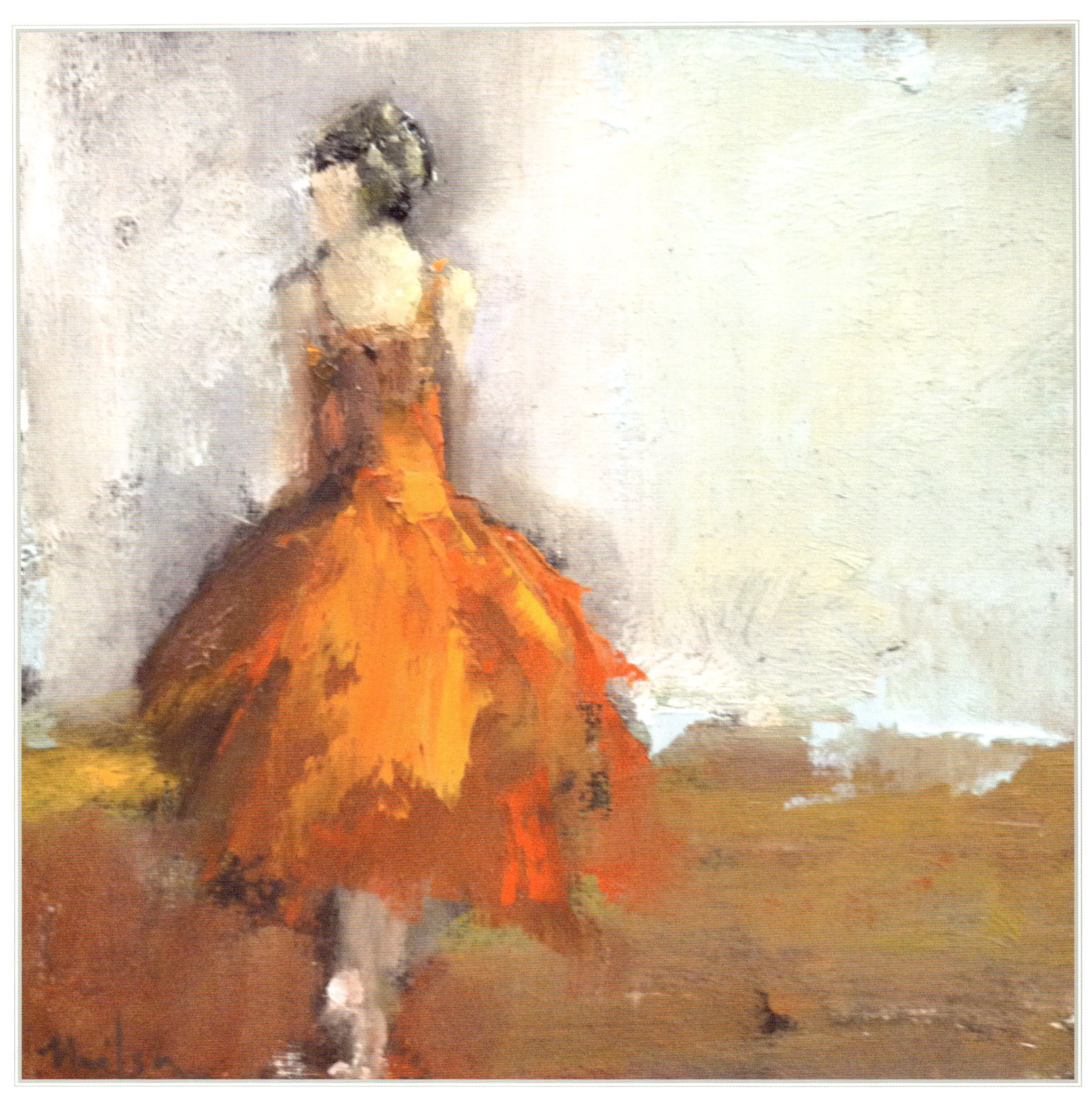

IF YOU COULD SAY IT IN WORDS, THERE'D BE NO REASON TO PAINT.

—EDWARD HOPPER

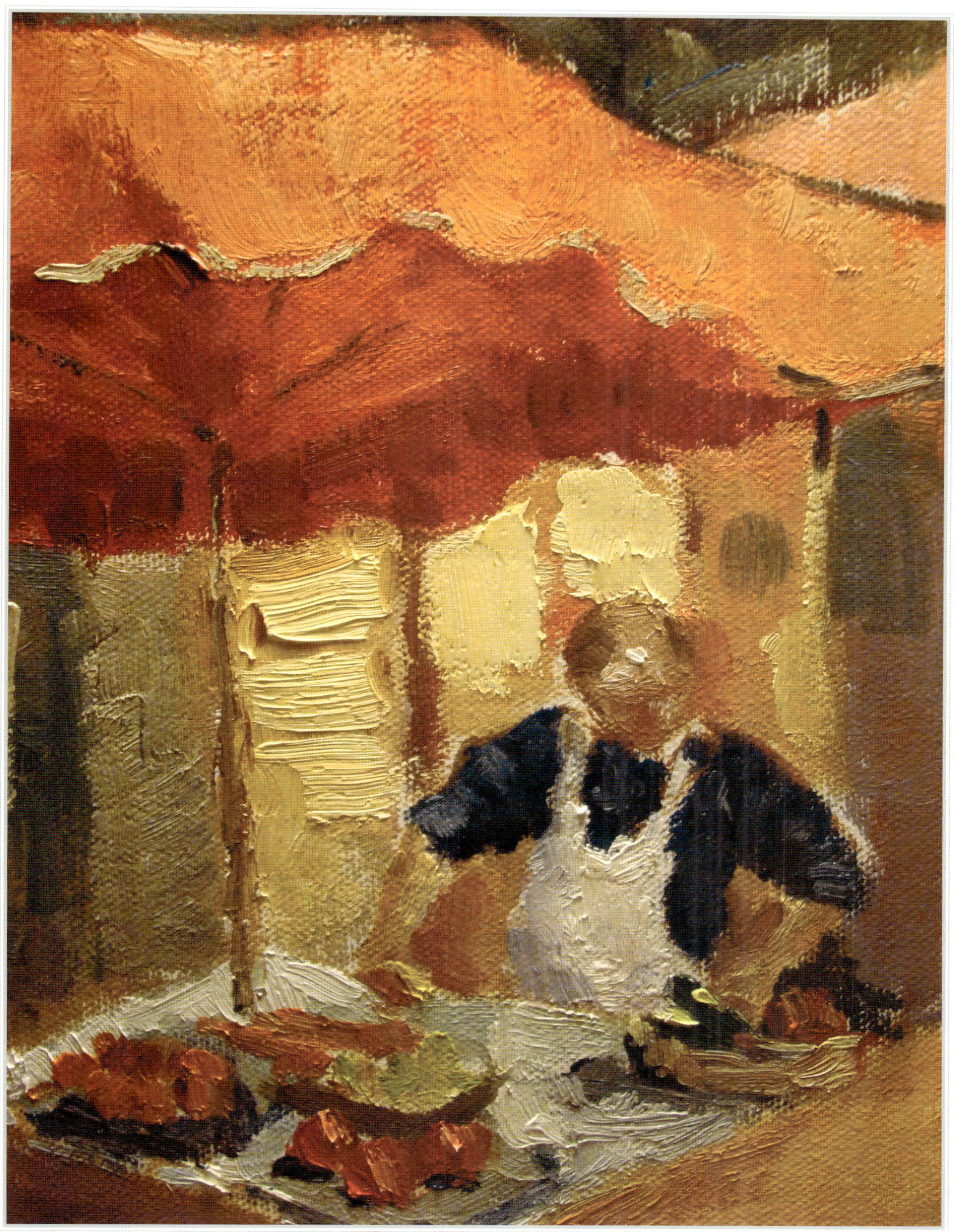

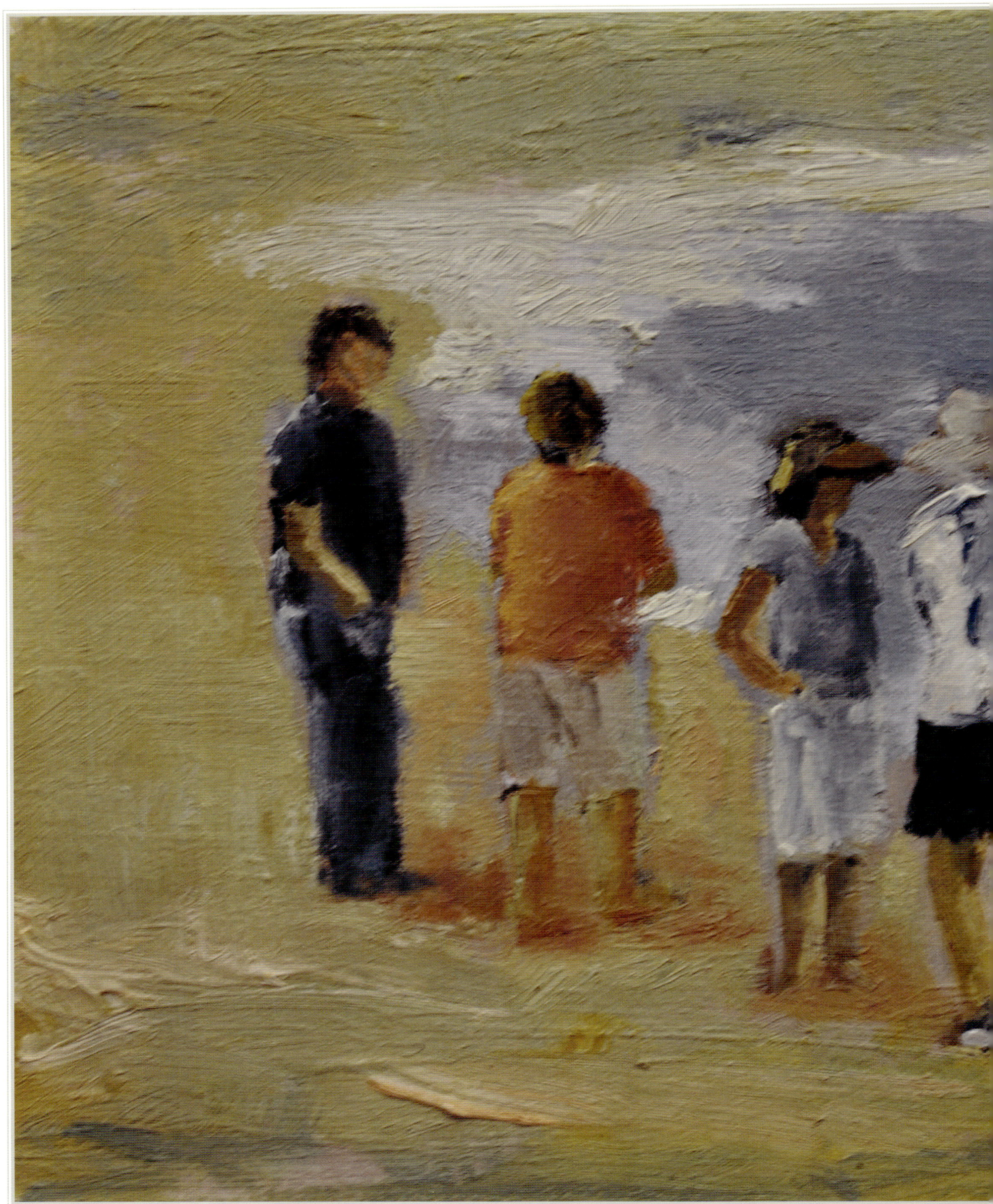

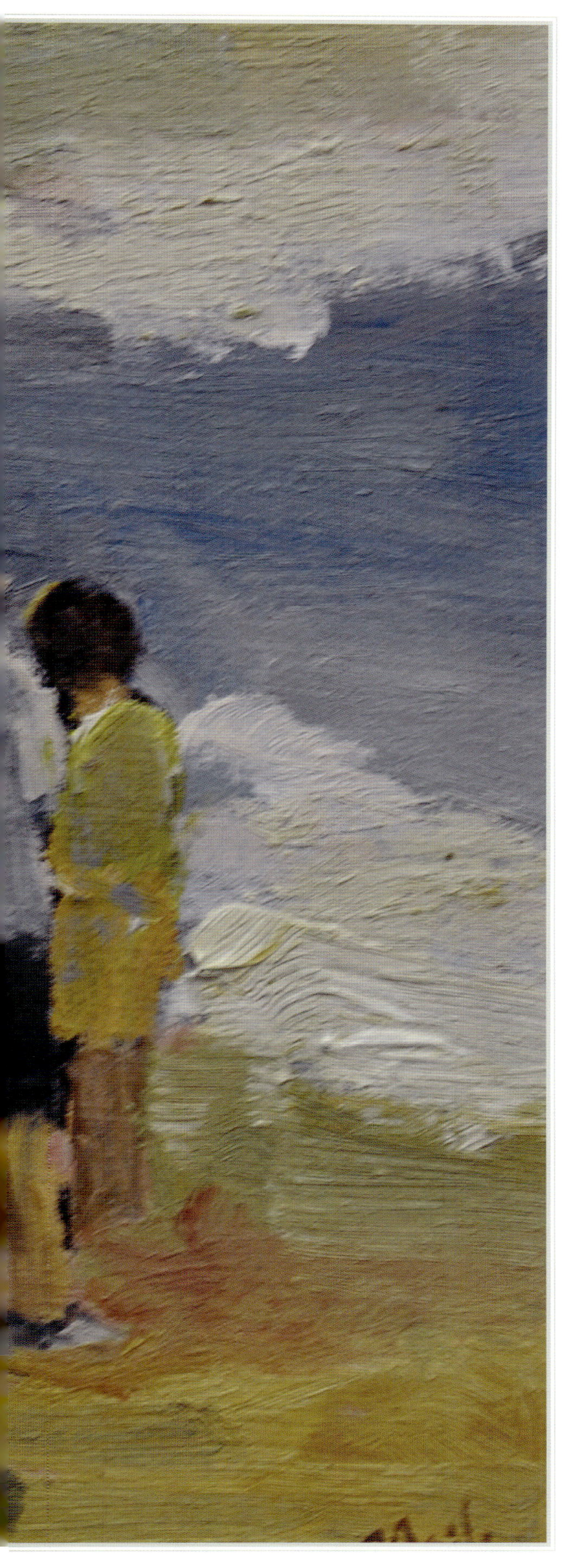

DO NOT BE ANXIOUS
ABOUT ANYTHING, BUT IN
EVERYTHING BY PRAYER
AND SUPPLICATION WITH
THANKSGIVING LET YOUR
REQUESTS BE MADE KNOWN
TO GOD. AND THE PEACE OF
GOD, WHICH SURPASSES ALL
UNDERSTANDING, WILL GUARD
YOUR HEARTS AND YOUR
MINDS IN CHRIST JESUS.

PHILIPPIANS 4:6-7

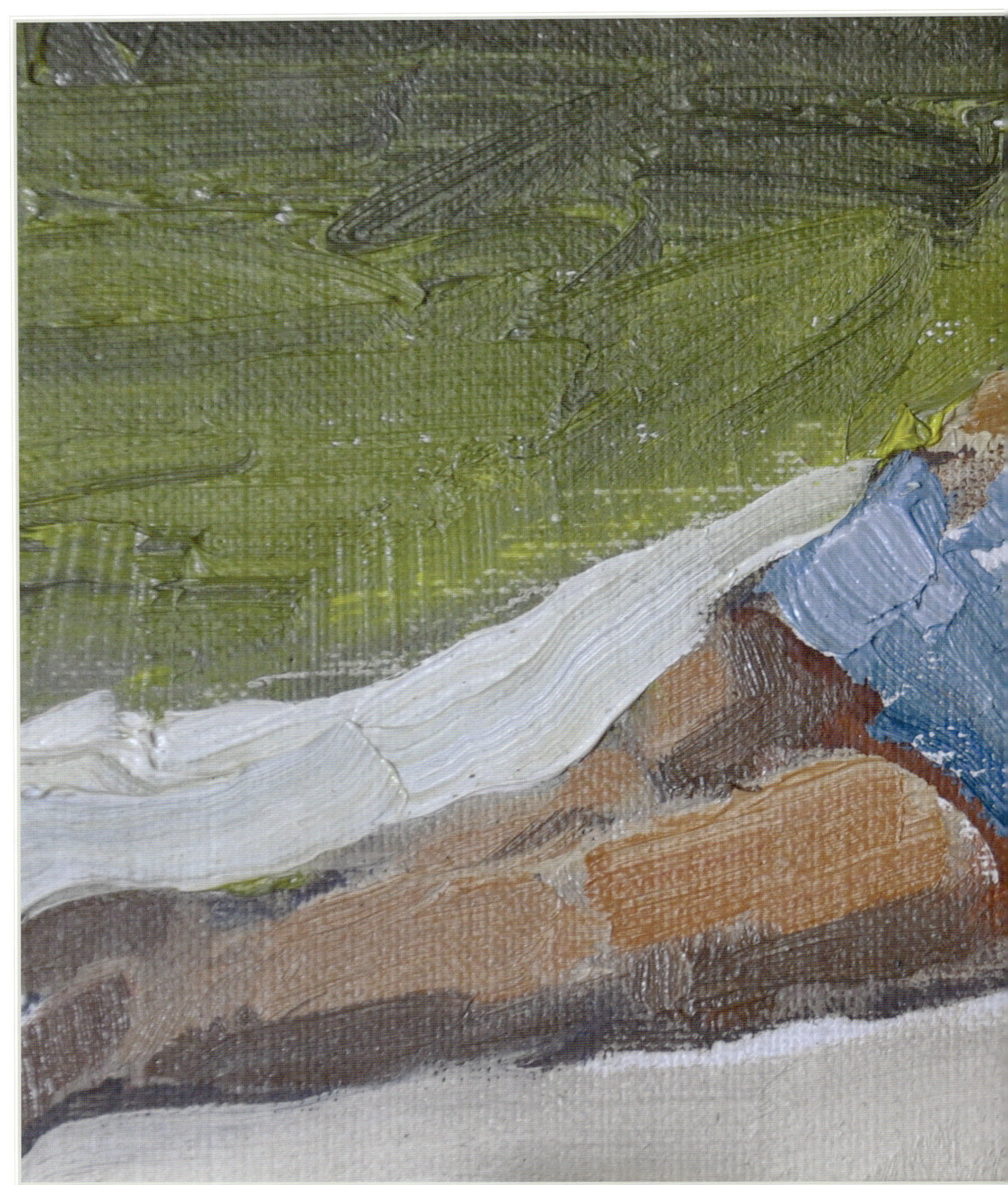

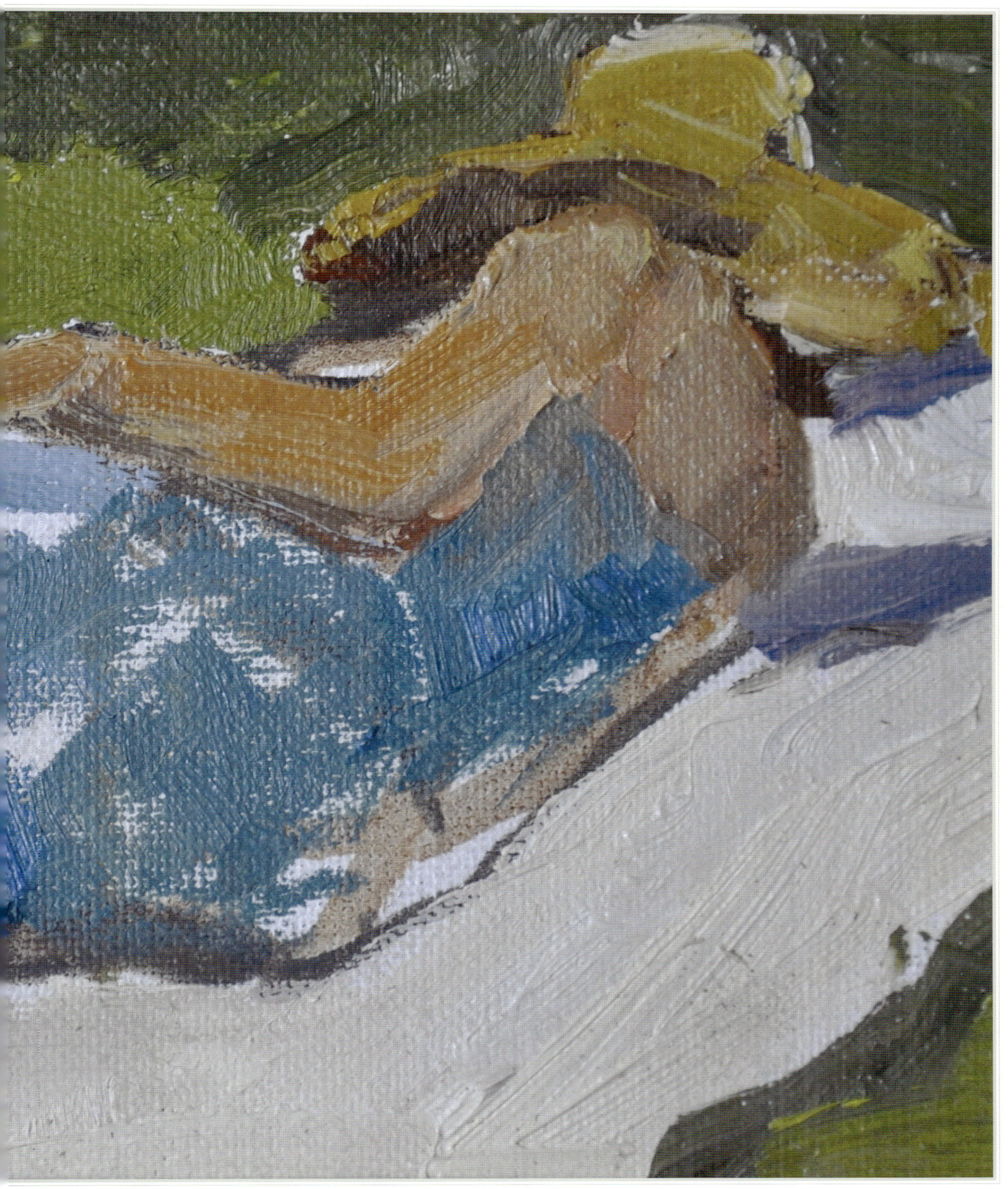

Train Up A Child

My husband and I had somewhat of a fairytale courtship. It was a time in my life where I had totally surrendered my life over to the Lord, and walking in his will, trusting that he would bring me a husband at his appointed time...not my time. We were set up on a blind date in June, 1993. Clark and I had about ten dates over the course of two months. That August, he invited me to the beach to meet his parents and hang out for the weekend. Again, at this point we had only about ten dates, and were just good friends going to the movies and having an occasional dinner. That Saturday at the beach, I can remember sitting in the surf with my prayer sheets praying for friends and family members. I distinctly remember, as I was watching the tide roll in and out, hearing in my mind the Lord speaking to my heart about a mate. "What do you want in a mate, what are your expectations . . ." and my response in my heart was that I wanted someone who loved the Lord, who was kind and had a great sense of humor. I heard the Lord whisper in my spirit: "Are you ready to trust me?"

Forty-eight hours later, Clark sat across from me saying: "I love you. I want to take care of you for the rest of my life. Will you marry me?" Wow! That was quick, Lord!

We have been married 18 years, have four children (three girls and one boy) and live a full life. I always wanted a big family, and I absolutely love our life and the four gifts that were given to me in my children. The three girls came in three years, and the son three years later. Life was physically exhausting, but we pressed on,

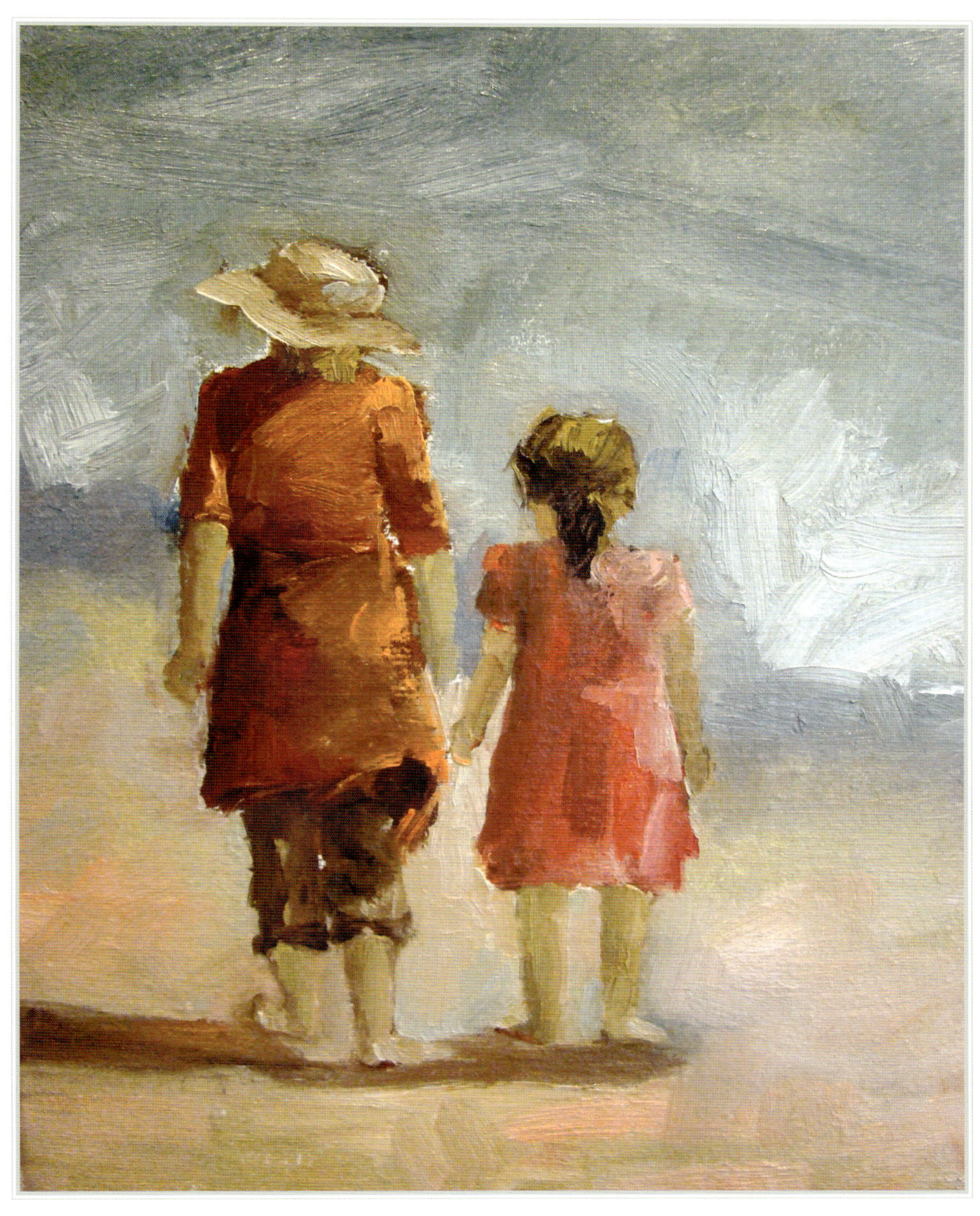

TRAIN UP A CHILD IN THE WAY HE SHOULD GO:
AND WHEN HE IS OLD, HE WILL NOT DEPART FROM IT.

PROVERBS 22:6

knowing that life was precious and we cherished each moment. As parents, we so want them to be happy and do the right thing in life and be kind and loving and compassionate towards others.

My job as a mother is to nurture these precious gifts, sowing seeds of God's truth into their hearts from an early age. My oldest daughter went off to boarding school in the tenth grade, and I was just devastated that someone else would be involved in raising my child on a daily basis. She would not be under my roof with our guidance and it was killing me. As I was driving home after getting her settled in her new home, I sobbed at the idea that she was slowly leaving us. I got home and opened my devotional book, *Jesus Calling*, and these are the words that were gently spoken to my heart:

Entrust your loved ones to ME; release them into MY protective care. They are much safer with Me than in your clinging hands . . . When you release loved ones to Me, you are free to cling to My hand. As you entrust others into My care, I am free to shower blessings on them. My presence will go with them wherever they go, and I will give them rest. The same presence stays with you, as you relax and place your trust in me. —Jesus Calling by Sarah Young (August 23)

I know that these precious gifts - my children - are on loan from a Heavenly Father who loves them far more than I could ever imagine. My job is to train up my children. They are my joy. I know that no matter what — God holds them in the palm of His mighty hand.

TRUST IN THE LORD WITH ALL THINE HEART;
AND LEAN NOT UNTO THINE OWN UNDERSTANDING.

PROVERBS 3:5

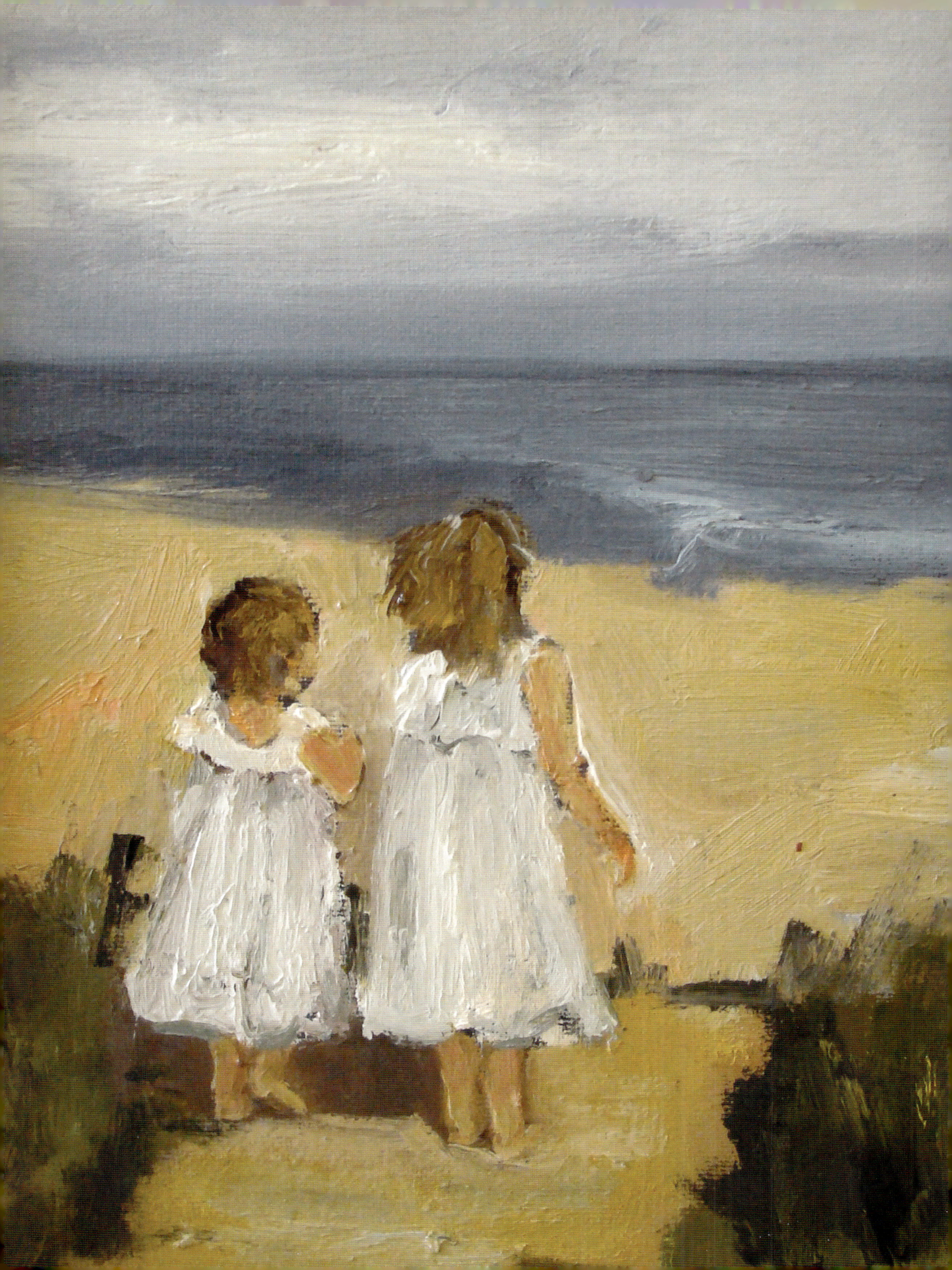

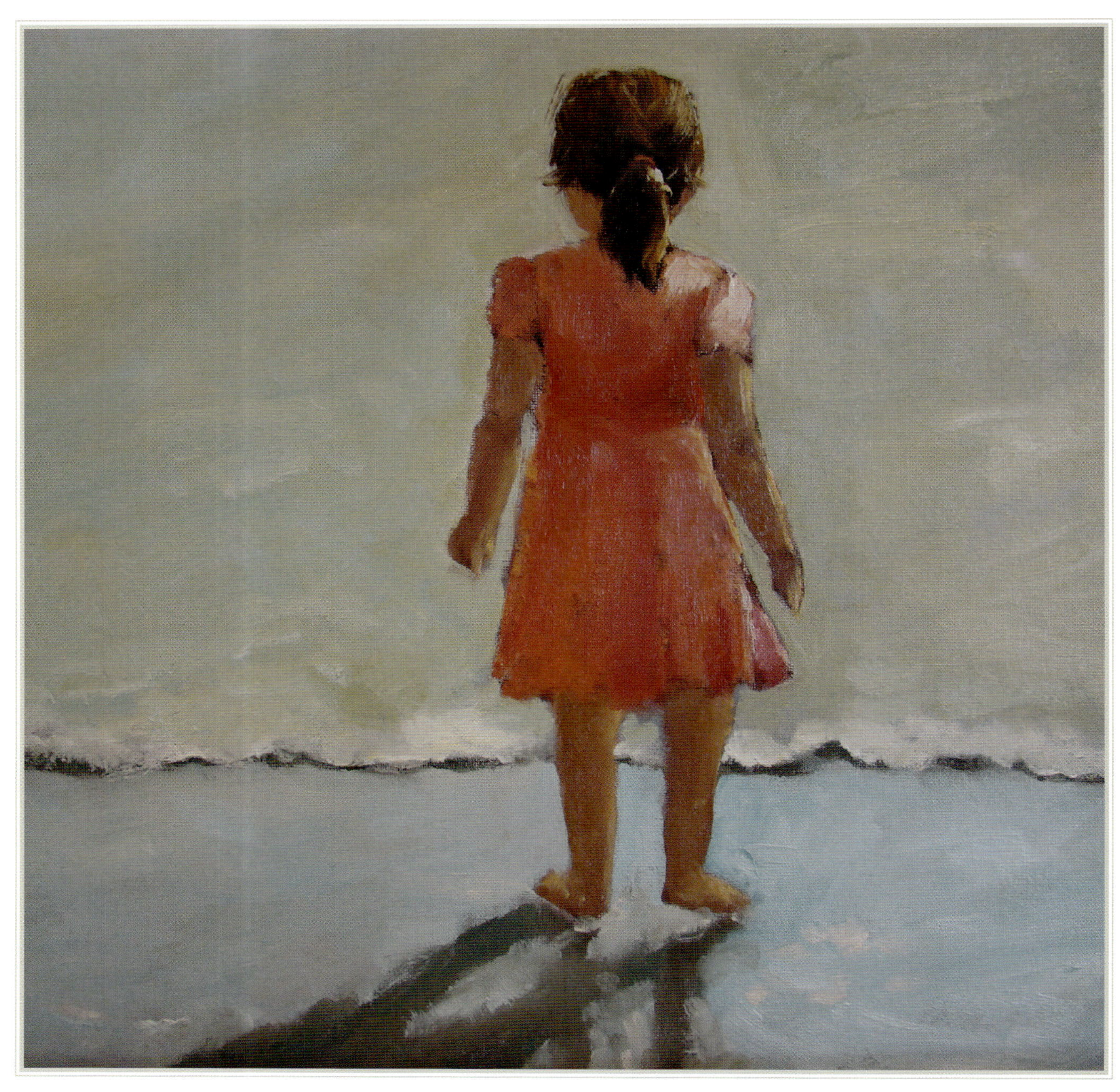

THE DAY THE CHILD REALIZES THAT ALL ADULTS ARE IMPERFECT, HE BECOMES AN ADOLESCENT, THE DAY HE FORGIVES THEM, HE BECOMES AN ADULT, THE DAY HE FORGIVES HIMSELF, HE BECOMES WISE.

—ALDEN NOWLAN

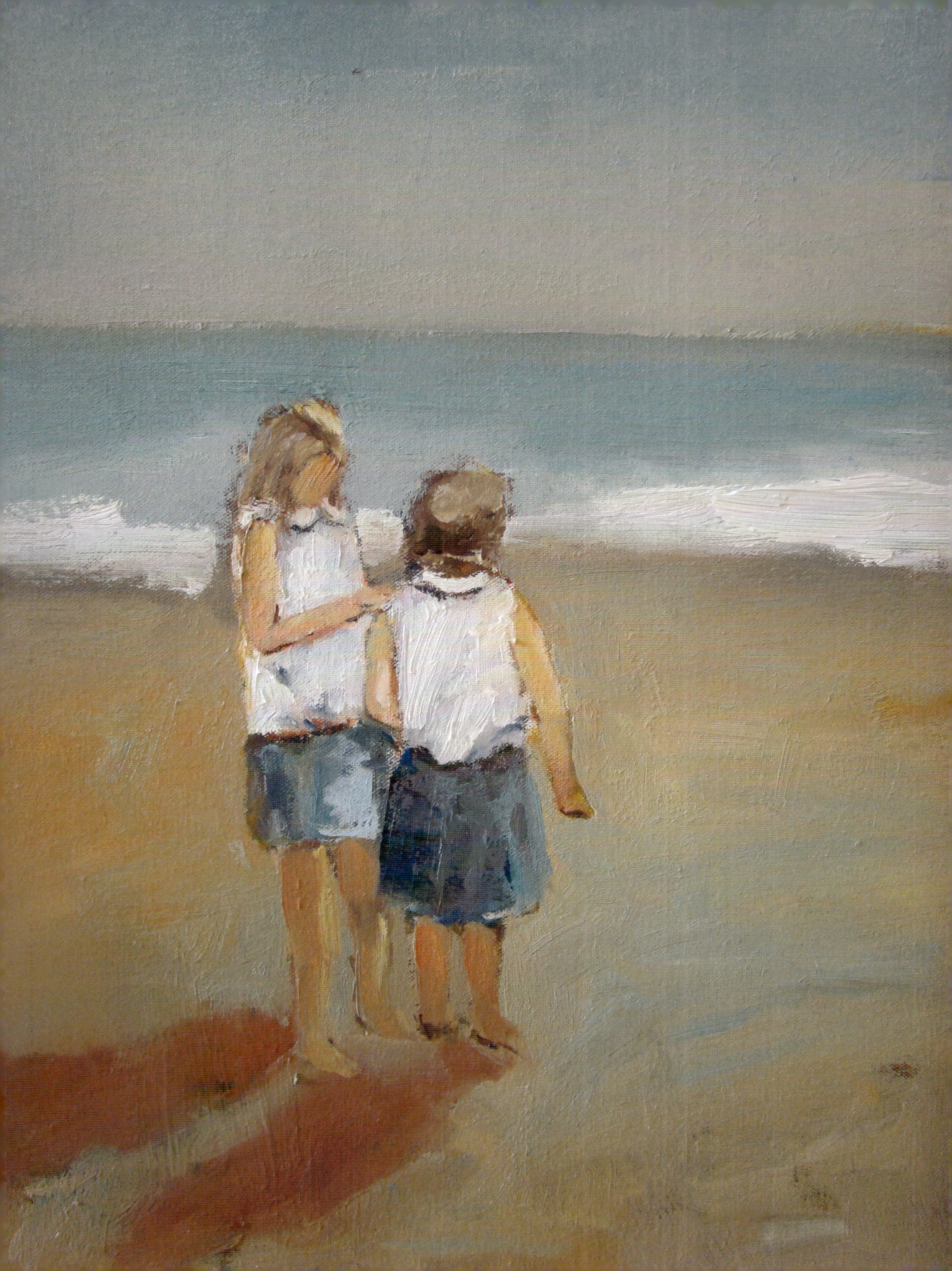

STILL-LIFES

Seek and Obey

There are days when life seems to be clicking right along and everything is good. The kids are not fighting, the house is clean, work gets done, and there are no glitches in your day. Ahh, life is good. Then there are days that you don't even know what happened, with hard bumps and interruptions all day long. Short tempers. Dirty laundry everywhere. Disgruntled kids. You know what I am talking about. Well, I have learned that when I seek God first in ALL that I do, in work, in family, in my marriage, then all things will fall into place. Seek first and Obey.

My daughter Catherine was about nine years old when she lost a little black stuffed animal at Church one Sunday. This broke our rule that our kids were never to take their "love item" out of the home, because if they lost it or left it somewhere the nighttime routine would be a nightmare. Catherine shed many tears as the church's halls and classrooms were searched, and we still could not find our lost stuff animal. We prayed that God would help us find our little lost love item. Nights were not fun, but eventually we found another animal to snuggle with and all was well.

A few weeks later, I was having my morning prayer time in the chapel at our church. Deep in prayer for our clergy, my family and people in need, I felt a slight interruption and need to pray for the lost stuffed dog.

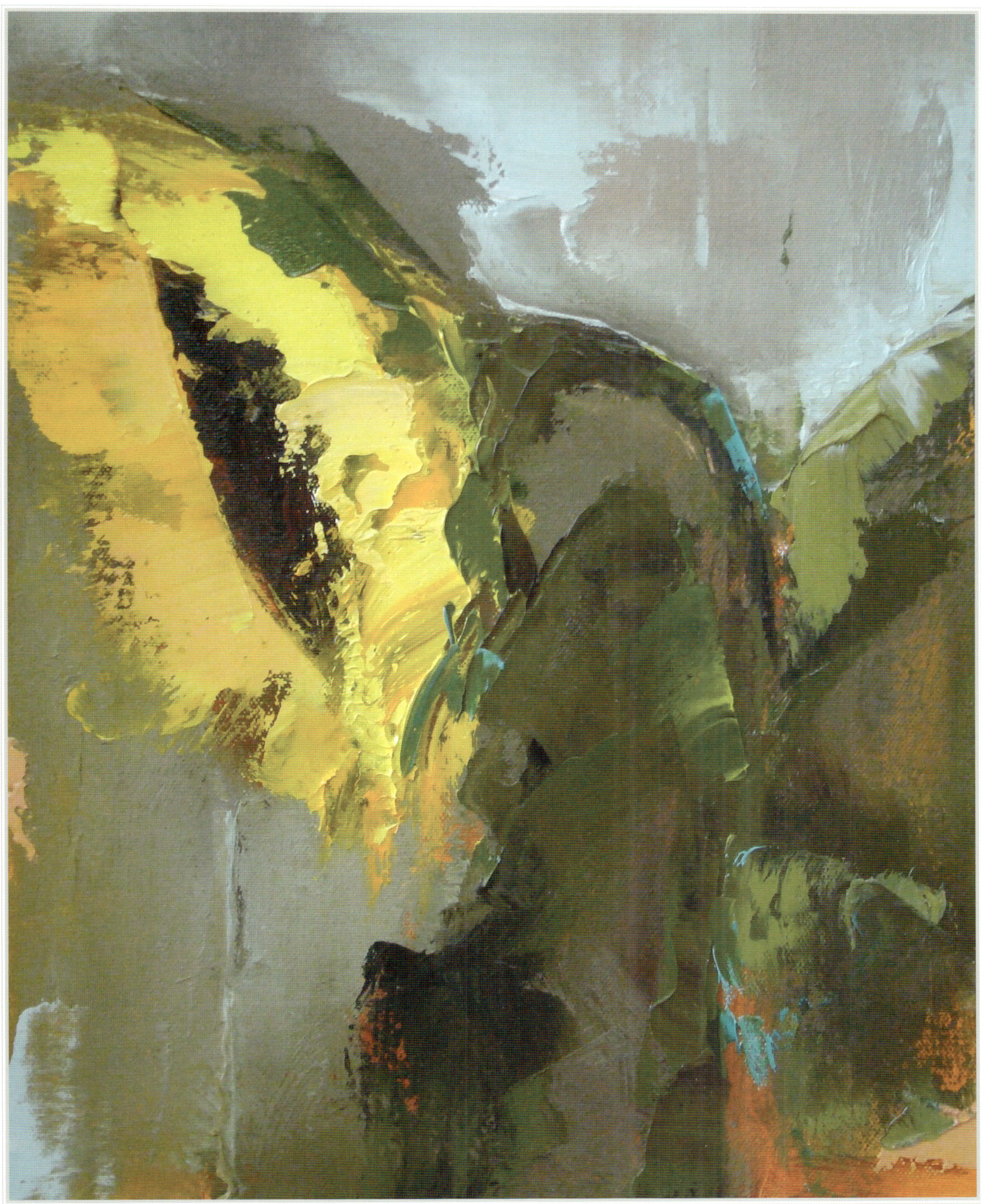

I questioned myself: Really? I mean, there are so many more important things to pray for. But, I felt the urge again, so I gave in and started praying for the lost dog. When I was finished praying, I packed up my things and headed to the car until I felt a nudge to head to the front office. I had a busy day ahead, and almost dismissed the nudge for more important things to do, but I headed to the office and asked Stella, the secretary, if there were any other places in the church that had a lost and found. The previous weeks we had covered all the other lost and found areas, but not one stuffed animal showed up. Stella asked me what I was looking for, and when she heard she opened her bottom drawer and pulled out the little black dog. Attached was a note to call the little girl who had found the dog by 10 am on a specific date if it had not been claimed. I happened to show up at 9:50 on that date.

I left the church, dog in hand and a very important message pressed on my heart: No matter what Seek HIM in all things and for all things. Pray without ceasing for the big things in my life, as well as the small things in life. Obey when you hear that still small voice. Be obedient in all things. What a great message to share with my children. Even though we don't always get answers to our prayers right when we what them or need them to be answered . . . God is always in control and He is always on time. Seek first the Kingdom of God and His righteousness and all things will given unto you. Pray for needs, whether they are too big or too small, TRUST Him and OBEY Him every day.

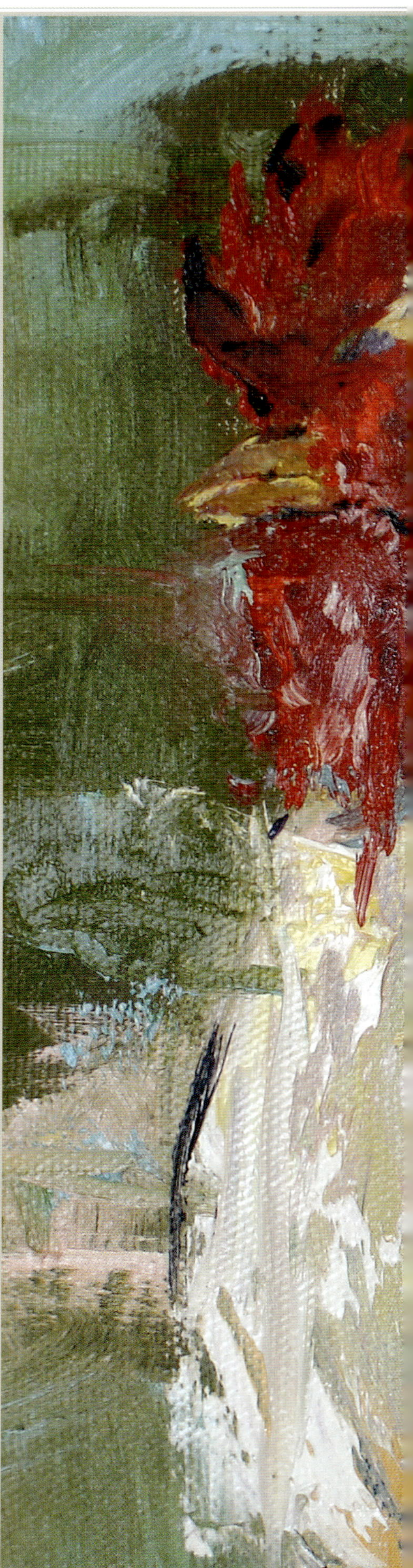

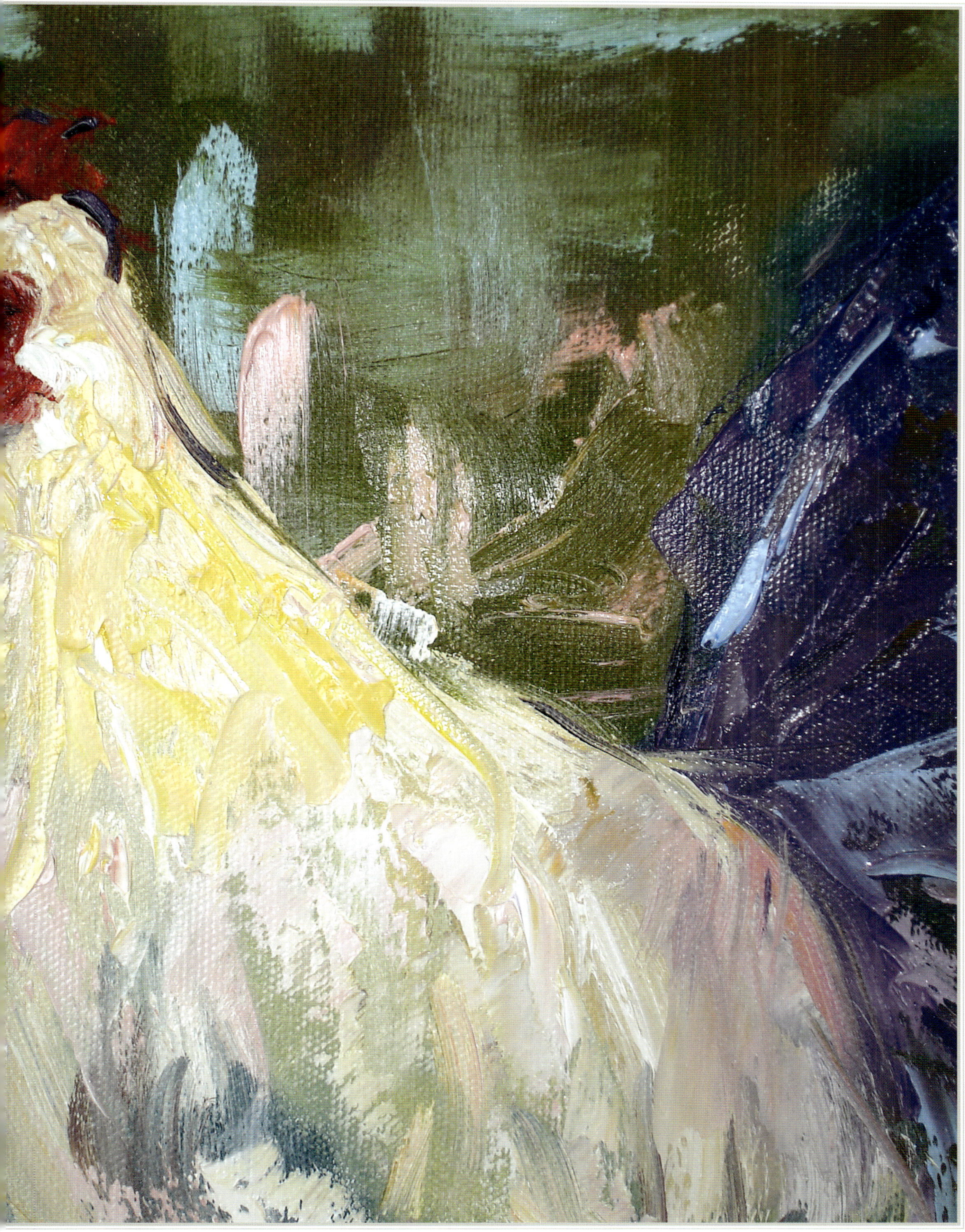

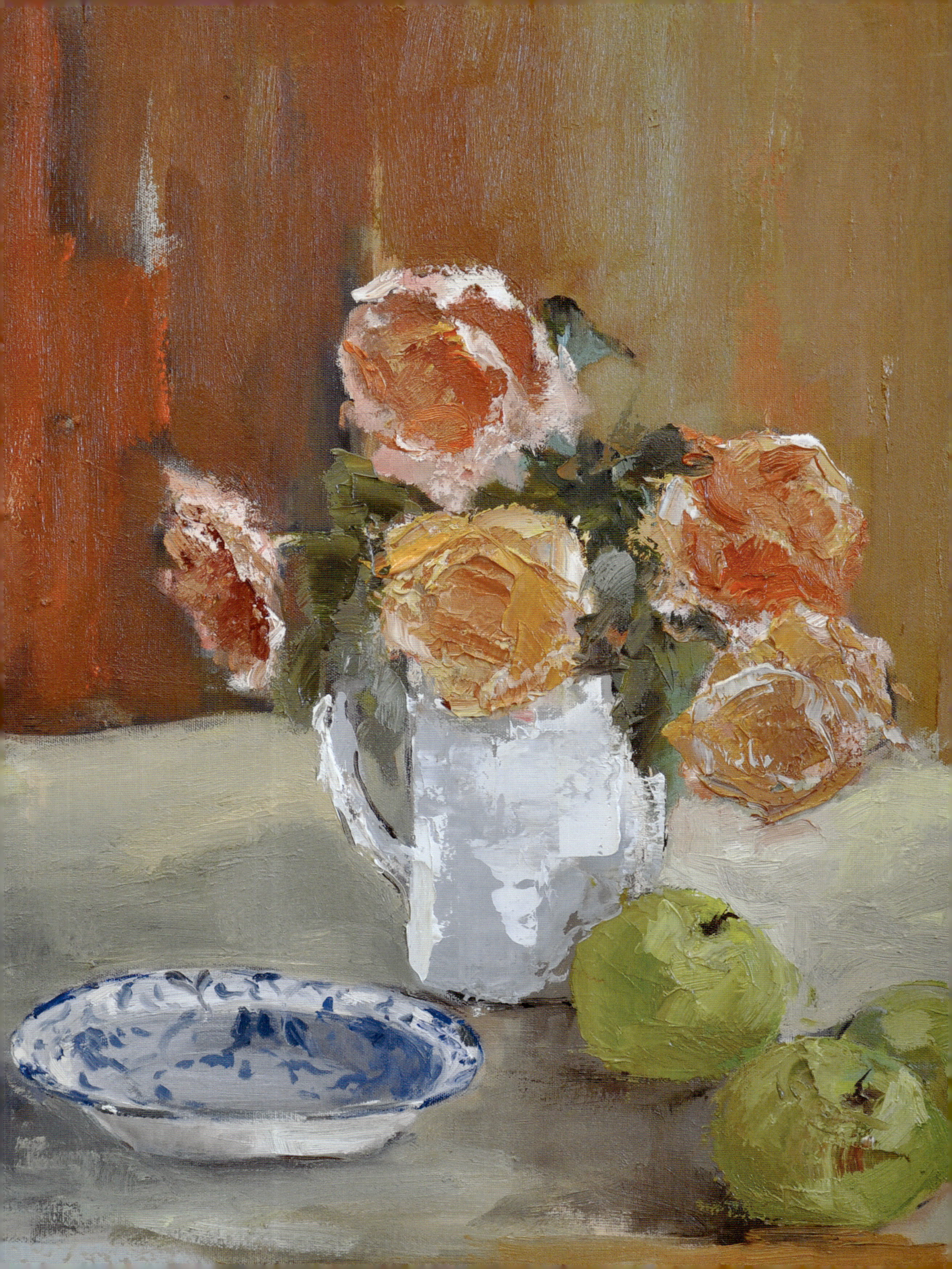

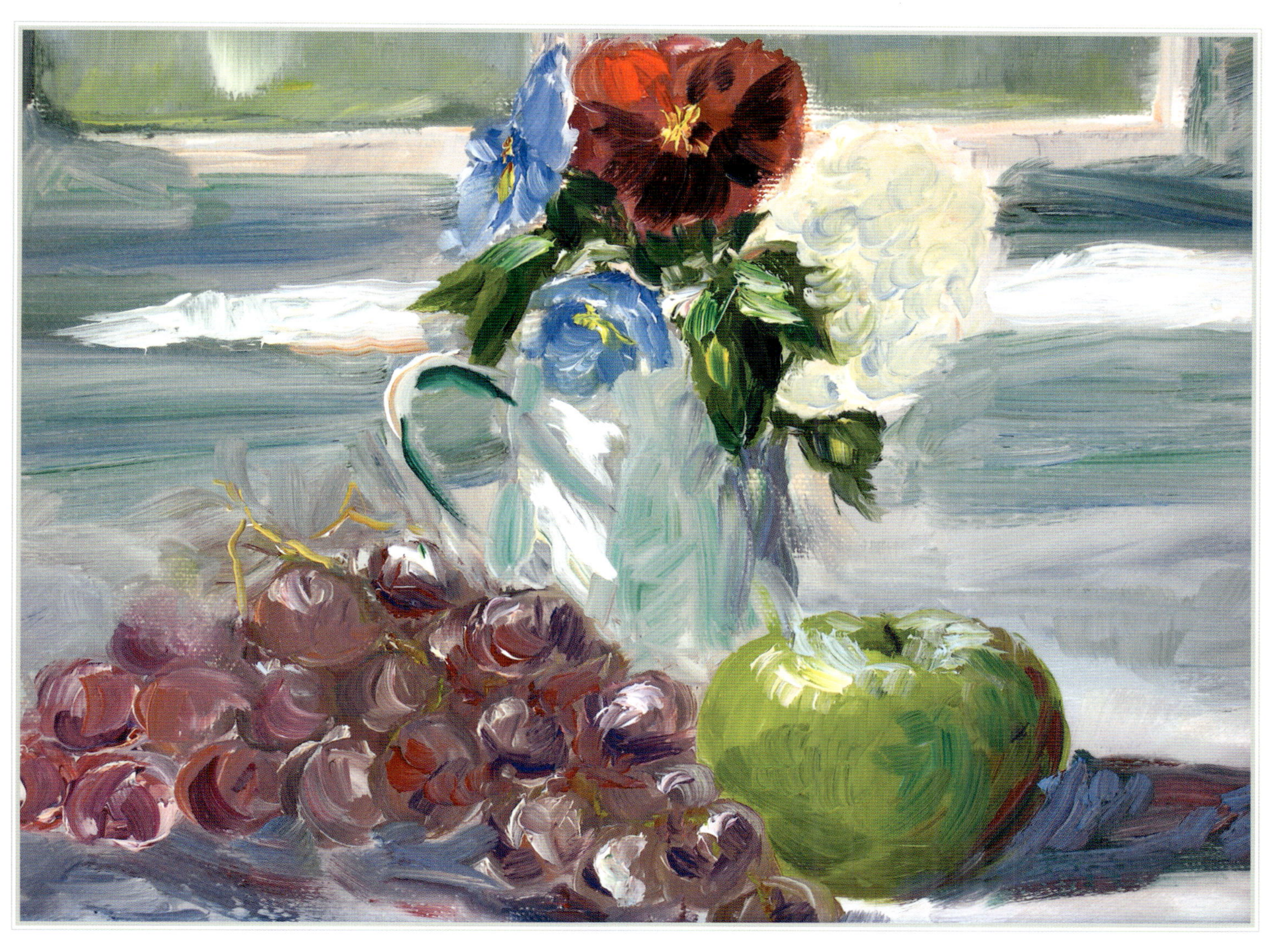

PAINTING IS JUST ANOTHER WAY OF KEEPING A DIARY.

—PABLO PICASSO

Too Much Baggage

Our family loves to travel. We have created a website to share our journeys with friends and family called thetravelingsix.blogspot.com. Several years ago, our family set out for a month to explore Europe. We were each given one small bag to pack for the entire trip. We were determined not to check any bags but only travel with what each could carry on their own. With ease, we traveled throughout Europe on planes, trains and walking through city streets rolling our simple luggage behind us. Free from the extraneous burdens of all the material possessions with which we daily load down our lives, we were able to fully live in the moment and appreciate every facet of the journey.

Fast-forward three years as we set out on a quick trip to the west coast. Over seven days we planned to combine a little business (visiting the gallery that sells my work in Carmel), check out some colleges for my daughter, and take in the sights of San Francisco. We packed the same bags that we had used for our European adventure.

Bags packed and car loaded, we headed to the airport early that morning for a 6 A.M. departure. As we boarded the plane with our carry-on bags and proceeded to attempt loading them in the overhead bins, we realized that the bags were just not going to fit. As the flight was filling up, the frustrated glares of our fellow passengers did not help as we furiously pushed and shoved, trying to cram our stuff in the too-small overhead compartments. We ended up having to take the bags to the back of the plane and remove some items from each bag, finally finding

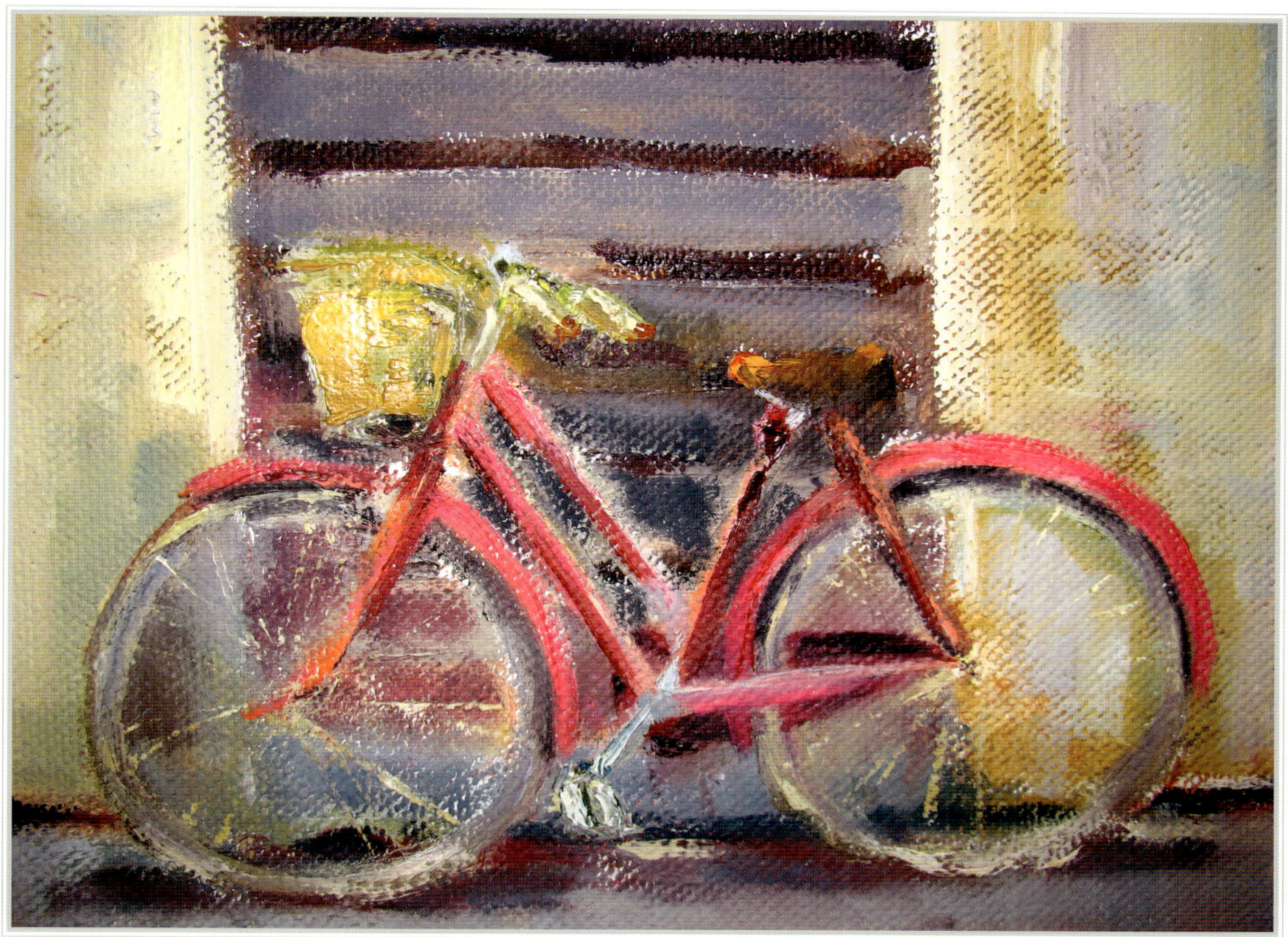

room and making them fit, only to do this all over again on our connecting flight. Whew! All of a sudden it hit me: "There's just too much baggage." We had forgotten the simplicity and luxury of traveling light.

I began to think and ask myself: "Do I have too much baggage in my life? What do I need to take out of my life that does not fit with my relationship with Jesus? What sin needs to be removed from my life to have a better relationship with my husband and my children? What do I need to do in my life to live a lighter life full of joy and peace?"

Our next adventure will be a trip to Peru for a part-mission trip with Samaritan's Feet, and part-touring another part of our world that intrigues us. When we head to Peru I know that we will be traveling light. Leaving a life of luxury to go and serve others, to wash the feet of children who have never owned a pair of shoes - we will slowly let go of the baggage that weighs us down in this world.

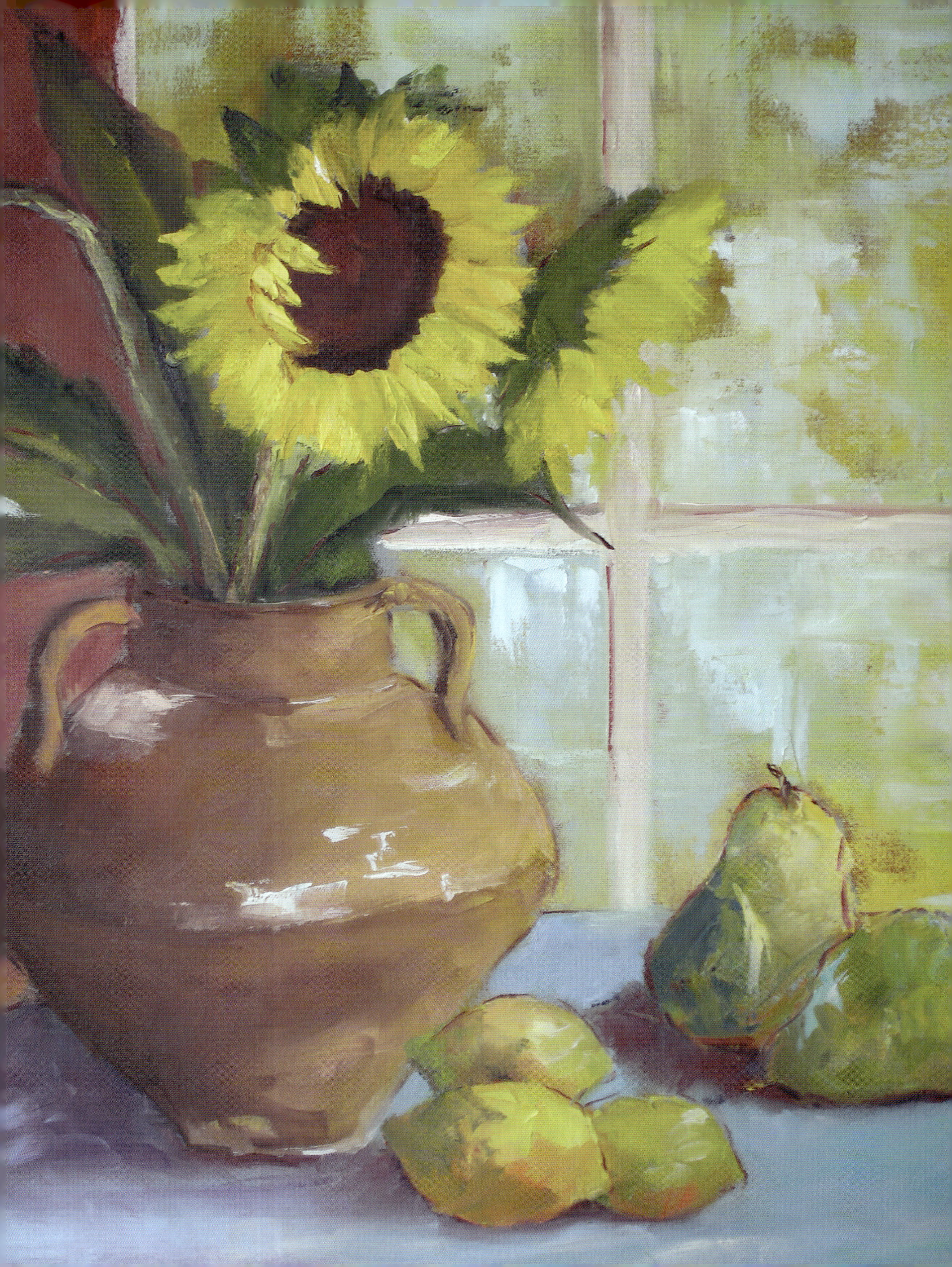

THEREFORE, SINCE WE ARE SURROUNDED BY SUCH A GREAT CLOUD OF WITNESSES, LET US THROW OFF EVERYTHING THAT HINDERS AND THE SIN THAT SO EASILY ENTANGLES. AND LET US RUN WITH PERSEVERANCE THE RACE MARKED OUT FOR US, FIXING OUR EYES ON JESUS, THE PIONEER AND PERFECTER OF FAITH. FOR THE JOY SET BEFORE HIM HE ENDURED THE CROSS, SCORNING ITS SHAME, AND SAT DOWN AT THE RIGHT HAND OF THE THRONE OF GOD. CONSIDER HIM WHO ENDURED SUCH OPPOSITION FROM SINNERS, SO THAT YOU WILL NOT GROW WEARY AND LOSE HEART.

HEBREWS 12:1-3

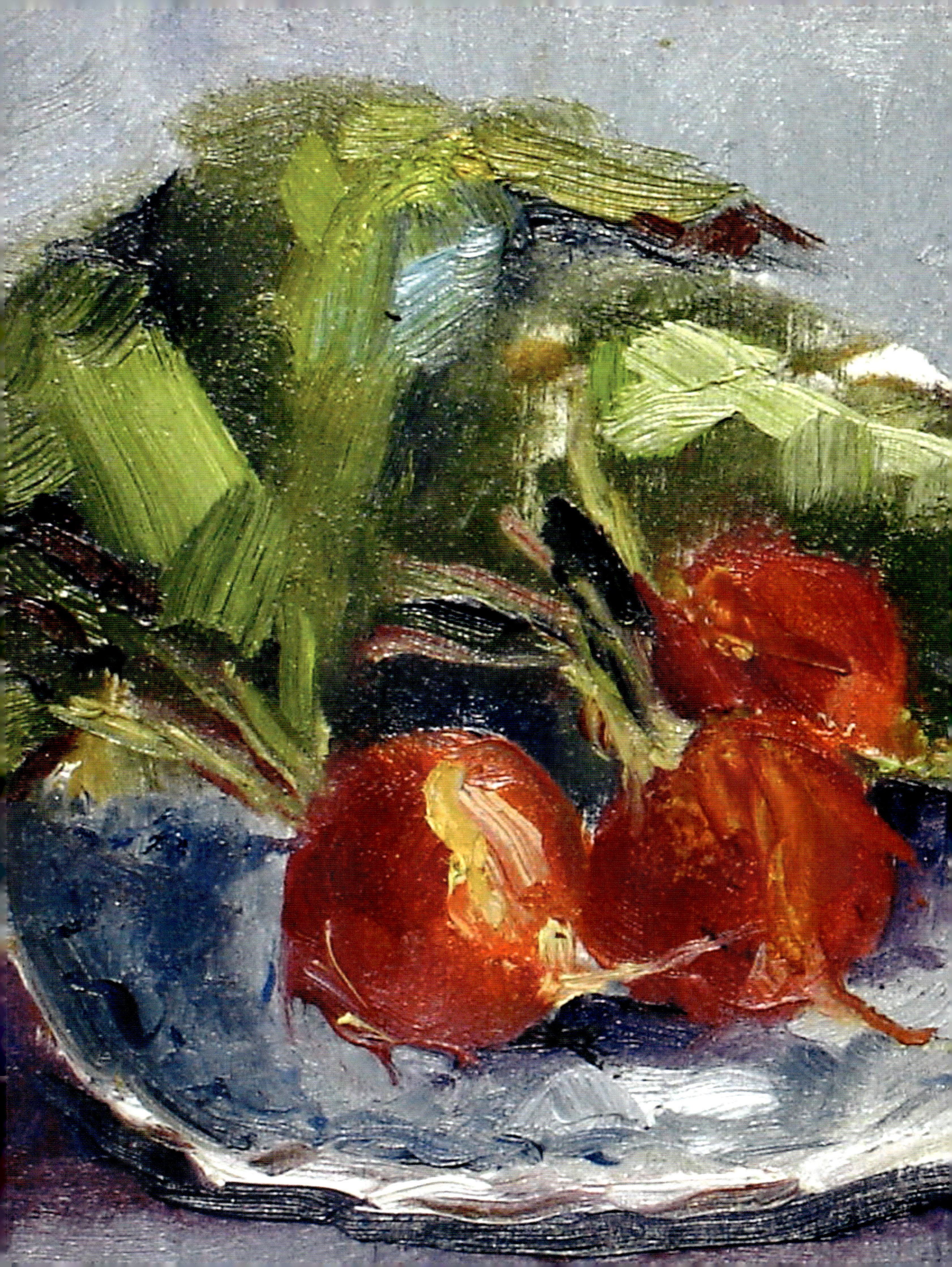

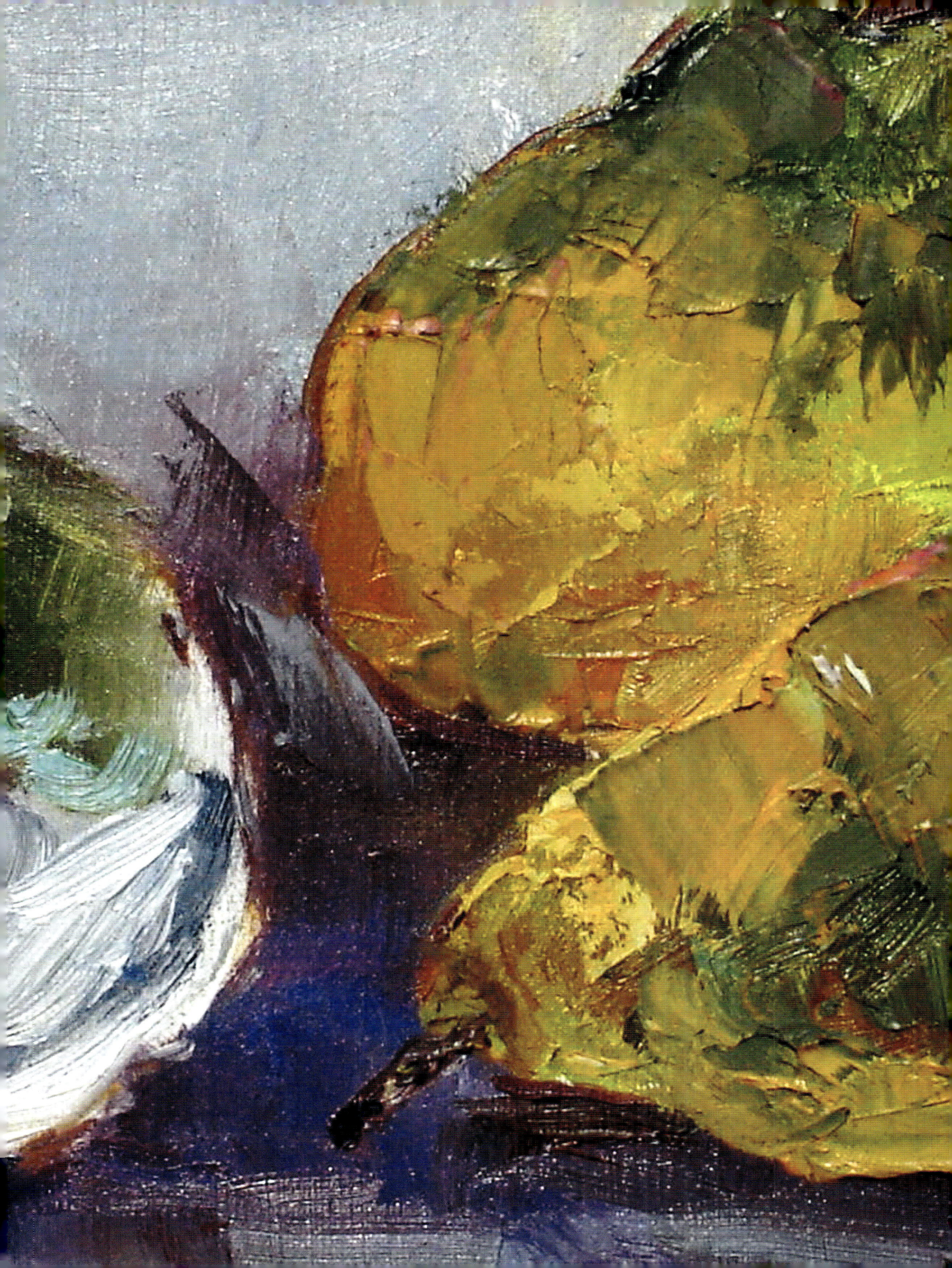

ACKNOWLEDGMENTS

A Special Thanks

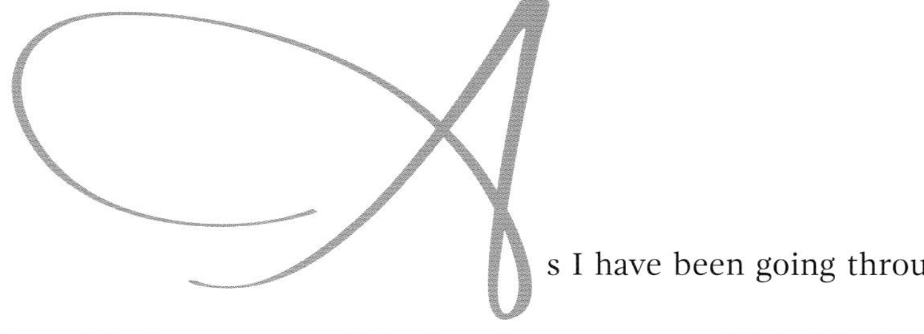

s I have been going through this writing process I realized that not only did I want to become an artist when I was a young girl, but I also had a burning desire to write a book. I give God the Glory for all things in this process. He has been the one directing my path and I give Him all the glory and honor! Along this journey there have been countless people who have supported me and my art career. First and foremost my family. My patient husband, Clark, who allows me to stay up late working and typing. My precious children, Blakely, Catherine, Taylor and Ford, who encourage me to continue on when I want to quit. I love you all so very much and I am so thankful for each of you and the individual talent that God has deposited into your hearts!

To Betsy Thorpe my incredible editor, and to my baby sister, Beth Bowen, whose literary skills flavored these words! Thank you, Angela Harwood for hanging in there with me through all my tedious attention to details, and for designing this amazing book! For my awesome Marketing and Graphic Designer Christine Dryden: without your vision and talent I am not sure I would be where I am today. Our countless late nights editing back and forth on the computer for marketing cards and shows . . . you are a gift to me and I want to thank you from the bottom of my heart! My PR cheerleader Gwen Poth: you are the best!

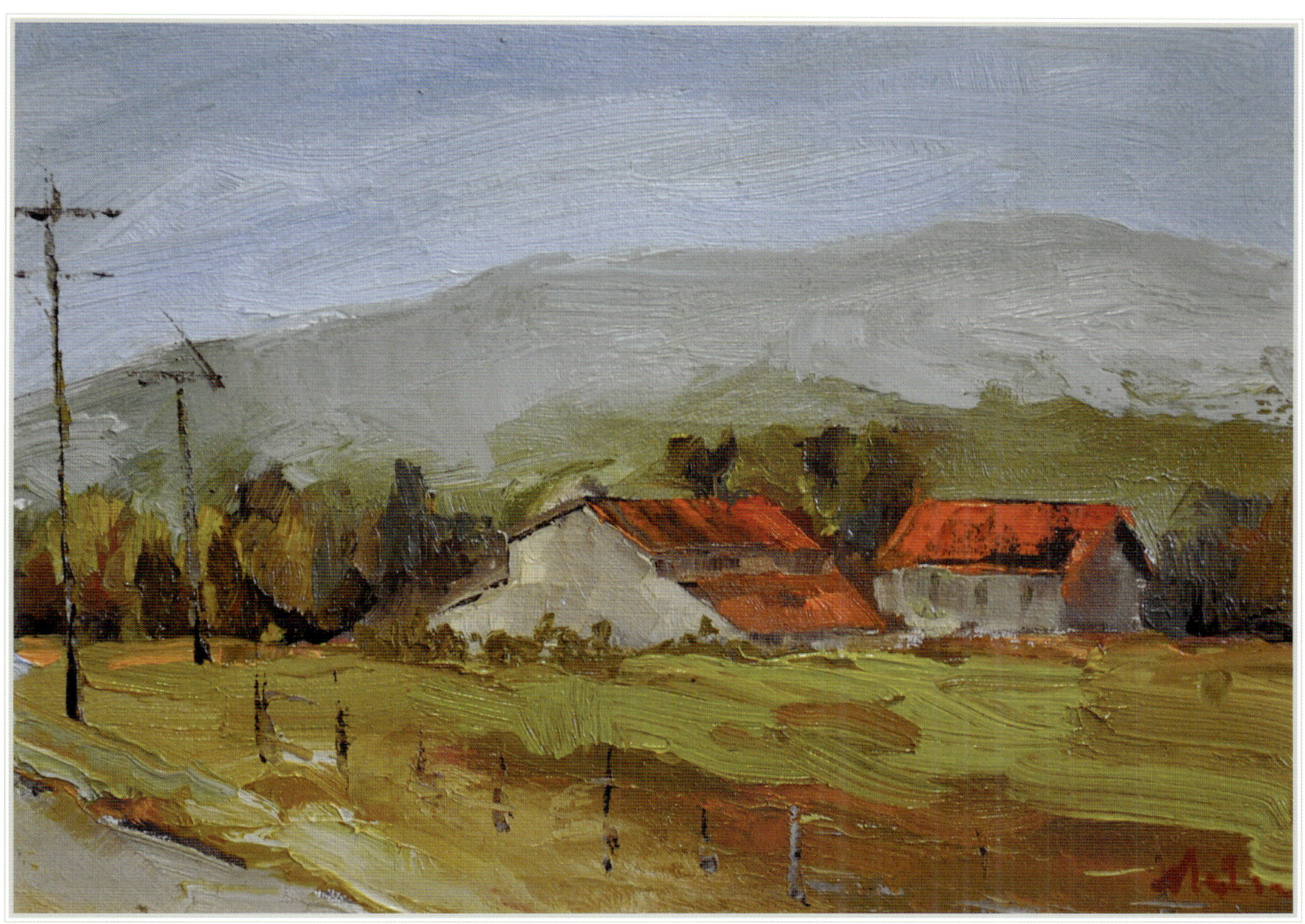

I am so thankful to have you by my side cheering me on and guiding me on this journey each step of the way. To my prayer warriors who stand in the gap and lift me up, your strength and encouragement inspire me. I am blessed by the countless people that I have met through my endeavors of giving back and all the discerning art collectors who are moved by my art. Thank You for believing in Angels and giving me the encouragement to keep on painting. To God be the glory now and forever!

RESOURCES

CHARITIES

The Harvest Center
www.theharvestcenter.org

Union Gospel Mission of Tarrant County
www.ugm-tc.org

Allegro Foundation
www.allegrofoundation.net

Levine Cardiac Kids
www.levinecardiackids.com

With Open Eyes
www.withopeneyes.net

Presbyterian Hospice and Palliative Care
www.presbyterian.org/hospice

GALLERIES

Anne Neilson Fine Art
www.anneneilsonfineart.com

Gallery Elite
www.galleryelite.net

Granville Antiques
Charlotte, NC

3 French Hens
www.3frenchhens.biz

COMMUNICATIONS

Stir Studios – Christine Dryden
www.stirstudios.net

Gwen Poth Communications
www.gwenpoth.com

Everidge Designs
www.everidgedesigns.com

ARTISTS | BUSINESSES

AndyBraitman Studios
www.andybraitman.com

BD Jefferies
www.bdjeffries.com

Campbell's Greenhouse
Charlotte, NC

Szeredy Photography
www.szeredy.com

K-Interiors
www.k-interiors.com

Charlotte Living
www.charlottelivingmagazine.com

SCRIPTURE | INSPIRATION

NIV Translation
The Message

Jesus Calling: Enjoying Peace in His Presence
by Sarah Young, published by Thomas Nelson, 2004

The Sword of the Spirit The Word of God
www.theswordofthespiritbook.com

Steven Curtis Chapman
www.stevencrutischapman.com

K-Love Radio Station
www.klove.com

Air 1 Radio Station
www.air1.com

Elevation Church
www.elevation.org

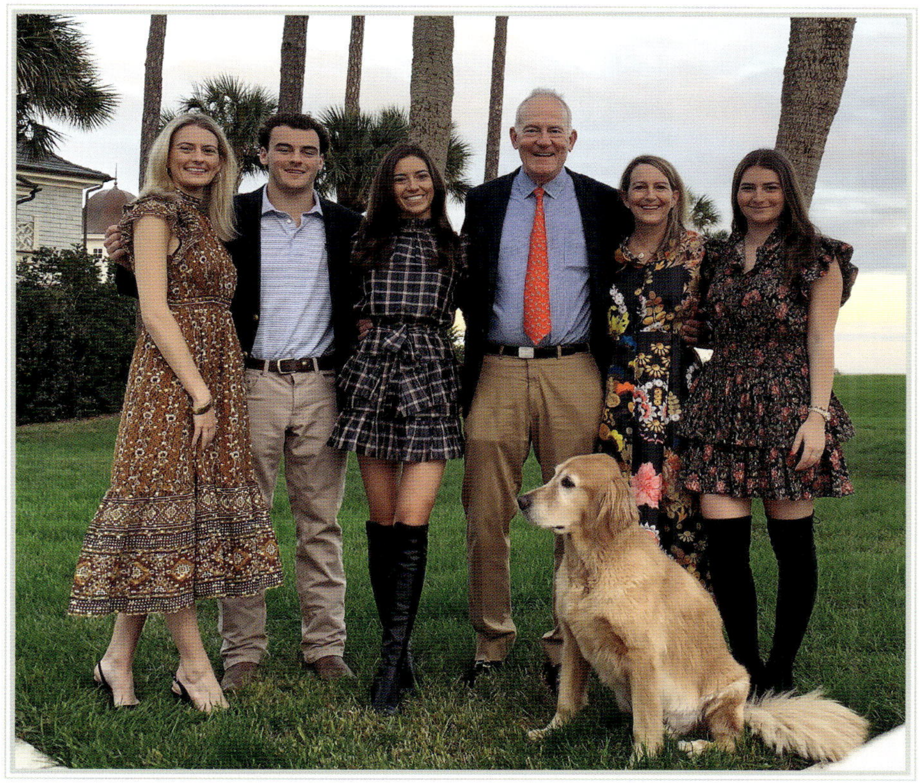

ABOUT THE AUTHOR

A lifelong artist, Anne Neilson began painting in oils in 2003 and quickly became nationally renown for her ethereal Angel Series paintings. A favorite of individuals and private art collectors, Neilson's paintings are inspiring reflections of her faith, recognized for their innate flair for color and light. In 2012, Neilson self-published *Angels In Our Midst*, an inspirational coffee table book, which has sold more than 30,000 copies. Following its success, and the demand for more access to Neilson's acclaimed Angels, Neilson released follow-up book, *Strokes of Compassion*, and launched Anne Neilson Home – a growing collection of luxury home products, which includes candles, note cards, scripture cards, prints, and journals. In 2020, Anne released her newest book, *Anne Neilson's Angels*, a 40 day word devotional to encourage, refresh and inspire. Neilson paints with both passion and purpose and always seeks to give back to those less fortunate through the sales of her products and art.

ISBN: 978-0-9853362-1-9

Book design by Angela Harwood, Greensboro, NC

Published by Anne Neilson Home
532 Governor Morrison Street, Suite 110, Charlotte, NC 28211
anneneilsonhome.com

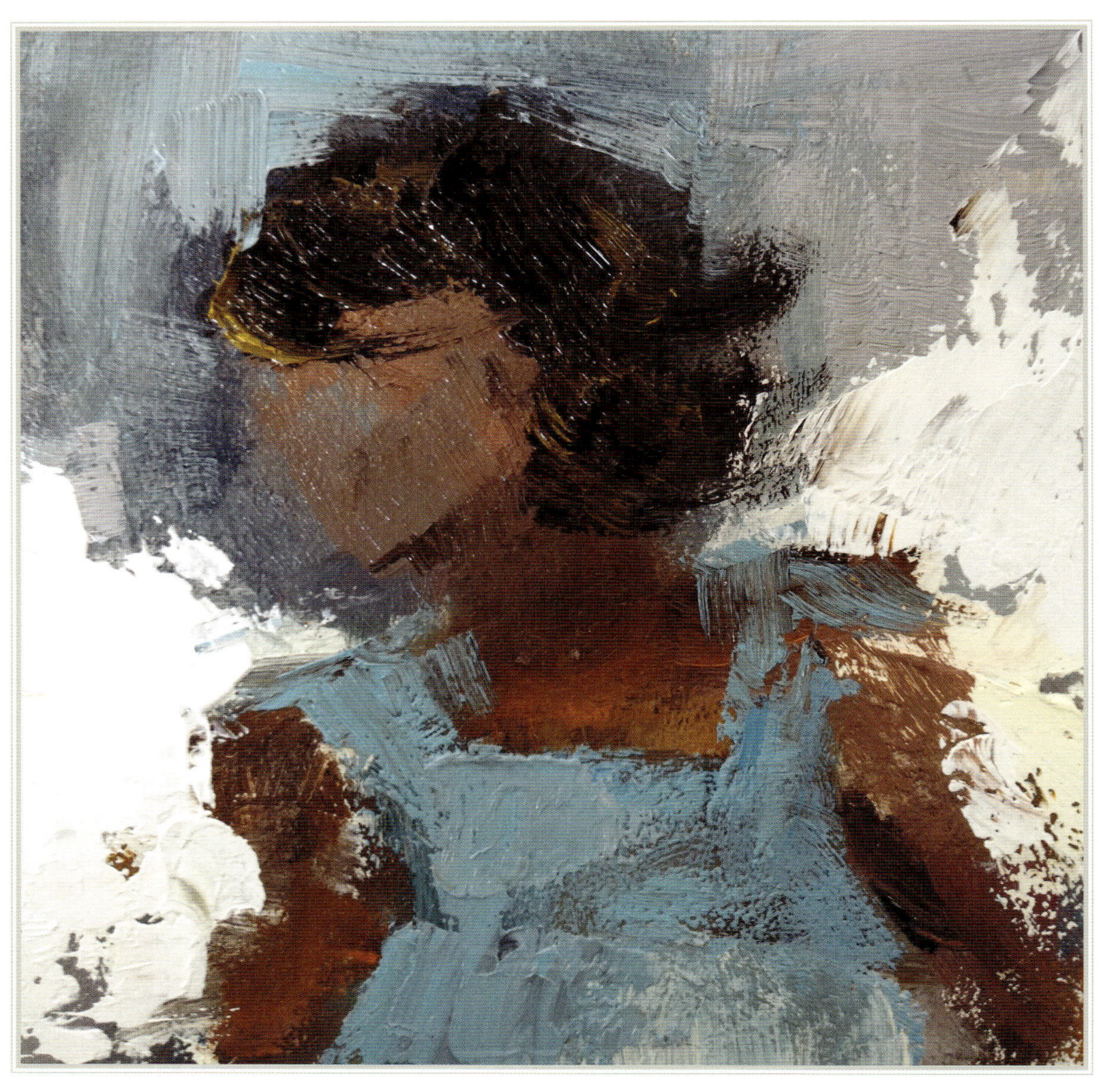

THIS BOOK IS DEDICATED TO MY INCREDIBLE FAMILY;

MAY YOU CONTINUE TO WALK IN FAITH KEEPING YOUR EYES FIXED ON JESUS, THE AUTHOR AND PERFECTER OF YOUR FAITH. MAY HIS ANGELS SURROUND YOU ALL THE DAYS OF YOUR LIFE.